The Breakthrough

PENNSYLVANIA STUDIES IN HUMAN RIGHTS

Bert B. Lockwood, Jr., Series Editor

A complete list of books in the series is available from the publisher.

The Breakthrough

Human Rights in the 1970s

Edited by

Jan Eckel and Samuel Moyn

PENN

UNIVERSITY OF PENNSYLVANIA PRESS

PHILADELPHIA

Published by
University of Pennsylvania Press
Philadelphia, Pennsylvania 19104-4112
www.upenn.edu/pennpress

Printed in the United States of America on acid-free paper
10 9 8 7 6 5 4 3 2 1

Library of Congress Cataloging-in-Publication Data
The breakthrough : human rights in the 1970s / edited by Jan Eckel and Samuel Moyn. — 1st ed.
    p. cm. — (Pennsylvania studies in human rights)
  Includes bibliographical references and index.
  ISBN 978-0-8122-4550-9 (hardcover : alk. paper)
  1. Human rights—History—20th century. I. Eckel, Jan. II. Moyn, Samuel. III. Series: Pennsylvania studies in human rights.
  JC571.H76919 2014
  323.09'047—dc23
                                                    2013011619

Contents

The Breakthrough

Chapter 1

The Return of the Prodigal:
The 1970s as a Turning Point
in Human Rights History

Samuel Moyn

The history of human rights is a new domain of inquiry. Until recently, this emerging field focused intently on distant origins, from the Bible to medieval philosophy, and from early modern natural rights theory to the age of democratic revolution. Above all other eras, it favored the 1940s, reasonably enough given the framing of the Universal Declaration of Human Rights (1948), on which the historical literature has concentrated.[1] About the trajectory of human rights after its ancient, medieval, early modern, and midcentury phases, however, little has been written.

When less rosy and more critical accounts of the emergence of human rights began to be produced—accounts that did not view the birth of the idea with the romanticized purity its first admirers had portrayed—they also concentrated on the 1940s.[2] Yet in this approach, too, how exactly it was that human rights acquired such considerable prominence in today's world remained hazy. After all, both the positive and critical accounts, which at least agreed in assigning great significance to the midcentury as the moment of the breakthrough, also concurred that it was immediately snuffed out: the Cold War supervened, as a struggle in which idealistic norms had no purchase. It was as if the history of human rights were the parable of the prodigal son (Luke 15: 11–32) but only narrated his birth and departure—even though it is his return that really mattered.

In recent years, historians of human rights have moved beyond the 1940s to give further thought to the period of the later Cold War, which was as responsible for the salience of human rights as the early Cold War was to their marginality.[3] In particular, historians have begun to focus on the era of the 1970s, when—initial indications suggested—the idea of international human rights achieved a prominence that far outstripped even that of its founding epoch thirty years before. Amnesty International, the first human rights nongovernmental organization of note, achieved striking visibility, especially through its Campaign Against Torture. Soviet dissidents rallied around human rights, attracting a massive global audience for their heroism in facing down a totalitarian state. After coups in the Southern Cone of the Americas beginning in the summer of 1973, appeals to human rights became a slogan of local response and international solidarity. The Helsinki Accords were signed in 1975, incorporating what became a fateful "third basket" of human rights principles.[4] And President Jimmy Carter, beginning in January 1977, gave the United States a "human rights policy." Contemporaries registered these separate but converging events as an explosion.

Yet if these events gave human rights an unprecedented new prominence in world affairs, only now are historians examining them both on their own and in their synergy with one other. This volume reflects some of those steps toward the present. Nothing is settled in the chronological shift forward to examine the contemporary era alone as the one in which the most cherished moral notions in international politics today exploded into relevance. This volume's first goal, therefore, is to pool the results of researchers focusing on disparate areas of the globe and to pose basic questions about advancing the clock of scholarship.[5] Everyone agrees that there has been a mismatch between the massive attention to prior periods in human rights history and the absence of any focus on our time—when, arguably for the first time, human rights gained traction in international political life, both as a matter of public consciousness and enacted law and policy.

Beyond beginning to redress this imbalance, the main hope is that this volume, which samples fascinating new research about key developments, also poses some important questions about how to interpret them against the backdrop of human rights history over the long term as well as in the framework of the 1970s. Most of all, the book illustrates the need for further research, as well as the reconceptualization that always goes along with it. Some chapters showcase findings that will be presented fully in ongoing research projects. In many instances the empirical results respond to outstanding controversies of interpretation in what has become an unusually controverted historiography. Other essays suggest the need for new controversies, whose resolution will require investigation that has not yet been undertaken. This introduction will proceed by posing and discussing both kinds of questions.

There is one paradox worth mentioning before canvassing human rights history in the era. The general history of the 1970s is usually treated as one of disaster or even "nervous breakdown," not of the moral breakthrough of human rights.[6] In the American case, the rise of the political right seems the currently most interesting feature of the period; in the United States and in the rest of the north Atlantic region, the crisis of social democratic consensus and the explosion of neoliberalism, with the failure of the Bretton Woods system and associated events, were far more visible than human rights. How was it, then, that human rights experienced a turning point in and through "the age of fracture," as historian Daniel Rodgers has famously dubbed our era?[7] Jan Eckel's synthetic concluding chapter turns to this subject in an over-all portrait of human rights in the 1970s. It suggests how to relate this era in human rights history, narrowly conceived, to the broader history of the period, which is also receiving new attention from historians whose primary emphasis falls on the more general contours of the years of economic crisis, geopolitical détente, and other social movements in which human rights began to be prominent.[8]

The Long 1970s in Human Rights History

Any decade, of course, is just an arbitrary demarcation in flowing time, and as historians often talk of "short" and "long" centuries, there is no reason not to do so with decades. Currently, the 1960s are probably the most famous recent decade, even boasting a scholarly journal devoted to it, and typically defined in a "long" way that spills over to recognize the antecedents and aftermath of generational rebellion and countercultural experimentation. The same, however, is probably true of the 1970s, as Bruce Schulman has argued.[9] No critical era can occur ex nihilo, and certainly the 1970s in human rights history did not. Discontinuous events depend on long-term preconditions and medium-term novelties as well as short-term triggers. And the complicated bequest the 1970s left for the future began to be bitterly fought over almost immediately, if not during the decade itself.

Even a generous definition of the 1970s has to begin and end somewhere.

Looking back, even if the human rights explosion seemed to come out of nowhere, its antecedents in the 1950s and 1960s, after the Universal Declaration of Human Rights, remain important. With the activation of civil society in the new social movements of the 1960s, such as Amnesty International (founded in that decade), it is clear that the explosion of human rights did not begin on January 1, 1970. International Human Rights Year was 1968, and the history of détente, which ran through the Helsinki Accords so critical in human rights history, similarly began in diplomatic openings in the earlier decade, as the treatment of European diplomacy in this book shows. Every chapter in the volume comments implicitly on when to begin the story of the 1970s in human rights history and when to end it.

Beyond the chronology of the 1970s, there is the difficult problem of how much of prior human rights history specifically it presupposed and whether, given the profusion of causes invoking the idea, the 1970s were in some sense the most critical period for the concept. The strong case for moving the clock forward to the 1970s that some contributors advance in this volume remains a hypothesis to be confirmed rather than a preordained conclusion, let alone some sort of orthodoxy to defend. Clearly, the existence of the basic idea of international human rights antedated the period, but how much else? Is that basic idea an eternal reference point or polestar merely glimpsed by transient human actors in various times and places? Were there strong existing traditions of affiliation with international human rights, by states or nonstate actors, which merely strengthened through the decade? Or, do the essays separately or together come close to suggesting that, had the Universal Declaration dropped from the sky at the beginning, most of the rest of the action in human rights history in the 1970s depended on short-term factors and gave the decade an altogether unprecedented centrality in world politics?

The essays in this volume consider these fascinating open questions. Some contributors are, like the editors, committed to a decisive and even discontinuous shift in the 1970s—defined in an extended way and without denying antecedents. Others simply want to add new chapters to the long saga of human rights, or, as in Daniel Sargent's provocative essay, they conceive of the 1970s in terms of the revival of an eternal possibility—a permanent ideological option that cannot vanish in world history except to be rediscovered later.

Biafra, Humanitarianism, and Human Rights

One place to begin is with Biafra. The Nigerian counterinsurgency in the late 1960s prompted widespread moral outrage across the West, including accusations of genocide. The Biafran case helps this volume thematize a currently simmering dispute about how to connect the history of human rights with the history of humanitarianism—which everyone agrees to be a nearly permanent feature of the modern political and moral landscape. In one of the founding works of human rights history, Lynn Hunt even claimed that humanitarian sentiment simply gave rise to the very idea of human rights.[10] Others have suggested divergences. Historians of antislavery in the Atlantic world and what was called "the Eastern question" of the Ottoman Empire's trajectory in the nineteenth century have shown how various movements sprang up around the succor of distant suffering, but these campaigns rarely invoked rights and seemed to have been based more often on Christian solidarity and hierarchical philanthropy.[11]

What, exactly, is the relationship of the history of human rights to this older history of sympathy, charity, and activism? Though this volume cannot take up that question in its necessary chronological sweep, Biafra provides a case that can be considered in detail. As Lasse Heerten narrates in his vivid chapter, the Biafran agitation involved some of the central moral ideas associated with human rights. The concern about genocide, of course, was in the air at the time, as Bertrand Russell's tribunal of the same moment indicting American prosecution of the Vietnam War makes clear.[12] The methods of publicity on behalf of the victims—including graphic images and emotional pleas—were familiar to nineteenth-century humanitarians and were later put to use in human rights campaigns. Famously, Biafra sparked the founding of Médecins sans Frontières, a subsequently central humanitarian group. Yet the importance of Biafra for this volume is to assess whether the episode drove the prominence of human rights or at least laid a foundation for it in the surprising events that were to follow.

Geographical Diffusion

The far-flung geography of events is the single most striking feature of human rights history in the 1970s proper. The world appears in the 1940s era of human rights history mainly in the form of diplomatic elites gathering in San

Francisco to finalize the United Nations Charter, at Hunter College and Lake Success in New York to initiate plans around the Universal Declaration the next year, and in Paris after two tortuous years of negotiation for the vote on December 10, 1948. Frequently, in other words, the world is present in the history of the 1940s merely in the persons of a few great envoys from non-Western states present for the sake of multicultural communion around consensus values.

The world of the 1970s in human rights history, by contrast, is a world of delocalized grassroots agents making claims, a global community far larger than that of the fifty or so nations that endorsed the Universal Declaration's principles in an era of reconsolidating empire. The Soviet Union provided a premier, and perhaps pioneering, initial site. Famously, Latin American nations soon followed. The 1970s, the essays show, offer a multitude of other actors, and the volume emphasizes the series of state entrants that rushed into the crystallizing field as well. Unlike in the 1940s, there was no center to developments, and indeed the cacophony of voices at the closure of decolonization raises the question of whether noise or music resulted.

Some of the sources remain so surprising as to still give pause. Most vividly in East Germany, Communist ideologues continued to proclaim fervently that their state was based on human rights, and U.S. politicians in the Republican Party, like their better-known Democratic counterparts, also turned to this language to frame foreign engagement. Even in the story of European diplomats, resisting the realist lead of American and Soviet principals of the Cold War struggle to stake out their own path, new details about states emerge. Finally, there is the "global South," which at the time of the framing of the Universal Declaration remained mostly under colonial rule. The 1970s in Africa involved the last battle against persisting empire for political freedom and collective self-determination—by this time a human right, too, though the Universal Declaration had omitted it.

Communist Europe

One familiar site of human rights dissent—by perhaps the first self-styled human rights movement in world history—was the Soviet Union, which Benjamin Nathans's essay takes up. As Nathans shows, something is lost if too decisive a caesura is placed at the beginning of the 1970s in explaining the background forces and events that led this to occur. After all, dissidence took place in other terms before the period. Nathans's cautionary remarks about the importance of local expertise shows that a unified history of human rights, if it is possible, will have to take account of multiple histories and fine-grained context.

A more radical departure for the field is provided in Ned Richardson-Little's essay, which shows that what was asserted against the state by inventive dissidents in Moscow and other Soviet cities remained a state discourse in Marxist-Leninist East Germany. To be sure, the USSR, though it had abstained in the 1948 vote on the Universal Declaration, advertised its own allegiances to human rights, up to and including in the period beginning in 1968, when it ratified the two international covenants on the subject (and bragged of doing so in its newspapers). Yet Richardson-Little shows that because the East German Communists had done so much work in claiming human rights or *Menschenrechte* as the authority for their socialist project, from high theory to low propaganda, the explosion of talk round the concept in international politics in the 1970s initially confronted them with no challenge. At least no human rights dissidents emerged, as they did early in the decade in the Soviet Union proper and later in diverse other Eastern bloc satellites. It was only in the 1980s that the language of human rights, which had worked for a while to stave off dissent, served dissenters as an even more powerful weapon.

Celia Donert's chapter attacks the east/west distinction in a different way, focusing on women's rights in the 1970s. Reviewing the contested intersection between gender and international human rights since the 1970s, Donert restores attention to women's internationalism without forgetting that it still came in rival versions in the 1970s. Developing a vivid contrast between the World Conference on Women during International Women's Year of 1975 and the East Berlin World Congress of Women, Donert shows that a concern with gender could lead as much to continuing worries about the famous abstraction of "the rights of man" as to a complete reorientation of all claims around the new global morality.

Latin America

Simultaneously with the Soviet birth of human rights, Latin Americans were also beginning to invoke the notion, which coexisted with and then slowly displaced other sorts of languages like Marxism and anti-imperialism.

Patrick William Kelly's excellent chapter puts the focus on Brazilian, Chilean, and Argentinean exiles from dictatorship who were driven into a period of extended experimentation. (Many Chilean exiles fled to Argentina, but the wave of coups followed them there.) As Kelly suggests, the putatively antipolitical language of human rights became valuable for such political activists for a variety of reasons.

One was purely accidental: activists who were not seeking it ran across the idea, as in the case of one who recalls happening upon a poster that mentioned human rights. Another was that human rights were coalitional, uniting not simply former disputants at home but also, and above all, people newly interested in forging transnational networks—an especially obvious strategy for exiles who have been driven from their country but hoped to influence it by finding new allies abroad.

Lynsay Skiba's essay focuses on this feature of emerging human rights activism by following the case of two Argentinean lawyers who eventually moved to the United States, where they testified before Minnesota congressman Donald Fraser's now celebrated human rights hearings. These hearings gave human rights some attention in North American political discourse before the rest of the Democratic Party began to debate the linkage of foreign policy and moral conditions. Skiba complements this focus with another on the transformation of the Organization of American States and the rise of the "inter-American system" for human rights protection.

In both cases, she shows, converging developments allowed novel spaces that individual Argentinean activists exploited, working in tandem with foreign supporters. Skiba's examination of Lucio Garzón Maceda and Gustavo Roca offers a fascinating personalized history of two trajectories that were microscopic instances of macroscopic change; and at the very center of her examination of these protagonists is the claim to expertise that lawyers could make in invoking international human rights. Ideologically flexible and maneuvering among rival political options, lawyers were able to find a path in which human rights impinged upon the "national security" rhetoric of dictatorships.

The United States in the World

In the geographical diffusion of the grassroots invocations of human rights such as occurred in the Soviet Union and Latin America, there is, however, no cause to romantically portray a "flat world" of ideologically and practically equal actors. As the Soviet Union battled dissidents and East Germany honed its ideological credentials at home, private citizens in the United States and Western Europe mobilized to join activists abroad, and states reoriented policy in tune with the new language.

Jimmy Carter, elected president of the United States in the fall of 1976, almost wandered into using the language. He barely mentioned human rights during his campaign, so that when he announced his commitment to human rights on the steps of the Capitol when he was inaugurated in January 1977, a months-long debate was sparked. Of course, Carter invoked old sources, as if the Cold War politics he denounced and to which—even in the policies of his own party—he presented human rights as an alternative were a temporary divergence from an ingrained national tradition. In his essay here, Daniel Sargent agrees, presenting human rights as an oasis around which Americans may wander. In Sargent's provocative view, historians need to account for how people come to drink its waters, as occurred in the 1970s, with Carter rightly reviving founding principles, albeit in contingent new circumstances. Sargent's paper offers a new analysis of how these conditions came about in a specific moment of fortunate conjuncture.

Carl Bon Tempo, meanwhile, demonstrates that the Republican Party is less well remembered as a partisan of human rights, in part because Carter has stolen the historiographical show and because Carter's successor, Ronald Reagan, is remembered as an enemy of human rights (perhaps largely because of opposition of the developing human rights community in the United States to his personnel and policies). Due to instant analysis—and some mythmaking—by Senator Daniel Patrick Moynihan, the negotiation of the Democratic Party platform in the summer of 1976 has passed into human rights historiography.[13] Bon Tempo shows that there was just as much action around human rights in Republican Party debates that summer. In his pioneering essay, he also shows how Reagan negotiated the minefield of Carter's elevation of human rights to a matter of controversy in American politics, beginning with a rejoinder to the famous Notre Dame commencement speech Carter gave in 1977.

The case of the United States remains of special importance in the human rights historiography of the 1970s. The role it had been assigned in the 1940s—to bring "a new deal to the world" in the form of human rights–based internationalism—has been challenged in recent years. Much depends on how the country's trajectory through the 1970s is narrated and evaluated.[14]

The country's hegemonic centrality to the world order, then and now, makes the United States a critical case to study as its old version of liberal internationalism based on containment and direct engagement evolved to incorporate human rights.[15]

The Helsinki Accords Between East and West

In recent years the origins of the Helsinki Accords have received a huge amount of attention from historians interested in how the determined inclusion by Western European powers of "human rights" in otherwise cynical diplomatic agreement led to unexpected but fateful change.[16] No one—not even the most enthusiastic Western Europeans—predicted the explosion of dissident appeals to human rights that the treaty sparked, or the role that the follow-up Helsinki Conferences would have in the creation of an international movement that worked into the next decade.[17] The Soviet Union signed the accords because they ratified its postwar takeover of Eastern Europe. (Americans also did not comprehend the significance of the "third basket" of human rights provisions.) However, Richardson-Little shows that Communist East Germany treated this part of the treaty not as a concession but as language in conformity with their own human rights principles at home.

Although an East German human rights movement did not emerge until the 1980s, Gunter Dehnert suggests how, across the border in Poland, a complex dialectic between prior social movements and state ideology unfolded in the 1970s, partly through the language of human rights. That the Polish civil society activists turned to human rights as a way to resist Premier Edward Gierek's normalization policies may have been due, Dehnert persuasively contends, as much to a process of internal disillusionment and self-reinvention after 1968 as to a "Helsinki effect." Dehnert likewise complicates the notion of an alliance between those internal groups—the KOR or Workers' Defense Committee most famously—and an external human rights community through which international norms affected governmental change.

North and South

The classic areas of concern for the transnational politics of international human rights in the 1970s were in totalitarian states to the east and authoritarian ones to the south. Still peripheral in this age, if not absent altogether, was the larger global South, notably sub-Saharan Africa along with South and East Asia. While Biafra certainly drew some attention to Africa, concern with human rights there was not the rule. (Human Rights Watch, created in 1978 as Helsinki Watch, added Africa Watch to its activities in 1988.) Yet today, countries of the global south are the most prominent forums of international human rights work.

To be sure, Amnesty International deployed northern grassroots attention to imprisonment and later torture in diverse southern locales. Brad Simpson's essay shows that a first wave of historiographical interest in such places—including his own prior investigation of the United States and political imprisonment—neglected indigenous articulations of human rights that stretched much further back in Indonesian history.[18] And when Indonesian activists became familiar with the burgeoning international human rights project of the 1970s, Simpson shows, they did not merely "translate" outside concepts and movements and import them from abroad.[19] They brought their own agenda to the table, exploiting zones of overlap and tweaking what they found in the directions they wanted to pursue.

Local activists, however, were not necessarily more authentic in their invocations of human rights than outside activists or state actors, whether in Jakarta or Washington. As the international history of the principle of self-determination suggests, the most prominent and powerful invocation of human rights by southern actors in this era occurred on the world stage in the form of the call for a "New International Economic Order," one with drastically different priorities from those that the meliorist politics of individual human rights were to imply in later decades in these same spaces.[20] The zeal to reclaim human rights as an indigenous or long-standing southern ideology is persuasive but should not oust the obvious fact that in diplomatic relations, formations like the Non-Aligned Movement championed self-determination for the sake of a very different global reordering than the human rights revolution of our time has involved. It also should not imply that human rights are like a moral Esperanto that transcends local meaning.

Indeed, Simpson's article suggests how much more is to be done to fully evaluate the interface between the burgeoning international language and movement of human rights and local meaning and agency. Nowhere is there more at stake in following these leads than in the global South, where, after the 1970s events this volume chronicles, international human rights politics now focus.

Simon Stevens's essay puts the north and the south in dynamic interrelationship in his well-grounded case study of the British movement against South African apartheid. Like Kelly and Skiba, Stevens emphasizes the role of exiles in transnational advocacy. In other ways his essay dramatizes distinctive dynamics that made the transnational activism around South Africa highly exceptional within the north-south relationship in the long 1970s and later. The protests of Stop the Seventy Tour and the City of London Anti-Apartheid Group, Stevens's case studies, were historically situated but also a sign of things to come. And Stevens's argument, when placed in the larger north/south contrast, mainly shows that the campaign against apartheid was not widely (or unilaterally) conceived either in the north or the south as a human rights struggle until the 1980s, as older visions of its character as a fight for self-determination, potentially through force of arms, gave way to a different self-conception and movement strategy.

In South Africa and elsewhere, this development transformed north-south relations, sidelining empathy with once prominent campaigns for justice, as apartheid finally became widely stigmatized as a human rights concern. It is almost as if the rise of human rights in the 1970s created an open portal through which many movements have later had to enter in order to gain acceptability and, sometimes, success, in their tangled relationships with external supporters and state power.

Lumping and Splitting

There is a familiar experience in which focusing on something that at first seems unified causes the object to disintegrate, and this risk is evident in a book of essays in which different authors take up disparate topics. To some degree, the determining role of local prehistories and conditions and specific states and institutions means that it will always be possible to disaggregate a general historical picture into a chaos of microscopic details. Put more positively, the particularities of different events are going to call for local, including national, research, since even an integrated view of the international scene demands inquiry into very concrete and small-scale forums. (Benjamin Nathans's essay demonstrates this familiar impulse at work.) When historians focus, it is often to show how different some moment rooted in place or time really was. It may be that a volume like this ends up proving that there is no alternative to a plurality of stories all happening at the same time.

It remains true that, from a bird's-eye view, accepting this necessary pluralism or "polycentrism" (as Eckel calls it in his magisterial synthesis) occludes the significant fact that so many different invocations of international human rights were occurring at the same time, and on a scale that dwarfed the percolations of the concept even in the immediately prior decade—to say nothing of before. A celebration of pluralism, or a rueful acknowledgment of its necessity, seems from this point of view more a failure of ambition. Historians of locales, jealous about the specificities of their geographical domain, risk losing the integrative view that the larger view tends to afford. Surely the very dissidents on whom Nathans focuses locally, for example, were actors of global significance, hewing out roles in a script later transported elsewhere.[21] And of course, there is no self-evident reason—beyond the fact that historians bring prior expertise to larger problems, even in an age of global history— that microscopic or temporary causation should prevail over macroscopic or long-term factors in explaining any particular event.

This does not mean that there is any obvious general perspective from which the explosion of human rights in the 1970s comes into view. Some authors—including the editors of this volume—have proposed the value of a framework stressing transforming ethical stances that suddenly made international human rights appealing, when it had been bypassed before. Others, like Daniel Sargent, claim that advancing globalization explains the real change that occurred. Readers of this volume will want to consider whether either story is right, whether some other explanation is better, and indeed whether there can be a single story at all.[22] Eckel concludes this volume with a careful history that cautiously balances local particularity and narrative integration, but the debate about whether to split or lump will continue in the future.

Antiquarianism, Monumentalism, and Criticism

A mere decade ago, no historians were working on human rights in any time period. Why are so many scholars, including the mostly younger scholars represented in this book, entering the field?[23] The question raises a final problem about the history of human rights in the 1970s worth dwelling upon: why write it, as opposed to something else? The answer follows almost immediately: the idea has played, and continues to play, a large role in world affairs, and knowing how it came to do so now seems exigent. (That it has gained urgency only lately suggests either that historians are only now catching up to old developments, or that the 1970s were merely the opening through which human rights came to occupy the moral imagination of contemporary citizens, before the end of the Cold War made the concept seem unavoidable.)

This volume offers a series of empirical contributions to historical knowledge that a wide variety of scholars may find useful. Far from dismissing the factual aspect of human rights history, it seems clear that this most basic and "antiquarian" agenda of these essays is a threshold or baseline for any other project. But now consider, to complete a famous tripartite distinction, two other sorts of historiography: monumental and critical. Where antiquarian history accumulates facts, and monumental history deploys them for the purposes of self-aggrandizing edification, critical history uses knowledge of the past to go on the attack.[24]

Though monumental and critical history have competed since early modern times, if not before, they have found themselves tussling again across the brief span in which the history of human rights has been emerging. Historians have used history to burnish the credentials of human rights idea and activism and to deromanticize or even depreciate them. A final point of interest in the volume is that it provides a barometric reading of where things stand in this ongoing dispute.

It is increasingly obvious as human rights history matures that in the beginning a monumental approach dominated, explaining how superior moral wisdom emerged, at least for the sake of the enlightened, in an obtuse world that still resists it. Critics have responded that human rights have been only one kind of ethical wisdom among others—including in the 1970s where, in places like Latin America, other projects were still alive—and matter as much for the better trajectories they rule out as for the evil ones to which their proponents contrast them.[25]

Once again, this volume provides no decisive resolution to this historiographical struggle, but it shows the variety of forms a critical approach might take. As the debate continues about the best forms of international human rights (indeed, whether to pursue that cause at all), this stimulating collection of historical inquiries shows what was at stake when people in widespread numbers around the world turned to human rights in the first place.

The Dystopia of Postcolonial Catastrophe: Self-Determination, the Biafran War of Secession, and the 1970s Human Rights Moment

Lasse Heerten

In the summer months of 1968, media reports of human suffering in the Nigerian Civil War (1967–1970) began to disconcert the "conscience of the world." Readers around the world were shocked when they were confronted with photographs of starving children in the secessionist Republic of Biafra.[1] Many contemporaries were soon convinced that genocide against Biafra's Igbos[2] was impending; the specter of a West African "Auschwitz" loomed large on the postcolonial horizon.[3] The war became the first postcolonial conflict to engender a transnational surge of humanitarian sentiment. A host of intergovernmental and nongovernmental organizations (NGOs), principally the International Committee of the Red Cross and a number of religious organizations under the umbrella of Joint Church Aid, organized an airlift to bring food into Biafra.[4] Biafra committees mushroomed in the West and began to raise funds for the relief operation and to lobby their governments.[5] Some of these ad hoc committees evolved into NGOs that play a crucial role in today's transnational human rights regime, the most prominent example being the French Comité de Lutte contre le Génocide au Biafra, which developed into Médecins sans Frontières (Doctors Without Borders).[6]

At least at first sight, this episode seems to be a perfect fit for the new body of scholarship on the history of human rights. Historians have recently begun to shed new light on the 1970s, reinterpreting the decade as a period of global transformation.[7] This is held to be connected to the rise of human rights as one of the lingua francas of international politics in the age of audiovisual mass media.[8] As a story of a globally transmitted humanitarian disaster, the Biafran crisis ostensibly matches this emergent scholarly master narrative. However, Biafra has played only a minimal role in the field so far. In one of its first major contributions, Samuel Moyn identifies the second half of the 1970s as the period of human rights' crystallization into a leitmotif of a political mass movement. For the intellectual historian, this was a new version of human rights. Contrary to its predecessors—natural rights and the rights of man—human rights were not tied to national sovereignty. To the contrary, the nation-state has become the supreme violator of human rights. A supranational law regime is envisioned as the guarantor of these rights, a safeguard against the excesses of sovereign power. However, one of the most extreme excesses of sovereign power does not play an important role in this account: for Moyn, genocide prevention was not a part of this new form of human rights activism before the 1990s. Yet conflicts that were understood to entail genocide had already happened earlier. Moyn mentions Biafra only once, but then his judgment is unambiguous: "Strikingly, . . . the crises in Biafra and Bangladesh . . . did not spark the creation of the international human rights movement."[9]

However, it is far from clear whether this is right. A brief glimpse at the history of the Biafran War indicates that the story is much more complicated. Thus the question needs to be raised whether the Biafran crisis did in some form contribute to the human rights moment of the 1970s. To define the place of the Biafran War in this history, I will analyze the rhetoric of human rights used by the principal actors during the Biafran War. The meaning of human rights is never clear-cut; human rights as a conceptual vehicle can accommodate divergent ideas.[10] Accordingly, it will be necessary to establish what people meant exactly when they were talking about human rights. The question is whether contemporaries agreed that human rights were at stake during the crisis. Otherwise, initiating a human rights movement could not have been prompted by the incident. Much of the scholarship on the emergence of global civil society treats its subjects as if individuals and groups discovered human rights causes quite naturally. But still, as Christopher Leslie Brown has argued with regard to British abolitionism, "It is one thing to notice an injustice and something else to act." To drive a wider movement, a cause needs to occupy a prominent place within the "complex of aspirations and concerns" of its key actors. Moreover, it is crucial how that cause is perceived by contemporaries. Only when a humanitarian cause is widely considered a good thing—and not, for instance, as an idle dream of a bunch of quixotic fanatics—is it thinkable to initiate a movement.[11] It is thus vital to establish in what ways the Biafran campaign was perceived. If it was not generally regarded as an unequivocally good cause, then it lacked the "moral capital" required to function as the myth of origins for a larger movement.

To analyze the different languages of human rights used during the Biafran War and perceptions of the Biafran cause, I first focus on how and in what guise the idea of human rights featured in the Biafran secessionists' campaign. Next, I analyze the modes in which the Biafran crisis was represented internationally, especially in the United Kingdom, the United States, France, and West Germany. I show how the conflict was turned into an international media event. Although represented as a purely humanitarian and accordingly apolitical issue, these accounts were widely understood as pro-Biafran. Then, I show how governmental officials in Lagos and London—Britain was the major foreign power supporting the Nigerian Federal Military Regime (FMG)—tried to counter these reports by casting doubt on the Biafran leadership. In conclusion, I try to situate the Biafran moment in the wider history of human rights in the 1970s.

Biafran Self-Determination: The Utopia of Rights of Man

After independence in 1960, Nigeria was widely considered one of the most promising Third World states. The potential for development—boosted by the discovery of oil on the eve of independence—seemed boundless in Africa's most populous country. Nigeria was divided into three main regions each dominated by one or two ethnic groups: Hausa-Fulani in the north, Yoruba in the west, and Igbo in the east. In January 1966, a series of coups and countercoups led to the installation of military rule and massacres against Igbos in Northern Nigeria. These outbursts of violence provoked a flow of some two million refugees to the Eastern Region. On May 30, 1967, the east's political leadership around the military governor-general Chukwuemeka Odumegwu Ojukwu declared their independence as the Republic of Biafra. The Nigerian Civil War began with the advance of federal troops into Biafran territory on July 6, 1967.[12]

The secessionist leadership, realizing their rather dim chances on the battlefield, tried to open a new front on the world stage of international politics and media and enlisted the services of international public relations agencies to coordinate their campaign.[13] The Biafran campaign for independence evolved around the classic anticolonial idea of the rights of man: the right to self-determination.[14] Tying their agenda to official Organization of African Unity (OAU) discourse, the Biafrans referred to the OAU Charter, which "states that the Heads of African States and Governments are 'convinced that it is the inalienable right of all people to control their own destiny.'" Integrated into pleas for independence and respect for human rights, the notion of genocide was a constituent element of the Biafran rhetoric. A pamphlet issued after the declaration of independence stated that as Biafrans were "victims of a continuing genocide . . . only a Government controlled and run by Biafrans can guarantee the people [the] basic human rights [of safety of life and property]." In the face of this most extreme violation of human rights, the Biafrans' right to self-determination could not be denied.[15] The Biafran genocide argument was hoped to be an effective tool to appeal to two audiences. First, the Biafran nation needed to be turned into an imaginable community for larger parts of the population at home. Evoking fears of a shared enemy is a widely used strategy to unify a heterogeneous population.[16] Second, the Biafran nation also needed to become an imaginable community in international diplomacy.

This, however, turned out to be too great a stretch of the imagination for most diplomats at the time. Almost all governments were reluctant to approve Biafra's right to self-determination. The only states that officially recognized the secessionist republic were Gabon, Haiti, Ivory Coast, Tanzania, and Zambia. In the OAU and "Third World UN," where many member states faced secessionist movements at home, fears of a balkanization of Africa were rampant. Biafran overtures thus fell on deaf ears in Third World diplomatic circles.[17] Accordingly, Biafran efforts to internationalize the conflict increasingly targeted Western audiences. International advocacy was initiated by Igbo expatriates, mostly young academics studying abroad.[18] But since Lagos also garnered support among Nigerian exiles, the efforts of the Biafran advocates did not tip the scales of international sympathy in favor of the secessionists.[19] In any case, even though casualties were substantial right from the start, the conflict did not engender a lot of international interest during the first year of fighting.

The humanitarian dimension was the issue that eventually changed that.

Already in late 1967 signs were discernible that Biafra would be threatened by a serious shortfall in food supply. After further advances in spring 1968, the federal army had created a blockade that left the secessionist state without access to the sea. The Biafran population was heading for a famine that would cost hundreds of thousands of human lives.[20] Foreign missionaries and other clergy were the first group of foreigners to be alerted to the threat. When foreign citizens were evacuated after the outbreak of war, most missionaries in Biafra decided to stay in their parishes. Many churchmen were convinced that their Christian Igbo brethren needed support in a religious war ignited by the Muslim Nigerian north, a perception that went back to Biafran rhetoric, which intertwined allegations against a Muslim north that "preached jihad" against Biafran Christians with the languages of genocide, human rights, and self-determination.[21] Irish missionaries of the Catholic Order of the Holy Ghost in particular began to "influence the message" dispatched from Nigeria and Biafra.[22] In the first months of 1968, more and more religious groups and humanitarian organizations were alerted to the event. Their support laid the foundation for what was later to become the Biafra lobby—a motley crew of supporters, mostly composed of nonstate actors rather than governments, united only by the rhetoric of humanitarianism.[23] This led to a move away from the sphere of politics into a purportedly nonpolitical sphere of humanitarianism. In the long run, that Biafra found support in a sphere allegedly transcending politics probably did not serve their political project. The Biafrans never achieved independence. After two and a half years of fighting, the secessionists surrendered on January 15, 1970. Biafran self-determination remained an unattainable utopia.

Representing Humanitarian Catastrophe

Within a few weeks in mid-1968, a dystopian vision of postcolonial catastrophe turned Biafra into an international media event. Starting in mid-June, newsstands across Western Europe and North America were repeatedly plastered with the pictures of haggard infants, emaciated skeletons with bloated bellies and eyes that seemed to condemn the passive beholder. A new icon of Third World misery was born: "Biafran babies."[24] The British station ITN was the first to broadcast television images from the area, other stations were soon to follow suit.[25] The images had an enormous effect on numerous contemporaries; many were reminded of the pictures taken during the liberation of the

Nazi camps in 1945.[26] For many observers, the images of starving children turned the Biafran rhetoric of genocide into reality. As Lady Violet Bonham Carter put it in the House of Lords, "not one of us can say, 'I did not know,'" because "thanks to the miracle of television we see history happening before our eyes. We see no Ibo propaganda; we see the facts."[27] However, the spheres of journalism, advocacy, and politics were deeply intertwined. Biafra's Swiss public relations agency Markpress organized the airlift of media representatives into the war zone, and the secessionist government made sure international journalists were given ample opportunities to take pictures of starving children.[28] The reports and appeals of humanitarian organizations and journalists entailed a change of what Biafra meant: it became a cipher for human suffering, typified by the icon of starving children.[29]

This new Biafra was decidedly at odds with the Biafra that had emerged in Third World international politics: a secessionist state seeking self-determination. The bifurcated understandings of Biafra are apparent in an exchange of letters between the Nigerian high commissioner in London, Babafemi Ogundipe, and Oxfam's general secretary H. Leslie Kirkley. Ogundipe wrote to Kirkley in June 1968 expressing his government's concern about Oxfam's "Biafra Emergency Appeal": the naming of the appeal would "add credence to the fiction that a State of 'Biafra' exists." Furthermore, this advertisement makes Oxfam appear to support "the propaganda of the rebels."[30] In his response, Kirkley explains that Oxfam "never take[s] political sides, and our one and only concern is to help those in the greatest need."[31] For the representative of the Nigerian federal government, Biafra was a political concept, a secessionist state; for Oxfam's general secretary, Biafra was a site of human tragedy, a hot spot on the humanitarians' mental map.

In the moment that the media turned Biafra into a burning issue in international politics, Western governments were forced to respond to the crisis. Discussions were especially intense in Britain, the former colonial power in Nigeria. Whitehall was the main foreign power supporting Lagos, providing the FMG with arms.[32] Criticism of Harold Wilson's Labour government was frequently formulated with recourse to the language of rights. Wilson, who had repeatedly expressed his government's "determination for human rights," was quoted in newspaper articles which concluded that "human rights mean nothing . . . when it comes to Biafra," or asked, "What about their Human Rights, Mr. Wilson?" accompanied by images of starving Biafran children.[33] A number of writers referred to the antigenocide convention, which had been recently ratified in the UK. In Nigeria, genocide is being perpetrated "with the positive support of the British government," as Britain-Biafra Association member Auberon Waugh, son of the novelist Evelyn Waugh, asserted, amounting to "the most hideous crime against humanity in which England has ever been involved."[34] For writers like Waugh, a reiteration of Auschwitz was happening in West Africa. In a *Spectator* editorial presumably written by Waugh, the Nigerian Civil War is described as "a war of extermination": the "final solution for the Ibos is well under way." Yet this time, Britain supported the wrong side: "If we were to stop arms shipments to Nigeria, says the Government, she would obtain them from other sources. Possibly so—but if Hitler had invited foreign tenders for the construction of his gas-ovens would Britain have applied, using the same excuse?"[35]

Similar, if less severe, criticism was voiced elsewhere, even if the allegations were not as strong as in Britain, since no other Western government opted so clearly for Lagos. "Severe violations of human rights such as genocide are a provocation to everybody dedicated to these human rights, and hence also to the Federal Republic," as the Aktionskomitee Biafra declared in a resolution to the Bonn government.[36] In a speech delivered at a Hamburg Biafra rally that was reprinted in *Die Zeit*, Günter Grass argued that "the knowledge of Auschwitz, Treblinka and Belsen" obligates every German "to speak out against the culprits and accessories of the genocide in Biafra."[37] In the United States the Committee to Keep Biafra Alive was the most vocal proponent of the secessionist republic. In a letter circulated to members of Congress, Paul Connett, the English head of the American group, suggestively addressed the politicians: "We are sure that you, as a congressman concerned with human rights, will see that Biafra is a test-case for humanity"; and argued that a system ensuring "that minority groups will not be eradicated or subjugated" must be established immediately.[38]

Many religious authorities, who continued to play a crucial role in the pro-Biafran campaign, argued along similar lines. Bishop Heinrich Tenhumberg, head of the Catholic Church's liaison office with the Bonn government, explained that the "principle of nonintervention is outdated in our time when the protection of fundamental human rights within a state is at stake." In such a situation, "no civilized state" could remain passive in a world after Auschwitz, given that modern transport and communication technologies automatically transform internal conflicts into international crises.[39] Officials of the Protestant church criticized the West German government for merely paying lip service to human rights and not acting on behalf of the Biafran population.[40] An internal memorandum of the German Catholic Church's

Arbeitskreis für Menschenrechte urged its members to advocate a more intensive discussion of the questions raised by the conflict, as this "should in the
long run lead to the erosion of the partly outdated principle of nonintervention in effective international law."[41]

Biafra lobbyists and intellectuals aligning with their cause questioned the
validity of national sovereignty in times of humanitarian crisis and called for
the rule of international law, invoking both the Universal Declaration of
Human Rights and the Convention on the Prevention and Punishment of the
Crime of Genocide. When the two conventions were passed in 1948, these
were competing projects: the gulf separating collective and individual rights
seemed impossible to bridge for the advocates of either cause.[42] In the language that the Biafra lobby used twenty years later, genocide and human
rights intertwined. Western sympathizers with the Biafran cause freely incorporated most of the elements of the secessionists' conceptual bricolage into
their rhetoric.[43] At the core of the activists' rhetorical mélange was the emergent belief that national sovereignty cannot be sanctified in a world after Auschwitz: to prevent genocide, human rights are needed to protect populations
from excesses of sovereign power. But in effect, it was only the sovereignty of
postcolonial states in the global South that was challenged. In his preface to a
volume on Biafra, noted German historian Golo Mann, the third child of
Nobel Prize laureate Thomas Mann, asks why the United States did not do
more about human suffering in Biafra. To leave no space for ambiguity, he
decided to answer the rhetorical question: "Because it would have been
against international law: 'intervention' in the 'internal matters' of a 'sovereign state.'" However, Nigeria was not a state like the United States, he argued,
since this legal terminology was foreign to African thinking. Intervention in
African affairs would thus be appropriate.[44]

Pleas for Biafra's right to self-determination generally featured much less
in the activists' rhetoric than in the secessionists' publicity. However, this was
different in France. French willingness to intervene went hand in hand with
pleas for self-determination. Paris never took the step of official recognition,
but the de Gaulle government was the main foreign power supporting Biafra
and repeatedly approved of the Biafrans' right to self-determination through
declarations and statements.[45] As a major postcolonial power in sub-Saharan
Africa, the Elysée's policy line was also motivated by the hope to weaken
Nigeria—the West African state biggest in population numbers, rich in oil,
and supported by the British.[46] Despite these overtones of power politics,
French rhetoric of the right to self-determination was echoed by some highly

optimistic voices among activists and journalists sympathetic to the Biafran cause. The French news magazine *L'Express* asserted that the French government initiated an international movement that would lead to intervention on behalf of the Biafran population.[47] As a number of French authors agreed, Republican ideals were the incentive for this intervention, which failed to materialize. Inscribing his account into a tradition of universalism *à la française*, Gaullist parliamentary delegate and former diplomat Raymond Offroy asserted in the first edition of the bulletin of the Comité d'Action pour le Biafra, which he headed, that France has "always defended the people's right to self-determination." "In Black Africa, the Fifth Republic carried out a decolonization that is the only complete success in this regard." Given that history, it is "normal that France is once more at the head of the battle line."[48]

French colonial republicanism had been fuelled by the ambition to turn imperial subjects into Frenchmen—or at least a chosen few, the so-called *évolués*. On the eve of decolonization, colonial republicanism turned from an ideal of assimilation to one of association. To come to terms with the end of empire, the story of French imperialism was now re-narrated as one of the benevolent guidance of colonial nations toward self-determination, rather than that of individuals towards "civilization" and, possibly, citizenship.[49] Perceived in these terms, the Biafran crisis seemed to call for a particularly French advocacy of universal rights—a stunning difference to the discussions in Germany, the United Kingdom, or the United States. In France, the emphasis put on the right to self-determination of the Biafran Republic added quite distinct tones to the dystopia of humanitarian catastrophe. The amount of identification with the political rather than just the humanitarian cause was remarkable, even more so in view of the cracks that formed in the façade of Biafran rhetoric soon after the conflict had become a humanitarian media event.

Representing the Biafran Government

The perception that the FMG deliberately starved the Biafran population to death posed serious problems for Nigeria's main ally in London. British officials were convinced that the Biafran allegations were unjustified. From their point of view, the problem was that the secessionists executed their propaganda campaign much more skillfully than their federal counterparts. In October 1968, a Foreign and Commonwealth Office (FCO) member of staff surmised that the "tide of unreasonable emotion" provoked by Biafran propaganda would obstruct a fair judgment of the conflict.[50] A colleague explained that "the Biafran rebels . . . thanks largely to the highly competent, if unscrupulous, activities of Markpress" made the most "of emotive issues such as the starvation of children." The FCO officials agreed that the Nigerian Government's task was much more difficult: they "have to rely on more intellectual arguments which do not possess the same headline value."[51] Accordingly, "one of our problems is that the Biafran case is an emotional one whereas the Federal case is an appeal to the intellect."[52] Officials of other governments that also faced a strong pro-Biafran lobby perceived the Biafran campaign in similar terms. In August 1968, German foreign minister Willy Brandt was informed by his right-hand man Egon Bahr about the "Church princes'" call for an arms embargo and the recognition of Biafra. According to the Social Democratic politician, it would not be in the interest of German foreign policy to give in to the wave of emotions. However, "emotions are always stronger than reason." Bahr advised that "the animal should be fed to control it."[53]

Most Western governments relied widely on information from the federal side; intelligence from Biafra was almost completely absent. Whitehall, which as the former colonial power would have been best prepared to produce more comprehensive information, relied almost exclusively on the high commissioner in Lagos, David Hunt, who from early on was dedicated to the federal side.[54] Despite this, the British government disseminated information itself and tried to convince journalists of the importance of Nigerian territorial integrity.[55] Measures taken seem to have been more drastic in the case of writers working for newspapers usually sympathetic to the Labour Party line. After Walter Schwarz had written "some frightful reports" for the *Guardian*, Whitehall "thought it was time to tackle him"; an FCO official wrote in a confidential report: "We had a good go at him."[56] These efforts were not restricted to releases in the United Kingdom. Through its embassies, London tried to influence coverage of the war in the foreign press by supplying editors with information and articles.[57]

Many contemporaries expressed their sympathies for Biafra in a language of affection. In a meeting with Ojukwu, Lord Fenner Brockway and James Griffiths, MP, leaders of the Committee for Peace in Nigeria, explained that they did not think they "have ever loved a country or a people more than we have during this last week in Biafra."[58] After their return, however, the two parliamentarians indicated their frustration with Ojukwu's tough position on negotiations of relief.[59] Others drew similar conclusions. Dame Margery

Perham, noted writer on African affairs and former Oxford tutor, initially sympathized with the Biafrans. Lagos invited her to visit the federally held parts of the country in the late summer of 1968. During her stay, she changed her mind and arranged for a radio talk during which she urged Ojukwu to surrender; after speaking to numerous military and political personnel on the federal side, she thought the fear of genocide after a military defeat was unfounded.[60] Many sympathizers with the Biafran side were quickly disillusioned with the secessionist leadership; their true intentions seemed to be veiled behind a smokescreen of do-gooder rhetoric. It was hard to grasp the reality behind the "emotions, illusions and slogans," as Bernard D. Nicholls from the Church Missionary Society commented in a letter to the editor of the *Times* that was not accepted for publication. Nicholls laconically explained to Oxfam's Leslie Kirkley that it was "not a very good letter," as it "didn't ride along on the present tide of emotion about the business."[61] Some even argued that the Biafrans willingly sacrificed millions of innocent lives in order to gain international attention. In August 1968, the California-based public relations agent Robert Goldstein resigned as Biafra's public relations consultant in the United States. After a February 1968 conversation, a U.S. State Department official noted that despite "his original desire only to 'make a dollar,' he admitted that he had now become 'emotionally involved' in 'Biafra's' cause."[62] This emotional involvement apparently reverted to disappointment. In a May 1969 interview on the BBC show *24 Hours*, Biafra's former spin doctor explained that "Ojukwu was using these starving children to get military concessions, possibly, at the negotiating table."[63]

Accordingly, the Biafran leadership soon lost much of its international esteem. Their unwillingness to allow relief into the enclave through a land corridor especially cast serious doubts on their trustworthiness. Already in late June 1968 the secessionist leadership felt impelled to issue a statement that it was not their intention "to play politics with the mass suffering of the victims of Nigeria's war of genocide."[64] Secretary of State for Commonwealth Affairs George Thomson, a "mild-mannered" politician, according to a U.S. State Department diplomat, mused in an August 27, 1968, House of Commons debate "that genocide is by no means the Federal intention, though I am afraid that I gloomily have the feeling that suicide for their people sometimes seems to be the intention of the Ibo leaders."[65] The question whether genocide was actually happening or was merely an invention of Biafran propagandists became a major issue. Certainly, the accusation of genocide had a real core in the massacres of 1966, and starvation was a problem indeed.

However, many Igbos lived unmolested in parts of Nigeria controlled by the Federal Military Government.[66] Lagos was understandably anxious to respond to these claims. One of the FMG's most effective diplomatic moves was the decision taken in late August 1968 to invite an international observer team to examine their troops' military conduct. This was, to a large degree, due to pressure from a British government concerned about its own international reputation. The team, comprised mainly of military servicemen sympathetic with the Nigerian cause, came to the conclusion that no genocide had occurred.[67] Nigerian propaganda relied quite heavily on the reports issued afterward.[68] Even if the Biafran lobby tried to counter these reports, they widely discarded the Biafran genocide claims internationally.[69]

Some Biafran sympathizers argued that this did not at all rebut the core of the allegations—innocent civilians were still dying. Discussions of what this should be called were nothing but a rhetorical exercise of "splitting hairs."[70] The problem was, however, that the secessionist campaign itself put so much weight on the genocide argument that, once this allegation was discarded, a rhetorical pillar of the Biafran representation of the conflict came tumbling down. Many tried their best to redeem this claim and answered with new forms of conceptual nit-picking—if it was not genocide, than at least it must be something comparable, they argued. One Tom Garrett wrote in the *Church Times* that, "genocide or no, the . . . Biafrans most certainly face the danger of 'hegemonocide,' if one may coin this word, i.e., the elimination of their most eminent men, many of whom are distinguished sons of Africa as well as of Biafra. This to the African mind, with its deep sense of family and tribal solidarity, is tantamount to genocide."[71]

Apart from the wider cultural-relativist structure of his argument, Garrett was right, to a certain degree: what was about to be killed was perhaps no tribal elite but at least an elite project. In a piece entitled "Who Killed Biafra?," published in the *New York Review of Books* a few weeks after the end of the war, the eminent anthropologist and Biafra lobbyist Stanley Diamond acknowledged that "premeditated biological genocide . . . was not officially sanctioned," even if "it was no doubt the policy of this or that field commander in localized areas." Yet, according to the New School for Social Research professor, "cultural genocide was being perpetrated." For the Biafrans, a successfully forged new nation, as the argument went, "genocide meant both more and less than physical extinction. It meant the collapse of their symbolic universe."[72] For Raphael Lemkin, who had developed the concept of genocide, the idea of cultural genocide was crucial for the definition of the crime. Yet it never formed part of the UN's genocide convention.[73] Even if it had, the Biafran case for cultural genocide rested on feet of clay—the "symbolic universe" of Biafra was a construction of very recent date and fragile composition. Moreover, it evolved around the notion of genocide; just like Israel, Biafra was a nation born in genocidal death. The danger of genocide was not real, however. Since both were mutually dependent, it was thus questionable whether the concept of Biafra was real at all. Were both just fictions created by an inventive secessionist leadership? Was there a Biafran people?

With these questions on the minds of contemporaries, the Biafran rhetoric of Holocaust comparisons backfired. Nigerian propagandists soon began to compare the secessionist leadership with that of Nazi Germany. Chief Anthony Enahoro, the FMG's commissioner for information, explained in a June 1968 letter to British MPs that the "rebel command" is "a régime which compares, in many respects, with the Hitler-Goebbels phenomenon."[74] Ojukwu's move to engage press agencies "to sell the idea to the world that there was a country called Biafra whose twelve million inhabitants were threatened with genocide by Nigeria" was an invention solely serving the Igbo elite, "a whopper on the grand scale that a connoisseur of mendacity such as Hitler would have appreciated."[75] More detached observers also came to such conclusions. Bernard Nicholls commented in one of his letters to Oxfam's general secretary that the "very general fear in Biafra of what has been called genocide is, I'm sure, real, but I am also sure that it is misguided, and that the bulk of the people are as much victims of a wicked and deliberate propaganda line as were the Germans under Hitler."[76]

Mainstream media also began to portray the Biafran leadership in an increasingly negative light. In an article after the Biafran surrender, *Der Spiegel* sketched Ojukwu as a dandyish man about town: unlike the "traditional leaders of Africa," this rakish bon vivant "was never put into the prisons of the colonial powers, never suffered from hunger or misery." Instead, he enjoyed the pleasures of student life in Oxford, where he was known as a "playboy driving fast MG sports cars." Only in his propaganda efforts did this "double-tongued" politician remain successful. To convince publics around the globe of his case, he and Markpress "invented . . . a 'religious war' between the Islamic Hausas and the Christian Igbos and cried genocide at a time when talk of this was unreasonable."[77] Doubts about the secessionist leadership seem to have been confirmed at the end of the war: "Ojukwu Flees as Biafra Faces Total Collapse," readers of the *Times* read on the front page on January 12, 1970.[78] Contrary to the expectations of many supporters of the Biafran cause, the Nigerian army did not "kill off" the Igbos after the Biafran surrender three days later.[79] Journalist Karl-Heinz Janßen explained in an article in *Die Zeit*: "the end was despicable." In view of the behavior of Biafra's "beloved *Führer*" during the days of the secessionist downfall, "many Germans may have thought of the May days 25 years ago." However, for the *Zeit* journalist, these associations were misleading: "Ojukwu was no Hitler and Biafra not a police state." The newspaper had been widely sympathetic to the secessionists' cause throughout the war. Now, Janßen attempted to defend previous frameworks of representing the conflict. He tried hard to disentangle the Biafran cause of self-determination from the associations flowing from the secessionist's regime's characterization as mendacious artists of propaganda: "This war was not a rebellion of a clique of officers avariciously snapping power and profits while fooling their people and large parts of the world's public by summoning the bogey of genocide. This was a tragic people's war for self-determination."[80] Certainly, Biafra was not a police state or a dictatorial regime of terror. But it was also not the birth of a new nation, molded out of the clay of tribal groups. That the *Zeit* writer goes at this length to redeem the Biafran cause testifies rather to the opposite: the tenacity of the doubts casted upon this program. Too many visitors to the secessionist state had returned disillusioned. As a political project, Biafra had become dubious.

Biafra and the 1970s Human Rights Moment

In 1972, the British journalist Suzanne Cronje published *The World and Nigeria*, one of the first accounts of the international history of the war. Like many other writers, Cronje highlighted the connection between propaganda and foreign policy. The war began to impinge on the consciousness of the general public "only in 1968, when starvation in Biafra had produced horrifying visible effects. . . . When people in Europe persisted in believing the evidence of their own eyes . . . it was claimed in London and Lagos that Ojukwu was using starvation for his own political ends." This was not "altogether unjustified," Cronje explained. "The Biafrans certainly did not manufacture starvation, but it soon became evident to them that world interest could be aroused more easily by evidence of suffering than by political arguments." However, not only Biafra's position at the negotiation table remained unaltered. The same would apply to Nigeria. Yet "official circles in London, Washington and elsewhere . . . took up and publicized the Federal 'concessions' while the Biafran suggestions received little public attention."[81]

It is doubtful whether the Biafran suggestions received "little public attention." What is interesting in this passage, however, is the apologetic tone in Cronje's portrayal of the Biafran position. Throughout the book the British policy line is continuously challenged. Cronje had been a staunch critic of the Labour government already during the conflict. As a member of the Britain-Biafra Association, she had, jointly with Auberon Waugh, penned a publication titled "Britain's Shame."[82] In her 1972 book, Cronje does not mention her membership in the association. The omission of her Biafra lobbyist past is a hint toward a changed perception of this cause. If she had still been convinced that being perceived as a part of this campaign would have bestowed her with the "moral capital" of the righteous humanitarian, she might have decided to take credit for her dedication. Yet she decided not to.

And indeed, the perception of the Biafran campaign changed decisively within a relatively short time after mid-1968. At the heart of Biafra's global moment lay a basic friction: observed through the lens of humanitarianism, the conflict appeared to be a solely humanitarian problem. Biafra, however, was first and foremost a political project. The dominant humanitarian representations depoliticized the civil war. Yet identification with the Biafran cause often went alongside empathetic reactions to the suffering of the "Biafran babies." The humanitarians were widely perceived as a constituent part of the Biafra lobby. However, during the course of the war, it became increasingly questionable whether the Biafran cause merited any support at all. Moreover, the staging of the conflict as a humanitarian media event made capturing the reality behind it incredibly difficult. To this day, the actual extent of the famine remains unknown. But the conflict made clear that governmental actors— probably on both sides—were willing to gamble with human lives in a poker game of power politics.

In spite of the loss of esteem of the Biafran cause, some activists had hoped to translate the campaign into an international network of human rights activists in a post-Biafra age. On a weekend in late May 1970, representatives of Biafra committees from twelve countries met in Liège to try to create "an International coalition to work on other human rights problems." Tying the agenda of International Conscience in Action (ICA), as the coalition was christened, to the imagery of borders and blockades so present during the Biafran crisis, Paul Connett envisioned "a coalition which would aim to break the blockade which separates man from human rights, human needs and human compassion." The coalition's charter specified that its aim is "to protect human rights (and to reintroduce the idea that they are as important as the rights of states)." These human rights are not those of individuals, however: "In particular the ICA will fight any attempt to destroy a group of people, its right to life, property, identity, and future."[83]

However, this coalition never met any success. After Biafra had been consigned to history, the Biafra lobby dissolved as well. The tenacity of the activists who remained convinced of the Biafran cause raised serious doubts among informed contemporaries—not a good basis to gather the moral capital that such a movement needs.[84] The only group of the coalition to outlive Biafra for more than a few months was the Hamburg-based Aktion Biafra-Hilfe (Biafra Help Campaign), which in 1970 evolved into the Gesellschaft für bedrohte Völker (Society for Threatened Peoples). Yet even if its success story is exceptional, it is also paradigmatic for the changes in the field of rights-based activism. Keeping in tune with the Biafran campaign, the work of the organization focuses on minority rights and genocide prevention.[85] Due to its emphasis on collective rights, it never formed part of the mainstream of human rights activism as this emerged as the "last utopia" in an age of the demise of ideologies—this utopia was one of individual rights, into which genocide prevention was not absorbed until the 1990s.

However, there was one major exception to the international dissolution of the campaign: France. Already shortly after the secessionists' surrender, *Guardian* journalist Walter Schwarz, who had initially been sympathetic to the project, evoked "Biafra's embarrassing ghost" that still "lingers on" on the other side of the channel. "A Biafra lobby without a Biafra is odd enough in itself." Yet French activist groups like Offroy's Comité d'Action pour le Biafra, also one of the driving forces behind the quickly defunct International Conscience in Action, continued issuing warnings of the genocide in Biafra.[86] In addition, humanitarians like Bernard Kouchner, cofounder and figurehead of Médecins sans Frontières, also kept telling the same story about Biafra. In their narrative, certainly based on heartfelt sentiments, young French doctors experienced the suffering of a group of innocent victims firsthand in the secessionist enclave and returned to Paris to revolutionize international politics.[87] In these accounts, the Biafran experience emerged as the myth of origins of a new movement aiming to end global suffering.[88] This narrative was based on the perception of the Biafran campaign as an unquestionably good thing—a conviction that had collapsed virtually everywhere else already during the war. With the possible exception of Ireland, France is the only country where Biafra indeed seems to mark a caesura in human rights politics.[89] Translating a distinctly French universalism into a postcolonial age, French republicanism was the hotbed of these ideas, which, however, could comprise the belief in a right to self-determination as well as the right to intervene.[90]

The model of the proliferation of human rights in the 1970s as part of a move toward transnationalism, which seems to underline much of the current literature, is too simplistic. It has to be borne in mind that the French case was special right from the start. Paris was the only Western government that supported the Biafran cause. Accordingly, a space for a much more positive apprehension of Biafra as a *political* cause was opened up there. The inscription of the human rights idea into national traditions of political thought is just as crucial as the liaison with national governments—at least Western governments. Otherwise, human rights politics often remain toothless, as evinced by Whitehall's policy line during the Biafran War. The Wilson administration did not change its position decisively in spite of severe criticism for supporting an allegedly genocidal regime.

Nevertheless, the Biafran case is an indicator for a change that fits quite well into the framework put forward by Moyn. The failed Biafran campaign for self-determination was one of the last efforts to keep alive anticolonialism as a "rights of man" movement. Yet in the political environment of postcolonial Africa, this politics could not thrive. Since then, movements that framed their project in the terms of postcolonial self-determination "fell outside the pale of empathy."[91] The Biafran failure put one of the final nails in the coffin of anticolonial rights of man. The civil war was also an indicator—perhaps a catalyst—of a wider loss of trust in postcolonial states. In a time when Third World governments turned toward authoritarianism, many of their erstwhile sympathizers in the West were disappointed. With the hopes for postcolonial liberation buried under the flags of Third World regimes, anticolonial revolution as the formation of new states lost its utopian allure.[92] The decades of the 1950s and the 1960s had been a time when very different futures were imaginable for Africans.[93] The Biafran case is evidence for the political space opening up in the moment of imperial dissolution: Biafra was a community imagined somewhere in between the Nigerian nation and the ethnic collective of the Igbos. However, this case also testifies to the limitedness of this space of political imagination: the Biafran program was still entirely dependent on the notion of the nation. This project turned out not to be viable, also because the Igbos did not equal Biafra. There was not only no genocide of the Biafran people, but also no Biafran people.

Even if this was not foreseeable, decolonization universalized the principle of the nation-state: it was perhaps not the universalization of the rights of man but of the nation-state as a guarantor of rights, whether it fulfilled these duties or not. Of course, an endless chain of secessions is virtually possible. But Biafra indicated that at that historical moment no further secessions—in Africa—would gain sufficient international support. Internationally, self-determination and secession were and still are thinkable in Europe.[94] But this is not the case in Africa, where minority rights are deemed dangerous. Deeply embedded in colonial stereotypes and politics, African ethnic groups are mostly perceived as tribes rather than nations.[95] Balkanization may be okay for the Balkans, but not for Africa. The territorial borders of the postcolonial nation-state became sacrosanct. Its political sovereignty, however, was about to erode. Biafra was a moment when the nation-state, or perhaps more precisely the postcolonial sub-Saharan African nation-state, failed to protect the human rights of a part of its population. In this case, the formation of a new nation-state was not a viable option. However, the closure of this political space, of secession as a viable alternative to the conditions of African nation-states, also opened up new spaces for political claim making. In a world of nations that did not leave much space for the emergence of new nations, the global, or the international, became increasingly attractive as entities called on as guarantors of the rights of individuals. Yet these individual rights could not simultaneously be group rights any longer. To legitimize a politics of interventionism into the conduct of sovereign nation-states, a language of moral demands transcending politics was needed, and the language of individual rights, detached from the revolutionary political project of building new states, proved more effective in this regard.

The paths toward the global human rights regime of the present were convoluted; the junctions, divergences, and dead ends were numerous. One of these paths, however, passed through the secessionist Republic of Biafra. This did not turn out to be the main path—human rights politics as genocide prevention were not the version of human rights that led to their breakthrough. But without considering the Biafran campaign, we cannot fully understand the transformation occurring in human rights politics in the last decades of the past century. The Biafran crisis was a step toward the conceptual erosion of the sovereignty of non-Western states. Because it had also proven that secessionist projects were not viable alternatives to the postcolonial state, the crisis helped to pave the way toward the late twentieth-century regime of transnational human rights as individual rights.

Chapter 3

The Disenchantment of Socialism:
Soviet Dissidents, Human Rights,
and the New Global Morality

Benjamin Nathans

Since at least the eighteenth century, the hallowed story told about human rights is that human beings are born in possession of certain claims to moral worth that are bound up with the essence of being human and therefore are not limited to particular times, places, or political arrangements. Over the last several decades, historians of human rights, bound by the axioms of historicism and antiessentialism, have tempered this story by insisting that human rights were constructed, or even invented, by human actors responding to historically specific circumstances, whether the struggle between feudal aristocracies and overweening monarchs, the building of republican nation-states, or the moral abyss of genocide. Instead of the timeless narrative that human rights imply about themselves, in which they "always already" exist (if only in latent form), historical scholarship has emphasized origins and change over time, typically within an assumed framework of moral progress. Rather than being cast as transcendent values, human rights have been brought down to earth and given a history.

But what kind of history? By selecting certain emblematic texts (while passing over others in silence), one can trace the origin of human rights to the Bible, to Greek and Roman antiquity, to medieval doctrines of natural law, to the Enlightenment, or to other privileged (read Western) sites. One can form a great chain of being that links these various sites to the present, or to parallel texts from non-Western traditions. In this manner, the accumulated legacy of decades (or centuries, or millennia) of human rights history can be mobilized to help explain (or buttress) their remarkable authority in our own time, whether in international affairs or in the way hundreds of millions of people articulate basic moral and political claims.

One of the goals of the present volume is to take a close look at what is gained and lost in this transition from mythological to genealogical ways of thinking about human rights. In separate works, Jan Eckel and Samuel Moyn have cast doubt on the claim that human rights in their current form—as a "central organizing principle of global modernity"—have a deep history in any meaningful sense. From different vantage points, they have proposed that the global prominence of human rights today is the result not of an accumulation of historical momentum starting in 1215 or 1789 or 1948, but of a rupture, a "tectonic shift" that gave rise to a new "morality for the world" in the 1970s.[1] For Eckel, the transnational synergies that distinguish the recent blossoming of human rights activism demand a "polycentric" approach to their history as a methodological imperative for understanding the globalization of rights-based idealism. For Moyn, invocations of the "rights of man" prior to the twentieth century were invariably bound up with citizenship-based projects that served to buttress, rather than constrain, the power of emerging national states. The swelling human rights rhetoric in the aftermath of World War II was stillborn precisely because none of the major actors proved willing to move away from the nation-building functions of rights inherited (at least in the Atlantic world) from the eighteenth century. Only in the 1970s did human rights succeed in transcending the framework of sovereign national states to become a truly transnational set of norms. For Moyn, moreover, the implosion of earlier utopian projects (such as socialism or world government) was an indispensable precondition for the human rights revolution of the 1970s. Not, however, because human rights are post-utopian: on the contrary, while the genealogical approach may have rescued human rights from their precarious mythological origins (which placed their foundations outside historical time), Eckel and Moyn caution that human rights remain a fundamentally utopian project (which places their fulfillment outside historical time).

Stimulated by these bracing arguments, which have helped inaugurate a kind of rupture in scholarship on human rights, I propose to explore their application vis-à-vis one of the key arenas in which the alleged revolution in human rights unfolded, namely, the Soviet Union. The world's first socialist society is important for the global history of rights in the post–World War II era for several reasons. As a superpower, and as leader of the "second world," the Soviet Union played an active role in nearly every forum in which international human rights accords were negotiated. Even in instances such as the 1948 Universal Declaration of Human Rights (UDHR), which in the end Moscow declined to endorse, the Soviet position profoundly shaped the final document, ensuring that economic, social, and national rights entered and remained part of the emerging ensemble of international norms. Unlike South Africa and Saudi Arabia, two other states that abstained in the voting on the UDHR, the Soviet Union offered an alternative vision of global rights (under the rubric of "socialist internationalism") to rival that of the Atlantic countries. Cast by those countries in the role of sole surviving totalitarian state, moreover, the USSR functioned as the conceptual antipode against which Cold War rights were articulated in the West. Finally, and contrary to all expectations, the USSR became home to an indigenous human rights movement, the first such movement in a socialist country, one further distinguished by the fact that it targeted human rights violations not in other people's countries but at home. Soviet dissidents' struggle to defend rights of free speech and assembly, freedom of worship, and emigration captured the imagination of Western publics like no other story of its time and thereby became a persistent factor in the Cold War—the era's preeminent international rivalry. By measuring the history of the Soviet human rights movement vis-à-vis new transnational interpretations of the 1970s offered by Eckel and Moyn, this chapter assesses important new global-historical hypotheses through the lens of local history, in effect proposing a dialogue between the two. Does the Soviet case fortify the claim that human rights represent a utopian platform whose sudden elevation in the 1970s depended on the collapse of prior, competing utopian projects? How might the Soviet human rights movement illuminate the dynamics of Eckel's polycentric model of the globalization of human rights?

The Soviet Seventies and the New Global Morality

Since much depends on the specific timing of the breakthrough of global human rights, we would do well to begin with the problem of periodization: what do we mean when we say "the seventies" in the Soviet context? As in other advanced, industrialized societies, in the USSR the sixties left a far stronger imprint than did the period that followed. The idea of "sixties people" (the so-called *shestidesiatniki*) became part of vernacular Soviet culture well before that decade was over.[2] By contrast, only in hindsight did the seventies become known for anything in particular, and then as "the era of stagnation," a term made famous by Mikhail Gorbachev in an obvious effort to contrast it with his own program of "acceleration" and "restructuring" (perestroika). For the Soviet Union, the seventies would seem to have begun in August 1968 when Soviet tanks smothered the Prague Spring and with it the dream of a more humane version of socialism in the USSR itself. Their end can plausibly be dated to December 1979—when the Soviet army invaded Afghanistan in an effort to shore up that country's Communist Party in its war against Islamic insurgents, an act that effectively put an end to détente—or more expansively, to March 1985 with Gorbachev's selection as general secretary of the Communist Party of the Soviet Union.[3]

The hinge year of 1968 and the transition to new ideas and practices in the 1970s help explain important aspects of the history of Soviet rights activism. As the standard narrative has it, that history evolved through a series of stages, beginning with the prepolitical or literary dissent of figures like Vladimir Dudintsev (*Not by Bread Alone*, 1956), Boris Pasternak (*Doctor Zhivago*, 1957), and Alexander Solzhenitsyn (*One Day in the Life of Ivan Denisovich*, 1962).[4] The Soviet government's arrest of two nonconformist writers, Andrei Sinyavsky and Yuli Daniel, marked a transition to the civil rights phase of the movement. A December 1965 "glasnost [transparency] meeting" in the heart of Moscow famously demanded that the government live up to its own constitution by holding an open trial of the accused men and releasing from prison those who had legally protested their arrest.[5] Here was born the counterintuitive strategy of deploying Soviet law, including the liberties enshrined in the Soviet Constitution, to counteract violations of the civil rights of Soviet citizens by their government. Thousands of individuals signed petitions calling for "socialist legality" in the treatment of nonconformists. The arrest or dismissal from their jobs of those who protested the heavy sentences imposed on Sinyavsky and Daniel sparked a chain reaction of further protests, more arrests and trials, and new rounds of protest.

Three years of such activities, however, failed to produce a victory (e.g., an acquittal in a political trial or a visible concession from the Soviet regime) for the self-styled rights defenders (*pravozashchitniki*). At this point, in 1968, so the argument runs, the struggle for rights took a decisive turn: it went global. The failure to gain traction by invoking Soviet civil rights and other domestic laws; the crushing of reform socialism in Prague, killing any hopes for a parallel Moscow Spring; and finally, the designation by the UN General Assembly of 1968 as the International Year of Human Rights, marking the twentieth anniversary of the UDHR—all these allegedly combined to produce a fateful shift in dissident strategy. Now, instead of invoking civil rights guaranteed by the Soviet constitution, dissidents cited international human rights covenants in an attempt to leverage world opinion for the purpose of containing the lawless behavior of the Soviet state toward its own population. It was a strategy that found expression in the samizdat periodical *Chronicle of Current Events*, founded in 1968, the cover page of which reproduced verbatim Article 19 of the UDHR: "Everyone has the right to freedom of opinion and expression; this right includes freedom to hold opinions without interference and to seek, receive and impart information and ideas through any media and regardless of frontiers." Shortly thereafter, in May 1969, activists grouped around Petr Iakir—the son of a Soviet army general executed on Stalin's orders in 1937 during the Great Terror, and himself imprisoned for nearly two decades in the Gulag starting at age fourteen—founded what came to be known as the Initiative Group for the Defense of Human Rights. Over the next decade, the Initiative Group would send dozens of letters to the United Nations (many of them via Western journalists), alerting Secretary-General U Thant, his successor Kurt Waldheim, and the UN Commission on Human Rights of violations of the UDHR suffered by Soviet citizens.[6] As with the Sinyavsky/Daniel trial, there ensued a chain reaction whereby members of the Initiative Group found themselves facing arrest and imprisonment. Within a year of the group's formation, more than half of the original fifteen founders were under arrest or detained in psychiatric hospitals, and much of the group's attention turned to the plight of its own members.

That plight failed to deter others from following a similar path. In November 1970, Valery Chalidze, Andrei Tverdokhlebov, Andrei Sakharov, and a handful of other scientists formed the Committee on Human Rights. More scholarly in orientation than the Initiative Group, the committee took upon itself the task of producing detailed analyses of various aspects of international human rights and Soviet law, all for the purpose of providing expert advice to the Soviet government and bringing attention to individuals falsely accused of anti-Soviet activity.[7] The Kremlin had no intention of accepting advice from the committee, but as KGB chairman Yuri Andropov reported to Brezhnev two months after its founding, Western shortwave radio broadcasts had already informed large numbers of Soviet citizens of the committee's existence. "Rumors about it are spreading," Andropov wrote; "the flow of letters addressed directly to Sakharov and to the 'Committee,' approving the creation of such an 'organization' in the USSR, is increasing."[8] Indeed, the committee soon found itself flooded with letters, petitions, and complaints from individuals across the USSR, overwhelming the capacities of its members to respond, much less take action on behalf of their correspondents.[9] The establishment in October 1973 of a Moscow section of Amnesty International, led by Tverdokhlebov and ten other dissident figures, offers further evidence of the turn to transnational frameworks and institutions among Soviet human rights activists.

The best-known examples of human rights activism in the USSR during the seventies are the Helsinki Watch Groups that sprang up in Moscow, Kiev, Vilnius, Tbilisi, and Yerevan following the Soviet Union's signing of the 1975 Helsinki Accords. Leaving aside overwrought claims of a "Helsinki effect" having brought down the Soviet bloc,[10] the Watch Groups proved considerably more effective than their predecessors, such as the Initiative Group or the Committee on Human Rights, at raising international concern over Soviet human rights violations. Part of the reason for this, of course, was that their letters and reports were addressed not to the toothless United Nations but to the USSR's Cold War rivals, sovereign Western states that had cosigned the Helsinki Accords and in principle had an interest in those accords' fulfillment. Another factor, wholly unforeseeable at the time of the Watch Groups' founding, was the election of Jimmy Carter in 1976 as president of the United States and his willingness to draw global attention to the small cohort of beleaguered Soviet dissidents. Founders of the Helsinki Watch Groups, people like Yuri Orlov, Elena Bonner, Anatoly Shcharansky, and General Petro Grigorenko, were predictably subjected to harsh repression. By now, however, the technique of documenting and publicizing contradictions between the Kremlin's formal commitment to rights norms and its actual behavior toward its own citizens had taken on a momentum of its own. Moscow's standard public defense, invoking the principle of noninterference in the domestic affairs of sovereign states, was powerless to stem the flood of negative publicity, including the possibility of cancelled scientific and cultural exchanges, trade barriers linked to human rights issues, and other threats to the carefully crafted scaffolding of détente.

As this brief summary suggests, the Soviet seventies, understood as stretching from 1968 to 1979, were indeed a crucial decade in the history of human rights activism in the USSR and beyond, insofar as that activism embraced the new "morality for the world" that was taking shape beyond the

Soviet Union's borders. But did this development actually represent a sharp break with the aspirations and practices of the preceding era? Did it require the collapse of previously held ideals, substituting for them something that was similarly utopian in nature?

Local and Global Dimensions of Human Rights Activism

There are multiple grounds for skepticism, or at least greater nuance, vis-à-vis the above account. To begin with, in the Soviet setting, the transition from civil rights activism—that is, rights functioning within a defined political community or citizenship space—to human rights activism not only did not require a "tectonic shift" but marked less a transition than an expansion of the dissident repertoire. In fact, the same protagonists took part in both the civil rights and human rights strategies. As early as 1967, Alexander Volpin, the initiator of the 1965 glasnost meeting, began circulating samizdat copies of the UN rights covenants signed by Moscow the year before. As late as 1977, Petro Grigorenko, one of the founders of the Initiative Group for the Defense of Human Rights in 1969, helped produce a samizdat journal of uncensored commentary on the draft of the new Soviet Constitution, focusing on the civil rights and duties contained therein.[11] In fact, the first appeal sent by the Initiative Group to the United Nations, dated May 20, 1969, exhibits not just a remarkable conceptual fluidity but what appears to be considerable confusion as regards civil vs. human rights. Identifying itself as "The Initiative Group for the Defense of Civil Rights [sic] in the USSR," the fledging organization called on the UN to defend the "human rights that are being crushed in our country": "We are turning to the UN because our protests and complaints, sent over the course of several years to the highest state and judicial organs of the Soviet Union, have remained unanswered. Our hope that our voice might be heard, that the authorities might put an end to the lawlessness to which we have repeatedly drawn attention—this hope has exhausted itself."[12] As this passage makes clear, the Initiative Group consisted of individuals who themselves had taken part in civil-rights-based campaigns and who, for the time being, continued to include that strategy in their repertoire. In a number of its subsequent appeals, the Initiative Group (which by June 1969 had quietly renamed itself the Initiative Group for the Defense of Human Rights in the USSR) addressed not the UN or other international organizations but the Soviet Procuracy, citing violations of Soviet law.[13] One such appeal, protesting

the arrest of one of its members (Viktor Krasin), referred to his work "in defense of the civil rights of man."[14]

The Initiative Group's mixing of appeals to civil and human rights, and its
mistaken claim in one appeal that the Soviet Union had "officially approved" the
UDHR,[15] were almost certainly symptoms of one of its distinguishing features:
the complete absence of lawyers from its ranks. One would be hard pressed to
name a Western human rights organization in the post-1945 period—the golden
age of human rights professionalization—in which this was the case. While the
Chalidze/Sakharov Committee on Human Rights and the Moscow Helsinki
Watch Group informally consulted the defense attorney Sofia Kalistratova (an
expert in Soviet, not international law, who stayed on the sidelines in order not to
jeopardize her ability to represent clients in political trials), it remains the case
that rights activism in the USSR—civil as well as human—was fundamentally the
work of legal amateurs. A hard-and-fast distinction between the two arenas appeared to Soviet dissidents as a luxury they neither needed nor could afford.

As the Initiative Group's first appeal intimated, the turn to the UN was
driven not only by the prospect of human rights serving as an added resource
in the struggle against political repression, but by the fact that numerous petitions and appeals to Soviet authorities "have remained unanswered." When
more than a year's worth of appeals to the UN similarly went unanswered—a
circumstance bitterly noted in subsequent announcements—the Initiative
Group began to set its sights elsewhere: the World Health Organization and the
International Congress of Psychiatrists (for cases involving dissidents imprisoned in psychiatric hospitals), the Papacy (regarding the arrest of religious dissenters), Reuters and other media companies, and in many instances "public
opinion" (*obshchestvennost'*). According to one former dissident, what was
shocking about the Initiative Group, beyond its open violation of the ban
against unauthorized organizations, was that it disregarded the unwritten taboo
against "airing dirty laundry in public, looking abroad for defense against our
own country's authorities."[16] And yet even this was not entirely new: for over a
decade, Soviet writers from Pasternak and Volpin to Sinyavsky and Daniel had
published abroad works whose content was deemed "anti-Soviet," typically
with grave consequences for their authors. It is also possible that the long-
standing internationalist strain of Soviet ideology itself, with its emphasis on
transnational solidarities (based, to be sure, on class rather than occupation,
religion, or "humanity"), unintentionally nourished the dissidents' turn to a
global audience and the emerging global morality of human rights.

To get a glimpse of how that morality appeared to dissidents, how the encounter of global and local (or, to put it somewhat differently, Western and Soviet) norms took shape, let us turn to a document stemming from the period leading up to the formation in 1973 of a Moscow affiliate of Amnesty International. A year earlier, Amnesty had (privately) estimated the number of political prisoners in the USSR at "between 5,000 and several hundred thousand." Of those, it had adopted several hundred as "prisoners of conscience," restricting itself to cases for which documentation—often in the form of smuggled samizdat texts—was available.[17] Amnesty was still feeling its way when it came to adopting Soviet prisoners and the attendant publicity: an internal 1968 memorandum discussing the adoption process had noted that "strong doubts have been expressed whether this can do any good in Soviet cases."[18] Nonetheless, prisoner adoptions proceeded, and word of Amnesty's work began to reach dissident circles inside the USSR. On September 10, 1973, a group led by Andrei Tverdokhlebov calling itself Gruppa-73 telephoned Amnesty headquarters in London in order to transmit a message to Amnesty's Sixth International Council, due to convene shortly in Vienna. Five days later, Amnesty delegates and observers from twenty-four countries who attended the council meeting at Albert Schweitzer Haus listened to the following words from Moscow:

> Greetings to the International Council of Amnesty International. Since childhood we have been accustomed to hearing such phrases as "political action of the masses," "the active foreign policy of the government and party," "the struggle for social rights and the social reconstruction of society," "the scientific and technological revolution"—and these are the things we imagined the world was preoccupied with. As for words like "conscience," "dignity," "conviction"—we are accustomed to apply them exclusively to the exertions and strivings of individual human beings. For who can help one to value such words, and to preserve their value, other than oneself and those to whom one is closest? At first we were astonished, and could not grasp, that in fact total strangers can help, people who live in the most distant countries, in conditions utterly different from one's own, in other cultures. It is this above all that we value in your example and your activity, insofar as we are in a position to judge them. Please accept our best wishes.[19]

For Tverdokhlebov and other members of Gruppa-73, Amnesty International represented not so much a new morality as a new way of deploying familiar, in fact intimately familiar, moral ideas in decidedly nonintimate settings. The kindness of strangers stood out all the more starkly against Soviet citizens' widespread cynicism vis-à-vis the Communist Party's omnipresent (and by the 1970s, largely hollow) rhetoric of moral exhortation. It suggested a recasting of the division of labor between public and private morality.

To the Soviet government, of course, the kindness of strangers looked suspiciously like a violation of the principle of noninterference in the domestic affairs of sovereign states. As Moyn emphasizes, it was precisely the willingness to bend that principle in the name of human rights that distinguished the global activism of the 1970s from its citizenship-based precursors in the late eighteenth century and the UDHR's toothless universalism. To Soviet rights activists, "interference" from abroad was merely one lane on a two-way street. From the very beginning—whether the story starts in the late 1950s with the publication of uncensored works abroad, or in 1966 with the appearance of Alexander Ginzburg's *White Book* on the trial of Sinyavsky and Daniel—Soviet dissidents actively engaged in outreach to foreign audiences, not just inviting but enabling and fostering specific kinds of attention to Soviet internal affairs. Amnesty International's adoption of Soviet prisoners of conscience, for example, would scarcely have been possible without the crescendo of data provided by samizdat texts smuggled abroad. Preeminent among these was the *Chronicle of Current Events* (1968–1982), the dispassionate underground journal of the dissident movement. An internal Amnesty memorandum from March 1970 described the challenge of "going through the large volume of Soviet documents originating in the USSR," for which volunteers with knowledge of Russian, and eventually a full-time researcher, were being brought on board.[20] In an unparalleled gesture—one that generated considerable controversy inside the organization—Amnesty sponsored the English translation and publication of the *Chronicle* starting in October 1970 (issue number 16), producing over a thousand copies of each issue for sale in the West and ensuring that every member of the International Executive Committee received a copy.[21] As Eckel notes, there was a basic asymmetry in the new global morality: "Only in the West did [human rights activism] since the 1970s take the form of global moral interventionism, while everywhere else it remained a form of self-defense."[22] And yet, at least in the Soviet case, local actors played an indispensable role in shaping that intervention. Or to put it another way, the local and global dimensions of human rights activism were mutually constitutive, if still highly asymmetrical.

The Evolution of Human Rights Activism

The trajectory of Soviet human rights activism thus begins to look less revolutionary than evolutionary, tracing a relatively continuous line of development (in terms of protagonists, ideas, and practices) from the 1960s to the end of the 1970s. At no point, it seems to me, was there a repudiation of, or break with, civil rights or citizenship-based strategies. Socialist rights grounded in Soviet citizenship were part of the USSR's nation-building process (in the sense of building a "Soviet people" rather than promoting the development of individual ethnic and national groups that comprised the Soviet Union). While it had not been the intention of their authors that constitutionally enshrined civil rights be used by ordinary citizens to contain the power of the state, this was precisely the purpose to which they were put by dissidents starting in the 1960s. Rather than marking a "transcendence" of the state, international human rights became an additional method for achieving the same purpose—from outside as well as from below.

The argument for the 1970s as marking the birth of a new human rights utopia, for which the collapse of previous utopias was a necessary precondition, would seem to find its strongest anchor in the loss of faith in socialism induced by the Soviet invasion of Czechoslovakia in 1968.[23] The crushing of the Prague Spring, while considerably less violent than the suppression of the uprising in Budapest in 1956, was far more consequential precisely because it strangled the dream of a humanistic socialism (rather than anticommunist secession from the Soviet bloc, as in the Hungarian case), not just in Czechoslovakia but among reform-minded socialists throughout the bloc—and beyond. Nowhere was the sense of humiliation more acute than in dissident and reformist circles in the Soviet Union, where in addition to grief and anger over the dream's demise, there was guilt over being a citizen of the country responsible for its death. The founding of the Initiative Group and the Committee on Human Rights in the wake of the Prague Spring would appear to exemplify the broader pattern that played itself out in numerous countries, as various leftist, revolutionary, and/or Third Way utopias of the 1960s collapsed, to be superseded by a new global morality of human rights.

As with the issue of discontinuity between civil and human rights activism, however, close attention to the particulars raises questions regarding the supersession thesis (which is of course related to the discontinuity thesis). Well before 1968, the idea of returning to a revolutionary Leninism untainted by Stalin's "deviations" had ceased to be the principal animating force among those dissatisfied with Soviet realities. A remarkable number of memoirs by Soviet dissidents capture the turning point in this process via an archetypal vignette: the young protagonist, troubled by Khrushchev's revelation in 1956 of Stalin's enormous crimes or by other symptoms that all is not well in the land of socialism, seeks enlightenment by returning to the Soviet Union's holy writ: the works of Lenin. Immersion in Lenin's thought—now as a solitary reader, rather than as a pupil in a teacher-controlled classroom—proves a transformative experience. The Founding Father is repeatedly found to contradict himself; he appears as a supreme tactician but utterly lacking in principle; he condones violence and his language itself is violent.[24]

The most influential accounts of the intellectual exit from communism are undoubtedly those penned by former converts in the West, above all the luminaries of *The God That Failed*, such as Arthur Koestler, André Gide, and Ignazio Silone. "The day I left the [Italian] Communist Party," Silone wrote, "was a very sad one for me, it was like a day of deep mourning, the mourning for my lost youth. It is not easy to free oneself from an experience as intense as that of the underground organization of the Communist Party."[25] With their shared metaphor of the death not just of a particular faith, but of faith itself, autobiographical narratives by Western ex-communists form a distinct genre that the philosopher Sidney Hook (himself an apostate from Marxism) dubbed "the literature of political disillusionment."[26] For most Soviet dissidents of the post-Stalin era, by contrast, the exit from communist ideology produced no such moral or spiritual crisis: on the contrary, it was construed as a coming of age, a liberation.[27] Unlike Koestler and company, they had never converted to communism, never experienced the intensity of underground conspiracy. What they came to reject was the validity of the Marxist-Leninist utopian worldview, far more than socialism as a system of actual economic relations. In this respect they were not so different from many of their fellow Soviet citizens, who as late as the 1980s continued to express support for key elements of the Soviet economic system even as they began to voice discontent with the Communist Party and its leaders.[28]

Even if one focuses on socialism as a moral utopia, a regulative ideal rather than a "real existing" system, it cannot be said that Soviet human rights activists were in any meaningful sense postsocialist or antisocialist. However convenient it was for the KGB to paint dissidents as anti-Soviet or anticommunist—a charge often uncritically embraced by the dissidents' allies in the West—one rarely finds criticism of collective ownership within the corpus of dissident writing, let alone arguments asserting an indispensable link between private property and liberty. One of the most trenchant dissi-dent analyses of the topic can be found in the 1975 samizdat essay "Is a Non-Totalitarian Type of Socialism Possible?" by the physicist and Helsinki Watch Group cofounder Yuri Orlov.[29] Even Orlov, after subjecting Soviet-style so-cialism to a withering critique, answered the essay's guiding question affirma-tively. He further argued that the safest and most realistic means to reform the Soviet system would require the decentralization of the command econ-omy while preserving state ownership of its critical sectors. To this end he called for the creation of an "ethical antitotalitarian" (not antisocialist) movement.

I have yet to discover a dissident text criticizing either the theory or prac-tice of the USSR's elaborate system of socialist rights guaranteed by the state—from free child care, medical care, and education (up through the postsecondary level) to subsidized housing and vacations. Paradoxically, the most common position among Soviet dissidents seems to have combined an unspoken acceptance of socialism as a system of coordinated, egalitarian public welfare (the "base," to use Marxist terminology) with a determination to emancipate the sphere of culture, politics, and ideas (the "superstructure") from the grip of official ideology. They were, one might say, good socialists but poor Marxists.

Something indeed happened in the post-Stalin era to the superstructure of socialism, to its commanding role as organizer of ideals and aspirations, but terms such as "collapse" and "implosion" are probably too blunt (and anachronistic) to capture it. I propose instead that we think about what hap-pened in terms of a much longer historical trajectory, the process identified by Max Weber as governing the evolution of social authority from person-centered charisma to tradition-based monarchies to more or less rational-ized, modern bureaucracies—namely, the process of disenchantment. Weber defined disenchantment as the process whereby "the ultimate and most sub-lime values retreat from the public sphere into either the transcendental realm of mystical life or the brotherliness of direct and personal human rela-tions."[30] More broadly, it involves the relative retreat of supernatural elements and modes of explanation from public life and their replacement by a this-worldly perspective.[31] To be sure, there is something peculiar about the idea of disenchantment in the Soviet setting, insofar as Marxism-Leninism was built on a radical critique not just of religion and superstition but of meta-physics in general. Soviet ideology, however, had its own metaphysics in the form of the "new Soviet person" and the "bright communist future," which served as transcendent values providing ultimate meaning to both past and present experience. These values did not exactly retreat from public life in the era after Stalin's death, but they became hollow and formulaic, thereby losing much of their aura. This is not the place to attempt an explanation of this development;[32] suffice it to say that modernizing processes encouraged by the Communist Party—rising literacy and education (especially scientific education), urbanization, the expansion of privacy made possible by tens of millions of new single-family apartments—contributed powerfully to the retreat of communist metaphysics from the public realm. If, during the formative period of Soviet human rights activism, it makes more sense to think in terms of the disenchantment rather than the collapse of the ideal of socialism, then the original precipitating event was not the crushing of the Prague Spring in 1968 (as important as that was) but Khrushchev's "unmasking" of Stalin's charisma-based cult of personality in 1956. Well before the 1970s, then, Soviet dissidents had begun to shed their faith in the socialist utopia even as—or perhaps because—they had come to take socialism for granted.

Human Rights and Utopia

Was the movement for human rights in the Soviet Union utopian? There are two very different questions embedded in this one. Did the specificities of the Soviet setting make human rights there a utopian project? Or are human rights by nature—as Moyn and Eckel claim—a utopian undertaking, regardless of setting, and akin to earlier utopian schemes?

Needless to say, very few people identify their own ideas as utopian; that label is usually attached by skeptics or opponents. When Yuri Orlov, in his essay "Is a Non-Totalitarian Type of Socialism Possible?" called for "the gradual transformation of the general moral atmosphere" so as to put an end to the totalitarian "use of force in the sphere of spiritual life," he insisted that "this program should not be considered utopian."[33] I confess that, as a general matter, I don't regard human rights as utopian, if we use "utopian" not simply to mean any project that aspires to make the world a better place but in the nontrivial sense of aspiring to a perfect (and hence implicitly unrealizable) order. One of the hallmarks of modern utopian thought has been the desire to fashion not only a perfect society but perfect human beings. Nowhere was the project of transforming human nature itself more assiduously cultivated (indeed, transformed into a cult) than in the Soviet Union. By contrast, Soviet human right advocates, like their counterparts elsewhere, insisted that rights belong to human beings just as they are, in all their diversity and with no necessary alterations.

To my mind, the human rights agenda represents a nontotalizing approach to eliminating certain perceived evils (admittedly, the list has grown exponentially over time) without claiming that doing so will come anywhere close to solving all problems, let alone produce a perfect society. Unlike utopian movements, the human rights agenda has tended to emphasize minimalist rather than maximalist claims. Moreover, the very nature of claims regarding civil and political rights (the so-called negative liberties) is such that, even as they insist on protecting their bearer's freedom to express his or her thought, practice his or her religion (or none at all), or form an association with others, they have absolutely nothing to say about the content of that thought, that religion, or that association, or whether it is wise or good to exercise a given right in a particular manner or in a given situation.[34] These observations, it seems to me, apply to nearly all human rights movements, regardless of setting.

The question of the utopianism of human rights in the Soviet setting is complex, because that setting itself was utopian insofar as it constantly sought to direct its inhabitants to a perfect communist future. Certain dissidents, including rights activists such as Alexander Volpin, bore traces of Soviet utopianism in their thinking about rights, insisting on the potential for perfect mathematical clarity in legal language and deriving absolute moral imperatives from it. Even Sakharov initially favored a kind of moral technocracy. In general, however, the language of rights activists, whether in their public appeals or in the *Chronicle of Current Events,* displayed an understatement and sobriety (Václav Havel called it "self-limiting") that are difficult to reconcile with utopian thought. The appeal to human rights was almost always conservative in the literal sense, calling for the defense of existing rights rather than the creation of new ones. Behind the remarkable idealism of the Initiative Groups for Human Rights and the Committee on Human Rights, moreover, lay a shrewd capacity to engage in cost-benefit analysis—hardly the hallmark of utopianism. When Yuri Orlov announced to a dissident friend in 1976 his plan to form a committee called "The Public Group to Support Compliance with the Helsinki Accords in the USSR," she retorted, "Your committee's name is outrageous. Supporting these accords means supporting the Soviet regime." Orlov disagreed: "These are political accords; that's their defect but also their value. Political levers can be used to defend human rights."[35]

In its colloquial meaning of "wildly unrealistic," the charge of utopianism—typically expressed in the Russian idiom as "Don Quixotism"—was often leveled against rights activists by sympathetic but skeptical friends.[36] Dissidents themselves often seemed to embrace this view in a spirit of bittersweetness: at gatherings around kitchen tables they would raise their glasses "to the success of our hopeless cause." Does this self-irony not gesture in a direction far, far away from utopia?

Conclusion

The experience of Soviet dissidents in the post-Stalin era highlights the need to take seriously the polycentric character of human rights history. In this chapter, I have explored the ways in which the thought-provoking new genealogy of human rights developed by Samuel Moyn and Jan Eckel sheds new light on one of those centers, as well as on the ways in which that center—outside of but increasingly linked to the West—might alter our understanding of the dynamics behind the globalization of human rights. This dialogue between the global and the local has much to do with the long-standing debate between lumpers and splitters, between those who propose grand syntheses and specialists who question the analysis of their particular neighborhood. Fully recognizing that synthesis is usually the harder and more significant of the two tasks, I nonetheless hope that the exchange will foster the collective advancement of an exciting new stage in human rights scholarship.

Chapter 4

Dictatorship and Dissent:
Human Rights in East Germany in the 1970s

Ned Richardson-Little

Most accounts of the rise of human rights in East Germany (German Democratic Republic, or GDR) regard the 1975 Helsinki Accords as a crucial turning point that created the conditions for the events at the Berlin Wall in the
fall of 1989.[1] This argument contends that by signing on to a major international treaty with human rights provisions, the ruling Socialist Unity Party
(Sozialistische Einheitspartei Deutschlands, SED) inadvertently ignited a dissident movement that would ultimately orchestrate the peaceful revolution
and the end of the communist system in Germany in 1989.[2] While the Helsinki Accords and the proliferation of the idea of human rights during the
1970s were important developments, they did not represent the definitive
breakthrough for either antiregime agitators or the broader idea of human
rights in the GDR.

Contrary to the popular narrative, the SED adopted the language of
human rights well before the 1970s, first as a means of propaganda in its conflicts with the nascent West German state immediately following the Second
World War and, by the 1960s, as a means of securing legitimacy within the
international community. Prior to the 1970s, East German citizens had begun
to employ the language of human rights to press their claims for greater religious freedoms, free expression, and the right to travel during the United
Nations' International Human Rights Year (1968). Yet by 1980, there was not
a single independent human rights organization in the GDR, nor had

dissidents widely adopted the discourse as a means of making claims against the state. An independent human rights movement would only emerge in East Germany in the mid-1980s, a full decade after the signing of the Helsinki Accords.

The absence of a human rights movement in East Germany until the 1980s can be attributed in large part to the early adoption of human rights discourse by the SED. During this period, dissidents who sought to use human rights language or international human rights agreements against the state were not doing so in a discursive vacuum but had to grapple with the hegemonic conception of socialist human rights that legitimized the SED's dictatorial rule and denied the autonomy of the individual. While the international human rights movement blossomed in the late 1970s, the SED was able to effectively either stamp out or co-opt efforts to challenge both state policy and its hegemonic discourse of human rights.

In the GDR, the notion of human rights was not a fixed idea naturally unfolding toward the ultimate goal of liberal democracy but a collection of competing universalistic discourses. Instead of one single breakthrough, there were four distinct periods in the evolution of the discourse of human rights in the forty years of East German history: First, the SED initially claimed that it represented "real" human rights in comparison to Western capitalism's fraudulent human rights. Second, the SED developed a separate conception of "socialist human rights" as a means of arguing for membership in the international community, which in turn provoked the first challenges to this new hegemony in the late 1960s. Third, these challenges to the dominant human rights discourse expanded over the first half of the 1970s and contributed to the short-lived outburst of dissent following Helsinki. Fourth, an independent human rights movement emerged in the mid-1980s that directly led to the mass protests of 1989, which brought SED rule to an end.

A Dictatorship for Human Rights

Immediately following the end of the Second World War, the SED began to use the rhetoric of human rights to justify its singular rule and the establishment of socialism in the Soviet Zone of Occupation. Such a tactic of embracing the idea of human rights, even on a purely instrumental level, was complicated by the gulf between this rhetoric and political reality. SED leaders had no intention of allowing any actual electoral competition for power, nor were they willing to create a system with legal protections for those who opposed a transition to socialism. As SED leader Walter Ulbricht said upon his return to Germany from exile, "it should look democratic, but everything must be in our hands."[3] The party sought to endorse the idea of human rights and claim its inherent legitimacy while simultaneously thwarting every effort by the East German populace to create a liberal democratic society.

The idea of reconciling the concept of human rights with the creation of a socialist dictatorship had few historical precedents. Karl Marx never theorized on the nature of human rights under socialism, and his only writings on the subject condemned liberal enthusiasm for the "rights of man" as a rhetorical trick of the bourgeoisie to portray its class interests as the rights of all humanity.[4] Vladimir Lenin's writings contained not a single mention of human rights.[5] Within the specifically German communist tradition, Rosa Luxemburg, the founder of the German Communist Party (Kommunistische Partei Deutschlands, KPD), had endorsed the idea of bourgeois democratic rights as an integral part of socialist democracy. However, her attacks on Lenin and the Russian Revolution meant that much of her work was heavily censored and consequently largely unavailable in the GDR. Communist activists had fought for democratic rights and freedoms during the Weimar period, but human rights were regarded as tools to advance the revolution only within the context of overthrowing the bourgeois political system.[6] The closest the SED came to an ideologically acceptable endorsement of human rights was in the lyrics to the late nineteenth-century socialist anthem "The Internationale," which promised to "win the human right" (*erkämpft das Menschenrecht*), a line unique to the German version likely included only because it rhymed with the previous verse.[7]

Rather than hewing to the examples of its ideological forebears, the SED initially improvised its particular conception of human rights in response to political pressure stemming from the competition for legitimacy in the three Western zones of occupation and later with the newly formed Federal Republic of Germany. This competition first incorporated the idea of human rights in 1946 during the first, and only, joint East-West Berlin elections and the first electoral contest for the recently formed Socialist Unity Party. While the SED was the product of the coerced amalgamation of the Social Democratic Party (SPD) and the Communist Party (KPD) in the Soviet Zone of Occupation, it was forced to compete against the still independent branch of the SPD operating in the Western Zones of Berlin for the same bloc of working-class and antifascist middle-class voters. Running on the slogan "No Socialism

without Human Rights," the SPD won a decisive plurality with nearly 49 percent of the vote, compared with a humiliating share of less than 20 percent for
the SED, in spite of the SED's full backing by the Soviet authority in its zone
of the city.[8]

Following this embarrassing defeat, the East German legal theorist Karl
Polak refuted these attacks on the SED and its brand of socialism in the SED's
theoretical journal *Unity* (*Einheit*). Polak addressed the SPD's slogan and
claimed the exact reverse: there could be "no human rights without socialism." He declared, "Socialism is by definition the realization of human rights;
and human rights are, if they are not to remain an empty principle, only realized insofar as socialism has been made a reality."[9] Although Polak invoked
Karl Marx's denunciation of the rights of man as a rhetorical trick of the
bourgeoisie, he argued that under socialism, real human rights could finally
flourish in place of the sham rights being peddled by West German
politicians.

This simplistic equation of socialism with human rights and the denunciation of liberal democratic rights as mere tools of bourgeois hegemony provided the basic outline of official ideology for the next two decades. SED
cofounder and later East German prime minister Otto Grotewohl picked up
the slogan "No human rights without socialism" for use in the propaganda
supporting the proposed constitution, which would form the political foundation for the new German Democratic Republic. The constitution contained
an extensive list of basic rights, with an emphasis on traditional social rights
such as the right to work and the right to leisure. Although these had no real
legal implications for the populace in the early years of the GDR, Grotewohl
proudly proclaimed that "the basic rights, which we have placed at the center
of our constitutional draft, are so much more than mere 'individual rights' or
judicial claims which the individual has against the state." Indeed "they are
the fundamental principles of the future of German state politics."[10] The
founding document of the GDR, following the lead of Karl Polak, simultaneously rejected the tenets of liberal democracy while embracing the language
of human rights.[11]

In the latter half of the decade, the West German Ministry for All-German
Affairs and other anticommunist organizations in the Federal Republic of
Germany (FRG) began to publish reports on human rights violations in East
Germany. Following heightened tensions between the two Germanies due to
the Federal Republic's decision to outlaw the West German Communist Party,
the SED crafted a single response to both problems. In 1959, the SED created

an organization to deal with the publicity efforts and material aid for communists and other left-wing activists imprisoned in West Germany: the GDR Committee for Human Rights.[12] The initial group—twenty jurists, cultural notables, and representatives from various party organizations assembled to assist "victims of the Cold War"—was given no clear mandate and was provided with almost no resources with which to take action.[13]

The committee's importance suddenly increased following the construction of the Berlin Wall on August 13, 1961. West Germans of all political stripes responded to the division of the city by attacking the SED in the language of human rights. Willy Brandt, the SPD mayor of West Berlin and future chancellor of West Germany, declared that "above all we [citizens of West Berlin] must seize the initiative in order to denounce this flagrant violation of international human rights."[14] Mass-produced pamphlets from the Ministry for All-German Affairs and from right-wing civil society organizations such as the Council for Central German Culture presented the GDR as a mass violator of international norms and laws.[15] Adding to this pressure was the creation of the West German chapter of Amnesty International in 1961 and the reorganization of the Frankfurt-based German League for Human Rights following years of mismanagement and corruption.[16]

In response to this outside pressure, the budget of the GDR Committee for Human Rights tripled from 1961 to 1962 and its activities vastly increased.[17] The small staff of the committee produced propaganda material for use in the GDR and abroad, while volunteers formed smaller groups in factories and workplaces to coordinate petition-writing events and contribute to donation drives to support the families of imprisoned communists and fellow travelers in the FRG.[18] The committee organized an annual fund-raising radio concert "Dem Frieden die Freiheit" to coincide with the annual International Human Rights Day on December 10, as well as other cultural events usually featuring honoured foreign guests and generous amounts of poetry by the recently deceased Bertolt Brecht.[19]

Although neither the GDR nor the FRG were members of the United Nations, the GDR Committee for Human Rights repeatedly petitioned the UN Commission on Human Rights to launch inquiries into human rights abuses in West Germany. In numerous pamphlets, they requested the assistance of the UN Human Rights Commission "in view of the danger which the violation and the threatened destruction of human rights in the German Federal Republic presents."[20] According to these petitions, the FRG sought "to create a graveyard atmosphere in internal politics permitting undisturbed nuclear rearmament, to prevent if possible the spreading of truth about its aggressive and revenge-seeking plans, and to cripple the rightful resistance of the people to these plans."[21] These petitions concluded with lists of detained and incarcerated activists in the Federal Republic often running to more than two hundred names.

The campaigns to free imprisoned "antifascist" activists and communists in West Germany resonated deeply with dedicated supporters of socialism. Some took part, wanting a chance to relive the glory days of the working-class struggle against Nazi persecution, while for others it was a chance to emulate the actions of those who had heroically stood fast against fascism and now held positions of economic and political power in the GDR.[22] Instead of pointing out the chasm between the state's rhetoric and its actions, many took it upon themselves to organize protest-letter-writing circles at their workplace, or engaged passively by privately tracking the progress of campaigns by checking off freed activists from lists of political prisoners in West Germany included in the committee newsletter.[23]

Socialist Human Rights

While committed socialists found the SED's human rights claims convincing, diplomats at the East German Ministry for Foreign Affairs and officials within the SED's Central Committee were concerned with the GDR's lack of a coherent positive conception of human rights in conflicts with West Germany.[24] As an ideological tool, Polak's simplistic formulation of socialism as the realization of human rights had limited appeal beyond the party faithful. Propagandists had no convincing explanations for how they could denounce West Germany's record on human rights when at the same time in the GDR there were no free elections, no freedom of speech, and very limited freedom of religious practice.

The solution to this problem of coherence came in 1964 when Hermann Klenner, a young and somewhat unorthodox legal philosopher, developed a conception of human rights that balanced international norms, Marxist theory, and the political needs of the SED. Klenner argued that while bourgeois human rights were clearly fraudulent, the abolition of capitalism in East Germany and the resulting liberation of humanity had ushered in a new phase in the history of human rights. Human rights in a socialist society moved beyond the destructive egoistical right to act out of pure self-interest promoted by legal rights in a liberal democracy. Socialist human rights were instead the natural outcome of the new socialist economy and social order that the SED had created in East Germany.[25] This did not mean that East Germans had the right to vote or organize as they pleased but that their human rights would be inherently fulfilled by their full participation in the socialist economic and social system.[26] Since capitalist states were still in the bourgeois phase of history, denial of voting rights or censorship could be attacked as a violation of human rights, while these same actions by a communist regime could be justified as necessary to protect the achievements of socialism and the realization of the true interests of the people.

Instead of speaking only within a Marxist vocabulary, Klenner sought to connect the virtues of SED rule with the two pillars of the United Nations' rights system—self-determination and international peace. He claimed that the East German people had realized self-determination and were now in total control of their society and state due to the success of socialism. The resulting end of class difference and domestic confrontation represented an important step toward international peace and harmony.[27] According to Klenner, human rights, peace, socialism, and self-determination were a single unified goal: "Wherever in the world the people are fighting against the exploitation, ignorance, and oppression brought about by the imperialist, they are fighting a just struggle for their self-determination. Wherever in the world there is the struggle against the threat of war, it is a struggle for the most important human right, the right to a peaceful life!"[28]

The SED sought to deploy Klenner's conception of socialist human rights as a means of not only counteracting West German attacks domestically but also gaining recognition and legitimacy on the world stage. Since the late 1940s, the FRG had employed the threat of cutting diplomatic ties and economic aid to Third World and nonaligned nations as a means of denying broad diplomatic recognition to the GDR.[29] By the late 1960s, however, the growing power of the emerging Afro-Asian bloc at the United Nations provided a new opportunity for the SED to break out of its diplomatic isolation and to gain membership in the UN. Klenner's emphasis on anti-imperialism and self-determination as core principles of socialist human rights allowed the SED to claim a kinship with the new Afro-Asian members of the international community by equating their claims to independence from colonial powers to the East German struggle for statehood in the face of Western European and American objections.

In order to claim its superior commitment to human rights, the SED launched a massive propaganda campaign in 1968 to coincide with the UN's Year of Human Rights. In addition to a flurry of propaganda pamphlets, speeches, and even commemorative stamps, the SED used the occasion to create a new constitution and criminal code, heralded as evidence of the triumph of human rights under socialism. The new criminal code explicitly mentioned human rights (the violation of which led to the harshest punishments, including the death penalty) more than a dozen times. Although the new constitution actually removed several basic rights, including those contained in the original 1949 version regarding religion, free expression, and movement, Klenner himself presented it in the East German media as the historical fulfilment of human rights in Germany.[30] In addition to these domestic measures, the SED also publicly announced its readiness to sign on to the UN's 1966 covenants on human rights.[31]

On the international stage, the SED's claims to represent a superior form of human rights fit well with the increased emphasis on the right to self-determination by the newly independent Afro-Asian states. The GDR attended the United Nations' Tehran Conference on Human Rights in 1968—hosted by the Shah of Iran, himself an antidemocratic dictator—at which many of the participants held political power as the result of revolutionary nationalist movements. As Roland Burke has written of the conference, "concentrated state power was lauded as the path to freedom, as opposed to a serious threat to it."[32] Most of the delegates echoed the GDR's calls for anti-imperialism and self-determination, as well as its repudiation of liberal democratic norms in the name of general economic well-being.[33]

This broad push for international recognition in the name of human rights finally provoked a reaction from the East German populace, but it was limited to official channels of complaint and did not result in public opposition. As part of the release of the new "Socialist Constitution" of 1968, the SED decided to hold several thousand consultations with the people across the GDR and accept petitions with suggestions for changes prior to a plebiscite on its adoption. Officials viewed this mass consultation (*Volksaussprache*) as a chance to educate East Germans and bring them on board with the change in order to provide greater legitimacy to the foundations of the state. Although citizens were careful to avoid any attacks on the political dominance of the SED or socialism in general, the consultations were used by a variety of groups as an opportunity to defend their interests or advance some limited freedoms. Although they represented a distinct minority, several hundred East Germans sought to advance their position through appeals to the international human rights documents that the SED claimed to embrace.

In particular, the Catholic and Protestant communities of the GDR sought to maintain their religious freedoms by appealing to the human rights instruments of the United Nations. While the 1949 constitution contained eight sections on the rights of the church and freedom of belief, only a single section in the draft presented to the people in 1968 provided any guarantee of religious liberty. The churches launched a massive campaign to prevent the further erosion of their position. Widely circulated letters, one from the Catholic bishop of Berlin and another from a group of Protestant bishops, called on the state to maintain the freedoms contained in the old constitution and invoked the promises made by the SED to the UN in honour of the International Year of Human Rights.[34] Hundreds of lower-level church officials and citizens followed suit in demanding their rights in the name of the Universal Declaration of Human Rights and the UN Conventions. Some smaller communities submitted petitions with more than two hundred signatures.[35] Although the churches failed to gain the full restoration of the rights contained in the previous constitution, this mass campaign resulted in the SED expanding two articles of the new version to include greater protections of religious communities and freedom of belief.[36]

Others sought to leverage the state's commitments to human rights to gain greater freedom of movement or increased freedom of expression. Although some letters were confrontational in tone, most citizens presented their claims to human rights as a helpful suggestion or reminder to the state. One citizen seeking to emigrate first offered reassurances that the right to work and living standards in the GDR were greatly appreciated before politely pointing out that it could give the mistaken impression to the West that "the GDR is similar to a prison that no one can leave," if citizens did not have a right to exit.[37] Official reports on feedback from the citizenry did not deem these human rights–based critiques to be problematic or "provocative." The language of human rights was powerful at this time not because it clearly contrasted with state policy but because it flattered the SED's conception of itself as a champion of human rights and of the GDR as respectable member of the international community.

Prior to the 1970s, the SED had effectively incorporated the idea of human rights into its ideology and used it as a discursive tool in its campaign to gain international recognition and legitimacy. Likewise, a small number of GDR citizens also discovered that international human rights norms could be a useful if limited means of demanding change and protecting personal freedoms. The discourse of human rights did not spread explosively and in most cases was deployed in a purely instrumental manner. In this period, the SED adopted and developed a unique ideological conception of socialist human rights in response to pressure from the West and utilized it when the international community provided opportunities for political gain. Similarly, East Germans began to adopt human rights language when threats to their personal freedoms coincided with the SED's increased claims of respecting international norms. The idea of human rights did not so much change the political discourse of East Germany; instead both the SED and the citizens of the GDR used the idea of human rights to legitimize their claims and promote their own specific interests.

Human Rights in the 1970s

The language of human rights gained great prominence in East Germany following the SED's signing of the Helsinki Accords in 1975, but in many ways this was simply an amplification of the human rights discourses of the late 1960s. East Germans applying to travel to the West and religious adherents seeking some space outside of official ideology ratcheted up their use of human rights language as official channels and methods of complaint failed to produce meaningful results. The idea of human rights did not instigate dissent but rather provided a means of last resort when other strategies of petitioning the state had failed. Although human rights became a far more common means of registering dissent in the 1970s, it mostly remained a tool that individuals used to apply pressure on the state for single issues such as emigration. Unlike in most other Eastern Bloc countries, no human rights organizations were formed in East Germany in the 1970s, and those within the intelligentsia who did speak out for democratizing reforms avoided using the discourse of human rights to justify their aims. Rather than representing a breakthrough decade for human rights, the 1970s in East Germany were decidedly more ambiguous.

Although many historical accounts portray the SED's decision to sign on to the human rights provisions of the Helsinki Accords as a major concession to West German pressure, to the party itself the accords represented merely a reiteration of the SED's position rather than a decisive shift in policy. West German political analysts saw the GDR as holding a superior position on the matter of human rights in the international arena in the early 1970s. As one report from the Christian Socialist Union party lamented, "the free world has almost cleared off the field without a fight: the United States by its human rights abstinence, the Western European countries by their regionalism. Above all, the GDR has incorporated from the beginning and with great aggressiveness its concept of human rights in its foreign policy."[38]

The SED was similarly confident that it had nothing to fear in a conflict with West Germany over human rights. Politburo instructions to GDR negotiators expressed some reservations about explicit language regarding freedom of expression, but as long as the treaty language was consistent with UN documents they were unconcerned.[39] A follow-up report to the SED's Central Committee described the human rights provisions of the accords as a compromise but declared that the negotiators had "foiled" efforts to prioritize "bourgeois" freedoms through the emphasis on self-determination and cooperation. Negotiators had formulated the section on human rights so that "the Western states have no basis for the interference or defamation of the internal order of the socialist countries."[40] The SED believed that its representatives had signed a document that would uphold its sovereignty and a socialist vision of human rights, not any kind of concession to the principles of liberal democracy.

In spite of the seeming nonchalance with which the SED restated its commitment to human rights, there was an explosion in public requests to exit the GDR on the basis of the contents of the Helsinki Accords. In the fall of 1975 the number of applications jumped by 40 percent, with every fourth letter explicitly mentioning the Helsinki Accords.[41] By 1976, the number of applications grew to nearly eight thousand (another 40 percent increase) and the office in charge of processing petitions became convinced that it was facing "increasingly organized subversive activities of the class enemy."[42] In addition to the massive influx of applications through official channels, some East Germans chose to make their petitions public through the West German media so as to put greater pressure on the SED. In July 1976, Dr. Karl-Heinz Nitschke, a physician from the small town of Riesa, smuggled out a blistering denunciation of GDR policy and a demand to depart to the West signed by over a hundred residents, many of whom were workers.[43] The published complaints of citizens in the wake of the Helsinki Accords represented the first major open dissent since the Berlin Uprising of 1953.

Although this move to open dissent in the name of human rights was significant, it was not so much a break with the past as the culmination of the repeated frustrations and disappointments suffered by East Germans seeking to travel to West Germany to see family and friends cut off by the construction of the Berlin Wall. Following the demands for a right to exit the GDR at the constitutional consultations in 1968, applications to depart the GDR first jumped in 1972 as the GDR eased travel restrictions, though the vast majority were rejected.[44] When the GDR became a member of the United Nations the next year, and thus a signatory to the Human Rights Conventions of 1966, the number of applications for exit visas once again shot upwards, with a growing number citing the accords' human rights provisions or threatening to appeal to the UN's Human Rights Commission. Applications that invoked international human rights norms came from citizens who had previously been rejected, sometimes repeatedly. Frustrations with official intransigence ran so high that 15 percent of applicants in 1973 actually informed state authorities that without an exit visa they would be forced to depart the GDR illegally.[45]

The burst of exit applications in the name of human rights following Helsinki was short-lived, as the number of petitions dropped sharply by the end of the decade. While the SED eventually allowed some applicants to emigrate, it continued to reject most applications and subjected petitioners to retaliatory harassment, unemployment, and even imprisonment. Although in 1978 the rapidly proliferating human rights organizations in Western Europe and North America began to bombard the SED with letters supporting East German requests to emigrate, in that same year petitions from GDR citizens fell by almost half.[46] When the usage of human rights language proved to be ineffective in pressuring the SED it was largely abandoned.

Furthermore, the increased engagement of the church with the field of human rights was similarly ambiguous in its effects. The Protestant Church in particular sought to integrate the ideals of human rights into its theology in the late 1970s. Spurred on by their involvement in human rights–friendly international organizations such as the Lutheran World Federation and the ecumenical World Council of Churches, East German Protestants overcame their traditional hostility to the idea of human rights (associated with anticlerical liberalism or atheistic socialism rather than theology).[47] The embrace of human rights by the church did not, however, imply rejection of the core tenets of the SED's conception of human rights or its right to absolute political control. Instead, the church ultimately chose to endorse and legitimize the state's claims to fulfill human rights so as to gain the opportunity to criticize the SED's actions in individual cases and to assist people on the margins.

Church officials began to see human rights as both a matter of pressing moral importance and a political opportunity. In 1973, the National Committee of the Lutheran World Federation in the GDR argued, "advocacy for humanity and human rights will provide legitimacy for our activities . . . even if efforts to implement human rights are inherently illegal."[48] After Helsinki, the leadership of the Protestant Church saw human rights as an effective means for their community to promote peace and to combat racism abroad as well as to protect religious believers and military draft resisters at home. The church leadership distributed copies of the Helsinki Accords and other international human rights documents to churches across the GDR and organized educational seminars to teach local pastors how to integrate human rights with Protestant theology.[49]

Yet this new engagement with human rights took a very conciliatory position toward the SED and its policies. In order to solidify a more active position in East German society, senior church officials sought to reassure the SED that they would not challenge its political legitimacy. In a 1976 paper on church policy toward human rights, Manfred Stolpe, head of the Secretariat of the Federation of Evangelical Churches, claimed that the GDR had actually fulfilled all of its human rights obligations demanded by international law and that criticisms of the SED "usually come from a one-sided individualistic understanding of human rights."[50] While seeking to assist conscientious objectors at home, the Protestant Church actively rejected working with foreign human rights organizations with similar goals, such as Amnesty International.[51] Church officials also punished local pastors whose human rights rhetoric was deemed overly contentious or insufficiently vetted by the church hierarchy.[52]

The adoption of the discourse of human rights by the Protestant Church in the 1970s represented a break from theological tradition, but the public efforts of the church to promote human rights were co-opted by the state as a means of reinforcing the legitimacy of the socialist position. SED propagandists quickly incorporated positive statements by the church on the compatibility of state socialism with human rights to buttress their own claims of legitimacy. Guidelines produced by the Ministry of Justice on combating pacifism actually cited church publications to claim religious backing for state defense policy.[53] Although the church was able to carve out a space for a non-socialist conception of human rights grounded in Christian ethics, it did so at the price of reinforcing and legitimizing the hegemonic state discourse of human rights.[54]

East German intellectuals, like their counterparts across the Eastern bloc, expressed increasing dissatisfaction and disappointment with the failings of "real existing socialism" in the 1970s, but unlike in Moscow, Prague, and Warsaw, the intelligentsia of the GDR did not turn to the language of human rights. East German dissidents sought to reform the GDR from within while remaining convinced of the need for a system of true antifascist socialism, divorced from the "bourgeois" liberal democracy of the West. When the popular East German singer Wolf Biermann was stripped of his East German citizenship for his remarks critical of the SED, GDR intellectuals petitioned the state to reconsider citing his loyalty to East Germany instead of posing any abstract right of free expression.[55] The chemist Robert Havemann, a formerly committed Stalinist and victim of Nazi persecution who had turned to open dissent in the 1960s, called for greater freedom of expression and open exchange of ideas but only as a means of reinforcing and advancing the goals of utopian socialism.[56] Rudolf Bahro, an SED functionary, imprisoned and then deported from the GDR following the publication in West Germany of his 1977 eco-utopian treatise *Die Alternative*, was outright dismissive of the growing international human rights movement. He attacked dissidents who "see themselves forced back into making straight liberal, democratic demands, and campaigning for human rights, that is, into a position which is at the same time the broadest and most insipid and, in any constructive sense, the most vacuous."[57] For Bahro, it was simply beyond the pale for socialist activists to be following the lead of American president Jimmy Carter by calling for liberal democratic human rights.

The SED viewed these outbursts of dissent not as the logical outcome of the citizenry holding the state accountable for its promises but as the result of capitalist agitation in violation of the spirit of international peace and cooperation. East German foreign minister Oskar Fischer viewed Western demands for greater openness as a ploy to diminish and violate the sovereignty of the GDR and reinterpret the terms of Helsinki to include "absolute freedoms" that were not intended by the signatories.[58] Rather than evading the subject of human rights, the SED believed that it needed only to continue educating East Germans on the subject to end their complaints. Loyal intellectuals argued that the real problem was that "old and obsolete bourgeois concepts often still persist, especially regarding the problem of basic rights and duties as met in socialist actuality."[59] SED officials viewed human rights complaints as a purely ideological problem and suggested that a more persuasive justification of socialist human rights would solve the problem.

At the close of the 1970s, the SED's socialist human rights discourse remained dominant, while alternative interpretations were co-opted or marginalized. Although East Germans seeking to exit the GDR now had far greater support from the international human rights movement, the state security apparatus effectively stamped out internal efforts to gain the right to emigrate through public appeals to the Helsinki Accords. The Protestant Church, although it had decided to contend with the problem of human rights, also chose to avoid conflict with the state by refusing to press for political or legal reforms that might threaten the SED dictatorship. Members of the East German intelligentsia were beginning to push for greater openness and free expression, but their continued devotion to the possibility of a "better Germany" through antifascism and socialism made them averse to the individualized and liberal democratic language of the budding international human rights movement. Although the idea of human rights proliferated in this period, through a combination of coercion, threats, and ideological inertia the SED ensured that there would be no decisive shift away from an entrenched state socialist conception of human rights.

The 1980s and the Dissident Turn to Human Rights

The dearth of human rights–based dissent in the GDR continued through the early 1980s, even as East Germans began to come together to form grassroots peace organizations in response to rising Cold War tensions. While next-door neighbor Poland was in turmoil following the organization of the independent trade union Solidarity, East Germans were forming small groups calling for disarmament, the end of nuclear proliferation, and the general demilitarization of society. Rather than challenging SED rule, GDR peace activists were more concerned with the nuclear arms race and the impending deployment of intermediate-range missiles in West Germany. In 1982, dissident Robert Havemann and Protestant pastor Rainer Eppelmann launched an independent peace movement with the publication of the *Berliner Appell*, a one-page declaration calling for dialogue with the SED and for the cessation of military parades, mandatory military courses in public schools, and compulsory armed service.[60] The discourse of human rights was noticeably absent from these activities as GDR citizens sought protection from reprisal by focussing on ostensibly apolitical causes, such as peace or environmentalism, which the state officially endorsed.

Despite the peace movement's avowedly apolitical stance, the SED did not tolerate these overtly nonthreatening efforts to form civil society organizations outside the purview of the state. The GDR security services imprisoned and deported activists, in addition to sending agents to infiltrate and disrupt their organizations.[61] By the mid-1980s many peace activists concluded that even a movement grounded in purely moral issues of peace and disarmament was doomed to failure until the East German political system permitted its citizens to speak, associate, and travel freely.[62] Frank Eigenfeld, a peace activist from Halle, later recalled, "We had little opportunity to articulate ourselves in public. . . . The focus changed from the arms race towards human rights . . . [but] only after we had begun to run into enormous organizing difficulties did our focus begin to change."[63]

The shift in focus toward domestic political reform in the name of human rights came to the fore in 1985 when a group of prominent peace activists came together to organize a human rights organization that would operate outside the confines of the Protestant Church and would directly challenge the SED. In January 1986, dissidents Ralf Hirsch, Wolfgang Templin, and Peter Grimm issued a statement announcing the creation of the Initiative for Peace and Human Rights (IFM), the first human rights organization in the GDR.[64] Having determined that the "goals of peace initiatives depend upon the implementation of basic democratic rights and freedoms," they called for assistance from the various dissident communities as well as cooperation from the peace movement in developing the idea of human rights in relation to social justice, the right to work, the protection of the environment, and the rejection of obligatory military service.[65]

The human rights advocated by the Initiative for Peace and Human Rights represented an important synthesis of political aims and ideologies. In its founding document the founders sought to bring together activists to discuss such wide-ranging problems as international peace, education, religious freedom, the environment, the military draft, and the right to work. Instead of focussing on a single issue or grievance in the name of human rights, the IFM pulled together the concerns of the peace movement, religious believers, the growing environmental movement, draft resisters, and workers all under the umbrella of the concept of human rights. Members of the IFM stressed the importance of legally guaranteed political and civil rights as a means of achieving these broader goals in the name of social well-being and harmony rather than to promote the autonomy of the individual. These dissidents did not hope for a transition to liberal capitalism but rather sought to promote democratic rights alongside the existing commitments to social and economic rights.[66] In particular, they argued that the human right to peace, which had so long been the centrepiece of SED propaganda, actually contradicted the rule of the party as it required democratic participation by the people as a whole. In a petition to the Eleventh SED Party Congress in 1986, the IFM wrote, "Peace and security policy cannot only be a matter of party and government. For peace is a human right, and therefore every member of society must be able to discuss and take part in the decisions regarding anything relevant to this right."[67] Whereas the SED argued that human rights and peace were the natural products of socialism, the IFM made human rights the starting point for a just society and the precondition for peace, not just socialism.

This new generation of human rights activism rapidly caught on with a broad cross section of East Germans in the next few years. Human rights organizations proliferated, not only in major cities like Berlin and Leipzig that had large dissident populations but also in smaller towns where people would gather in living rooms and church basements to discuss their problems and organize demonstrations. The concept of human rights was crucial to the emergence of a successful dissident movement in that it created a political space in which a heterogeneous coalition could form in opposition to one-party rule by the SED. The blend of peace, workers' rights, and guaranteed legal rights to political participation promoted by the IFM and other human rights groups in the GDR appealed to those who sought the political and civil rights of a Western-style liberal democracy, while also accommodating idealists who had tired of "real existing socialism" but were not disillusioned by the socialist project as a whole. Most important, it appealed to frustrated low-level party functionaries and high-level communist reformers who sought a way of breaking with the past without wholly rejecting it.[68] Implementing political and civil rights to allow the population to fully participate in the affairs of state held out the possibility of redeeming the unfulfilled promise of socialism as a more humane alternative to the capitalism of the West rather than as a capitulation to it.

This shift in the 1980s represented an important break with the past as East Germans stopped making claims in the name of human rights and began to act as if they had inherent rights to express themselves, assemble, and politically organize. Although only a small number of the hundreds of independent civic groups that sprang up in the years leading up to 1989 specifically dealt with human rights, these citizens were all behaving as though they had a right to call for environmental reforms or international peace, even if it was still illegal to do so. Yet, this new human rights consciousness did not mean the total displacement of socialism as a utopian project as it did in much of the West.[69] Many dissidents and members of the SED hoped that a turn to individual human rights could provide a source of renewal for the tired and ossified state socialism of the GDR.[70] The new utopia of human rights was to be the salvation of the old utopian project, not its replacement.

In response to this destabilizing shift from below, the SED redoubled its efforts to promote the GDR as a champion of international human rights. At a 1985 meeting of ideology ministers from across the socialist world, GDR representative Kurt Hager called for a rallying of the socialist nations to fight back against the West on human rights, specifically calling for a socialist convention or declaration of rights to match that of Western Europe.[71] The SED organized a panel of experts from across the Communist bloc, the Academic Council of Fraternal Parties of Socialist Countries on the Issue of Human Rights; however, its efforts to find a path forward on the matter while maintaining the political status quo ended in ignominious failure following an initial burst of enthusiasm. Socialist allies pulled their support as they discovered articles in the draft that appeared to threaten their domestic stability.[72] The project was indefinitely postponed in 1988 when the SED Politburo determined that the section on freedom of movement in the prepared draft was simply too dangerous to publish due to rising unrest.[73] In the spring of 1989, as human rights demonstrators were taking to the streets in Berlin, Leipzig, and other East German cities, the council turned against the ruling party dogma and concluded that the socialist world needed to reintroduce the rule of law and an independent judiciary, and to abandon the fallacy that the transition to socialism automatically resulted in a system of human rights superior to those found in bourgeois societies.[74]

Facing huge street protests and the mass exodus of citizens in the fall of 1989, many in the SED came to accept, with varying degrees of enthusiasm, the idea that socialism had to embrace political and civil rights if an independent GDR was to survive. The hundreds of thousands of East Germans fleeing the country or publicly chanting in protest gave the lie to any kind of claims that there existed a true harmony between the state and society following the abolition of capitalism. After months of growing protests in the name of human rights, on November 9, 1989, the Berlin Wall, the great symbol of the abuse of human rights in the GDR, was opened, setting off a series of reforms granting liberal democratic rights. After the top echelons of SED leadership were forced out or resigned, East Germany was now in the hands of Hans Modrow, the SED's best-known advocate of reform, who set about dismantling the party's monopoly on political power, legalizing the creation of independent newspapers and printing houses, and organizing the first (and last) free elections in the GDR. In promoting his reforms in December 1989, Modrow singled out for attention "especially the strict respect for human rights without exception, which demands a new attitude of the state toward the individual."[75] After forty years of rule, the SED had ceased to believe its own human rights rhetoric.

The 1970s were important for the development of the idea of human rights in East Germany but not the decisive turning point in the political history of the GDR. The SED's early embrace of human rights language and its steady development of a doctrine of socialist human rights immunized it against the potentially destabilizing effects of the Helsinki Accords and the international explosion of human rights activism in the 1970s. The SED had already demonstrated its ability to aggressively defend its claim to represent the ideals of human rights from foreign opponents, well before its own citizens sought to use human rights to justify their claims to greater freedom or political participation. Challenges to the hegemony of the SED's human rights conceptions in the 1970s were quickly suppressed or co-opted. While the SED's early embrace of human rights delayed the appearance of a reformist human rights discourse in the 1970s, when it did finally emerge in the 1980s it claimed to represent the highest ideals of socialism rather than their repudiation. The human rights ideals that dissidents used to challenge the SED dictatorship stemmed from diverse sources and grew not only from Western liberal democratic sources but also from the hegemonic official discourse of human rights that the SED had long employed to justify its dictatorial rule.

Chapter 5

Whose Utopia?
Gender, Ideology, and Human
Rights at the 1975 World Congress
of Women in East Berlin

Celia Donert

The United Nations Decade for Women (1976–1985) laid the foundations for a global campaign to recognize "women's rights as human rights" that culminated at the 1995 Fourth World Conference on Women in Beijing.[1] During the 1970s the number and type of women's nongovernmental organizations (NGOs) around the world increased exponentially, and their alliances, networks, and coalitions increasingly crossed Cold War ideological and geographical divides.[2] Marginalized within the UN human rights institutions since World War II, women's rights moved center stage during this decade. Second-wave feminism, along with new social movements pressing for fundamental rights of economic and social development, launched a far-reaching critique of the UN human rights system and its claims to universality.[3] Conventional narratives have written the history of the UN Decade for Women from the perspective of Western women's movements.[4] This essay focuses instead on the neglected role of the Soviet bloc in promoting gender equality as a human right during the 1970s, through a case study of a forgotten episode: the East Berlin World Congress of Women in International Women's Year, which was organized by communist governments and international NGOs as a riposte to the first UN World Conference on Women in Mexico City in 1975.[5]

Since World War II, governments and nongovernmental organizations in the Soviet bloc had integrated women's rights into cultural diplomacy promoting social justice, security, and world peace.[6] The East Berlin congress represented both the climax and the nadir of efforts to internationalize a vision of women's rights through the United Nations that would be recognized as specifically socialist.[7] Indeed, the Soviet bloc—acting together with the Third World states in the Group of 77—played a significant role in shaping women's rights at the UN during the 1970s. The landmark 1979 Convention on the Elimination of All Forms of Discrimination Against Women, which the UN describes as the first international bill of rights for women, reflected these disparate ideological influences.[8] Yet the impact of Socialist mobilization around women's rights was not confined to the role of states, institutions, and international law. International events like the World Congress of Women—or the much larger and more boisterous World Youth Festivals—were supposed to foster new forms of political activism and solidarity in the spirit of socialist internationalism.[9] The era of détente was rich in transnational exchanges across the Iron Curtain in which East European and Soviet women were key participants.[10] Unlike dissidents' protests against violations of civil rights following the celebrated Helsinki Final Act—signed only months earlier—these social movements did not necessarily lead to the creation of organized opposition to communist rule in the 1980s.

Women's equality was conceptualized at the East Berlin World Congress as the true embodiment of the socialist conception of human rights.[11] Thus this essay chimes with recent histories that analyze "rights regimes" in the German Democratic Republic or the Soviet Union on their own terms—as a reflection of the changing relations between socialist states and societies—rather than measuring them against Western ideals.[12] Long before Helsinki, Paul Betts has recently written, socialist publicists found a way of reconciling socialist ideals with human rights by conceptualizing them as "fundamental elements of social justice and entitlements" that were always politically determined rather than natural or inalienable.[13] The history of the World Congress thus complicates narratives that reduce local human rights politics in Eastern Europe during the 1970s to a narrowly conceived "Helsinki effect."[14] Histories of the Helsinki network—Soviet and East European dissidents using the Conference on Security and Cooperation in Europe (CSCE) to criticize their governments for violations of civil rights—lend weight to the argument that human rights emerged as a global politics of morality in the 1970s as a result of disillusionment with the failed utopias of postwar politics, not least revolutionary socialism.[15] In contrast to the glaring absence of civil and political rights under state socialism, however, the vision of gender equality it promised still retained a certain allure for women's organizations around the world during the era of détente, despite the widespread recognition of the "double burden" that women shouldered under state socialist rule.[16] Women's rights seemed ripe for promotion by East German diplomacy in the first half of the 1970s, when the GDR had recently achieved its long-sought goal of diplomatic recognition as a sovereign state and East German society was enjoying the material benefits and cultural détente of the early Honecker era.

Drawing on the archives of the East German Socialist Unity Party (Sozialistische Einheitspartei Deutschlands, SED), the mass Democratic Women's League of Germany (Demokratischer Frauenbund Deutschlands, DFD), and the Ministries for Foreign Affairs (Ministerium für Auswärtige Angelegenheiten, MfAA) and State Security (Ministerium für Staatssicherheit, MfS), this article reconstructs the history of the East Berlin World Congress. The final section considers the emergence of new social movements stressing sexual and reproductive rights, as well as the question of violence against women, issues that paternalist socialist regimes and the international Marxist left found irrelevant to their visions of social justice. Histories of women's rights that focus exclusively on Western feminism seem to have obscured a more complex and contested history of conflicts over gender, ideology, and human rights in the 1970s. It is this contested history that this chapter seeks to explore.

Internationalizing Women's Rights Since World War II

The historical context for understanding state socialist concepts of international women's rights in the 1970s is the attempt of the Soviet bloc to incorporate women's rights into cultural diplomacy as part of its broader ideological contest with the West after the Second World War. At a moment when the prewar liberal women's movement was in disarray after the massive upheaval of the war, state socialism conceptualized women's equality in terms of social rights for producer-citizens against the liberal feminist understanding of civil, political, and property rights constituting women as political subjects. The Soviet bloc internationalized this vision of women's rights through mass women's organizations, governments, international NGOs, and the UN, emphasizing that gender equality could never be separated from political and economic conditions such as national independence, economic development, and the absence of war.

The UN Charter was the first international declaration to refer to equality between the sexes as a "human right," marking a decisive break from the interwar era when women's rights were seen as a national rather than international concern.[17] Ironically, however, the near-universal achievement of women's suffrage and the crisis of Western internationalism seemed to sound the death knell for the liberal feminist organizations that had championed women's rights before World War II.[18] When the United Nations was founded, the international women's movement was deeply divided over the best way of accommodating women's interests within the new human rights institutions. The International Alliance of Women, one of the largest prewar organizations, claimed credit for the sex equality clause on behalf of two women members who lobbied strongly for its inclusion in the UN Charter at the San Francisco conference. Yet many female delegates had actually opposed the clause, and the Brazilian Bertha Lutz, one of the few women delegates to San Francisco, later berated British and North American women for their resistance while expressing her surprise at the unexpected support her proposals received from the Soviet Union, Ethiopia, India, Lebanon, and several Latin American countries.[19]

State socialist regimes emerged after the war as a powerful new voice speaking in the name of women's rights.[20] Lobbying from Soviet delegates in alliance with the women's movement ensured the inclusion of sex equality provisions in the Universal Declaration of Human Rights.[21] In 1945, a coalition of antifascist women established the Women's International Democratic Federation (WIDF) in Paris, which appropriated the language of women's rights used by the prewar women's movement while removing any references to feminism.[22] With the expansion of Soviet influence into Eastern Europe, the ranks of the WIDF were swelled by the mass women's organizations of the Soviet bloc.[23] As the Cold War intensified, the WIDF headquarters were transferred to East Berlin. From the divided German capital city of the major Cold War battleground within Europe, the WIDF secretariat coordinated the activities of a global umbrella organization that claimed staggeringly huge membership figures. One Soviet publication boasted about 135 million members in sixty-four countries by 1951.[24] The title of the WIDF journal summed up the image that it sought to project: *Women of the Whole World*.

Women's rights at the UN were polarized by the ideological cleavages of the Cold War during the late 1940s and 1950s. The U.S. State Department nervously viewed the Commission on the Status of Women (CSW) as a "bat-tlefield" over competing Soviet and American ideals of women and the fam-ily.[25] Feminist and socialist traditions were the two main influences on gender equality provisions in human rights law after 1945. Formal nondiscrimina-tion on the basis of sex—the goal of "equality feminists"—was incorporated into Article 7 of the Universal Declaration of Human Rights. Legal equality was the main aim of the UN Commission on the Status of Women in the early years, resulting in the adoption of conventions on the political rights of women (1952), the nationality of married women (1957), and consent and minimum age in marriage (1962). Meanwhile equality in employment was pursued partly through protective labor legislation that sought to balance women's roles as mothers and workers, which had been pushed by the inter-national labor movement and socialist women's organizations since the early twentieth century. Such measures included maternity pay or prohibitions on night work, as set out in Article 25 of the Universal Declaration.[26]

Soviet-sponsored organizations like the WIDF were not simply the com-munist "fronts" that they appeared to be during the Cold War. Supported politically and financially by the Soviet Union, the WIDF offered scope for transnational networking between women of different ideological persua-sions, even though Cold War politics narrowed its potential membership and activities.[27] Women's rights remained high on the WIDF agenda, especially after the death of Stalin. Soviet and East European regimes continued to ex-ercise a high degree of control, however, and sought to use the WIDF—which regained consultative status with the UN Economic and Social Council in the late 1960s, as Cold War tensions ebbed—as a channel of influence at the UN. The WIDF played a crucial role in wooing women from postcolonial coun-tries with information about the apparent success of the communist model in integrating women into economic development in Eastern Europe and the Soviet Union. Publications, conferences, study visits, exchanges, and material assistance targeted women in the newly independent states in Africa and Asia.

In 1963, delegates from developing and Soviet bloc countries called on the UN Commission on the Status of Women to draft a new declaration on eliminating discrimination against women.[28] In the same year, the General Assembly adopted a resolution on women in development, proposed by the UN Economic and Social Council, which expanded the range of questions addressed by the CSW to include women's economic and social development as well as legal status. Based on a draft submitted by Poland and working papers from Ghana and Mexico, the CSW began to draft a declaration at its meeting in Tehran in 1965. The visibility of women's issues at the UN increased with the 1970 publication of Ester Boserup's *Woman's Role in Economic Development*, which highlighted the need to include women in projects promoting economic growth in the Third World.[29] In 1973 the U.S. Congress passed the Percy Amendment to the Foreign Assistance Act, requiring that women be integrated into programs promoting economic growth. The perceived vulnerability of Third World women to communist propaganda, suggests Kristen Ghodsee, was one of the factors that pushed Congress to adopt these changes in the provision of foreign aid.[30]

Gender, Ideology, and Human Rights in the Era of Détente

The era of détente and the resurgence of international feminism in the United States and Western Europe produced a multitude of alternative perspectives on women's rights that fundamentally challenged the claims to universality of the existing UN human rights system. Initially, the new feminist groups paid little attention to the UN. Radical, socialist, black, and anti-imperialist feminists looked instead to revolutionary politics and psychological consciousness-raising, at the same time seeking to connect gender to other axes of injustice such as class, race, and sexuality.[31] State socialism in the Soviet Union and Eastern Europe was a reference point for socialist feminists in the West, although by the 1970s it was cited frequently as a negative example, as many observers concluded that neither Leninist parties nor "really existing socialism" had liberated women.[32] Second-wave feminism, emerging from the New Left while contesting the latter's sexism, rejected "Marxism's exclusive focus on political economy and liberalism's exclusive focus on law" to unveil injustices outside the classic public sphere: in the family, everyday life, cultural traditions, and civil society.[33]

In response, Soviet bloc governments continued to use diplomacy, foreign aid, and international NGOs in an effort to redefine women's rights in line with communist ideology and foreign policy. From 1968, the Soviet Union coordinated the international activities of the mass women's organizations through regular meetings of East European, North Korean, and Cuban functionaries in charge of the official "women's movement" in each member state.[34] Women's rights were the main theme of the 1969 WIDF World Congress in Helsinki, for example, although socialist governments were adamant that sexual equality should never be separated from what they termed "political problems," such as European security or peace in the Middle East.[35] During the 1970s the WIDF turned its attention to influencing the women's rights agenda at the UN, and it is now acknowledged that delegates from the Soviet bloc put forward the intitial proposal for a UN global campaign specifically targeting women.

In 1972 the WIDF observers at a meeting of the UN Commission on the Status of Women (CSW) proposed that 1975 be designated International Women's Year. With the support of sympathetic government delegates in the commission, the proposal passed.[36] Raluca Popa has convincingly demonstrated that the WIDF and its member organizations viewed women's rights and the equality principle as crucial elements of International Women's Year, a finding that challenges the Cold War assumption that Soviet-sponsored women's organizations were focused exclusively on the defense of "peace."[37] At a meeting in Warsaw in April 1974, Popa notes, the council instructed its members to "review the *de jure* and *de facto* rights of women" in their countries.[38] Rights and inequality, according to the WIDF, were an inseparable part of the other goals of socialism such as national independence, democracy, social progress, and peace. Western feminist organizations quickly sought to establish control over preparations for International Women's Year, with the result that two rival NGO subcommittees were set up, one in New York (strongly influenced by liberal, Western feminists) and the other in Geneva (controlled by East European and working women's representatives).[39] Each NGO subcommittee vied for influence at UN headquarters in New York, seeking to win official recognition as the sole NGO organizer for International Women's Year.[40]

At a February 1975 meeting in Berlin, functionary Inge Lange, head of the Women's Department in the SED Central Committee, declared that the UN conference in Mexico City offered a unique opportunity to publicize what socialist society "means for women."[41] According to Lange, the SED "was of the opinion that our socialist countries should exert more effort to strengthen our influence over the work of the WIDF." Efforts should be made to ensure that the WIDF concentrated purely on women's issues and did not duplicate the work of the World Peace Council or the World Council of Trade Unions. Lange reassured her audience that this focus on "women's work" would not lead inevitably to the "depoliticization" of the WIDF. In particular, she argued, the socialist countries should help the WIDF extend its influence in Asia, Africa, and Latin America. The head of the international department of

the Communist Party of the Soviet Union's Central Committee declared that
the congress should go further than the 1973 Moscow World Congress of the
Forces of Peace in reaching out to a broader range of potential collaborators—
for example, members of the International Council of Social Democratic
Women, or even the Catholic women's movement—"if it advances our interests." Moreover, the Soviet representative emphasized the importance of winning the UN as a "partner" and maintaining a "flexible" approach to ensure
that "our other partners feel equally treated," in the interests of strengthening
international cooperation. He emphasized that the UN had adopted the International Women's Year themes of equality, development, and peace "on our
initiative and not on the initiative of our opponents."[42]

The East German Ministry for Foreign Affairs (MfAA) carefully moni-
tored the preparations and proceedings of the Mexico City World Conference
on Women. Two main UN documents were adopted at the conference: a
World Action Plan for implementing the objectives of International Women's
Year (equality, development, and peace), and the more controversial Declaration of Mexico, which was proposed by the Group of 77 with Soviet bloc support. The declaration sparked heated debate by linking the subordination of
women to the New International Economic Order and describing Zionism as
a form of oppression akin to colonialism, racism, or apartheid. Ahead of the
conference, Soviet bloc diplomatic representations to the UN coordinated
their responses to the Secretariat's draft action plan. In May the East German
permanent representative to the UN reported back to Berlin that "the proposed social-political points put forward by the socialist states during the
consultative committee meeting have been largely accepted." However, diplomats identified a weak point in the action plan, namely a lack of attention to
the "political aspects of women's equality and the connection between the
struggle for freedom, détente, disarmament, and the role of the woman."[43] In
a report to the SED Central Committee, the MfAA presented the first UN
World Action Plan for Women as a triumph for socialist diplomacy, describing it as the "first UN document" to link the "basic rights of people, men and
women" to peace, international security, peaceful coexistence, anti-
imperialism, anti-racism, and national liberation.[44]

In June 1975 some 1,200 delegates took part in the intergovernmental
conference for International Women's Year in Mexico City, and a further
6,000 attended the parallel tribune for nongovernmental organizations. Soviet bloc countries were intent on pushing the message that women's issues
were inherently political. U.S. liberal feminists and the Ford administration

took the line that women's equality was separate from issues like economic development or world peace, in response to the perception that the Soviets were attempting to hijack women's issues for the cause of world communism by linking gender equality to world peace, anti-Zionism, or national independence. By contrast, communist governments scorned the "capitalist" approach to women's rights for reducing the roots of social and economic inequality between the sexes to a question of biological difference. At the same time, the East German Foreign Ministry claimed in reports back to Berlin that the Socialist bloc had also managed to exert its influence over the Third World nations at Mexico by shaping the content of the controversial Declaration of Mexico. The declaration was the outcome of fierce polemics over Zionism at the conference and listed Zionism as one of the barriers to women's emancipation.

The East German Foreign Ministry described the Declaration of Mexico as the result of 'intensive cooperation' between the socialist and nonaligned blocs: "It was possible to include all the fundamental political questions proposed by the Soviet Union and other socialist countries into the documents introduced by the Group of 77." The Foreign Ministry proudly reported the "complete failure" of the United States, Great Britain, and West Germany to divorce the question of sexual equality from "its socio-economic context."[45] Debates at Mexico City raged over whether women's emancipation was best achieved by integrating women into economic development or pursuing legal equality.[46] According to socialist publicists, there was no necessary contradiction between the two under state socialism. The East German media meanwhile reported to domestic audiences on how convincingly the GDR delegation to Mexico City had delivered its message. As the daily newspaper of the SED reported, "In socialism the rights of women are a reality."[47]

Women's Equality and "Socialist" Human Rights at the World Congress of Women

The World Congress of Women was a five-day event during which international delegates filled the conference halls and hotels of East Berlin. Delegates were under constant surveillance by uniformed and plainclothes police acting on instructions from the Ministry for State Security (MfS, commonly known as the Stasi) to monitor contacts between East German citizens and foreign visitors and to oversee the security of delegates from politically sensitive areas in the Middle East, Africa, or Latin America, some of whom could only attend the congress under conditions of strict anonymity.[48] Unconfirmed rumors of infiltration by foreign intelligence agencies filled the secret police reports. East German citizens were prohibited from entering the conference venues located in hotels used by international visitors, including the Intershop chain selling foreign and luxury goods, and tighter surveillance was exercised over the state borders.[49] Meanwhile, international delegates were escorted on tours of factories, schools, hospitals, and kindergartens around the country. Delegates were met by members of the official women's league, the Democratic Women's League of Germany (DFD). On a daily basis, DFD officials solicited opinions about the congress from its members. The ideal type of answer came from a DFD member from Berlin: "We'll gladly show them what we've achieved under the leadership of the party of the working class. I mean, everyone can see for their own eyes that women's rights are fully realized here."[50]

In the mid-1970s the GDR had one of the highest rates of paid female employment in the world. Legislation had helped establish social services for working mothers, enabled huge numbers of married women to work outside the home, laid down the principle of equal pay for men and women doing equal work, and sought to open up traditionally male-dominated occupations to women.[51] By the 1960s, East German citizens—especially educated, working women—possessed a hardy sense of the entitlements conferred by their rights as women, which they used to press their claims against the state.[52] By the mid-1970s, however, the capacity of the socialist regime to deliver on its promise of material guarantees for these social rights and entitlements was flagging. The GDR Human Rights Committee publicity materials for International Women's Year had characterized the "right to dissolve a shattered marriage," for example, as proof of the humanitarian character of socialism.[53] Such statements fuelled the standard criticism in West Germany that socialism was destroying the family, reflected in press coverage of the World Congress by conservative West German newspapers, such as the *Frankfurter Allgemeine Zeitung*, which used the occasion to refer once again to the soaring divorce rates in the GDR.[54] Meanwhile, the social and sexual revolutions that influenced postwar European societies, East and West, were causing East German women to question the meaning of equality as it had been defined by the paternalistic SED state.[55]

Propaganda for International Women's Year published by the GDR Human Rights Committee claimed to have stamped universal human rights with the mark of socialism. A brochure, *Equal Rights for Women in the GDR*, linked the East German conception of women's rights to human rights at the UN, asserting that "numerous UN Human Rights documents have been initiated by the USSR or that their content bears the unmistakable imprint of the attainments of socialism in the field of human rights."[56] This argument was pursued in the working papers prepared by East German officials ahead of the congress. The position paper for the congress working group on "Women's Equality in Society, De Jure and De Facto" claimed that the international legal status of women "has without doubt substantially improved as a result of the constant efforts of the progressive forces, men and women pursuing justice and progress, the activities of national and international organizations, as well as of cooperating women's organizations working for the achievement of this goal." Moreover, the national legislation on women's rights adopted by the socialist countries was presented as a model for the "drafting and adoption of a number of conventions and declarations for the improvement of the status of women."[57]

Congress working papers referred to the gender equality provisions of the UN Charter as an example of the dialectical relationship between human rights, "including also the rights of women," and the preservation of world peace, international security, and the development of friendly relations between nations. Socialist governments were credited with shaping international norms that had spread progressive ideas to both developing and developed countries, inspiring legislation on gender equality in the developing countries while also contributing to a "progressive change in the legal regulation of the status of women in the developed countries."[58] Officials in charge of drafting the conference documents meanwhile worried that overly legalistic texts would alienate their audience of women. While preparing the draft statements for the congress, the SED and working group members warned that "a simple, popular, less legalistic language" should be used for the declarations issued by each working group, and if "laws, conventions, and covenants are referred to, they must be explained in a way that is generally comprehensible."[59]

The opening speech by SED general secretary Erich Honecker referred interchangeably to "rights" and "needs," reflecting the socialist conception of "welfare rights." The 1966 International Covenant on Economic, Social, and Cultural Rights was one of the main reference points of East German discourses of human rights, along with the Final Act of the 1968 Tehran Conference on Human Rights, with its reference to the "indivisibility" of political and economic human rights.[60] Honecker presented the World Congress, along with the UN Conference on Women and the Helsinki Final Act, as proof of the socialist commitment to "the struggle for peace, détente, social security, and equality" that would fulfill the needs, desires, and hopes of humanity.[61] In part this reflected the tendency in communist propaganda to associate women and peace. The tone of Honecker's speech mirrored the paternalism built into socialist conceptions of "welfare rights."[62] Honecker also placed the GDR commitment to gender equality in the context of antifascist East German humanism, a favorite trope in socialist propaganda aimed at the anti-imperialist convictions of Third World audiences.

During the congress debates, the Working Group on Equal Rights presented the socialist model of gender equality as the true embodiment of human rights, in contrast to the "new women's liberation movement," which was characterized as a resurrection of the old women's rights movement.[63] The Working Group on Equal Rights was composed of experts in the theory of state and law from the SED Central Committee, the Humboldt University, and the Academy of Sciences. Misconstruing second-wave feminism as a bourgeois ideology that privileged the interests of elite women over the class oppression of working women and men, the congress working papers referred to the "great significance" of locating the principle of women's equality within the general UN human rights framework. This achievement in universalizing women's rights was claimed as a victory for socialist diplomacy and international cooperation, and the UN documents were described as "effective instruments" in the hands of the "progressive forces" represented by international socialism. The UN Commission on the Status of Women was invited to participate in the work of the preparatory committee but—to the chagrin of the SED—did not attend. However, an official from the GDR Human Rights Committee reported that the most heated debates in the Equal Rights Working Group did not concern equal rights at all but rather references in the final report to international cooperation, peace, national liberation movements, and above all, Zionism.[64] This raises the question of how activists responded to the World Congress.

The Solidarity of Sisterhood? New
Social Movements and Alliances

The sheer diversity of women's interests and experiences represented at the UN World Conferences on Women exploded feminist myths about "global sisterhood" premised on the notion of a universal female subjectivity.[65] But the massive increase in grassroots women's activism during the 1970s also challenged the Marxist view that gender equality was purely contingent on economic and political factors. The loosening of restrictions on transnational exchanges between activists and social movements allowed new ideas about gender and sexual rights in Eastern and Western Europe to circulate across the Iron Curtain. During the cultural détente of the early 1970s, Josie McLellan has recently written, the massive Tenth World Festival Games of Students and Youth in East Berlin provided a forum for creating transnational alliances built around international gay solidarity.[66] At mid-decade, the World Congress of Women was a far more official affair, but hosting an international conference under UN auspices nonetheless forced the GDR to open its doors to human rights organizations like Amnesty International, whose representatives were normally refused permission to enter the country.[67]

Although many feminist groups boycotted the congress, the concerns voiced by the human rights' and women's organizations that did attend were indicative of a new awareness of gender as a category of oppression that transcended Cold War conflicts over the relative importance of political or economic rights. The perception that the pursuit of social justice was incompatible with the recognition of sexual rights had been a major ideological cleavage at the UN Mexico City Conference on Women. Sexual rights had been the source of vitriolic conflicts between First- and Third-World women at the NGO Tribune, notes Jocelyn Olcott, particularly when perceived as part of the liberal equal rights ideology that Western feminists were presumed— often erroneously—to espouse.[68] From a variety of perspectives, these organizations called attention to the psychological and cultural factors that prevented women from achieving full equality, even when the economic causes of women's subordination had theoretically been removed by the socialization of the means of production. Stasi officers were dismissive of these "feminist" claims, yet such critiques resonated with new forms of domestic activism within the GDR itself, ranging from gay and lesbian activists to the antimilitarist women's and peace groups that emerged in the late 1970s and early 1980s.

The legacy of socialist internationalism influenced the varying forms of activism, exile, emigration, and international solidarity that connected women's NGOs and activism at the congress. Solidarity campaigns for oppressed women around the world were central to the international activities of the WIDF and mass organizations in the GDR, exemplified in the "Million Roses for Angela" campaign.[69] Angela Davis was a starring guest at both the World Youth Festival and the Women's Congress. The warm welcome extended to Chilean political exiles living in the GDR, especially Hortensia Bussi de Allende, was presented as proof of East German solidarity with the victims of imperialist aggression (even if the everyday experiences of "political émigrés" in the GDR did not correspond to this image).[70] Based on ethnographic and archive research, Ghodsee writes of the sentiments of solidarity with Third World women that Bulgarian women reported after attending the World Congress, in their shared reaction against American warmongering, imperialism, and racism in the wake of U.S. interventions in Vietnam and Chile, as well as continuing U.S. support for the apartheid regime in South Africa.[71] Kanak Mukherjee of the West Bengal Communist Party of India (Marxist) dismissed the UN Conference in Mexico City as a "big festival" while praising the approach toward women's rights in East Berlin.[72] The Northern Ireland Women's Rights Movement—founded by women members of the Communist Party of Ireland to take advantage of the publicity surrounding the UN Decade for Women—travelled to East Berlin to denounce the British Army for torturing prisoners in Long Kesh and shooting down women and children. The British Foreign Office, who recruited a woman delegate to act as an informal observer at the congress, concluded that the Women's Rights Movement was a communist organization exploiting women's issues for political goals.[73]

On the last day of the East Berlin Congress, the Stasi observed some thirty-five women gathering in the lobby of the main conference hall for an unofficial protest meeting. The women, who claimed to come from twelve different countries, later sent an anonymous note to the congress presidium: "We have heard many protests in the name of our sisters in the national liberation struggles here, but we have heard hardly any protest in the name of our sisters in their personal struggles against old attitudes, outdated structures, and crimes against women, which are taking place in every country in one form or another. We need both forms of solidarity, if we want to achieve equality, development, and peace."[74] Internal Stasi reports claimed feminists from the United States had arranged the protest by distributing handwritten invitations. True to the paternalistic mindset of the East German state security, which tended to assume that women were not capable of political protest, the Stasi classified the meeting as an unimportant event that failed to interest the other delegates in its discussion of matters such as "sexuality and lesbian love."[75] The East German women's magazine *Für Dich* reported on the protest, warning that feminist obsession with "sexual problems" diverted attention from the issues that could really improve women's lives, namely the struggle against oppression and discrimination: "imperialism" was the enemy, not men.[76]

Feminists also complained that the "highly-organized" congress had not helped women "to speak out against continual violations of women's rights such as rape, domestic violence, murder, and sexual exploitation."[77] The discussions about gender equality failed to consider the "new female types" created when women enjoyed equal rights alongside their traditional roles as mothers, wives, and workers: "There are more and more women who choose to remain single, not to have children, to do non-traditional work, to regain control over their own bodies—sexually and in other ways." A delegate from Women Overseas for Equality, an NGO associated with the Brussels-based International Tribunal on Crimes Against Women, similarly objected: "Nowhere in the Declaration is there reference to the fundamental psychological attitude that is known as sexism and defines a person's role on the basis of their gender rather than their capabilities, and thus remains a huge obstacle to achieving true equal rights for women in all political systems, in national liberation struggles, in war and in peace, as women adopt the stereotypical role modes defined for them by men."[78]

Explosive questions about the intersection of class, race, and gender in reproductive rights simmered under the surface of discussions on family planning. The Center to End Sterilization Abuse (CESA), a New York–based advocacy group founded by women affiliated with the Marxist, pro-independence Puerto Rican Socialist Party, distributed flyers to delegates protesting the coercive sterilization of women in Puerto Rico. Following from its Puerto Rican campaign, CESA was the first reproductive rights advocacy group to draw attention to sterilization abuse against poor Latina and black women in New York City.[79] Emotively, *Für Dich* reported "horrifying words from Maritza Arastia from Puerto Rico: 'Women's ignorance in family planning prevents them from participating in social development and contributes to poverty.' And she reported how women's ignorance is exploited and women are sterilized without their consent. Every third woman in Puerto Rico is already sterilized today."[80]

The sole Amnesty International representative granted permission to attend the congress was Irmgard Hutter, an Austrian woman.[81] Hutter brought with her six hundred copies of a four-page memorandum in English on the torture of women, and a draft resolution calling on all nations to consider the specific experiences of women political prisoners. With an emphasis on violence against women political prisoners that was relatively unusual for Amnesty at this time, the memorandum spoke emotively of the "male world" of the interrogation chamber in which, "degraded to the status of helpless objects, detained women very often are subjected to the most brutal sexual abuses and insults." The report highlighted the sexual abuse of women prisoners and physical violence against pregnant women, noting that "women raped by their interrogators have been refused abortion. Thus, the female identity of the torture victim is exploited in the most cynical way to humiliate their human dignity." Furthermore, the report claimed that "the close emotional relation of women to their families is misused in the most inhuman way. Women are often detained and tortured not because of their own activities, but because of the alleged activities of their relatives and friends."[82]

At the congress, Hutter tried to distribute copies of the Amnesty memorandum in the working group devoted to discussions of international cooperation. During an afternoon discussion session in a hotel owned by the GDR trade union confederation, Hutter left some eighty copies in a pile in the corner of the room. Swiftly, plainclothes Stasi officers removed some sixty copies, after which she attempted to distribute more by hand to other congress participants. A later Stasi report also claimed that an English-language poster had been discovered in circulation—printed in the name of the WIDF—with an appeal to release several named women prisoners, who were supposed to be "political prisoners" (including four from the USSR, Bulgaria, and Cuba).[83] Hutter later claimed that she used the opportunity to speak about women prisoners with other participants during the congress. Regarding GDR political prisoners, she only managed to telephone the attorney Wolfgang Vogel about a number of cases adopted by Amnesty International.[84]

Amnesty International had launched an action in International Women's Year focusing on some 250 female prisoners in 28 countries, including 25 in the GDR. Most had been charged with *Republikflucht*, or illegally attempting to leave the country.[85] In the context of the Helsinki Final Act, official restrictions on emigration—which so flagrantly violated the right to freedom of movement—were politically explosive. This was true for all socialist states but particularly for East Germany in connection with the issue of family reunification, since the closely guarded internal German border had divided thousands of communities and families since 1961. The Stasi placed Hutter under close surveillance with the aim of establishing whether Amnesty International planned to name political prisoners being held in the GDR or other Soviet countries.

The Amnesty report was clearly deemed subversive even though it did not refer specifically to rights abuses committed by socialist regimes. It reminded the congress participants "that in many countries women who exercise these rights [of participation in political, economic, and public life of their own society as well as of the international community] run great personal risks and in fact are punished for exercising them by arbitrary arrest and by the infliction of torture and degrading treatment." A draft resolution called upon all nations not only to abolish torture but to provide "medical care, including pre-natal care, for pregnant women prisoners, and safe and adequate facilities for their infants and small children," and recommended that the UN Committee on the Status of Women "create an ad-hoc working group to receive reliably attested information on the detention, torture, and cruel, inhuman and degrading treatment of women."[86]

The interventions of groups as diverse as Amnesty International, the Center to End Sterilization Abuse, or Women Overseas for Equality confirmed that women's rights could no longer be confined to the preexisting ideological frameworks of the Cold War, which viewed women's issues as a secondary concern.[87] In 1975 Stasi reports suggest that the East German regime did not view women's protest as a serious political threat. What the socialist regimes did not foresee was the rapid growth of nongovernmental women's organizations, which proved ever more resistant to the imperatives of ideological conformity and geopolitical alliances. The NGO Tribunes at the UN women's conferences testified to the explosion of transnational women's networks: 6,000 participants at Mexico City in 1975, 8,000 in Copenhagen, 13,500 in Nairobi, and 30,000 in Beijing in 1995. Groups such as Las Madres de Plaza de Mayo, an association of mothers who courageously protested the disappearances of family members during the Argentine military dictatorship's Dirty War , played a crucial role in publicizing gendered violations of human rights within women's transnational networks.[88]

Conclusion

The East Berlin Congress of Women in International Women's Year represented the culmination of postwar efforts by state socialist regimes to use women's rights for the purpose of gaining international legitimacy. Despite the failure of the congress to impose a hegemonic state socialist vision on the increasingly fragmented global discourse of women's rights, the GDR continued to present state socialism as the vanguard in the promotion of women's equality. Reflecting in 1987 on the first ten years of the UN Human Rights Committee, the seasoned East German expert in international law Bernhard Graefrath noted that women's equality had been one of the first themes discussed by the committee after its creation in 1977. Noting the increasing importance of women's issues for the Human Rights Committee, for years previously "a purely male assembly," Graefrath emphasized "how greatly the international women's movement, the numerous resolutions of the UN General Assembly, the actions of the Decade for Women, and the efforts for a convention against the discrimination against women have contributed to placing the problems of women's equality ever more clearly in the center of international attention."[89]

Long-established Western women's organizations such as the Young Women's Christian Association (YWCA) moved swiftly to write the World Congress of Women out of histories of International Women's Year. For example, the International Women's Tribune Centre, set up in 1976 to organize follow-up activities after International Women's Year, refused to refer to the East Berlin Congress in its reports.[90] Meanwhile, GDR officials remained suspicious of NGO activity at future UN women's conferences: Shortly before the Copenhagen conference the SED Women's Department authored an internal report noting that the NGO tribune in Mexico City had been hijacked by national women's organizations from the United States who tried to turn it into a "feminist forum" as well as an anti-Soviet tool.[91]

The documents adopted by the Copenhagen World Conference on Women in 1980 were dominated by debates about economic development and strongly influenced by postcolonial and Soviet claims, referring explicitly to the advances made by women in centrally planned economies.[92] In more lasting ways, however, the influence of Socialist governments and mass women's organizations continued to shape the movement for recognizing women's rights as human rights. The landmark Convention on the Elimination of All Forms of Discrimination against Women (CEDAW), adopted by the General

Assembly in December 1979, bore the influences of Soviet perspectives on gender equality and human rights.

The convention established women's rights to property, financial credit, and choice of marriage, education, and work, as well as full participation in all aspects of political life. CEDAW also contained provisions that recognize the need for special provisions based on women's biological or gender difference. Blurring the distinction between the public and private spheres in previous human rights conventions, the convention not only expanded states' accountability for discrimination against women by "any person, organization or enterprise" in economic and family life but bound state authorities to take measures to prevent abuses by private persons, including the adoption of temporary special measures to accelerate equality between men and women.[93] But Jean Quataert reminds us that CEDAW "has the largest number of reservations attached to it of any international human rights treaty—reservations that in good measure undercut the letter of the law. Most are raised in defense of family (the personal status codes) and religious laws at the heart of assumptions about the specific cultural identity of a particular state."[94]

Only after the end of the Cold War did the movement for women's rights as human rights fully materialize, and then in the form of a global campaign that sought to increase the visibility of gender in the UN human rights system by privileging reproductive rights and protection against violence over social justice.[95] Charlotte Bunch, whose Center for Women's Global Leadership at Rutgers University became the motor of the women's human rights movement, has claimed that after the collapse of the Socialist bloc the transnational appeal of human rights swelled to such an extent that, she felt, women had to "claim it and be in on it."[96] Indeed, the 1990s rather than the 1970s appear to be the heyday of human rights mobilizations for women's advocacy groups and NGOs.[97] Gender emerged as a legally protected category, and violence and reproductive rights were recognized as legitimate areas of concern for international human rights law. The definition of crimes against humanity was broadened to include rape. Yet social feminists have criticized the "women's rights as human rights" movement for focusing "overwhelmingly on issues of reproduction and violence, as opposed, for example, to poverty. Ratifying the Cold War split between civil and political rights, on the one hand, and social and economic rights, on the other, these efforts, too, have privileged recognition over redistribution."[98] Thus the 1970s were a breakthrough decade for women's rights, setting up the institutional and organizational networks for the global campaign to frame women's issues in terms of rights—rather than concepts such as development or discrimination—that triumphed after the end of the Cold War.[99] The history of this campaign was no simple linear narrative but a deeply contested process of negotiation between numerous competing factions over the relationship between gender, ideology, and human rights, which continues to the present day.

Chapter 6

"Magic Words"
The Advent of Transnational Human
Rights Activism in Latin America's
Southern Cone in the Long 1970s

Patrick William Kelly

> Upon hearing the word "right," Doña Susana kept looking at him as if she were Alice in Wonderland, but thinking deeply.
> "Rights? 'My rights'? . . .
> "Rights for those who don't have them? How can people claim rights if they don't have them?"
> —Juan Rivano, *Época de descubrimientos* (*The Age of Discovery*)

In March 1972, members of the Division for Latin America of the United States Catholic Conference, relying on information from Brazilian exiles, directed a letter to Brazilian president Emílio Médici that challenged the detention of "famed" peasant leader Manuel da Conceição. They urged the president to "allow an international team of impartial observers" into the country to "investigate the long-standing and widespread charges of systemic repression, torture and violation of basic human rights."[1] A mere two years later, a collection of Latin American and European activists used a comparable discourse when they formed the International Commission of Enquiry into the Crimes of the Military Junta to protest the arrival of military rule in Chile. "Every attack on human rights in Chile," remarked the chairman of the commission at its first meeting, "has its victims and its guilty men who should and must be identified."[2] And in December 1975, as political order was unraveling in Argentina, a group of political and religious activists founded the Permanent Assembly for Human Rights. The group's official protocol announced in hortatory language its mission to "promote the vigilance of the human rights enumerated in the Universal Declaration of Human Rights."[3] What unites these activist claims was an unprecedented convergence in the 1970s on the use of human rights as a depoliticized framework to apprehend and intervene in alarming events unfolding in Latin America.

This chapter investigates the advent of a transnational politics of human rights in the "long 1970s," when social activists raised global awareness about violence and repression during military dictatorships in Brazil, Chile, and Argentina.[4] It asks a seemingly simple question: why did activists begin to speak the language of human rights? "Before the 1970s," Argentine human rights activist Emilio Mignone reflected, "no one spoke of human rights in Argentina."[5] While not unknown, the language of human rights was not widely used in the Americas or in most places throughout the globe prior to the 1970s.[6]

By synthesizing existing scholarship on South American authoritarian rule and related exile diasporas—which often treats each country or case in isolation—to largely unexplored material from North and South American archives, this chapter explains the turn to human rights by foregrounding the transnational. It is only through analyzing the border-hopping nature of transnational activism that we can begin to grasp why human rights surged in the 1970s. By the end of the decade, human rights would come to transform not only the activist vocabularies but also the moral imaginations of many throughout the world. It would be invoked by an array of activists, civil society designers, and state bureaucrats as a set of globalized norms, even if there was profound disagreement over what constituted those norms. At the same time, we must shy away from triumphalism in cataloging the rise of transnational human rights activism in the 1970s: the turn to human rights represented a significant scaling back of the parameters of social change, especially for Latin Americans who once longed for revolution and the enactment of a socialist state.

The shift to a human rights sensibility in this period was neither self-evident nor rooted in a timeless past.[7] A second related question this chapter explores, then, is why did human rights have staying power? In other words, once it began to circulate, how did it catch on as an activist vocabulary? While transnational advocates came to use the explicit language of human rights, it was by no means the only moral vocabulary they employed. Activists were often equally at ease in the idioms of humanitarianism, anti-imperialism, civil liberties, and the rights of man. The multiplicity of moral appeals in the late 1960s and early 1970s attested to a moment when human rights floated through the sea of a fluid activist vocabulary.

In many senses human rights was always an embattled concept, jostled around on the battleground of transnational politics to fit the fancy of the political soldier. For some, especially activists who questioned the nature of the capitalist world order, the appropriation of human rights rhetoric was far more tactical than ideational. Many Marxists in Latin America had little trouble making human rights claims at the same time as they saw revolution as the ultimate solution to society's ills. But for others, the appeal to human rights moved beyond mere tactics: it became a fundamentally new moral paradigm through which they saw the world. Activists from each of these broadly defined groups at times cobbled together coalitions to work in the name of human rights, but at other times they found their ideas about human rights competing against one another.[8] Most obviously, activists at Amnesty International shunned the use of violence and refused to adopt prisoners of conscience (Amnesty's term for a detained victim who would have letters written on his or her behalf) who had advocated or employed violence. Many Marxists, although not all, would take offense at such a limited view of what they considered to be necessary means of social activism.

This chapter argues that answers to these two questions can be found in the inherent versatility of human rights language: it doubled as a depoliticized language that seemingly hid its politics. Activists took advantage of this dual nature to develop a series of depoliticized arguments. It was not that activists concerned about events in South America in the 1970s were not political—they never ceased being political—but they articulated their claims in language that stressed the moral priority of ending human rights abuses.[9] This chapter speaks to this tension of human rights as a language that is at once political and allegedly beyond politics.

The chapter is divided into four sections. First, it surveys the range of human rights activism that developed in response to the waves of violence that struck Brazil, Chile, and Argentina in the late 1960s and 1970s. While these are not the only potential examples—Uruguay could also be easily included—I see them as playing a critical role in the development of transnational human rights activism in the long 1970s. Second, it analyzes the creation of a transnational solidarity movement comprised of exiles, scholars, and clerics who used the language of solidarity as a political organizing concept. These advocates also began to utilize the vocabulary of human rights, and the third section looks at the myriad ways solidarity activists approached human rights as an activist language, one which they were not always fluent in, committed to, or even fully comfortable with. The fourth section turns to a few examples of human rights networks that emerged as transnational activists from a variety of places throughout the Western world worked with domestic groups in Brazil, Chile, and Argentina to ameliorate rights abuses.

Case Studies: Brazil, Chile, Argentina

Protest against the Brazilian dictatorship in the late 1960s was among the first instances of nascent human rights advocacy in Latin America, if not the world. Although the 1964 coup was indeed violent, the institutionalization of a set of draconian acts in 1968 produced a sharp increase in state repression.[10] Notably, most opposition to the Brazilian dictatorship did not at first take the form of an activism expressed in the language of human rights but rather focused almost uniquely on the state practice of torture.[11] Where too often scholars have conflated torture and a response to it based on human rights in an era before they were so intricately enmeshed, the Brazilian case shows how a rise in concern over torture could at times take place outside of a broader human rights vision. When human rights rhetoric began to shape these campaigns more directly, it came initially from enterprising transnational church activists in Brazil and the United States—Archbishops Dom Hélder Câmara and Paulo Evaristo Arns and the National Conference of Brazilian Bishops stand out—and from the pioneering efforts of Amnesty International. Meanwhile, the idea of human rights was absent among the Brazilian left in large measure due to the permanence of a belief in armed struggle and Marxist revolution. But when it did enter into usage among the left, primarily through the influence of exiles and the church, it was appropriated and transformed by Brazilian activists, who grafted it on top of Marxist theory and often used both idioms interchangeably.

If the Brazilian case set these processes in motion, the Chilean military coup of 1973 served as the critical fulcrum in the shift to an avowed activism couched in the language of human rights. Chilean military leader Augusto Pinochet swiftly reorganized Chilean society, turning to torture, summary executions, and exile to silence dissenters and inculcate widespread fear.[12] Since criticism of the junta was largely stifled in Chile, activists at first organized in the international arena (the important efforts of the Pro-Peace Committee (Comité Pro Paz), as explained below, were initially based more on humanitarian than human rights concerns). Fueled by waves of Chilean exiles, activists formed a series of solidarity groups throughout the world, adopting names like the Chile Committee for Human Rights. Although they organized for unique political reasons, solidarity groups collaborated with NGOs like Amnesty International to shine the spotlight of international publicity on rights abuses in Chile.[13] As the key hub in a larger transnational advocacy network, Amnesty developed coalitions with solidarity groups, which in turn opened up a space for the growth of domestic human rights organizations in Chile, particularly the Vicaría de la Solidaridad. These alliances, while not without tensions over the role of politics in the moral appeal to human rights, often worked through the Organization of American States and the UN to denounce violations of human rights.[14]

The 1973 coup and Chilean oppositional politics augured a future of transnational human rights activism. Activists throughout the world—and even national governments, notably in the United States under President Jimmy Carter—latched onto the rhetoric of human rights to "name and shame" governments, as they did during the Argentine dictatorship (1976–1983). Although more than ten organizations would form in Argentina, the Permanent Assembly for Human Rights (Asamblea Permanente por los Derechos Humanos, APDH) and the Center for Legal and Social Studies (Centro de Estudios Legales y Sociales, CELS), formed in 1975 and 1979, respectively, as two of the most important oppositional voices to the dictatorship. The APDH compiled vast lists of victims of unwarranted detentions and *desaparecidos* that supplied the documentary evidence to protest the junta. In response to a perception that the APDH was too cautious in its work, a group of activists created CELS to more aggressively confront the dictatorship. Strains in the relationship emerged between these two dueling visions over the proper place of politics in human rights. If not always on the same tactical page, these groups enabled transnational NGOs like Amnesty International to make its appeals in the international arena. While many of the same international bodies organized against the Argentine junta, Amnesty International, again, stands out for its local investigation and subsequent report.[15]

These three cases from the Southern Cone show that different actors approached the idea of human rights in different ways, falling somewhere on a sliding scale between outright rejection and forthright embrace. Leftist activists were responding not only to the collapse of their political utopia with the death of Chilean president Salvador Allende—the turning point at which many saw the futility of armed struggle—but also to the brutal torture and murder of family and friends. The next section more directly focuses on the role that South American exiles and transnational solidarity played in the construction of a novel form of transnational human rights politics.

Exiles and the Transnational Solidarity Movement

In the early 1970s, a constellation of activists in Europe, the United States, Canada, and Latin America formed a transnational solidarity movement to raise global awareness about escalating violence in Latin America. If virtually ignored so far in the existing literature, or discussed only with reference to specific diasporas, the transnational solidarity movement, and exiles in particular, played a key role in the shift to a global language of human rights.[16] The Brazilian, Chilean, and Argentine coups produced massive and multiple waves of exiles that circulated throughout the world. In their insightful study of the politics of exile in Latin America, Mario Sznajder and Luis Roniger point to exiles' denunciations of the horrors of authoritarian regimes in the Southern Cone in the 1970s as a "voice not to be silenced by distance, time, or international censorship."[17] A close examination of exiles' trajectories, both physical and ideological, in the transnational solidarity movement opens a revealing window on the making of human rights politics in the long 1970s.

Depending on the particularities of the moment, exiles left for varying destinations and for varying reasons. In the best-researched case of Brazil, Denise Rollemberg distinguishes between the exile generations of 1964 and 1968. Whereas the former consisted of reformist politicians who believed in democratic politics, the latter was much more revolutionary. In the first period following the 1964 military coup, reformist Brazilians primarily went to Montevideo, Uruguay. Following the crackdown by the dictatorship in 1968, the second period saw Brazilians heading to Santiago de Chile, especially after the election of the world's first socialist president, Salvador Allende, seen by many as a symbol of transnational solidarity and the Non-Aligned Movement.[18] Once Allende fell in September 1973, a third wave of Brazilians, fearing that no place in the Southern Cone would be safe, left in large numbers for France.[19] Estimates for the numbers of Brazilian exiles range from five thousand to thirty thousand.[20] They interacted with like-minded exiles and leftists in solidarity groups throughout the world, especially in Santiago, Buenos Aires, and eventually Paris. But the leftist laboratory in Allende's Chile stood out as especially central to the development of a transnational solidarity movement, where leftists found common cause in the fight against imperialism and state violence.

Like the Brazilian one, the Chilean case is well studied. According to Thomas Wright and Rody Oñate, between 1978 and 1988 some two hundred thousand Chilean exiles (a conservative estimate) formed a transnational diasporic community in over 140 countries. Exiles principally settled in Sweden, France, Italy, East Germany, and Moscow in Europe, and in Mexico City, Venezuela, and Cuba in Latin America.[21] Chilean exiles ranged from radical Marxists, like members of the Movimento de Izquierda Revolucionaria (MIR), to Christian Democrats, and exiles regularly chose their point of destination based on party affiliation.[22] They injected new life into the solidarity movement, propelling linkages among more ad hoc solidarity organizations, NGOs like Amnesty International, and intergovernmental organizations like the Inter-American Commission on Human Rights (IACHR) of the Organization of American States, and the Commission on Human Rights (CHR) at the UN. These networks helped to construct a "global arena" for the voicing of human rights violations in the Southern Cone.[23]

Unlike the Brazilian and Chilean examples, the Argentine exile story has not yet received a systematic review, as existing accounts focus on specific countries, communities, and tactics.[24] But as Sznajder and Roniger show, Argentines left for many of the same places as the Chileans, although they were less driven by party identification in the selection of destination cities. In Latin America they traveled to Mexico and Venezuela; in Europe to Italy, Spain, France, and Sweden; and they even went as far as to Australia and Israel.[25] Argentines more commonly chose the same destinations as their Brazilian and Chilean counterparts, the majority settling in Spain and Mexico.[26] They also struggled with many of the same questions about the use of violence as the most effective way of bringing down an authoritarian regime. Most notably, regardless of the place they were fleeing, and despite ideological, national, generational, and class tensions, exiles grew increasingly politically conscious through their experiences as enemies of the anticommunist military juntas in South America. The exile experience thus became a shared political learning environment in which exiles educated one another, promoting enduring bonds across national borders and political cleavages.

As the carriers of personal experiences and knowledge of the repressive reality of authoritarian governments, exiles were the engines of the transnational solidarity movement. Between struggling to find a safe haven, adjusting to an unfamiliar land, and longing to go home, they engaged in a series of political activities that would come to define the sociopolitical landscape for solidarity groups. They formed a diverse array of organizations, such as the Comité de Solidaridad con la Lucha de los Pueblos Latinoamericanos (Committee of Solidarity in the Struggle of the Latin American People). They held symbolic "Weeks of Solidarity" with different "oppressed" nations of the Americas numerous times throughout the year, in various locations throughout the globe, and alternately expressed a pan-American sense of solidarity with the "Latin American people."[27]

Through their physical diaspora, exiles underwent a series of ideological journeys. In many ways, the exile experience was a metaphorical classroom for the assimilation and articulation of new ideas. Through studying the publications of Brazilian exiles, specifically *Debate*, a monthly periodical that appeared first in Paris in February 1970 and lasted until July 1982, Rollemberg shows that the exile experience was an intellectually generative environment that welcomed the production and consumption of new global paradigms, such as internationalism, feminism, racism, democracy, and human rights. The idea of democracy and rights, especially, provided many Brazilian exiles with a new way of interpreting old Marxist debates.[28] For example, Antonio Leal, an exiled Chilean politician in Italy, explained how he discovered through his first-hand experience in exile that "the socialist bloc had serious defects" and that "there couldn't be democracy without human rights."[29] For their part, Argentine solidarity groups split over the use of violence. When solidarity groups in Mexico led by radical revolutionary leaders of the Montoneros and the Popular Revolutionary Army (Ejército Revolucionario Popular) refused to moderate their position on armed struggle, one faction of exiles turned to a more rights-based approach to found the Human Rights Coordinating Committee (Coordinadora de Derechos Humanos).[30]

Parallel debates played out in other places as exiles relied on the printing press as a cheap and effective way to foment transnational solidarity. Exile publications offer a compelling perspective on how activists in the transnational solidarity movement negotiated the language and practice of human rights. Publications can be roughly divided into two types: those whose main purpose was to disseminate information about violence and repression under dictatorships, and those that took a more theoretical approach to the future of the left in Latin America and beyond. The first cluster of publications adopted depoliticized names like the *Brazilian Information Bulletin*. The point here was to deemphasize ideology in favor of the cold, hard facts. Activists believed this was the best way to raise awareness about the abrogation of the rule of law and widespread use of torture under military dictatorships.[31]

The second cluster forthrightly took on the question of ideology and the left. Prior to the appearance of human rights, as noted above, many exile organizations expressed solidarity in the language of anti-imperialism. In October 1972, for example, *Brazil Hoy* placed a picture of Marxist Angela Davis on its cover. Following her trip to Santiago de Chile, Davis was quoted speaking in typically Marxist terms about the "fight of the Chilean workers to construct socialism" as part of a broader effort to fight against the "citadel" of U.S. imperialism. In activist circles and publications, the language of anti-imperialism and the language of human rights competed for predominance. Whether or not activists decided to use one or the other or both reflected the growing salience of both the local and global meanings of human rights in the 1970s.

The 1973 Chilean coup marked perhaps the essential turning point for transnational human rights activism. While a small solidarity movement existed before the coup, it saw its ranks grow exponentially in its aftermath, fueled by waves of Chilean exiles that spread throughout the world.[32] As one activist put it, "the September 11, 1973, coup changed everything, pushed every other concern to the background, and Chile came to dominate our work for years to come. It was *the* event that catalyzed everything else."[33] More so than the other cases, Chile served as the critical hinge for the transnational solidarity movement in the co-optation of both a distinct vocabulary of human rights and a consciousness of the power of the term "human rights" as a way for the movement to legitimize its claims.[34]

But why Chile? Chilean president Salvador Allende, elected with a plurality of the vote in 1970, launched a gradual and democratic transition to socialism. In so doing, he challenged the binary visions of high modernism that the United States and the Soviet Union offered to the world by adopting a "third way" approach to a socialist state that resonated with the nonaligned nations of the global South.[35] Allende also appealed to a transnational culture of revolt of the late 1960s that was disenchanted with the slow struggle for change and the empty promises of reform from Cold War leaders.[36] In deposing Allende, Chilean military leaders ended his democratic experiment in socialism, which in turn collapsed the dreams of many throughout the global left who saw Allende's path as perhaps the only viable way forward.

The shattered dreams of the left fostered the creation of new solidarity organizations in Europe, the United States, and Latin America. It also promoted cooperation among existing NGOs like Amnesty International, the International Commission of Jurists, the Ford Foundation, and other more ad hoc structures of the transnational solidarity movement. International groups often turned to domestic activists for information. Church organizations in particular, such as the Vicaría de la Solidaridad in Chile, compiled vast amounts of evidence of arbitrary detentions and instances of torture. This information was handed off to activists at NGOs, who turned the IACHR as well as the UN into key forums to denounce the dictatorships. The Commission on Human Rights at the UN, to take only one example, issued successive reports on the "protection of human rights in Chile" as well as votes of condemnation of human rights violations.[37] Before the Chilean coup, the supranational structures of the IACHR and the UN were not commonly seen as forums where abuses of human rights by states should be addressed. It is remarkable how quickly they became relevant institutions.

In addition to the international sphere, early human rights activism took many different local forms. Typical of the transnational solidarity movement's embryonic coalition building were a series of action groups that were formed in college towns throughout the United States in 1971. The United Ministries of Education of the National Council of Churches provided the funding for four such groups in the progressive college communities of Berkeley, Ithaca, Austin, and Madison. A look at the Madison-based Community Action on Latin America (CALA) illuminates the importance of these grassroots solidarity organizations in explaining the local-global dynamics of human rights in the 1970s. A collection of church activists, cosmopolitan leftists, and intellectuals formed CALA as a solidarity organization concerned with Latin America.[38] CALA activists, in the tradition of Marxists-Leninists, initially worked to expose what they perceived to be the exploitative effects of multinational corporations and the insidious interventions of U.S. imperialism in Latin America.

Following the 1973 coup, CALA began to campaign more directly in a human rights idiom. "The demands," argued CALA members, "must be twofold: that the UN take action to ensure an end to the violation of human rights in Chile and that all U.S. economic and military aid to the junta be cut off."[39] For CALA members, as for all members of the transnational solidarity movement writ large, it is not so much that a human rights consciousness was born in the wake of the Chilean coup—solidarity groups did not one day awaken to being concerned with human rights; they were always concerned with what today we call human rights. But rather they developed a new awareness of the rhetorical fluidity, adaptability, and utility of human rights language.[40] These appeals not only galvanized national attention to the cause but also show how CALA served as one hub in a larger transnational network of Latin American solidarity. In this way, CALA served as an interlocutor for local activists trying to grasp global events.

Approaches to Human Rights

The shift toward human rights in exile publications mirrored a larger transformation in the work of transnational solidarity activists as they contemplated whether and how to use such language. What were human rights? How and why should they be incorporated into existing doctrine and practice? The documents from activists during this period provide a set of preliminary answers. First, we must acknowledge that some solidarity activists rarely spoke in human rights terms. In large part, this was due to the continued belief in armed struggle. In his handwritten notes, Brazilian exile Jean Marc van der Weid, the president of the banned União Nacional dos Estudantes, responded to the question, "How do we fight against this [the Brazilian dictatorship]," with the answer, "armed struggle."[41] To these activists, the specter of Che Guevara loomed large. Human rights were nowhere on their moral radar.

Another approach to human rights was to simply reject them, and some activists refused to wave the human rights flag. For instance, Brazilian leftist students at the State University of Campinas (UNICAMP) debated the use of such discourse before a planned Human Rights Week in 1976 to draw attention to repressive government practices. One hard-line section of the student group argued against the invocation of human rights because they felt it hewed too closely to a bourgeois philosophy of liberal rights.[42] To these absolutists, human rights were nothing but mere "magic words" that would not change the capitalist reality. In response, a more moderate group of socialist students, calling themselves the Permanent Commission for the Defense of Human Rights, considered human rights a savvy propagandistic tool that did not subvert the greater cause of socialism but rather extended it. From an "immediate tactical perspective," argued the moderates, Human Rights Week would broaden the appeal of the student movement while not subverting the ultimate goals of revoultion.[43]

The moderate retort revealed a second stance toward human rights: the acceptance of rights language as one component of a much larger struggle for socialist revolution. Human rights were therefore seen as a strategic device that did not foreclose a revolutionary future but rather worked to create the conditions to make revolution possible. The purpose would be to amplify to the greatest extent possible the number of trajectories toward overturning the existing system. Human rights, in that sense, furthered the eventual goal, but they were not seen as an end in themselves. Marxists should work to expand the fight on "every possible front," the moderates thought.[44] In this rendering, the struggle for human rights and democracy were often called "tactics" that would ameliorate the abuses and the extremes of the dictatorship, which was considered the first step toward a revolutionary future.[45]

In opposition to these more calculated responses, the third approach toward human rights reflected what Silvina Jensen characterizes as a global shift in the "ideological matrix" of the left in the 1970s—a "rupture" that saw the left arriving at a general "consensus" on human rights.[46] However, born in an age of deep division on the left, the transition to human rights was neither smooth nor inevitable. Disillusioned with the collapse of an international socialist vocabulary, the failure of revolution in Latin America, and the rise of moderated approaches like social democracy and Eurocommunism in Europe, the concept of human rights for many on the Latin American left became gradually more appealing. If human rights once smacked of a bourgeois fantasy, many Latin American activists began to view it as a useful new paradigm, if a far more limited program for social action.

A fourth approach showed how human rights could easily be appended to existing belief systems and reinterpreted in a new light. Catholic and Protestant groups spearheaded the turn to human rights as the chief means of moral opposition to the dictatorships of the Southern Cone. As early as 1963, Pope John XXIII's encyclical *Pacem in Terris* called for a reorientation of Catholic doctrine and praxis and mentioned the need to defend human rights, using that explicit language. Throughout the 1960s, driven by the reforms of the Second Vatican Council (1962–1965), some Catholics, both in the Americas and more globally, grew increasingly comfortable viewing their work in human rights terms. To Tom Quigley, a solidarity activist for the U.S.

Catholic Conference, human rights were "the air we breathed at the time."[47] However, it would not be until the late 1960s and 1970s that different coalitional groups would form a social movement based on the language of human rights. Once that happened, Catholics were often at the domestic epicenter of these new transnational coalitions that emerged in the 1970s. This was especially so in Brazil under the Comite de Defesa dos Direitos Humanos para os Países do Cone Sul CLAMOR, led by Cardinal Paulo Arns, and in Chile under what would become the Vicaría de la Solidaridad, led by Cardinal Raúl Silva Henríquez.[48]

Transnational Coalitions

The Brazilian, Chilean, and Argentine campaigns relied on the creation of transnational coalitions. Starting in the late 1960s, as the Brazilian state instituted a series of authoritative reforms including the widespread use of torture, transnational solidarity activists developed new networks, technologies, and strategies to raise awareness about state repression in Brazil with the hope of ameliorating and ultimately ending such abuses. Although activists worked in Europe, the United States, and Latin America, the best documented example of these efforts has revealed the work of enterprising Christian and academic activists in the United States.[49] James Green explains how the Latin American departments of the National Council of Churches (NCC) and the United States Catholic Conference (USCC) denounced torture in Brazil.[50] These protests, however, were only made possible through the transnational circulation of information by a variety of exiles and organizations in the late 1960s and early 1970s.

Crucial to their efforts was the information gleaned from emergent exile networks. One key exile in this network was Márcio Moreira Alves. A former Brazilian politician, he fled to exile after publicly speaking out against the crackdown in post-1968 Brazil.[51] From his initial post in Santiago, according to his personal testimony, he "distribute[d] information" he had obtained from clandestine Brazilian networks "to the media in the United States and Europe about repression and torture."[52] As an affluent Brazilian who spoke both English and French, Márcio revealed the reach of transnational solidarity activists in their efforts to denounce authoritarianism in the Southern Cone. In June 1969, Márcio traveled to New York and Washington in collaboration with Brady Tyson, a professor at American University, and to the

USCC, and even spoke with Senators Mike Mansfield and Edward Kennedy in hopes of persuading them to apply pressure on the Brazilian junta.[53] In April 1970, Senator Kennedy would deliver a speech in Missoula, Montana, calling into question U.S. foreign policy for "support[ing] regimes in Latin America that deny basic human rights."[54]

In April 1970, activists at the NCC and the USCC, with information gathered from Brazilian exiles and the World Council of Churches, published "Terror in Brazil." It was one of the first dossiers to relay the pervasive nature of torture as a Brazilian state practice. The eighteen-page pamphlet, signed by thirty-four American religious and academic activists, detailed the history of rights abuses in Brazil since the 1964 government takeover.[55] "We cannot remain silent," the declaration read, "to the flagrant denial of human rights and dignity coming to us from Brazil. . . . To do so would make us accomplices of those who are the authors and perpetrators of this repression." The group's efforts produced supportive editorials in the *New York Review of Books*, the *Washington Post*, and the *New York Times*.[56]

Provoked by this account, a number of Catholic-led organizations sprouted up in the United States in the early 1970s. Following the example of groups in Algiers, Paris, and Santiago, a small coterie of Catholic and exiled solidarity activists including William Wipfler, Ralph Della Cava, Brady Tyson, Tom Quigley, and others established the American Committee for Information on Brazil in February 1970 in Washington, D.C. In addition to helping to orient exiles in their visits or transition to the United States, the committee spoke out against torture in Brazil. It was joined by the USCC's Latin American Bureau, led by Louis M. Colonnese until 1972 and then Fred McGuire, which sent letters to Brazilian military officials and the Inter-American Commission on Human Rights.[57]

Solidarity activists at the USCC and the NCC engineered a novel plot in 1970 that sought to redefine the meaning of human rights monitoring at the Organization of American States (OAS). As Quigley recalled it, after locating the number of the OAS in the phone directory—"nobody in the human rights community had as yet availed themselves of [that] entity"—five activists walked over to the offices of Charles Moyer, the staff director of the IACHR. They held a "three-inch-thick dossier" of incidents of torture and repression, which they presented with a petition on behalf of torture victims. Secretary Luis Reque of the IACHR was "nonplussed," especially as they had brought a photographer from the *Washington Post*, but Moyer was secretly pleased that "someone had discovered the IACHR." Once one of the cases was accepted, the Brazilian government was forced to engage in international volleys over its human rights record, albeit behind closed doors. Although the process was slow and "torturous"—lasting over three years—the IACHR would end up delivering a damning report to the OAS General Assembly on the political environment in Brazil. While ultimately ignored by the OAS General Assembly, in that organization predicated on the sovereignty of the nation-state, these early solidarity activists pioneered a number of tactics that future human rights activists would pick up and expand upon.[58]

Building on these earlier efforts, activists played a pivotal role in the establishment of a human rights community in Washington, D.C., in the early 1970s. Tom Quigley and Brady Tyson, in conjunction with Márcio Moreira Alves, organized the Latin American Strategy Committee (LASC), which presaged the later and more formalized Washington Office on Latin America (WOLA); not incidentally, many LASC members helped to form WOLA out of a desire to more directly influence U.S. foreign policy.[59] Quigley and Tyson developed relationships with early champions of human rights activism, such as John Salzburg, who proved instrumental in the focus on human rights by Representative Donald Fraser's House subcommittee. These contacts would result in many future House and Senate sessions on human rights violations in the Southern Cone, events which served as the seeds of what would become the human rights lobby in Washington.[60] (Amnesty International, for instance, did not have an office in Washington until 1976.)

Unlike the relatively small Brazilian campaigns of the late 1960s and early 1970s, the Chilean coup galvanized people throughout the world. Exiles and solidarity activists formed a series of informal groups in protest. For example, the International Commission of Enquiry into the Crimes of the Military Junta in Chile first met in Helsinki in early 1974 and was comprised of exiled Chileans, politicians from Western European governments, international lawyers, academics, clerics, and others concerned with the situation in Chile.[61] The commission would meet almost every year throughout the 1970s in an assortment of cities throughout the globe: Helsinki (1974 and 1976), Copenhagen (1974), Mexico City (1975), and Algiers (1978).[62]

To push back against the official story in Pinochet's Chile, which whitewashed human rights abuses, commission members pieced together a narrative of massive violations of human rights in Chile. They did so by accumulating stories from survivors about their experiences in Chile, at times sensationalized for effect. Steve Stern has argued that this "testimonial truth" provided "personal experience and personal witnessing, told as living memory of the authentic, [which] could bring out a collective truth denied by the official story."[63] The "official story," promoted by the Chilean junta, claimed that intervention was necessary to rid the country of the communist "threat" and as a hyperbolic propaganda conspiracy by the forces of international communism. At their annual meetings, the International Commission of Enquiry deployed the testimony of Chileans who had been tortured, imprisoned, raped, or subjected to other human rights abuses not simply to gain information but as a form of propaganda and international diplomacy to put pressure on the Pinochet junta. Going forward, human rights activists would use the power of testimonial truth as a trump card that could not be turned over, in effect constructing a powerful story of human rights abuses to counter the official story. By systematically documenting these abuses, they established a track record of evidence that then was forwarded to the Ad-Hoc Working Group on Chile, a subsidiary body of the Commission on Human Rights at the UN.[64]

Transnational activism as represented by the International Commission of Enquiry also provided cover for the expansion of domestic human rights organizing. In the early years of the Pinochet dictatorship, however, the church was the only institution permitted to organize. Almost immediately after the September 1973 coup, an array of Christian groups formed an ecumenical rights organization, the Pro-Peace Committee, to offer legal and social relief to victims of state repression.[65] Especially important was the work of the legal department, headed by José (Pepe) Zalaquett, which filed habeas corpus petitions on behalf of detained prisoners. Even though few appeals were granted—3 out of 2,342—the Comité collected a great deal of information that was then passed to transnational advocates at the International Commission and Amnesty International. The relationship between domestic and international activism was thus symbiotic. From the beginning, the Comité Pro-Paz received the majority of its funding from the World Council of Churches.[66]

Under pressure from Pinochet, who saw a challenge to his legitimacy, the Comité was forced to close at the end of 1975. Almost immediately after, Cardinal Silva Henríquez founded the Vicaría de la Solidaridad as an official act of the Catholic Church of Santiago. In an "entirely new departure" for the church, the Vicaría, again with the lion's share of its funding coming from the World Council of Churches, expanded on the work of the Comité to offer legal, social, and economic care to needy Chileans.[67] At the same time, the Vicaría served as a unifying force between competing factions of the Chilean left and promoted closer alliances with leftist groups, although obviously not without some tensions over how far to push these associations. Church activists were always divided over how radically they should oppose the Pinochet regime. Both the Comité and the Vicaría debated at length whether each should use the testimonies of victims and families to publicly denounce the junta, or if they should negotiate with the military behind closed doors. The Vicaría, like Amnesty International, refused to work on behalf of Chileans who had committed acts of violence. Thus the Vicaría adopted the same depoliticized stance of neutrality that guided the work of Amnesty International. To transcend politics, both groups argued, one had to be against violence in all situations.[68]

Where did the discourse of human rights figure into the work of the Comité and the Vicaría? José Zalaquett pointedly remembered that international activists from the OAS and Amnesty International "brought with them the language of human rights."[69] Similarly, in an interview with Pamela Lowden, Fernando Salas, the executive secretary of the Comité, recalled a fascinating anecdote that attests to the contingent nature of human rights activism in the 1970s. At the end of the 1973, Salas found a poster of the Universal Declaration of Human Rights in the office of a friend who worked for the UN. Excited about the discovery, he apparently took it to a copy shop to make duplicates to be placed at the Comité's headquarters. Comité members saw this as a "daring new departure." According to Salas, it was only then that he discovered the "potential of the Declaration."[70] That said, the turn to human rights by an ecumenical association of church activists in Chile was part and parcel of a broader Christian embrace of human rights, which began at least initially during the Vatican II reforms of the 1960s and expanded exponentially in the chaotic months after the 1973 Chilean coup.

In Argentina, activism in the language of human rights against the Argentine dictatorship grew quickly, building on the newfound global currency of human rights as an activist vocabulary following the Chilean coup.[71] The first organization to employ human rights language in any sustained fashion in Argentina in the 1970s was the Permanent Assembly for Human Rights (APDH), formed in December 1975 by a group of political and religious figures. The APDH pushed a depoliticized argument front and center, as evidenced by its explanations of its origins and its denunciations of "terrorism" regardless of political affiliations. Noting the diversity of "points of view," APDH members were united in their hatred of "the devaluing of life and the dignity of man that is made manifest in the kidnappings, attacks, harassments, and torture" by the Argentine junta.[72] The APDH crafted exhaustive lists of the detained and disappeared, which they would use to confront the Argentina junta when it claimed no knowledge of missing persons or refused to respond to such allegations.

Not all Argentines agreed with the measured approach developed by the APDH. In respectful, deferential letters to Argentine military junta members, the APDH proceeded cautiously. It avoided outright accusations against the government, always speaking of the "disappeared" in quotation marks. Emilio Mignone, who began to work for the APDH shortly after his daughter was kidnapped and disappeared, described how he "never agreed with that type of usage." Mignone would later leave to found the Center for Legal and Social Studies (CELS), which adopted more aggressive tactics in confront junta leaders.[73] CELS more actively pursued alliances with international NGOs and governments. It was joined by other enterprising Argentine groups that turned to the international sphere to protest against the dictatorship (see Lynsay Skiba's chapter in this volume). Likewise, the Mothers of the Plaza de Mayo (Madres de Plaza de Mayo) toured throughout the United States and Europe to draw attention to the flagrant disregard for rights occurring in Argentina. Although the Argentine junta subsumed these groups under the dismissive label "paladins for human rights," each group, from CELS and APDH to the Madres, had very different visions of the role of politics in human rights activism.[74]

Conclusion

When the idea of human rights came onto the political stage in Latin America in the 1970s, it was fundamentally a minimalist solution to political cataclysm. Transnational activists deployed human rights language with increasing regularity throughout the 1970s because it appealed to many as a depoliticized language in an era when the political status quo was not seen as providing actionable solutions. If some activists once dismissed human rights as mere "magic words," they gradually began to recognize its versatility as a depoliticized language. Even as activists remained profoundly political, they articulated their campaigns against authoritarianism as a critique of the amorality of politics as usual. And yet the transition to human rights as the primary moral compass that oriented social activists concerned about rights abuses in Brazil, Chile, and Argentina was riddled with tensions and contradictions. Human rights did not immediately supplant rival ideologies and moral vocabularies in Latin America, but rather it had to compete for primacy among an array of activist paradigms. In the most cynical reading of its transformative potential, the construction of human rights in the 1970s served to elevate the neoliberal world of the future as a model of global citizenship while subjugating alternative visions that emphasized social or economic rights or the right to self-determination.[75] In response, some prominent Latin American activists would reject the discourse of human rights as an "ideological weapon" used by rich countries to perpetuate imperialism and capitalist inequality.[76]

But human rights, in many senses, did win out. As the last third of the twentieth century unfolded, the lexicon of human rights gradually snowballed, expanding to encompass a range of issues that were far outside its minimalist inception.[77] In the Southern Cone, as each country struggled to confront the legacies of an authoritarian past, the language of human rights became widespread as it shifted from being the language of opposition to the language of national unification. "What unites us," reads the preamble to Chile's National Commission for Truth and Reconciliation Report, released in 1994, "is the same fundamental principle: respect for the human being by virtue of being . . . [Human] rights are those than no power . . . can trample."[78] One could rightfully celebrate this turn of events. At the same time, such depoliticized platitudes amounted to a retreat from more ambitious conceptions of social change in the late 1960s. The socialist dream of revolution, by the end of the 1970s, had morphed into the minimalist cry not to be tortured. While we should recognize the 1970s as a critical breakthrough era for global human rights politics, we must at the same time register it as coming at the expense of far more robust panoramas of social change now discarded.

Chapter 7

Shifting Sites of Argentine Advocacy and the Shape of 1970s Human Rights Debates

Lynsay Skiba

Thirty years after testifying before the U.S. House Subcommittee on International Organizations in September 1976, Argentine lawyer Lucio Garzón Maceda recalled the hearings with satisfaction and surprise: satisfaction because he viewed the two-day proceedings on human rights conditions in Argentina as the first international defeat of the military junta, contributing to its subsequent loss of U.S. military aid and turning the tide of world opinion. Surprise because he and his fellow Argentine witness and lawyer, Gustavo Roca, never imagined that they would confront the junta from the capital of its most powerful supporter.[1] Three years later, the astonishment on the part of both the Argentine military government and its opponents was perhaps no less when the Inter-American Commission on Human Rights proved to be a formidable critic of the junta. The commission—the investigative body of the Organization of American States human rights system, assumed by many to be controlled by cynical U.S. foreign policy interests—became in the 1970s a vocal defender of human rights.[2]

Centered on these two moments and their reception in Argentina, this chapter explores the broader question of the causes and consequences of a changed international landscape for activism, examining the ways in which the creation of human rights institutions in the 1970s, and activists' strategic use of them, transformed the debate about state violence. The selected case studies, drawn from the early years of Argentina's 1976–1983 military dictatorship, highlight the construction and operation of some of these institutions and illuminate how human rights entered public discourse in the country. To be sure, information about human rights in Argentina was filtered through mass media subject to censorship and government repression.[3] Nationalist messages against international human rights criticism were rampant.[4] But a debate was developing, with messages from human rights advocates also circulating and substantive human rights concerns beginning to come to light.

Scholars have noted the importance of international human rights initiatives in bringing public attention to government abuses in Argentina during this period. Political scientist Héctor Ricardo Leis, for example, explains that during the first three years of the dictatorship, the profound silence around human rights violations started to break due to media coverage of events like Patricia Derian's trips to the country as a U.S. State Department human rights official during the Carter administration and the visit of the Inter-American Commission on Human Rights analyzed here.[5] My goal is to explore this process as it unfolded. I argue that new governmental, intergovernmental, and nongovernmental bodies facilitated public awareness and discussion of human rights by opening new spaces of protest and legitimation for advocates, making the international setting increasingly challenging for governments accused of abuses. In Argentina, the military government was forced to talk about human rights as it defended itself against allegations of abuse from internationally powerful institutions.[6] Certainly the new role of the United States in human rights politics in the 1970s, first on the part of Congress and then the White House, was a major force behind some of the period's human rights venues. But other state and nonstate actors crucially shaped the changing environment for advocacy and debate.

New Openings for Argentine Human Rights Advocacy

With significant public support, a military government took power in Argentina on March 24, 1976. Its leaders pledged to combat political violence blamed on leftist "subversion," restore order, and turn around a troubled economy.[7] Portraying themselves as messianic defenders of Western civilization and Christian traditions, the junta brutally rolled back the power the urban working class had won under Peronism.[8] The unprecedented state-sponsored terrorism that this military dictatorship employed—widespread torture, mass murder, and the enforced disappearance of many thousands of people from all sectors of society—compelled the creation of the country's modern human rights movement.[9]

While the 1960s and 1970s marked a particularly tumultuous time in Argentine political history, government repression against perceived subversives and advocacy strategies to protect the rights of the persecuted were not entirely new. Before the leftist and Peronist guerrilla groups that formed during the 1966–1973 dictatorship, earlier de facto and democratic governments subjected anarchists, communists, and labor activists to imprisonment, deportation, and extrajudicial violence.[10] Advocates often operated in legal teams with connections to a targeted political group. La Liga Argentina por los Derechos del Hombre formed in 1937 as an initiative of Argentina's Communist Party to organize legal defense for political prisoners.[11] It became the country's first human rights group, counting among its ranks and advocating for people from a range of political backgrounds.[12] Efforts to protect the rights of those persecuted included the submission of writs of habeas corpus to challenge unlawful detentions.[13] Paired with this traditional legal activity, lawyers, like those affiliated with the anarchist Federación Obrera Regional Argentina in the early twentieth century, and La Liga beginning in the 1930s, published and publicized their legal work, taking their advocacy beyond the courtroom and into the realm of public opinion.[14] Prior to the 1970s advocates for political prisoners also sought support from international nongovernmental and intergovernmental bodies, as was the case in 1949 when La Liga announced that it would report the detention of a labor lawyer to the International Association of Democratic Lawyers, a nongovernmental organization (NGO) whose work included advocacy before United Nations bodies.[15] Rights activists also turned to the United Nations directly, despite its limited capacity to respond to reports of human rights abuses in its early years.[16]

In 1970s Argentina, methods of challenging government abuses changed as increasing repression choked off domestic channels of political participation and legal protection. Established sites of advocacy constricted. Amid left-wing and, especially, right-wing violence, a particularly consequential change occurred in the law itself, which had been an important domestic arena for efforts to protect the rights of political prisoners, and, for some sectors of the legal profession, a site of resistance to the 1966–1973 military dictatorship.[17] During a brief and tumultuous interim of democracy (1973–1976), and especially after it was brought to a close with the 1976 coup, attorneys were increasingly unable to exercise their profession or defend people's rights in court.[18] Identified with their "subversive" clients, hundreds of lawyers were victims of harsh state-sponsored repression, from arrest without charge to kidnapping and assassination.[19] Lawyers and legal organizations were hardly the only targets of state repression, but they played an important and internationally prominent role in the early work of Argentina's modern human rights movement.[20] Legal institutions came under fire as well during this period. After seizing power in 1976, the military government populated the Supreme Court and appeals courts with its chosen judges. Under a state of siege in which many judges accepted the suspension of basic rights, the writ of habeas corpus was converted into a "mere formality, rendering it totally ineffective," and the judicial process became "almost inoperative as a means of appeal."[21]

Under these conditions—and with institutions including political parties, the church, and unions offering limited responses to the mounting violence— human rights organizations were pushed to innovate while building on established methods.[22] Joining La Liga, multiple new groups were formed during the 1970s by family members of political prisoners and the disappeared, civil libertarians, and religious activists.[23] With hundreds of thousands of people fleeing the country, Argentines also joined human rights organizations in exile.[24] While united in their application of universal rights to challenge government abuses, Argentina's human rights groups and individual activists differed in their political orientations and approaches to the junta, with some more confrontational and others striving for evenhandedness by speaking out against left-wing as well as right-wing political violence.[25] Their tactics also varied. The military's reliance on clandestine violence made careful documentation of abuses and their scope crucial. The Asamblea Permanente por los Derechos Humanos (APDH), founded in 1975, collected thousands of reports of disappearances from family members.[26] An important innovation came in the form of new styles of protest, most notably the public vigils of the Madres de Plaza de Mayo, whose demands for the return of their disappeared children challenged the military government's purported protection of traditional Christian values of family and motherhood.[27] Legal channels, though limited, provided another path for domestic human rights advocacy under the dictatorship. Though the courts regularly denied writs of habeas corpus, activists—like members of the APDH and Centro de Estudios Legales y Sociales (CELS), a group formed in 1979 to go beyond the collective petitions and tempered approach of the APDH—continued to submit habeas corpus petitions demanding information about the detained and disappeared.[28] Advocacy around these cases did not end with unsuccessful outcomes in court but were publicized by human rights organizations through their own publications and, when possible, the press, a strategy reminiscent of earlier advocacy efforts.[29]

As in the past, Argentine activists also created ties with organizations abroad, but in the 1970s these connections proliferated as part of a new transnational advocacy network.[30] During the last dictatorship, Argentine human rights groups became engaged in a multifaceted, geographically widespread process in which the opportunities were growing for international denunciation of Argentina's military government through prominent institutions—governmental, intergovernmental, and nongovernmental. At the United Nations, by the end of the decade the Commission on Human Rights was increasingly able to investigate allegations of human rights abuses, first through a problematic confidential process introduced in 1970, and then, more publicly, through the efforts of commission working groups like those established in 1975 to address conditions in Chile and in 1980 to address enforced disappearances.[31] Individual governments also expanded opportunities for the promotion of human rights. In Europe, for example, some countries established human rights advisory committees that brought together nongovernmental organizations and government entities.[32] Argentine human rights groups inside the country and in exile made use of these openings, traveling to Europe, the United States, Mexico, and elsewhere, providing information to foreign officials and representatives from the newly prominent NGOs of the period (including Amnesty International and the Washington Office on Latin America), communicating with the media, testifying before United Nations bodies, and soliciting funds from U.S. and European foundations.[33]

The U.S. Congress

The United States became an active site for international human rights advocacy in the 1970s. By the start of the decade, the civil rights movement, Vietnam, and Watergate had raised questions about human rights, abuse of power, and the excessive simplicity of the communist/anticommunist binary that previously dominated the policy agenda. Motivated as well by revelations of CIA abuses and human rights violations in Latin America, Chile especially, some members of Congress made human rights a foreign policy priority.[34] The House Subcommittee on International Organizations and Movements (later renamed the Subcommittee on Human Rights and International Organizations) and its chairman, Minnesota representative Donald Fraser, played a central role in congressional action by proposing legislation, designing bureaucratic structures, and gathering information across national borders through hearings to inform the development of a new kind of foreign policy rooted in principles of international human rights law.[35] Fraser's subcommittee held more than 150 hearings between 1973 and 1978, providing a platform for more than five hundred witnesses to share their experiences and recommendations on a wide range of human rights issues and national cases.[36]

In addition to the hearings themselves, the policy tools that came out of them were instrumental in facilitating human rights activism. From 1973 to the end of the decade, with the active participation of NGOs including the Washington Office on Latin America, Congress passed legislation linking most-favored trading status, military and economic aid, and loan approvals to countries' human rights records.[37] These laws reflected Congress members' mounting frustration with the executive branch's failure to respond to their human rights concerns. Military aid in particular became a focal point for congressional action.[38] In 1974, disturbed by the continued provision of U.S. aid to governments abusing human rights, Fraser introduced an amendment, Section 502B of the Foreign Assistance Act, that called on the president, "except in extraordinary circumstances," to reduce or terminate security assistance to governments engaging in "a consistent pattern of gross violations of internationally recognized human rights."[39] As a "sense of Congress" statement, Section 502B was not at first legally binding, but it has been called one of the most important legislative measures that came out of the first round of Fraser hearings, serving as "the yardstick for the Fraser subcommittee's consideration of human rights policy."[40] Transformed in 1978 into a truly mandatory requirement, Section 502B would also help link foreign human rights advocates, like Argentines Lucio Garzón Maceda and Gustavo Roca, to the U.S. government.[41]

The willingness of members of Congress to act on foreigners' human rights insights was not just facilitated by new legislative and bureaucratic mechanisms, however. The incredible state-sponsored violence in Latin American countries, recounted by victims in meetings and testimony, moved some senators and representatives to join the activists calling for measures against abusive regimes.[42] Just a week before Garzón Maceda and Roca's congressional appearance, the bloodshed afflicting South America struck

Washington. Chilean diplomat Orlando Letelier and his U.S. colleague Ronni Moffitt, who were engaged in congressional lobbying efforts aimed at ending U.S. support for the repressive Chilean military regime, were killed in a car bombing on Embassy Row.[43] The assassinations were not confirmed to have been committed by Chilean government agents (although this was suspected) until a year after the event.[44] But the killings, so close in space and time to the hearings on Argentina, must have underscored for members of the Fraser subcommittee the incredible risks exiled human rights activists faced as well as the special role they themselves could play in confronting the carnage.[45]

The September 1976 Hearings Before the Fraser Subcommittee

Before fleeing their country in 1976, Garzón Maceda and Roca were part of a sector of the Argentine legal profession that challenged abuses during the 1966–1973 military government and the constitutional government (1973– 1976) that followed.[46] During a period of activism by labor lawyers, Garzón Maceda was an attorney for labor unions.[47] Notably, he was a legal advisor to the unions during the major 1969 riot in Córdoba, the Cordobazo, a watershed moment in popular resistance to the military regime.[48] Gustavo Roca was prominent in a national network of politically engaged defense attorneys and active in leftist politics.[49] The two shared a law office in Córdoba, where their main clients were labor unions. They also represented political prisoners, including members of guerrilla groups like the Montoneros, work that drew the ire of the military.[50]

After their law offices were repeatedly set on fire and houses raided, the men fled Córdoba. In August 1976 they made their way to Europe, Garzón Maceda to Paris and Roca to Madrid, where they connected with fellow Argentines working to denounce the junta. Garzón Maceda credits one such compatriot with suggesting the unexpected trip to Washington, urging him to meet in London with Amnesty International staff and individuals with good contacts in the United States to prepare to speak with members of the Congress. According to Garzón Maceda, Amnesty staff emphasized the potential impact of direct congressional testimony by a recently arrived Argentine about junta abuses, especially in the run-up to a presidential election that Jimmy Carter was likely to win.[51]

Roca and Garzón Maceda were associated with the Comisión Argentina por los Derechos Humanos (CADHU), an organization that played an early and active role in the international campaigns of the Argentine human rights movement.[52] At the Fraser subcommittee hearings, Roca, a founding member of the group, spoke as a CADHU representative, and together Roca and Garzón Maceda submitted a CADHU report to supplement their oral presentations.[53] Forced out of Argentina by violent political persecution, CADHU members worked in exile.[54] The organization opened offices in Madrid, Paris, Geneva, Rome, Mexico City, and Washington, D.C.[55] CADHU would later be among the NGOs credited with helping secure the cutoff of U.S. military aid to Argentina in 1977 and 1978.[56] In addition to U.S. lobbying activities, CADHU members provided testimony before the United Nations and helped to organize a colloquium on enforced disappearance in Paris in 1981.[57] As Iain Guest has noted, "CADHU was not only the best, it was the only source of information on Argentina during the first terrible year of killing. It was hardly surprising that people turned to it for information and ignored the 'political motivation' of its members."[58] Indeed, its ranks included advocates with established histories of challenging Argentina's military governments, including attorneys from the legal teams of leftist organizations,[59] and some sympathetic to guerrilla groups.

In late September 1976, Gustavo Roca and Lucio Garzón Maceda appeared before the Fraser subcommittee in a two-day session on human rights conditions in Argentina. Through an interpreter, Roca spoke on September 28 and Garzón Maceda the following day. Testifying with them were U.S. advocates with firsthand experience in Argentina. While Garzón Maceda has noted the improvisational aspects of his and Roca's appearance before the Fraser subcommittee, he has also shed light on the strategy that comes across in the testimony transcripts.[60]

Together, the presentations by Roca and Garzón Maceda took three steps in calling on Congress to pressure the Argentine state. The first was to challenge the depiction of junta methods as justifiable government responses to leftist violence. Roca and Garzón Maceda insisted instead that these were human rights violations, that is, violations of universally applicable laws that crossed national, and political, lines. Notably, both described the violation of economic and social rights to unionize and make a living. They focused, however, on precisely those violations of civil and political rights at the heart of the subcommittee's work: politically motivated and targeted kidnapping, murder, and torture.[61] Roca emphasized the attacks against attorneys and Garzón Maceda those aimed at workers and union organizers.[62] Both suggested that the junta's assaults on these groups reflected an effort to undermine not only the guerrilla forces but the rule of law and democracy itself.[63] In a revealing exchange, Roca addressed the argument that such state action might be a legitimate reaction to leftist terrorism. "It does not matter where the violence comes from. . . . If there is a civil war going on in Argentina, it should be regulated by the accords of the Geneva Convention which guarantee the human rights of soldiers and prisoners, norms which are of course not followed by the Argentine Military Junta."[64]

A second step taken by Roca and Garzón Maceda was to urge congressional action. Both witnesses described violence directed against them personally along with broader patterns of abuse. Credibility, established through professionalism and a law-based methodology, was fundamental to these efforts. Roca introduced the work of CADHU: "We have been able to put out a first report, which is serious, responsible, legally formulated, and which has sufficient proof to show that in the Argentine Republic at this moment grave, massive, systemic, and persistent violations of human, civil, political, economic, and social rights are taking place."[65] At stake in Fraser's subcommittee hearings was the continuation of military aid, with Section 502B of the Foreign Assistance Act in effect. Roca and Garzón Maceda testified that U.S. action would have a positive impact and described the sorts of government abuses that would classify as "gross violations of internationally recognized human rights."[66] This strategy of calling for a military aid cutoff, as noted earlier, was one that CADHU would continue to pursue with ultimate success.[67]

The efficacy of these two steps—presenting government violence in Argentina as a violation of human rights, and calling for Congress to cut aid to the junta—might have depended on a third. Their responses to Fraser's questioning suggest that Roca and Garzón Maceda were prepared for suggestions that any political affiliations undermined their credibility as human rights advocates, and the lawyers emphasized their apolitical aims. Given the Argentine junta's habit of labeling human rights advocates "subversives," as well as the lingering Cold War dynamics in the United States, Roca and Garzón Maceda's approach was astute.[68] The men flagged their status as attorneys as proof of their neutrality: "Our only crime, Mr. Chairman," Roca affirmed, "has been for many years to carry out the task of defending human rights in Argentina and to have exercised our right as lawyers in the courts of our country to defend citizens persecuted for political, social, or ideological reasons."[69] The debates sparked by the hearings would reintroduce politics into this moment of human rights advocacy.

Reactions to the Fraser subcommittee hearings in Argentina, as reflected in major newspapers and letters to the U.S. State Department, were swift and, for the most part, harsh. As Roca noted, the Argentine press practiced self-censorship in line with government directives.[70] But the strong criticism visited on Roca and Garzón Maceda cannot be blamed entirely on government influence. A more convincing explanation rests in the polarized political culture of 1970s Argentina, a setting in which the threat of revolutionary violence trumped human rights concerns for people across the ideological spectrum. Far from being universally applicable norms, human rights were presented as weapons wielded by and for subversive forces.

Argentina's military government was quick to denounce Roca and Garzón Maceda. A memorandum from Argentina's foreign ministry dated October 4, 1976, made its way to the State Department with a clear message of rebuke. After noting the long history of good relations between the two countries, it attacked the credibility of Garzón Maceda and Roca, whom it accused of "wide-ranging ideological activity in subversion and labor union activism." The memo concluded, "Independent of whatever judgment could be made about the individuals called to testify, it goes without saying that they lack any of the minimum objectiveness and impartiality necessary for their opinions to be taken into account in a serious investigation." In any case, the memo went on, Argentina was enduring an exceptional period in which the government was going to take any measures necessary to restore internal security.[71] Within weeks of the hearings, the Argentine government charged the men with "promoting political or economic sanctions against the state" and ordered them to stand trial.[72] Roca and Garzón Maceda were indicted in absentia in December 1976.[73]

Jacobo Timerman, who within months would become the junta's best-known political prisoner, also criticized Fraser and his subcommittee.[74] Though his newspaper turned more critical of the military government shortly before he was kidnapped in 1977, the publisher of La Opinión had been like many Argentines in his belief that the March 24, 1976, military coup was a necessary step toward restoring order in the midst of political chaos.[75] Timerman wrote to Donald Fraser to express deep misgivings about the direction the subcommittee hearings had taken. In the October 1, 1976, edition of La Opinión, Timerman published his letter, in which he asked to be invited to testify so he could provide a more objective perspective.[76] Timerman's accusation of partiality in the subcommittee's selection of witnesses was part of his newspaper's larger criticism of U.S. human rights policy, which centered on the potential cutoff of U.S. aid, the threat such a cutoff would pose to national sovereignty, and the meaning of human rights. But the messages circulating in the Argentine press were not necessarily blanket rejections of the concept of human rights. Alternative definitions of the term were put forward by commentators who evinced some acceptance of universal rights principles despite criticisms. An article published in *La Opinión* on November 12, 1976, for example, suggests the multiple channels through which human rights were given meaning during this period. Amnesty International sent a mission to Argentina in November 1976, whose members included U.S. Congressman and Jesuit priest Robert Drinan.[77] Jacobo Timerman met with Drinan and offered his own interpretation of human rights in light of the political violence gripping the country. Urging Drinan to propose that Amnesty modify its conception of human rights, Timerman argued that "given the idea sustained by guerrilla activity . . . that through political crime, no longer individual but collective, the course of the nation may be altered, the concept of human rights not as individual but as collective rights should be created."[78] Even the conservative paper *La Nación*, which criticized the Fraser subcommittee, suggested that human rights were of legitimate international concern as long as they were interpreted by international congresses of jurists "above suspicion of political inclination."[79]

Alongside the harsh reactions to Fraser's subcommittee hearings were calls for help from survivors, the families of victims, and advocates speaking on their behalf. One group of family members of prisoners sent the subcommittee a message of their own. In their letter, they described incommunicado detentions and worsening prison conditions. Invoking both Christian values and basic human rights standards, the letter's authors asked the U.S. Congress to put pressure on the Argentine government to stop these abuses.[80] Their message is a reminder that despite the fierce resistance of the junta and members of Argentine society, the Fraser subcommittee hearings—and U.S. human rights policy more generally—was recognized, appreciated, and seized upon by other Argentines compelled to look abroad to make change at home.

The Organization of American States

The Organization of American States (OAS) became in the 1970s another important forum in which Latin Americans would advocate for human rights. OAS member states expressed support for human rights when they signed the 1948 American Declaration of the Rights and Duties of Man, but the inter-American human rights system remained largely unchanged and lacked an enforcement mechanism until the Inter-American Commission on Human Rights was established in 1959.[81] Made up of seven experts elected by the OAS General Assembly, the commission was charged, in a vaguely worded statute, with advancing the observance of human rights in the region.[82] The commission's scope of work expanded significantly in the decade following its creation, with commissioners pushing the boundaries of their formal mandate by focusing on particular countries, accepting individual petitions claiming human rights violations, and publishing reports on OAS member states' human rights conditions.[83] The commission's 1965 investigation inside the Dominican Republic set the precedent for another consequential piece of the body's work: its visits to OAS member countries.[84]

After 1965, the legal structure governing the inter-American human rights system began to reflect more accurately the activities of the commission while strengthening its status.[85] The commission's ability to examine individual petitions alleging abuses and address human rights concerns in specific countries was affirmed and subsequently incorporated into the commission's statute.[86] With the 1967 Buenos Aires Protocol, which entered into force in 1970, the commission was made a principal organ of the OAS, and its authority to process individual complaints of human rights abuses and initiate investigations into alleged violations was given legal backing through the OAS Charter.[87] At the dawning of the 1970s, in short, the commission had tools at its disposal—through practice and law—should alleged human rights abuses come to its attention.

In the second half of the 1970s, facing a deluge of abuse allegations, the commission became a major player in hemispheric human rights politics.[88] The election of Jimmy Carter to the U.S. presidency was central to this conversion. Carter was a vociferous supporter not just of human rights generally but of the inter-American human rights regime specifically, signing the legally binding American Convention on Human Rights and urging other OAS member governments to become parties so it would enter into force, which it did in 1978.[89] Over the course of the 1970s, the commission published reports on the human rights conditions in countries including Chile, Uruguay, Paraguay, and Argentina, sometimes on the basis of onsite visits—as in Chile in 1974—or, when governments refused to consent to visits, using the information it gathered from afar.[90] Based on the precedent set during its 1977 visit to

Panama, the commission gained broad latitude to speak with whomever it chose, wherever it deemed necessary, including inside detention and interrogation centers.[91] In the estimation of Iain Guest, these changes "made the IACHR altogether more effective at fact-finding than the U.N., and thus more menacing to governments like the Argentinean Junta."[92]

The September 1979 Visit of the Inter-American Commission on Human Rights

Three years after the Fraser subcommittee hearings, international scrutiny once again fell on Argentina when the Inter-American Commission on Human Rights visited the country between September 6 and September 20, 1979. In the interim, pressure on the junta had mounted as nongovernmental organizations including Amnesty International published critical reports and, in 1978, launched campaigns to coincide with the country's hosting of the soccer World Cup.[93] Now an organization of fellow governments was turning the spotlight on conditions in Argentina. The commission's investigation and its 1980 report, like the congressional testimony of Roca and Garzón Maceda, sparked intense discussion about the meaning of human rights to the Argentine nation.

In December 1976, just a few months after the Fraser subcommittee hearings, the U.S. State Department began to formulate its plan to ask the junta to allow a commission visit.[94] Internal divisions within the junta, rising domestic dissent, and international condemnation were influential factors leading the Argentine government to permit the visit, but U.S. government pressure was instrumental.[95] At stake were a U.S. Export-Import Bank credit for the construction of a hydroelectric dam in Argentina and the issue of frozen military funds.[96] With both the U.S. and Argentine governments eager to improve bilateral relations, and Argentina seeking a fix for its international isolation, junta leader Jorge Rafael Videla and Vice President Walter Mondale struck a deal in September 1978.[97] The agreement promised Argentina the bank credits and allowed pending military sales to go through in exchange for the junta's invitation to the commission to conduct an unconditioned onsite visit.[98] Strengthening the hand of the U.S. government and OAS in these negotiations was the high profile that Argentina's human rights abuses had garnered due to the work of human rights groups and U.S. embassy officials, chief among them political officer F. A. "Tex" Harris.[99]

Nongovernmental advocates sought to make the commission a viable force for change in Argentina. In the United States, the Washington Office on Latin America had pushed the OAS to condemn the junta from the first year of the regime, writing letters, delivering boxes of affidavits from Argentine religious orders and human rights groups that documented abuses, and lobbying at OAS meetings.[100] Emilio Mignone, the director of CELS who had worked for the OAS in the 1960s and whose own daughter was among the disappeared, traveled to Washington to provide the commission with documentation of disappearances collected by the APDH.[101] Activists also offered relevant insights into Argentine politics. In an English-language bulletin that reached the U.S. State Department, for example, activists warned of the junta's likely foot-dragging on the visit after the invitation was issued.[102] Inside Argentina, activists distributed literature, published newspaper announcements, and held meetings to shape public opinion and maximize the number of testimonies that the commission received.[103] Groups that collaborated with the commission were subject not only to police surveillance but to judicially sanctioned raids of their offices the month before the visit.[104]

The commission finally arrived in September 1979 and began its work, interviewing government officials, religious leaders, union delegations, political organizations, victims of human rights violations, and others, and visiting detention centers.[105] Argentine human rights groups and individual activists helped facilitate the commission's activities. CELS leaders set up interviews for commission members and offered guidance throughout the visit.[106] Representatives from organizations including APDH, the Liga Argentina por los Derechos del Hombre, and the Madres de Plaza de Mayo met with the commission and provided evidence of rights violations, especially cases of enforced disappearance.[107] Activists also worked to connect family members of the detained and disappeared with the commission.[108] The quantity of information that ultimately reached the commission—and the extent of human rights violations it reflected—was staggering, with 5,580 complaints received.[109]

On April 11, 1980, the commission released its findings in the *Report on the Situation of Human Rights in Argentina*.[110] It concluded that "numerous serious violations of fundamental rights, as recognized in the American Declaration of the Rights and Duties of Man, were committed in the Republic of Argentina during the period covered by this report."[111] The abuses documented included enforced disappearance and violations of due process, labor, political, and religious rights. While the junta barred distribution of the full report inside Argentina and, through diplomatic machinations, managed to avoid an OAS resolution criticizing Argentina specifically, it could not hold back the report's revelations or its international impact. The report's findings were presented before the United Nations and national government bodies and publicized in media outlets around the world.[112] Inside the country, CELS managed to distribute copies of the report that Emilio Mignone smuggled in from the United States.[113] The junta responded with its own report. In *Observaciones y comentarios críticos del gobierno argentino*, also released in April 1980, the military government accused the commission of endeavoring to tarnish its reputation rather than promoting human rights.[114] The junta asserted that the commission had failed to take into account Argentina's war against subversion, a war that might have required the temporary restriction of human rights but which had been necessary for the survival of the nation.[115]

Though it rejected the commission's findings, the military government was clearly affected by the commission's investigation. The most tangible effect was on the junta's behavior. On the one hand, disappearances spiked just before the commission's visit, and the junta took steps to undermine the investigation by hiding detainees and demolishing clandestine detention centers.[116] On the other hand, some prisoners—including Jacobo Timerman—were released, and the number of reported disappearances declined following the commission's investigation.[117] One commentator describes the commission's visit to Argentina as "its most successful in terms of results."[118]

Another measure of the commission's visit is the way it, like the Fraser subcommittee hearings, influenced the debate in Argentina about human rights. Previously quiet members of Argentine society spoke publicly on issues only discussed until then by human rights groups. The lines of family members and victims stretching along city blocks to meet with commission representatives made mounting allegations of abuse hard to ignore.[119] But Argentina's military government was working to shape the discussion many months before the commission's arrival. The junta hired a U.S. public relations firm to manage its international reputation, and it produced propaganda for dissemination in the Argentine and international press.[120] The military upped its public relations efforts with the 1978 soccer World Cup, seizing on the widely popular event as an opportunity to improve its image in the face of human rights complaints.[121] Criticism of the government's human rights record was denounced as part of an anti-Argentina campaign, and Argentines were asked to defend the country against such attacks. Challenging the notion of human rights directly with a play on the Spanish term "derechos humanos," the dictatorship took up the slogan, "Los argentinos somos derechos y humanos" (We Argentines are human, and we are right).[122]

A major theme of public discussion sparked by the commission's visit, and one consistent with the coverage of Roca and Garzón Maceda's testimony before the Fraser subcommittee, was the relationship between national security and human rights. This was an issue raised in the press from the time the junta's invitation was issued. As reported in *La Opinión* in June 1978, Argentina's foreign minister complained at an OAS meeting that legitimate efforts taken by South American states to defend themselves from terrorism were being confused with human rights violations.[123] This argument was sometimes itself expressed in human rights terms, with the assertion that the true human rights violations were those committed by "terrorists."[124] The commission addressed this claim directly, explaining that its mandate did not allow it to consider acts of violence allegedly committed by nonstate actors.[125] By the time the commission visited Argentina, the military government had already declared victory against "subversion," but a counteroffensive launched by the Montoneros in 1979 provided the junta with evidence of an ongoing threat, and junta supporters frequently answered allegations of human rights abuses by pointing to the junta's need to fight terrorism.[126] The Argentine government and its supporters depicted human rights activists, and people who provided the commission with information in particular, as part of the subversive threat.[127] In keeping with this publicly expressed line of reasoning, a police intelligence memo described the collaboration of local human rights groups with the commission as a Marxist plot to seize power through the destabilization of the country.[128] The day after the commission left Argentina, *La Nación* published a statement signed by a long list of business and professional groups expressing their belief that "we were at war. . . . We want the world to know that the decision to enter the fight provoked and imposed by subversion was not the decision of the armed forces. . . . It was the decision of Argentines. . . . And just like any other war, ours had its price."[129] Human rights advocates responded. Demanding government accountability, the religious human rights group Movimiento Ecuménico por los Derechos Humanos (MEDH) explained in a newsletter, "When . . . traveling a path so painful . . . , the relatives (of the disappeared) do not deserve answers that range from 'the disappeared have disappeared by their own doing' . . . to 'this is an undeclared war to prevent the dissolution of Argentine society in which there are no answers to the questions being asked of us.' "[30]

Closely related to the issue of national security in debates about the commission's investigation was the concept of Argentina's sovereignty.[131] So prevalent was this theme that officials at the U.S. embassy in Buenos Aires concluded that it was sovereignty, and not the substance of human rights, that dominated public debate in the weeks before the commission's arrival.[132] Around the same time, in August 1979, a conservative political party, the Unión Conservadora de la Provincia de Buenos Aires, voiced its concerns on the topic in a statement they sent to the country's foreign minister. The group declared its opposition to the commission's visit, insisting that "everything relating to the internal life of the nation . . . is its concern alone and one of the attributes of sovereignty."[133] Human rights advocates addressed this argument as well. After the publication of the commission's report, the APDH argued that in fact there had been no violation of sovereignty since, as it noted accurately, the Argentine government had invited the commission to visit the country.[134]

Reflecting a long history of resistance to U.S. meddling in the region, sovereignty-based criticisms of the commission's visit underscored the United States' role in making it happen. Commentators across the political spectrum criticized U.S. interference in Argentine internal affairs. A pro-government publication dismissed the commission as a mere appendage of President Carter's policies.[135] Some activists on the left denounced the commission's visit as a form of imperialism.[136] These criticisms of the commission, however, did not necessarily result in the outright rejection of the body's involvement in Argentina. Worries of creeping U.S. interventionism could coexist with the hope that the commission's investigation might bring positive change. An August 1979 flyer from the Trotskyite group Política Obrera observed that "everyone knows that the OAS is an agency of Yanqui imperialism . . . , one of the principle supports of the dictatorship." Yet it went on to express its support for the commission's investigation, citing the need for a unified front against the dictatorship and embracing the position articulated by family members of the disappeared and detained: "The OAS visit, despite its pro-dictatorial purpose, will attract national and international attention to the problem of dictatorial repression and in this sense can be utilized as an opportunity to make great progress in the fight for democratic freedoms."[137]

Conclusion

To what degree did these two moments of human rights advocacy—and the new forms of human rights activism they represented—influence the broader history of Argentina's military regime, and what can they tell us about the operation of 1970s human rights politics? I suggest that these episodes and their aftermaths contributed to a larger, if nascent, discussion about human rights. When powerful governmental and intergovernmental bodies entered the fray on the side of human rights, informed by nongovernmental activists, the setting for debate was transformed. The visibility and influence of the United States Congress and Organization of American States, the two bodies considered here, raised the stakes for both advocates and the junta. Activists refined their demands, amplified their voices, and expanded their audiences through their use of these new venues, making the evidence they provided of human rights violations harder to ignore, even in Argentine media subject to junta controls. Newspapers printed at least some of the human rights groups' paid advertisements, covered their press conferences, and followed closely, if critically, the work of foreign and international bodies including the Fraser subcommittee and the Inter-American Commission on Human Rights. Human rights groups also distributed their own publications and provided testimony. Activists and family members communicated with U.S. government officials and commission members. Argentina's government found that its capacity to dismiss human rights allegations was diminished in this new environment by the possibility of U.S. aid cutoffs, the withholding of loans, and increased international isolation.

In the end, the demise of the military dictatorship in 1983 was due most directly to the junta's disastrous 1982 war with Britain over the Falkland/ Malvinas Islands. In that nationalist bid to bolster public support, the government proved itself inept at fighting, a fatal flaw in a military regime.[138] But the junta had suffered serious blows to its legitimacy before then. International human rights criticism in the early years of the dictatorship prompted the government to defend itself in the language of national sovereignty and security and drew it and its supporters into debate, and in the ensuing debate denials and justifications unavoidably brought attention to—and began to raise questions about—precisely those actions the government sought to deny and justify.

Chapter 8

Oasis in the Desert?
America's Human Rights Rediscovery

Daniel Sargent

An oasis in the Sonora desert begins with a fracture in the earth's crust. If the groundwater is high enough, liquid under pressure will seep through the cracks. With time, these trickles may support vegetation, even animal life. For travelers, the oasis offers a respite from the heat of the California interior. For historians, its provenance may spur reflection. Like oases, human rights breakthroughs are rare. In the expanses of world history, the idea of human rights has had limited relevance for most people. Yet ruptures do occur, as in the 1970s, and the oasis evokes the dynamics that create them. The groundwater stands for the elements that produce human rights, which I take to be the idea of inalienable natural rights and the sentimental humanitarianism that can nourish and universalize rights concepts. The desert represents forces arrayed against them.

For the historian Paul Gordon Lauren, by contrast, human rights are a river that courses through history, a river that has grown "larger and mightier" as new tributaries have flooded it.[1] This is appealing but too hopeful. Human rights flow, but they also ebb. The guillotine spilled streams of blood in the years that followed the *Déclaration des droits de l'homme*. The British Empire abolished the slave trade, but its imperial mission also culminated with heads on spikes. In recent years, human rights have been fickle. They proved a wedge against totalitarianism in Eastern Europe, but they brought no relief to victims of man-made apocalypses in Cambodia or Rwanda. To explain human rights is to grapple with omissions. In some places and at some times, they have borne consequences. At others, they have not. The oasis, which acknowledges both the specificity in place and time of particular human rights eruptions and their connectedness to deeper wells of action and thought, may be more apt a metaphor than the river flowing forward.

The question of genealogies is contentious. Some historians, such as Lauren, favor theories of origins that are deep and cosmopolitan. They reach back in time and take human rights for the common inheritance of humankind. Others argue for the Western origins of human rights but nonetheless trace the story back centuries, perhaps to the Renaissance or the Enlightenment.[2] Another approach rejects theories of deep origins altogether. Stefan-Ludwig Hoffmann calls long-term genealogies a "chimera" and argues that human rights became historically salient only in the twentieth century.[3] Nobody states this revisionist hypothesis better than Samuel Moyn, who locates the emergence of a recognizable human rights doctrine in the 1970s.[4]

There is a pattern to the interpretive wrangling, and it has to do with definitions. Those who argue for novelty define their terms more precisely than do those who emphasize the deep origins. For Moyn it is disentanglement from the nation-state that distinguishes late twentieth-century instantiations of human rights from earlier concepts. "The move from the politics of the state to the morality of the globe," he writes, "defines contemporary aspirations."[5] Those who trace deep origins define their subject with less precision. For Micheline Ishay, human rights are simply the litany of "rights held by individuals because they are part of the human species."[6] In both cases, the definitional precision (or lack thereof) serves an interpretative strategy. The desert oasis suggests a different way of looking at the problem. The groundwater represents continuity, a source of underlying connection. But the oasis metaphor also emphasizes the particularity of human rights moments, whether in the 1780s or in the 1970s. Crucially, it draws our attention to the geological circumstances—the tectonic pressures, the cracks in the earth, the historical topography—that permit human rights to flourish at certain times.

What comprises the groundwater? I see it as a compound of two elements. One, humanitarianism, is ethical and moral; the other, the idea of natural rights, is political and philosophical. Humanitarianism begins with empathy: the capacity to view others as fully human, equally capable of experiencing pain and no less entitled to life and its opportunities than oneself. Empathetic identification is not new; ancient religious and philosophical texts expound its virtues. Still, the emergence of a modern culture of sympathy, as Thomas Laqueur argues, reflects the effects of mass literacy.[7] Another historian, Lynn Hunt, calls empathy the basis on which political rights have been constructed.[8] She thus links humanitarianism with a doctrine of natural rights that also has a long genealogy. As far back as the thirteenth century, European charters of rights acknowledged that men retained rights against kings. The seventeenth century began the process of universalizing such rights. Hobbes made the right to self-defense the basis of legitimate political authority, while Grotius concurred that all people shared certain natural rights.[9] By that century's end, Locke had widened the scope of natural rights beyond self-defense and proclaimed the violation of them to be legitimate grounds for revolution.[10] Within a hundred years, Thomas Jefferson had inaugurated the era of rights-based politics. The idea that men are created equal and are endowed with certain inalienable rights remains the foundation of human rights today. For rights claims to become human rights applying to all peoples without distinction as to gender or pigment, however, requires a leap of moral imagination that human beings have often struggled to achieve.

As Jefferson's own shortcomings attest, the forces ranged against human rights have been strong. Among them is racism, which denies that all men are equals and thereby denies that they are entitled to equal rights. As late as 1857, the U.S. Supreme Court upheld this logic.[11] Racial distinction was the basis of colonial violence and was integral to Nazism, which, as Aimé Césaire wrote, was colonialism inflicted upon Europeans.[12] At the same time, the realities of political power have inhibited the transformative possibilities of rights. Until the modern era, traditional elites were usually able to rebuff whatever rights claims subjects might have made of them. Only with the dawn of the democratic state did rights-based politics become viable. Even then, democratic majorities inherited from their predecessors the capacity to trample upon minorities. Realities of power and perceptions of difference are not the only variables that inhibit human rights. Another crucial factor is distance. A European "man of humanity," Adam Smith proposed, would be more disturbed by the imminent loss of his own little finger than by an earthquake that swallowed millions of Chinese.[13] What rationalizes his callousness is distance. Geography, cultural as well as physical, has consequences for humanitarian identification, even though it is a dynamic variable and not an unchanging fact of nature. China may be closer to Edinburgh today than it was in Smith's times. Still, space ranks high among the factors that inhibit the scope of natural rights claims and of humanitarian empathy. For oases to blossom requires a collision of circumstances that permits the groundwater to break these restraints.

Human Rights in the Postwar Order

Hailed by Eleanor Roosevelt as the "international Magna Carta of all men everywhere," the 1948 Universal Declaration of Human Rights remains a point of departure for histories of postwar human rights.[14] The Universal Declaration inspired hope, and African Americans, among other oppressed peoples, invoked it to press their claims for emancipation and justice.[15] As far as international relations were concerned, however, the effects of the Universal Declaration were slight. Although virtually all nations signed it, the opportunities for realizing the Universal Declaration's aspirations were truncated by the realities of postwar international relations.

What emerged after the Second World War was not the integrated, liberal world order that American planners hoped to build but a world divided, not only between East and West but also between north and south. The structural realities of international politics were not propitious for the advancement of human rights. International law claimed minimal authority over the domestic conduct of nations, and the sovereignty principle was entrenched such that the pursuit of universal human rights would have been difficult even under political circumstances more favorable than were those of the early Cold War. As it was, the imperatives of superpower confrontation and the ascendancy of postcolonial nationalism both inhibited the willingness of American officials to emphasize human rights in foreign policy.

In a decolonizing world, U.S. foreign policy deferred to sovereign prerogatives. Although Cold War concerns led the United States to intervene against established governments in a few cases, American officials worked, for the most part, to rally a Cold War alliance of sovereign nation-states. The major military interventions of the era, in Korea and Vietnam, aimed to stabilize existing regimes, not to redeem them. For all its wariness over decolonization where Communists stood poised to inherit power, the United States was not about to offend postcolonial governments over the matter of human rights. At the same time, the United States demurred from making an issue out of rights violations in the Communist sphere. Some congressional Republicans toyed with the "liberation" of Eastern Europe in the early 1950s, but the Eisenhower administration settled for a pragmatic containment that acknowledged the world's division and recognized the sovereignty of Communist governments. The risks of military confrontation, American officials concluded, outweighed whatever interests the United States might have had in injecting the language of human rights into a precarious East-West standoff. The reticence of U.S. officials to promote international human rights during the 1950s and 1960s reflected the realities of postcolonial nationalism and Cold War geopolitics. But this was not all that inhibited the articulation of human rights in the foreign policy arena. During the 1950s and 1960s, the United States grappled with serious human rights dilemmas of its own. Running for office in 1960, John F. Kennedy declared the world "half slave and half free," but the enduring legacies of slavery meant that American efforts to export freedom to the world risked indictment on charges of hypocrisy.[16] More broadly, the West's legacies of racism and colonialism limited the U.S. government's ability to speak up for human rights in the world.

The 1970s transformed the profile of human rights in American diplomacy. Before the decade's end, President Carter would proclaim human rights to be "the soul of our foreign policy."[17] This pronouncement followed developments outside the executive branch. Beginning in 1974, Congress passed laws that circumscribed the delivery of U.S. aid to violators of human rights and required the State Department to issue reports on human rights conditions within foreign countries receiving American aid. Law schools began to teach human rights, while the American Bar Association, long skeptical of binding transnational law, endorsed the Genocide Convention.[18] These were developments that public officials could not ignore. Even Secretary of State Henry Kissinger, a notorious skeptic, acknowledged in 1976 that human rights had become "one of the most compelling issues of our time."[19]

Why did human rights reappear in American diplomacy and public debate a quarter-century after the Universal Declaration of 1948? Why did a marginal issue disrupt long-standing alliances with authoritarian regimes? Why did human rights reinvigorate an ideological style in American foreign policy? To understand the seventies' human rights moment, it may help to reflect upon the interplay of large-scale historical factors. These, I would argue, should include the acceleration of globalization, which helped human rights to surmount the barriers of sovereignty; the waning of Cold War politics in an era of détente, which created political space for human rights to flourish; and the ideological revival of individualist liberalism, which followed upon the completion of decolonization abroad and desegregation at home. Together, these developments cracked open space for a distinctive idiom of human rights to manifest itself in American diplomacy and, as this chapter argues, exerted durable influence on its contents.

Globalization and Transnational Humanitarianism

The connections between globalization and humanitarianism are not recent; we can trace them back to at least the nineteenth century. The Ottoman Empire's suppression of Greek nationalists in the 1820s and Bulgarians in the 1870s outraged Western audiences. The international media, as political scientist Gary Bass has shown, exposed atrocities like these to Western newspaper readers and repeatedly forced the hand of British diplomacy.[20] In the second half of the twentieth century, the opportunities for globalization to affect foreign policy only expanded.

In the decades after 1945, technological innovation enhanced the opportunities for the media to shape humanitarian sentiments. Television helped constitute what Marshall McLuhan dubbed the "global village."[21] By 1969, there were four televisions for every ten people in the United States; in Western Europe, there were nearly two.[22] While Western families acquired screens of their own, innovations in broadcasting technologies such as geostationary satellites made it possible for them to receive video from far-flung corners of the globe.[23] The relationship between cause and effect, however, was often convoluted. The Vietnam War became a landmark in the history of wartime broadcasting, but the appearance of war journalism on private television screens did not necessarily lead to antiwar politics or humanitarian activism. The media censored itself, as historian Daniel Hallin argues, while some Americans even approved of the violence that they encountered on screen. Vietnam was a complex case, especially for U.S. audiences.[24]

The Nigerian Civil War, by contrast, provides a clearer example of television's capacity to stir humanitarian reaction. In this conflict, which began in 1967, both the Nigerian government and the separatist Republic of Biafra used the international media and even Western advertising agencies to make their cases to the world.[25] Television and photojournalism energized distant humanitarian engagement. Some observers, like the French medic Bernard Kouchner, traveled to Nigeria to provide humanitarian relief.[26] Others stayed home and organized grassroots organizations to lobby for Biafra. In the United States, the conflict drew considerable attention. Trawling for votes, Richard Nixon called in 1968 for an active American response. President

Lyndon Johnson growled at his staff to send some aid to Biafra and "get those nigger babies off my TV set."[27] Uncouth as Johnson's language was, the president recognized the media's capacity to make distant suffering a charged political issue.

To invoke globalization as a partial explanation for the human rights breakthrough should not be to embrace technological determinism. Broadcasting can challenge sovereign control over information, as Radio Free Europe and Radio Liberty did in Eastern Europe during the Cold War. But states and demagogues alike can also use the media to mold mass politics. In Rwanda in 1994, for example, the genocidal Hutu elite used Radio Mille Collines to whip up a nationalist frenzy that contributed to the murder of eight hundred thousand Tutsis. Nor should it be assumed that technology flattens sovereignty. For most of the modern era, in fact, technological innovation has favored the consolidation of territorial sovereignty; only in recent years have the paths of technological innovation and political centralization seemed to diverge.[28] Technology rarely commands outcomes; at most, it changes the options that are available to human agents.[29]

The proponents of human rights in the 1970s embraced the structural opportunities that material changes presented. Here the role of nongovernmental organizations (NGOs) comes into particular focus. While technologies from the jetliner to the Xerox machine empowered their work, the era's human rights activists were the real globalizers. Through conscientious activism and the force of unarmed opinion they aimed to reveal abuses that sovereignty would otherwise have veiled. They constructed international networks to make abuses known to international audiences. They worked to reorient international law toward individual human subjects, affecting a radical transformation of institutions that had evolved to reconcile and guard the prerogatives of sovereign states. They had a crucial role to play in the decade's human rights conjuncture.[30]

Leading human rights NGOs included Amnesty International, the International Commission of Jurists, the International League for the Rights of Man, and Freedom House. These groups ranged in their foci and their biases. Amnesty sought neutrality in the Cold War. Freedom House and Helsinki Watch focused on the sins of left-wing regimes. Common to the NGOs, however, was an anti-statist idiom of human rights, an outlook that assumed individuals to be the bearers of rights and regarded governments as their potential violators. Within the United States, these organizations drew support mainly from an educated, modestly affluent elite. Berkeley and

Columbia professors led Amnesty International missions to explore human rights conditions in developing countries. The impact that the NGOs made belied their limited personnel. By the mid-1970s, NGO representatives were testifying in congressional hearings and interfacing broadly with legislators. Amnesty International even created a Washington office with the purpose of leveraging U.S. foreign policy as an instrument of human rights advocacy.[31]

Promoting a globalization of rights, the human rights NGOs played a vital role in the rise of human rights. Beliefs about globalization, meanwhile, conjured historical and moral imaginaries that helped to legitimate visions of human rights for all. While the word "globalization" became familiar only in the 1990s, the 1970s were abuzz with talk of "interdependence." The terms are not synonymous, but they are closely related: both evoke a structural convergence of human destinies and hint toward a common global civilization. Prophets of interdependence in the 1970s envisaged what Lester Brown in 1972 called a "world without borders"—a world in which the accelerating mobility of people, ideas, goods, and capital was making territorial sovereignty an anachronism.[32] From the late 1960s, interdependence became a powerful theme in international thought. It had important implications for the politics of human rights.

The conviction that an integrating world might become a unified social arena was a core assumption for many human rights proponents. While human rights remained a largely Western preoccupation, the moral imaginary that they projected was borderless. In this sense, human rights served as an ethical or ideational counterpoint to globalization's structural reconstitution of international society. In the United States, some proponents linked their enthusiasm for human rights directly to sweeping, metahistorical claims. The lawyer Richard Falk described the universalization of legal rights as a corollary to the globalization of sentiment. As interdependence unshackled the horizons of empathy from the borders of the nation-state, he argued, the "expression of public opinion on the world level" would undermine "traditional notions of territorial sovereignty."[33] Even the U.S. State Department saw the point. "We seem to be heading into a period of greater American awareness of world-wide interdependence," concluded one 1974 policy review. This augured "greater American interest in major issues of human rights."[34]

After 1977, globalization became for the Carter administration a conceptual rationale for human rights promotion. Zbigniew Brzezinski, the most conceptual of Carter's advisors, linked human rights to the historical circumstances that globalization was making. "Throughout the world," he wrote, "because of higher literacy, better communications, and a closer sense of interdependence, people are demanding and asserting their basic rights."[35] Richard Gardner, another Carter advisor, attempted a similar move. "Peace and security, economic and social development, and human rights," Gardner explained, "are three interrelated and essential developments in the triangle of world order."[36] The metahistorical assumptions of globalization shifted human rights out of the arena of policy debate and into the realm of destiny. Human rights offered a renewed sense of moral purpose after Vietnam, but that was not all they promised. As globalization proceeded, human rights were something even more powerful: an idea whose time had come. "We believe," Brzezinski explained, that "human rights summarize mankind's social progress; that they represent the genuine historical inevitability of our time."

The Cold War, Détente, and Human Rights

In May 1972 Richard Nixon traveled to Moscow. His summit with Leonid Brezhnev marked a high-water mark in superpower relations but a low point for human rights in the USSR. At that time, the Moscow Human Rights Committee, which the physicists Valery Chalidze and Andrei Sakharov founded in 1970, symbolized the promise of the Soviet Union's "democratic movement," but its membership comprised only a handful of westward-looking liberals.[37] The writer Alexander Solzhenitsyn was not especially liberal, but he was the Soviet Union's most famous dissident. Under constant surveillance, Solzhenitsyn had already lost his membership in the Soviet writer's union; soon he would lose his citizenship. Others fared little better. Chalidze would flee to the United States in the fall of 1972. Other dissidents faced jail or internal exile.

Speaking on Soviet television, Nixon had nothing to say about the embattled plight of Soviet dissent. Instead, he disavowed any desire to "impose" Western solutions on the Communist world.[38] This was not politesse. Nixon hoped to build what he called "a live-and-let-live world" in which hostile social systems could coexist.[39] He also followed a hardheaded conception of American interests. As president, Nixon sought to play the Soviet Union and China off against each other. Dividing the Communist monolith promised strategic dividends. By pivoting between Beijing and Moscow, Nixon would be able to dominate superpower relations. This gambit was the basis of détente, which was Nixon's strategy for waging the Cold War in an era of limits. In Moscow, Nixon talked peace but sought to push the Soviet Union into concessions on strategic arms control, conventional force reductions, and Vietnam. Nixon's leverage, as it was, derived from his travel itinerary. Months before he arrived in Moscow, Nixon had dined in Beijing with Mao Zedong. The implication was clear: the Soviets would deal with Nixon, or the United States would edge toward China.

Nixon's triangulation of Cold War politics created leverage for the United States vis-à-vis the two Communist superpowers, but Nixon did not use this influence to impress human rights upon either. Why not? His disregard contrasts, after all, with the attentiveness of successors like Jimmy Carter and Ronald Reagan to human rights in the Eastern bloc. How then to explain it? For one thing, Nixon's conception of international relations permitted little, if any, scope for the transnational claims that human rights made. Crucially, he and Henry Kissinger, his principal aide, shared an image of the world that comprised "one hundred and fifty sovereign states, profound ideological differences, and nuclear weapons."[40] A seasoned foreign policy hand, Nixon came to accept ideological diversity as a fact of international life after building his career as a Cold War ideologue. For Kissinger, the pursuit of stability among nation-states was an end that overrode other purposes, including human rights. Sovereignty for both men was an essential foundation of international relations. Even adversaries, they believed, might cooperate if they articulated their interests with sufficient clarity. To meddle in the domestic affairs of foreign powers exceeded the scope of legitimate national interests as Nixon and Kissinger defined them. For their part, Soviet leaders made their feelings clear, with *Pravda* indicting human rights as a "tool of ideological sabotage against the Soviet Union."[41]

Détente struck a balance between conflict and cooperation, but the compromise came under fire during the mid-1970s. Some critics argued that détente neglected human rights, and their challenge revealed the intrusion of globalizing, transnational forces upon stable patterns of interstate relations. U.S.-based NGOs focused attention on human rights in the USSR and provided dissidents with an international voice. Amnesty International, for example, translated samizdat narratives including the *Chronicle of Current Events*, the organ of the Soviet rights movement. Telephone calls enabled Soviet dissidents to speak with Western NGOs.[42]

Yet globalization did not make a backlash against détente inevitable. In the 1930s, Western journalists could have printed more than they did about the Ukrainian famine; for political reasons, they chose not to.[43] Politics in the 1970s, by contrast, created space for human rights to flourish. Nixon and Kissinger were victims of their own success. The stability that détente achieved made the threat of superpower conflict appear distant. It was "easy to posture against the Soviets," Kissinger rued, "because we have them all quieted down."[44] Détente thus undercut its own legitimation, which was that East-West peace had to be made because the stakes of conflict were so atrocious. Amid convivial summitry, such rationalization became more difficult to sustain.[45] The diminishing urgency of Cold War tensions thereby created space for human rights proponents to stake their claims.

Of course, not all Americans in the 1970s believed that the Cold War was passing. Some remained anti-Soviet hawks. But this hardly made them immune to the appeal of human rights. As a line of demarcation between American freedom and Soviet tyranny, human rights could invigorate the Cold War's ideological mission. The genius of human rights in American politics was the issue's capacity to appeal simultaneously to multiple constituencies. Doves could take human rights as the basis for a post–Cold War foreign policy; hawks could tether the same language to traditional Cold War concerns. Détente, which appealed to neither hawks nor doves once its novelty had worn off, was caught in the middle.

Consider the intrusion of human rights upon U.S.-Chilean relations, where the Nixon administration's policy followed Cold War preoccupations. Fearful of Communist advances, the White House condoned a 1973 coup d'état against an elected Marxist, Salvador Allende. (Nixon acknowledged no contradiction between his entreaties to Communists in Beijing and Moscow and his harassment of them in the developing world; only a strong Western bloc, he argued, could make détente with the East.) U.S. involvement in Chile was hardly more egregious than earlier Cold War interventions had been, such as those in Iran in 1953 and Guatemala in 1954. It nonetheless provoked a backlash that those misdeeds had not. Before 1973 was out, the U.S. Congress had convened an inquiry at which a Berkeley law professor testified on behalf of Amnesty International.[46] Over the coming years, Congress passed a series of laws restricting the provision of material aid to Augusto Pinochet, the general who ousted Allende. Kissinger could only apologize lamely that his hands were tied. "We face massive domestic problems," he explained, "over the issue of human rights."[47] Much had changed since the 1950s.

By the early 1970s, Cold War imperatives were ceasing to rationalize violent interventions in the global South. "Two decades ago," noted one State Department report, "the focus of public and Congressional attention was on those states with which we were engaged in a Cold War. Today it is directed at the human rights violations of regimes with which the U.S. Government is identified."[48] The point was crucial. The Cold War's urgency in the 1950s had excused dalliances with dictators. By the 1970s, such rationalization was becoming harder to sustain. The Pinochet coup made Chile a notorious case, but it was not unique. Authoritarian governments in South Korea, Greece, and the Philippines found themselves the targets of sustained human rights critiques. In some cases, Congress passed legislation that limited military and developmental aid to long-standing allies. This was a new departure.

Even as human rights cut against Cold War logics, the Soviet Union's status as an egregious violator created opportunities for anti-Soviet hawks to align themselves with the new moral idiom. The career of Senator Henry M. Jackson reveals the power of this elision. A fierce critic of the USSR and aspirant to the White House, Jackson in 1973–1974 led a congressional insurgency that made the normalization of U.S.-Soviet trade relations conditional upon human rights conditions. By the mid-1970s, other cold warriors were lining up behind human rights. That is not to say that the issue's use was always instrumental. Jackson accepted that human rights applied to right-wing regimes, and he sponsored a Senate amendment to curtail assistance to Greece's anti-Communist junta.[49] Progressive proponents of human rights also focused on Soviet abuses. Donald Fraser, a liberal Democrat from Minnesota who became especially associated with the cause, spoke against Soviet abuses. Jimmy Carter articulated a "strong concern for human rights, particularly in the Soviet Union."[50] The Soviet Union's superpower status, its fraught relations with the United States, and its visible dissident community all made it an irresistible target, especially for politicians like Jackson who saw a winning issue.

To emphasize the bipartisan reach of human rights in the United States is not to say that the issue was nonideological. Rather, human rights made ideological claims to which both Republicans and Democrats could subscribe. As their political appeal advanced, moreover, human rights circumscribed the opportunities for détente. During the presidential election of 1976, candidates from across the spectrum competed to exorcise détente's ghosts. Gerald Ford, the incumbent who inherited both détente and Henry Kissinger from Nixon, banished the word from his campaign. Ronald Reagan, challenging

Ford for the nomination, lambasted détente's accommodation with totalitarianism. Jimmy Carter, the Democratic candidate, made human rights a central theme in a foreign policy platform that otherwise resembled Ford's. Human rights did not determine the election, but the breadth of enthusiasm for them revealed the public's exasperation with détente. Still, the rise of human rights in the 1970s was not removed from Cold War politics. The stability that détente achieved created space for them to flourish, while the enduring specter of Soviet totalitarianism imparted to American human rights discourse an adversarial, almost Manichean content that would endure beyond the 1970s.

Human Rights and Individualist Liberalism

Human rights surged to prominence in the 1970s due to complex circumstances. Cold War détente created space for human rights to flourish, and a transnational social movement propelled the issue's march. These circumstances shaped the substantive content of human rights in the late twentieth century. Animated by globalization, human rights assumed in the 1970s an anti-statist thrust, which distinguished them from earlier natural rights formulations that took the nation-state more for a guarantor of human rights than for a likely violator of them. If human rights drew from deep historical springs, their distinctive content in the 1970s revealed the imprint of the political and ideological circumstances that framed their emergence.

The substance of human rights in the 1970s was liberal and individualistic. Proponents stood for liberty, limited government, and the free movement of ideas and people. Defenders of human rights in the West paid little attention to collectivist concepts of rights, such as the right to national self-determination that preoccupied the votaries of Third World opinion.[51] Cutting against the collectivist priorities of the Third World majority in the UN General Assembly, the revival of a liberal idiom of human rights in the 1970s was in some ways surprising. Prominent Americans had embraced the politics of collectivism in recent years: John F. Kennedy had told Americans to subordinate their individual aspirations to their country, while Martin Luther King, Jr. had privileged the nation-state as the framework in which rights and justice could be realized. Human rights, by contrast, offered not nationalist exhortations but an exaltation of the individual as the bearer of unique rights. Their ascendancy in the 1970s eclipsed collectivist visions of political justice, whether postcolonial nationalism abroad or the New Deal's communitarian liberalism at home.

How can we explain the individualist bias? The rise of human rights in the 1970s depended, as Samuel Moyn has argued, on the displacement of prior utopian visions.[52] This was obvious for the European left, which had to grapple after 1968 with the implosion of Marxist-Leninism's ideological credibility. In the United States, where Marxist-Leninism had been at most a fringe preoccupation, its eclipse does not explain the rise of human rights. Yet human rights in the United States also hinged on specific displacements. In world politics, the degeneration of anticolonial nationalism into Third World authoritarianism, a process that became manifest from the mid-1960s, cracked open space for human rights to flourish in American international thought. At home, both jurisprudence and politics experienced reorientations toward individual rights from the 1960s onward. This too involved displacement—of local self-governance and of legislative power. What was won for individual rights was often very good; at the same time, collective self-determination was diminished.

For Henry Kissinger, the problem with human rights was that they violated a basic assumption of statecraft, namely "the understanding that it involves relationships between sovereign countries."[53] While international law by the 1970s permitted some scope for surveillance, if not intervention, most governments still assumed that human rights remained "purely matters of 'domestic' concern."[54] Third World nations were especially sensitive to perceived intrusions on their sovereign autonomy. To promote human rights, advocates had to overcome the suspicion that they violated the most basic tenet of world politics, namely territorial sovereignty. This applied within the U.S. government too. Apart from a handful of Cold War interventions that evoked older colonial habits, U.S. foreign policy in the Cold War accepted pluralism as a fact of international life and sovereign autonomy as a principle of international conduct. Unlike human rights activists, U.S. diplomats did not seek to impose universal norms upon nation-states; they accepted foreign governments largely as they were and worked to promote American interests in a complex world. Before the 1970s the United States did not consider tethering military aid to human rights; in the view of U.S. diplomats, the issues that human rights evoked lay within the sovereign responsibilities of foreign states. Within the U.S. government, the State Department was especially deferential to the sovereignty principle, being accustomed to dealing with foreign governments and to representing their perspectives in Washington.

With the Portuguese revolution of 1974–1975, the last of the colonial empires collapsed. This shifted the political implications of human rights. In a postcolonial world, could the defenders of sovereignty still decry humanitarian meddlers as would-be colonialists? Meanwhile, the historical luster had worn off the postcolonial state. Most of the new nations by the 1970s had failed to fulfill the developmental goals that their founders defined for them. Many had slumped into authoritarianism. Others fought civil wars. "It is not Nehru who is taken for the Third World's augur," wrote Clifford Geertz, "but [Idi] Amin," referring to the clownish but brutal Ugandan dictator.[55] The south's struggles might have been a legacy of colonialism, but the failures of postcolonial states created new openings for universal human rights claims. Washington's ambassador to the United Nations Daniel Patrick Moynihan grasped the strategic opportunity. "Colonialism is over," he wrote in 1975; "human rights is our secret weapon."[56]

That fall, Moynihan and Amin became the central players in a drama that pitted universal human rights against postcolonial sovereignty. It began when Amin, speaking at the UN General Assembly, assailed Israel and denounced Amnesty International as a stooge of colonialism. This was too much for Moynihan, who dubbed Amin a "racist murderer." Moynihan's rejoinder breached diplomatic protocol, and the postcolonial world rallied around Amin. That only encouraged the U.S. ambassador. When the Soviet–Third World bloc introduced a UN resolution equating Zionism with racism later that fall, Moynihan reached for the language of universal human rights. Determined to expose the hypocrisy of the West's critics, he proposed a worldwide amnesty of political prisoners. A deliberate provocation, the effort spelled the end of Moynihan's UN career. But it marked the climax of his attempt to reorient American foreign policy toward human rights. The crusade earned Moynihan the ire of Henry Kissinger. "Now he is starting a brawl with South Africa on apartheid," lamented Kissinger, "[and] he says the UN has 130 dictators."[57] Yet Moynihan grasped something that Kissinger did not: with the waning of colonialism, the opportunity for a proactive human rights agenda had arrived.

Within the United States, meanwhile, the 1970s invigorated an individualistic, rights-oriented liberalism. This was especially clear in economic life, where deregulation and market reform proceeded apace. Conversely, the language of collective economic justice fell by the wayside. Individual freedom was a theme of the decade's emancipatory social movements, for women's and gay and lesbian rights. Was there a common logic? The historian Thomas Borstelmann argues that the seventies "granted greater formal recognition of the dignity and value of all persons, while permitting increasingly sovereign market forces . . . to further widen distinctions of wealth and class."[58] Connected or not, the ascent of individualistic human rights paralleled the eclipse of more communitarian vocabularies of justice, especially social and economic justice.

Martin Luther King Jr. in the last years of his life embraced the language of human rights. "We have left the realm of constitutional rights," he wrote in 1967, "and are entering the area of human rights."[59] Yet what he meant was not necessarily what the words would come to connote. King envisaged a "revolution of values" that would uplift the needy and end "the glaring contrast of poverty and wealth." Compared to this, human rights in their 1970s version would be a preventive doctrine, aimed at the inhibition of harm and not constructive uplift. Human rights did not necessarily mark a continuation of the civil rights agenda as King envisaged it. Still, civil rights were a precondition for human rights. The end of Jim Crow made it possible for Washington to promote human rights in the world without exhibiting rank hypocrisy. More substantively, civil rights reaffirmed liberal self-confidence, affirming that change could be achieved through gradualist methods. There were also continuities in personnel. Patricia Derian, who ran the human rights desk at the State Department under Carter, had scant foreign policy experience, but she had registered voters in Mississippi. Bayard Rustin, one of King's closest aides, became an active member of Freedom House and a pillar of the New York human rights community.[60]

Civil rights were one legacy of the 1960s that preconditioned the rise of individualist human rights, but there were others. Among them was the shift in the orientation of domestic law toward individual rights, which hinged on the judicial philosophy of the Warren Court. The emergence of the Supreme Court as the defender and champion of individual rights was a slow process. For the republic's first hundred years, after all, common law rights were a matter for the states. The Bill of Rights pertained only to the federal government; it did not apply to the states until 1868, when the Fourteenth Amendment guaranteed citizens' rights against the states to the due process of law and to equal protection under the law. The Fourteenth Amendment thereby created scope for federal courts to intervene in the affairs of the states to enforce individual rights. In a sense, it did to the American states what the proponents of human rights would later propose doing to the world's nation-states: it made them subject to a penumbral law of rights.

Ratified after the Civil War, the Fourteenth Amendment created a mechanism for the federal enforcement of individual rights against states. It was not until the mid-twentieth century, however, that federal courts began to use it with vigor. *Brown v. Board of Education*, which struck down segregated schooling in 1954, was a landmark.[61] It marked the beginnings of a historic shift in the Supreme Court's role. A court that had heretofore served mainly to resolve jurisdictional disputes and to adjudge the constitutionality of law became the guarantor of individual legal rights. From the 1960s, a culture of legal rights blossomed. Supreme Court decisions defined the rights of criminal suspects (*Miranda*) and the rights of citizens to privacy (*Griswold*) against states (Arizona and Connecticut, respectively).[62] Painful dilemmas such as abortion were engaged as issues of fundamental rights. The Supreme Court even concluded in *McDonald v. Chicago* (2010) that the Second Amendment applies to state and local authorities, making local prohibitions on handgun ownership a violation of constitutional rights.[63] Not everyone agrees that the ascent of individualist rights has been positive. The legal scholar Mary Ann Glendon argues that a rights culture has diminished American civic life.[64] Others disagree. Perhaps the most that can be said is that the proper scope of individual rights and the legitimacy of their constitutional foundations remain fraught dilemmas.

As far as human rights are concerned, the parallels between the rise of legal rights at home and the ascent of human rights in American foreign policy are striking. One did not cause the other; foreign policy remains one of the few areas in American life around which federal courts have steered a wide berth, considering it a "political question." Human rights nonetheless emerged as a foreign-policy concern while Americans were becoming attuned to the language of individual rights under law. It does not take a leap of imagination to perceive how domestic developments might have reinforced Norman Podhoretz's conviction that foreign policy ought to proceed from the belief that "ours is the culture based on the primacy of the individual [and] the claims of the individual against those of the state."[65] That the security and welfare of individual citizens might also depend upon the nation-state was left unstated.

The Oasis Blossoms: Jimmy Carter and the Politics of Human Rights

Though he became uniquely associated with it, Jimmy Carter did not claim to have invented the idea of human rights in foreign policy. Instead, he sought to ground human rights in the American past. "America did not invent human rights," he explained, "Human rights invented America." Others made similar claims.[66] For Senator Edward M. Kennedy in 1975, human rights were a "historic" commitment for a republic that had been "founded as a nation of liberty."[67] This rhetorical strategy was sensible. Rooting human rights in American tradition was likelier to secure public support than was Brzezinski's future-oriented globalism. Yet the recourse to tradition was not wholly instrumental. Carter was in a sense correct to argue that human rights invented America. The generation of 1776 depended on the language of natural rights to make its revolt against the British Crown; on this at least, both Jefferson and Hamilton had agreed. Nor was Ted Kennedy wrong to argue that altruistic concern for foreigners had recurrently animated American foreign policy. There are myriad examples, from the anguished American reaction to the Greek crisis of the 1820s, to the pro-Hungarian movement of the 1840s, to the outrage that Americans expressed over Tsarist pogroms in the 1890s. Human rights in foreign policy built upon familiar legacies.

There were indeed elements of powerful continuity in the human rights agenda of the 1970s. The claim that rights are inalienable and universal is not a twentieth-century invention. Human rights depend upon philosophical claims that trace back to Hobbes, Grotius, and Locke, if not earlier. Humanitarian engagement, a vital component of human rights politics, also has an ancient history. Mencius, Buddha, and Jesus Christ were all pioneering humanitarians, even if it took the Enlightenment and mass literacy to make humanitarianism a major political force. While human rights are not commensurate with humanitarianism, their rise depended on engagement with suffering human beings, from Biafran infants to Soviet political prisoners. Seeking to redress distant misery in the name of natural rights, human rights advocates plumbed deep historical wells.

At the same time, there are dangers in seeing human rights as an ahistorical essence that breaks through from time to time. Serving specific political agendas, human rights in the 1970s were neither a philosophical assertion of natural rights devoid of political content nor an apolitical humanitarian enterprise.

Their proponents made claims—political and ideological claims—about how power, law, and legitimacy should be structured in international society and in relation to the individual human subject. A political project grounded in time and place, human rights in the 1970s reflected the circumstances of their creation. Globalization imparted an antistatist accent, which made human rights a suitable moral vocabulary for a world in which the vectors of interdependence appeared to be erasing the barriers of territorial sovereignty. The Cold War injected an antitotalitarian bias, while some Americans began to take the global promotion of human rights for the prerogative of a post–Cold War superpower. Changes within the United States, meanwhile, invigorated an individualistic idiom of liberalism and facilitated the embrace of an ideological foreign policy agenda. Consequently, human rights matured in the 1970s as a doctrine that emphasized the prevention of harm and applied mainly to dissidents, political prisoners, and other opponents of Third World and Communist dictatorships.

Carter's own instincts on human rights were capacious. Moved by a humanitarian spirit and strong (some said rigid) moral commitments, Carter preferred to define human rights "in its broadest sense."[68] Despite a focus on civil and political rights, Carter did not disparage alternative visions of human betterment, and his administration included "economic and social rights" within the major statement of its human rights agenda.[69] That Carter could later describe the Panama Canal Treaty as an accomplishment of his human rights foreign policy suggests the breadth and subtlety of his vision.[70] Carter encountered pressure from those who sought to narrow the scope of human rights by limiting their application to totalitarian regimes.[71] He nonetheless attended to the Soviet human rights issue in ways that won plaudits from dissidents and irritated Soviet-American relations. The Carter administration struggled to implement an overarching human rights policy, but there were important innovations. Carter tethered U.S. voting in international financial institutions to human rights and made bilateral aid subject to similar scrutiny.[72] There were omissions and failures, such as Iran and China, to which historians have drawn attention.[73] Perhaps the best that can be said is what the International League for the Rights of Man said, which is that human rights became in the late 1970s "a subject of national policy debate in many countries [and] the focus for discussion in international organizations."[74] This was Jimmy Carter's contribution. His influence was more limited where the substantive or doctrinal content of human rights was concerned. Carter's own approach was broad and generous, but human rights in the 1970s became defined in ways that reflected the circumstances of their arrival, especially the antitotalitarian priorities of what became, from the late 1970s, a resurgent Cold War. That Reagan was able, against expectations, to appropriate Carter's human rights agenda for his own purposes after 1980 showed how malleable human rights could be.

Since the 1970s, human rights have assumed new burdens. During the 1980s, they became entwined with democracy promotion. In the late 1990s, they legitimated humanitarian interventions in Kosovo, Sierra Leone, and East Timor. While human rights did not cause the U.S. invasion of Iraq in 2003, George W. Bush styled his foreign policy as a crusade for human rights against the "wills of powerful states and the evil designs of tyrants."[75] His willingness to make military violence an instrument of human rights promotion was a radical departure from Carter's humbler and more reflective human rights agenda. Yet the left, so critical of Bush, has been hardly less radical in its own reinvention of human rights. The limited and antiauthoritarian doctrine that emerged in the 1970s has retained its fundamentalism and global purview while assuming substantive contents that increasingly imply affirmative duties on the state's part. Human rights are now said to include myriad social and economic commitments, including even high-speed Internet access.[76] There are excellent reasons to favor expansive social provision, but to make higher education a "human right" on a plane with bodily integrity is a reductio ad absurdum. There are serious risks to all this. Shifting complex policy issues into the arena of rights impoverishes our politics, but it also does inestimable damage to the idea of rights itself. Human rights in the 1970s served particular agendas, but they were at least able to rally broad reaches of American opinion. Human rights, by some accounts, were the most popular aspect of Carter's foreign policy.[77] As rights expand, on the other hand, they also divide.

In assessing the human rights moment of the 1970s after almost forty years, this chapter has argued that exigent historical circumstances conditioned the rise of human rights politics in the United States, molding their programmatic agenda and conditioning their content. This history should be cautionary. Attaching substantive political content to transcendent claims about natural rights and humanitarian responsibility is a fraught act, as much today as it was in the seventies. If human rights are to serve a useful purpose in a democracy, they will have to be framed so that a consensus of decent opinion can agree upon what constitutes them. Proponents in the 1970s largely accomplished this, I would argue, and this fact was crucial to their success at that time. Still, this does not mean that human rights will bear unlimited burdens. The reality is that particular idioms of human rights will always be political, even as they draw upon transcendent themes of natural law and humanitarian obligation. In practice, it will likely be the breadth of consensus that human rights are able to command that determines whether they flourish or wither, whether we have reached an oasis or simply a mirage.

Chapter 9

Human Rights and the U.S. Republican Party in the Late 1970s

Carl J. Bon Tempo

Historians of the United States recently have turned their attention to the 1970s. In the words of one chronicler, "something happened" during this decade that shaped the United States for the rest of the twentieth century.[1] As the essays in this book make clear, one of the things that happened in the 1970s—in the United States and around the globe—was a new emphasis on human rights. This is not to say that human rights emerged sui generis in the 1970s, but instead that human rights principles, politics, and policies enjoyed a greater standing, wider audience, and new meanings.[2]

While the human rights moment of the 1970s was a global phenomenon, it also was an American one. The Helsinki Accords brought human rights principles to the fore of the United States' Cold War policies in ways not seen since the late 1940s.[3] Nongovernmental organizations (NGOs) in the United States trumpeted human rights concerns with vigor. Amnesty International USA grew into a powerful grassroots force that shaped the perceptions, concerns, and actions of the public and policy makers, while Americans participated in transnational campaigns against government-sponsored torture in Latin America and Europe.[4] In American politics, Democratic liberals like Donald Fraser pushed human rights, as did the so-called neoconservatives, Democrats like Henry "Scoop" Jackson and Daniel Patrick Moynihan (as well as their intellectual allies nestled in vital think tanks and journals). These politicians, of course, tied human rights to sometimes vastly different policy and ideological agendas. Sensing the moment, President Jimmy Carter promised to make human rights a centerpiece of U.S. foreign policy, though his record of accomplishment was mixed at best.[5]

This standard narrative of 1970s human rights activism and action contains two blind spots, however. First, the human rights issues of the 1970s that rose to the top of the agenda in the United States were based mainly in foreign affairs: Helsinki and the Cold War, torture in the Third World and developing nations, and Carter's foreign policy, for instance. But did human rights concerns find a place in domestic politics and culture? Second, too often scholarly focus falls on human rights activists, politicians, and organizations from the left, liberal, or Democratic side of the ideological, political, and partisan divide.[6] There is good reason for this emphasis—some of the most important proponents of human rights came from the liberal Democratic left—but it also raises the question of whether, and how deeply, human rights talk penetrated the right's and Republican Party's agendas.

The Republican Party of the late 1970s provides answers to both of these questions and a fascinating case study of human rights' place in American political culture. Quite simply, the GOP in the late 1970s grappled with human rights, and some members of the party saw human rights concerns as an important element of domestic political and cultural issues, as well as foreign policy. The GOP was not the party of human rights, but more than a few in the party took human rights seriously.

This trend emerged clearly in two episodes. At the 1976 Republican National Convention, party members debated human rights issues, displaying remarkable diversity in their conceptualizations of human rights principles in both domestic and foreign affairs. That diversity often broke down along the party's ideological splits between conservatives, moderates, and liberals. By the end of the convention, however, the conservatives had emerged as the clear winners in the party's human rights battles. Then, in the aftermath of the convention, the GOP's most important figure, the conservative Ronald Reagan, began to outline his views on human rights. Reagan focused more on human rights' place in foreign affairs, but he also tied human rights to his powerful antistatist and antigovernment politics. Likewise, while at least part of his definition of human rights fell within the mainstream of 1970s activists and organizations, he advocated for human rights within a larger strategic and ideological framework that characterized Republican and conservative politics in the 1970s.

During the late 1970s, conservative Republicans stood on the brink of political power. In the next two decades they would launch a revolution that shaped politics and governance, the economy, social and race relations, and how Americans conceived of their society. Historians have spent the better part of the last decade explaining the rise of conservatism. These explanations focus, for the most part, on the domestic scene, and to a lesser extent on America's role in international affairs.[7] This literature on the rise of the right contains little about how conservatives and the Republican Party participated in and constructed the human rights moment of the 1970s. This lapse is understandable: conservative and Republican engagement with human rights language and principles did not power the larger conservative turn in American politics. Yet Republican participation in the human rights revolution of the 1970s is still revealing. First, it adds another element to the story of the ideological clashes in, and transformation of, the GOP. The human rights battles show how certain elements of the party might coalesce around ideas and policies, all the while driving out other factions. Indeed, the human rights activism of the 1970s in the GOP mirrored much of what disaffected conservative Democrats were offering at the same time. The politics of the 1970s, as constructed by conservative Republicans, set the stage for the marriage of those disaffected Democratic neoconservatives with the GOP in the 1980s. Second, the Reagan administration adapted many of these ideas in the 1980s, enacting them in Reagan's human rights policies. Third, the episode reminds us that human rights were not merely the province of the Democrats or liberals or the left. There was such a phenomenon as Republican human rights talk in the 1970s.

Republicans and Human Rights Prior to the 1970s

What makes the events of the late 1970s so surprising is that in the decades after World War II, Republicans were not at all in the forefront of the human rights revolution. The Roosevelt administration declared human rights an aim of the United States in the 1940s, and liberals were vital in writing the 1948 Universal Declaration of Human Rights. Some Republicans voiced support for human rights in the 1940s. The GOP's 1940 presidential nominee, Wendell Willkie, authored the popular 1943 book *One World*, which prefigured some of the themes at the heart of emerging human rights doctrine. At the same time, Republican foreign policy expert John Foster Dulles used appeals to human rights as one part of a campaign—formulated with Protestant organizations—to sway Americans toward internationalism. Dulles's interest in human rights continued in the postwar years as he joined with European conservatives to fuse human rights and Christian ideals during the larger European reconstruction project in the face of the Cold War threat of communism.[8] But Willkie's and Dulles's efforts proved exceptional; the GOP during the 1940s displayed little interest in human rights concerns.[9]

Republican opposition to human rights solidified in the 1950s. Senator John Bricker, a conservative Republican from Ohio, sponsored an amendment that would have placed strict limits on presidential power in foreign relations, specifically in treaty making. Bricker asserted that international agreements such as the United Nations Covenant on Human Rights were a "blueprint for tyranny" in the United States because they permitted international and foreign organizations to judge American legal and political practices, infringing on sovereignty and limiting basic rights and freedoms in the United States.[10] Likewise, Bricker and his allies argued that these treaties were merely communist fronts or that the emerging corpus of international human rights law would only pave the way for radical domestic economic and social reform. Although the Republican Eisenhower administration opposed (and ultimately defeated) Bricker's amendment, it did so to protect executive power. Eisenhower and his secretary of state John Foster Dulles joined Bricker in opposing human rights treaties. Dulles tried to end the Bricker controversy by publicly abandoning any pretext of support for international human rights covenants. Dulles also vaguely promised to pursue human rights through publicity and education. Likewise, in their Latin America policies, Eisenhower and Dulles stressed halting the advance of communism rather than promotion of democracy or human rights.[11]

The 1964 Goldwater campaign was even less hospitable to human rights. For liberal Republicans, this stance was too much. William Scranton, Pennsylvania's Republican governor, challenged Goldwater in 1964 as a "progressive Republican" and pledged support for human rights.[12] For Scranton, human rights—along with the welfare state, international organizations, and a restrained Cold War arms race—signaled a modern and relevant GOP. Other Republicans with similar ideological predilections would make similar claims in the late 1970s. Of course, Scranton lost, Goldwater won, and human rights remained outside the mainstream Republican Party.

In the early 1970s, though, human rights began its ascent into the mainstream of American foreign policy through the work of a variety of politicians and activists. Transnational nongovernmental organizations such as

Amnesty International used the language of human rights to protest and publicize torture, abuse, and the curtailment of individual rights around the globe. Liberal Democrats in Congress embraced human rights as an alternative to what they saw as the spent strategy of anticommunist containment and the amorality of realpolitik. In contrast, neoconservatives in both parties (but mainly residing with the Democrats) used human rights to blast détente with the Soviet Union as selling out both American ideals and the brave and courageous dissidents behind the Iron Curtain. Conservative Democrat Henry Jackson wanted to tie trade agreements between the United States and Soviets to the right of Soviet Jews to emigrate. Neoconservatives lamented that the Helsinki Agreement's human rights sections came at too high a cost: formal recognition of the East-West divide in Europe. Finally, neoconservative intellectuals embraced human rights because those principles resonated with their faith in democracy.[13]

The Nixon administration's policies spurred and accelerated the human rights activism of neoconservatives and liberals. The foreign policy of President Richard Nixon, constructed with his secretary of state Henry Kissinger, emphasized global power relations, détente, and maintaining American clout in a challenging world that saw U.S. power in decline relative to other nations. Unsurprisingly, the Nixon (and later the Ford) White House had little interest in human rights, instead viewing them at times with disdain. This was especially the case with Kissinger. He only very reluctantly agreed to the establishment of a human rights office in the State Department in 1975—largely to forestall further congressional action—and then spent the next nearly two years rejecting any and all of its initiatives.[14] When it came to Latin America, where rightist governments allied with the United States launched horrific campaigns to suppress internal dissent, Kissinger played a sly game. Publicly, Kissinger took to proclaiming the importance of human rights, largely to quiet domestic critics. Privately, however, he lambasted his department officers who supported human rights and reassured America's Latin American authoritarian allies that they had U.S. support and understanding.[15] Finally, while Kissinger helped convince the Soviets to accept some of the human rights provisions of Helsinki—which the secretary later saw as a vital part of the accords—he spent much of the actual negotiations downplaying human rights concerns and viewed them as secondary to larger strategic considerations.[16] As Kissinger himself stated in 1975, "I hold the strong view that human rights are not appropriate in a foreign policy context."[17] Not all Republicans, however, agreed with him by the mid-1970s.

The Republican National Convention of 1976

By the summer of 1976, Republicans focused on pending political matters, mainly the upcoming presidential election. The GOP faced a difficult political environment. The party still carried the stains of Watergate, which had damaged the GOP brand with voters; in 1974, a group of reform-minded Democrats, called the "Watergate Babies," had ridden public discontent to victories in the congressional midterm elections. Republicans held the White House, but President Gerald Ford's almost two years in office had been marked by economic troubles, foreign policy problems, and political tests (such as whether or not to pardon Nixon.) Moreover, Ford faced a stiff challenge for the GOP's 1976 presidential nomination from California's ex-governor Ronald Reagan. Reagan's supporters, the heirs to Goldwater's conservatism, held a dim view of Ford's supposedly moderate politics and policies. Ford capitalized on Reagan's early stumbles in the primary season and seemed on his way to locking up the nomination rather quickly, but Reagan climbed back into the contest with blistering attacks on Ford that played well with conservative voters. By the end of the primaries and on the eve of the convention, neither man had secured enough delegates to claim the nomination, but most observers believed that Ford had the inside track to it.[18]

Presidential politics was not the only source of discontent in the party. Republicans fought bitterly over social issues like abortion and the Equal Rights Amendment (ERA). The controversy over abortion was more recent—the 1972 party platform did not mention abortion rights—but in the wake of the Supreme Court's *Roe v. Wade* decision, pro-choice advocates battled with antiabortion activists to set the party's position. The question of equal rights for women had a longer history in the party. The GOP had long endorsed the Equal Rights Amendment and many of the party's most important female members believed passionately in the ERA. In the mid-1970s, however, as the nationwide drive to ratify the ERA picked up steam, some Republicans objected. Most striking, the conservative leader Phyllis Schlafly attacked the ERA as an assault on women's privileged place in society, which earned her the condemnation of Republicans who supported the amendment.[19]

Taken together, the Ford-Reagan contest and these divisive social issues were battles in a larger war within the GOP. In general, although exceptions surely existed, moderates and liberals in the party lined up behind Ford. Conservatives, many of whom had cut their teeth on the 1964 Goldwater campaign, gravitated toward Reagan; they liked his antistatism and critiques of the modern welfare state, his muscular anticommunism, and his opposition to the ERA. These divides almost guaranteed fireworks at the August Republican National Convention in Kansas City, Missouri. The party's chief task was to settle on a presidential candidate. Through adept maneuvering and the power of incumbency, Ford managed to take the nomination.

The GOP gathered not only to choose a candidate but also to write a party platform. That task proved difficult, largely because of the fractures in the party. But producing the party's statement of principles also proved tiresome because of the process by which the GOP wrote its platform. In the months leading to the convention, the party took testimony on issues from experts, interest groups, and party members at several meetings throughout the country. Informed by this testimony, subcommittees at the convention set out to draft relevant sections of the platform, which were then submitted to the larger Platform Committee (consisting of 106 members) and the Platform Committee's executive committee (consisting of 15 members, including the chairpersons of the subcommittees.) These latter two groups put all of the moving parts of the platform into place.[20]

Human rights emerged as a prominent issue during these platform discussions, but it did not dominate the convention. Nor, it seems, did human rights concerns emerge as a topic of discussion among Republicans in response to the Democratic Party's human rights stance, which very few seemed to notice. In fact, the Democrats at their convention a month earlier had not focused so sharply on human rights. Democratic presidential nominee Jimmy Carter made few mentions of human rights in his convention speech, and, while the party's July 1976 platform pledged to integrate human rights more thoroughly into U.S. foreign policy, this promise was consistent with what congressional liberals had suggested in recent years.[21] Republicans, then, came to discussions of human rights on their own initiative. While discussions of human rights had occurred in the platform subcommittees addressing foreign policy, the majority of human rights talk at the convention took place in the Human Rights and Responsibilities Subcommittee. Human rights concerns relating to foreign policy did receive an airing here as well, because Republican ethnic organizations (especially from Eastern Europe) testified before this subcommittee. But more revealing, the subcommittee's agenda was crowded with the most divisive social issues of the day: abortion, affirmative action, civil rights, gay rights, and the ERA.[22] The association of human rights with these issues made clear that Republicans conceived of human rights as having a distinctly domestic component.

The fireworks on the Human Rights and Responsibilities Subcommittee began quickly, first centering on the question of who would serve as chair. Ford ally Governor Robert Ray of Iowa had appointed Massachusetts representative Silvio Conte to chair. Conte, a Ford delegate, was a liberal Republican. But a week before the convention, Conte lost his position. Instead, Ray named Thomas Pickering, a state senator from Mississippi, as chair. Pickering remained uncommitted in the Reagan-Ford contest, though most thought he was very much in the governor's camp. His conservatism, however, was no secret. The Ford camp dismissed Conte's demotion as inconsequential, choosing to accept the official reason: the congressman had pressing legislative business in Washington. Conte, though, was not so sanguine. He issued a barely diplomatic press release that declared, "We can't afford a platform written for just one region of the country, or for just one segment of the party." When asked by a reporter about the situation, Conte dropped the diplomacy. He blamed his demotion on the pro-Reagan forces who he labeled "desperate." Then, Conte really opened fire, commenting: "They're just a bunch of rednecks from North Carolina and Oklahoma anyway."[23]

The Conte episode was not nearly as insignificant as some tried to assert. It neatly displayed the animosity between the Ford and Reagan supporters and the ideological and regional divides in the party. Representing a liberal district in Western Massachusetts, Conte was pro-ERA, concerned with job creation and the weak economy, and had no qualms blasting Republican policies that he believed were skewed toward helping the well-off. These positions put him in the line of fire of Reagan supporters, a spot he seemed happy to assume. Moreover, Conte in 1976 was in the midst of developing into a forceful advocate for human rights. At the convention, Conte voiced strong concern about the violation of human rights by U.S. Cold War allies. This position differed from the Ford administration's stance, but this divergence did not lessen Conte's support for the president. Conte's interest in human rights accelerated in the late 1970s, as he generally supported the Carter administration's human rights efforts and traveled extensively in South America to meet with human rights activists. In the 1980s, he was a leading critic of the Reagan administration's Central America policies and a strong proponent of the nuclear freeze movement. Conte's demotion, in short, sidelined one of the most vocal human rights supporters from the GOP's liberal wing.[24]

Even with the more conservative Pickering as the subcommittee's chair, GOP members brought human rights principles to the fore during the platform's public hearings and drafting process. In fact, the Republicans who testified during the hearings and participated in the platform discussions and drafting displayed remarkable diversity when it came to human rights. Some prominent Republicans embraced human rights as a path toward a more expansive vision of political and social rights in general. This was the case especially among Republican women who supported the Equal Rights Amendment. Here, the key figure was Elly Peterson, a long-time Republican activist who had spent decades trying to carve a more prominent place for women in the GOP. She was also a member of the party's moderate wing, a stance that would, by the mid-1980s, lead her to declare herself an independent. In 1976, Peterson was fully and equally committed to the party and to the ERA, but she worried about the anti-ERA movement led by Schlafly and conservatives.[25] She admonished her party "that at no time have I been more concerned that we are in danger of being left behind by the realities of the second half of the twentieth century if we fail to continue to lead the American people as primary proponents of individual freedoms and human rights for the common man and women." Foremost among those human rights for Peterson was the ERA, which she described as a "basic guarantee of citizens' rights" and saw as central to the party's and the nation's greatness. Peterson believed that human rights was a mark of modernity and that only by demonstrating its fealty to human rights by supporting women's rights and the ERA could the GOP remain relevant and powerful in contemporary politics. But beyond this political positioning, Peterson identified the ERA as a vital star in the larger constellation of human rights as she pushed for an expanded definition of "individual freedoms" and "citizens' rights."[26]

Other Republicans linked human rights to ethnic and cultural diversity. Benjamin Fernandez of the Republican National Hispanic Assembly of the United States urged the GOP to embrace Hispanic Americans, who "are organizing ourselves into a formidable Republican bloc so that we can effectively take our place at your side as full and equal partners." Fernandez then asked the party to "develop a solution to the illegal alien problem in this country . . . which is compassionate . . . which respects human rights."[27] Fernandez's use of human rights in this case was, in one sense, vague. He might have been equating human rights with basic decency and humanitarianism, or he might have been suggesting bolstering the political and civil rights of illegal immigrants by respecting their human rights, or perhaps both. On the other hand, Fernandez's larger agenda promoted cultural diversity and Latino participation in American life, and he asked Republicans to embrace human rights in attempting to integrate newcomers into American society. Echoing

Fernandez, Michael Buryk of the Republican Heritage Groups Federation of the State of New Jersey asked the GOP to support U.S. government policies that "actively encourage and support in every way the preservation of the ethnic heritage of all its citizens." Buryk next coupled ethnic diversity to human rights by examining superpower relations. He noted that "spirited folk dances, bright costumes, delicious national cuisine and displays of native folk art have shown all of us that the cherished tree bearing the fruits of the world's cultural past can take root and flourish on American soil." Soviet citizens, on the other hand, were denied these very opportunities, thus their "cry for human rights." It was perhaps both an overly complicated and too poetic comparison, but at the heart of Buryk's formulation lay the assertion that regard for human rights was based in a respect for ethnic diversity. Americans respected diversity, and thus human rights, while the Soviet Union assaulted both.[28]

Buryk's thinking pointed to the final way in which Republicans utilized human rights, mainly as a weapon in the Cold War. Buryk wanted Republicans to make the Soviets live up to the Helsinki Accords: "Western . . . concessions should not be sold at the expense of the basic human rights of people living under totalitarian regimes." American support for human rights in Eastern Europe, according to Buryk, would undermine the Soviet Union and its repression of political dissidents and ethnic nationalities. Daumantz Hazners of the Latvian-American Republican National Federation made a similar plea: "We urge the Republican Party to insist that the Soviet Union lives up to the spirit of the Helsinki Agreement and respect basic human rights."[29] Republican ethnic organizations, then, saw human rights both as a benchmark that the United States should force the Soviets to live up to and as a rhetorical, anticommunist hammer with which to pound the Soviets.

While Ford and Kissinger would have disagreed, it soon became clear in the final platform that others in the GOP also trumpeted this line. Jesse Helms and his chief aide John East—officially uncommitted to Ford or Reagan in 1976 but sympathetic to the latter and pushing a stringent brand of conservatism—wrote a plank called "Morality in Foreign Policy" that addressed human rights issues. Helms and East declared that the "goal of Republican foreign policy is the achievement of liberty under law and a just and lasting peace in the world." They asserted that any negotiations with the Soviets under the guise of détente "must not grant unilateral favors with only the hope of getting future favors in return." Finally, they went on to declare that Republican foreign policy had to respect "the rights of man, the rule of law, and guidance by the hand of god."[30] This section did not use the term "human rights" but instead offered detailed praise for the Soviet dissident and author Alexander Solzhenitsyn. Solzhenitsyn's writings described how the Soviet system crushed individuals spiritually and physically. His vivid portrayals of Soviet totalitarianism won him the Nobel Prize for literature in 1970 but also made him a target of the Soviet security apparatus. In 1974, the Soviets deported him and he began a long exile in the West. By 1976, Solzhenitsyn was a hero to conservative Republicans and practically the embodiment of the idea of human rights. Solzhenitsyn's prominence was amplified among conservatives because President Ford refused in 1975 to meet with him at the White House for fear of upsetting the Soviet government. Conservatives railed against Ford's decision, which they saw as the president helping the Soviet government to crush an individual's rights.[31] "Morality in Foreign Policy," then, was a human rights plank in all but name.

As Republicans debated foreign policy specifics, fault lines emerged on human rights issues that pitted liberal against conservative Republicans. The original draft of the platform's section on Korea read, "We encourage the Government of South Korea to institute domestic policy initiatives leading to the extension of basic human rights." This somewhat remarkable sentence had Republicans criticizing an anticommunist ally on the front lines of the Cold War. Albert Lee Smith, a conservative Republican from Alabama who would go on to Congress (1981–1983) and focus on social issues,[32] successfully amended the platform so that it encouraged both North and South Korea—the former being a thorn in the side of the United States—to work toward human rights.[33] Later, Smith won a change to the platform's statement on China, which was amended so that Republicans stated, "we are hopeful that basic human rights will be extended to the Chinese People."[34] But there were limits to this human rights talk in foreign policy. Representative Conte suggested that the committee adopt a basic amendment supporting human rights in all countries. Defeated on that score, he asked for a specific amendment recognizing the human rights violations in Chile, Argentina, and Uruguay, countries whose anticommunist governments allied with the United States in the Cold War. Conte's proposals resembled, in their approach and targets, the policies that congressional Democratic liberals advocated throughout the 1970s, though he did not acknowledge this connection. Conte lost that battle as well, largely because Republicans, led by the Goldwater ally Fred Streetman of Florida, worried that addressing human rights across Latin America would have the effect of watering down criticisms of communist

Cuba. The platform's message was clear: with the exception of the inclusion of South Korea, human rights would not be used to criticize America's Cold War allies or be held as a general benchmark of U.S. foreign policy, but instead would be a tool to criticize communist countries.[35]

The platform's foreign policy pronouncements must have looked familiar to one group of pioneering human rights activists: the neoconservatives. Neoconservatism was not quite the same as conservatism in the Republican Party. For instance, Republican conservatives despised the welfare state and wanted to destroy it, while neoconservatives objected to certain aspects of it, but approved of other social safety net provisions. More important, many neoconservatives in the 1970s were still Democrats, hoping that their party could be reformed to embrace a tough-minded and pragmatic liberalism at home and abroad. In other words, they were not Republicans. But, in the late 1970s, many neoconservatives were beginning their voyage into the GOP.[36] Part of the attraction was surely based on a shared definition of human rights and a common belief in how human rights principles ought to be applied in foreign policy.

On the domestic side, when the party platform addressed the questions of abortion and the Equal Rights Amendment, it most certainly did not embrace the human rights language that had found its way into the public forums. There was no mention of using human rights as a mechanism to expand the benefits of citizenship. Instead, the GOP took another path, one that had little to do with human rights talk during the previous months. Under a heading titled "Responsibilities," Republicans declared: "Finally, the most basic principle of all: Achievement and preservation of human rights in our society is based on the willing acceptance by millions of Americans of their responsibilities as free citizens. Instead of viewing government programs with ever increasing expectations, we must readily assume the obligations of wage-earners, taxpayers and supporters of our government and laws. This is often forgotten, and so it is appropriate to remind ourselves in this Platform that this is why our society works."[37] It is not clear from where, or from whom, this telling and significant language originated. Human rights were not a vehicle for expanding political or social rights, nor did they express rights consciousness or support for ethnic diversity. Human rights were the product of a certain type of active and engaged citizenship in which citizens fulfilled the "obligations" of work, of law and order, and of paying taxes. Just as important, the platform defined human rights in opposition to the state. That is, human rights were most clearly expressed and honored when individuals eschewed reliance on government and its programs in favor of exercising their "responsibilities as free citizens."

President Ford won the nomination, but in many ways he lost the platform. The same might be said of the hopes of moderates and liberals when it came to the party's statement of principles. On some issues, to be sure, Ford and his allies triumphed. On the ERA, the Rights and Responsibilities Subcommittee narrowly approved an anti-ERA plank, only to see it overturned by the larger Platform Committee as the Ford forces, moderates, and liberals exerted their strength.[38] The abortion issue was less clear-cut: the platform was more pro-life than pro-choice, though it recognized that both positions had advocates within the GOP.

But on human rights, in both foreign policy and domestic affairs, the platform reported the views of conservatives much more than the left wing of the party. Indeed, as the convention concluded, it was clear which definitions of human rights, and which faction within the GOP, was in ascendance. In the domestic arena, human rights concerns that referenced an expansion of political or civil rights along the lines of the rights-consciousness of the previous decade suffered setbacks, as conservatives in the party made real gains in reversing sometimes long-held Party stances on these social issues. Instead, the party's platform couched human rights, at least as a domestic issue, within the paradigm of citizenship, but with an emphasis on the citizen's responsibilities and obligations rather than rights. Just as telling, the GOP's foreign policy agenda pointed to the important link between anticommunism and human rights. Conservatives in the party repeatedly inserted human rights language that critiqued and criticized communist countries and lauded a human rights activist who blasted the Soviet system. At the same time, those conservatives turned back attempts by liberals to forge a place for a more expansive definition of human rights within the GOP's foreign policy.

Human Rights, Ronald Reagan, and the GOP in the Late 1970s

President Gerald Ford lost the presidential election of 1976 to Democrat Jimmy Carter. As president, Carter chose to make human rights a focal point of American foreign policy. While Carter and his supporters advocated a different definition of human rights than the GOP and conservatives in 1976, his foreign policy program gives more evidence of human rights' vitality in the late 1970s. The human rights movement outside the White House—in Congress and among transnational NGOs—continued apace as well.

Republicans, with a Democrat in the White House for the first time in eight years, began to plot their future course. The conservative movement in the late 1970s continued to gain momentum. Phyllis Schlafly's campaign against the ERA garnered more attention and success. An antitax movement that began in California and won a groundbreaking reduction in property taxes in 1978 spread across the country. Finally, Ronald Reagan emerged from the convention with his reputation intact and with a fervent base of supporters and admirers in the party. His position as the GOP's leader only solidified in the wake of Ford's loss in the general election. Over the next few years, Reagan prepared for a run at the presidency in 1980. He strategized with his political advisors, deepened his connections to key GOP leaders and the Republican faithful, and continued to introduce himself to the general electorate. This latter task was important: some polling showed that while Reagan was the most popular Republican among the GOP, Ford, at least in 1978, was more popular among all voters.[39] Thus, Reagan maintained an active public presence in the late 1970s. He wrote a newspaper column, delivered regular radio commentaries (which he often wrote) on current events, and gave speeches to almost every group and organization imaginable.[40]

These activities gave Reagan ample opportunity to comment on human rights. This appears to have been a real change for Reagan, because during his 1976 campaign he did not focus much on human rights issues or pursue human rights rhetoric with any real force. Reagan, unsurprisingly, frequently lambasted Ford's foreign policy. He lamented what he saw as the United States' failure to maintain its "military superiority" in the face of growing Soviet capabilities, and called for accelerated development of weapons systems.[41] He blasted détente as a "one way street" in which the Soviets accrued all of the benefits while the United States sacrificed its position and ideals.[42] And, famously, he critiqued Ford's negotiations with Panama over the canal, claiming, "We bought it, we paid for it, we built it, and we intend to keep it."[43] With détente and Panama, Reagan danced around some of the staples of human rights rhetoric and ideas. He claimed that the Helsinki Accords were "our stamp of approval on Russia's enslavement of the captive nations. . . . We gave away the freedom of millions of people—freedom that was not ours to give."[44] On Panama, Reagan objected to the United States negotiating with General Omar Torrijos. "The dictator of Panama," Reagan declared, "seized power eight years ago by ousting the duly-elected government. There have been no elections since. No civil liberties. The press is censored. Torrijos is a friend and ally of Castro and, like him, is pro-Communist."[45] In both cases, Reagan highlighted the sanctity of "freedom," "civil liberties," and "elections"— all hallmarks of human rights thinking on both the political right and left. But he never identified these explicitly as human rights, nor did he find a way to explore human rights' place in American politics and foreign policy.

Reagan's thinking began to change and to expand in 1977. In a series of speeches, radio talks, and newspaper columns that appeared over the next few years, Reagan started to articulate a human rights agenda. Why did Reagan begin to delve more deeply into human rights? A few reasons suggest themselves. His allies in the party—conservatives like Jesse Helms—had adopted certain human rights positions; thus, Reagan, as the country's leading conservative, had political reasons to think about human rights. Likewise, positioning himself on human rights allowed Reagan to differentiate himself from the Ford-Nixon wing of the party. At the same time, Reagan took up this task in part as a response to President Carter's human rights initiatives. Indeed, Reagan delivered a major speech on human rights in June 1977 in New York City that essentially offered a rejoinder to Carter's noteworthy speech on U.S. foreign policy, and the place of human rights within it, at Notre Dame earlier that spring.

Most important, Reagan addressed human rights as part of his larger program for U.S. foreign policy and his critical assessment of the state of world affairs. Reagan consistently praised patriotism and celebrated American exceptionalism as he urged the country to take a more forceful and righteous position in global politics. He bashed the Soviet Union and ridiculed the claims of communism. He promoted a strong American foreign policy and demanded enhanced American military capabilities in order to meet what he saw as a growing Soviet and communist threat. He offered encouragement to America's Cold War allies and scorn for those countries that either sympathized or allied with the Soviets. None of these positions were all that surprising as Reagan had made these points in the years before and would continue to do so into his presidency. But when Reagan spoke about human rights, he almost always placed it within this larger strategic and rhetorical framework. Human rights, as defined by Reagan, could be a part of (but by no means the centerpiece of) his larger ideological and policy agenda, especially in relation to the Soviet Union.

Reagan's thinking on human rights in the late 1970s consisted of a few elements. In Reagan's worldview, the countries and leaders who most violated human rights all were American opponents in the Cold War. East Germany and Cuba abused their citizens, while in "communist China . . . the violation of human rights is confirmed by literally thousands of stories told by escapees."[46] And of course, the Soviet Union, whose human rights abuses at home were matched, according to Reagan, by their efforts abroad. Reagan asked, "Is there any doubt about the fate of human rights if Southern Africa falls into the orbit of the Soviet Union and becomes, in the next few years, a series of Russian client states?"[47] The one exception was Panama, where Reagan continued his line of attack from 1976, wondering why the United States would turn over the canal to a government that routinely violated human rights.[48]

American human rights policies, Reagan, believed should reflect these realities. Thus, he decried what he saw as "hypocrisy" in U.S. policies: a willingness to excuse the human rights violations of adversaries in the hopes of improving relations with them while focusing on the supposed human rights shortcomings of American allies.[49] As Reagan declared in 1977, "the new Administration's foreign policy has aimed most of its human rights criticisms at governments which are no threat to others and which, despite not always behaving precisely as we might like, have nevertheless been our friends."[50] Reagan, then, accused the Carter administration of excusing Castro's human rights violations in Cuba in the name of opening a dialogue, but at the same time cutting off aid to President Somoza of Nicaragua for violating human rights. Reagan declared that he was not certain if Somoza had "violated our standards of human rights," but he was sure that the "revolutionary forces who are fighting against his regime are Marxists for the most part and many were trained and armed by Castro's Cuba."[51] It was this inconsistency—and its jarring departure from his larger strategic worldview—that Reagan found inexcusable.

Reagan made clear that while human rights were important, they were also somewhat of a secondary concern. "If our concern for basic human rights is to be fulfilled," Reagan explained, "there must be a favorable world environment in which we can pursue it. Only if we are ready to meet challenges—peacefully and effectively—from those who have a quite different view of mankind, can we meet our destiny as a free people. And, only by remaining second to none in our defense capability will we have that opportunity."[52] This line of thought—the larger strategic goal of creating a favorable world environment through a strong defense would create an opportunity for human rights to flourish—was revealing. In his speech at Notre Dame on human rights, President Carter had made a contradictory assertion, mainly that stabilization in world affairs would come only when the United States and others honored human rights. Thus, for Carter, unlike Reagan, human rights were of primary importance.[53]

On these scores, Reagan found common cause with the evolving neoconservative position on human rights. Neoconservatives despised Carter's Notre Dame speech, seeing it as too conciliatory toward the Soviets and not reflective of the hard-minded approach to world affairs that they advocated. Carter's foreign policy did little to assuage them in the years that followed.[54] By then, Jeane Kirkpatrick had articulated the most well-known neoconservative position in her November 1979 article "Dictatorships and Double Standards" for *Commentary*.[55] In that piece, Kirkpatrick asserted that Carter's foreign policy and human rights initiatives held American allies to higher standards of conduct than the Soviets, with whom the president was eager to seek détente and arms agreements. Kirkpatrick argued that Carter had weakened allies in Iran and Nicaragua instead of buttressing these stalwart (if flawed) authoritarian anticommunist allies who might, in time, reform politically. Ultimately, Kirkpatrick believed that Carter had applied human rights principles in a way that weakened America's strategic position in the Cold War. Reagan had made many of these same critiques as early as June 1977. Neoconservatives, then, found a lot to like in Reagan's human rights agenda.

Finally, Reagan outlined in these years a definition of human rights. At times, Reagan equated human rights simply with "freedom."[56] But, Reagan also made clear that the foundation of human rights was clearly political and civil rights. People had rights to "assembly, expression, and association," the right to a fair "judicial process,"[57] and the right to leave one's country.[58] Reagan also highlighted the sanctity of the body and the right to be free from torture and physical abuse as human rights. In Panama, "electric shocks . . . physical beatings . . . threat of rape . . . and long interrogation of prisoners while denying them food, water, or sleep" were regular occurrences. In East Germany, political dissidents and those hoping to leave were imprisoned, sentenced to solitary confinement, forcibly fed while on hunger strikes, and physically abused. This focus on political and civil rights, torture, and the sanctity of the body was not outside the norm of human rights language in the late 1970s. Other organizations like Amnesty International defined human rights in much the same way. The difference between these groups and Reagan was that the exgovernor seemingly applied these human rights standards only to communist nations.

Reagan's human rights' thinking, though, was not limited to foreign policy. Indeed, he unveiled one other aspect of his definition of human rights that was both uniquely domestic in orientation and the province of conservatives: he tied human rights to the distrust of government and the state. Reagan noted "the decline of the Western concepts of political responsibility and individual freedom" and suggested that "perhaps President Carter, in his quest for human rights, has recognized this decline and wants to reverse it." Even more clearly, Reagan asked that the United States continue to be guided by "our historic desire for all men and women to share in our tradition of individual human rights and freedom, with government the servant and not the master."[59] On this point, Reagan made the case, even more starkly than the 1976 Republican platform, that the foundation of human rights was a particular relationship between government and the individual that privileged the latter in comparison to the former.

Republicans and Human Rights at the End of the 1970s

While Republicans in the 1950s and 1960s largely avoided human rights issues, more and more of the party addressed—and even embraced—them after 1976. Some of this attention was surely expected; human rights had gained a more prominent footing in American politics by the mid-1970s, and Republicans would have been foolish to ignore their power. But given the Party's longer mid-twentieth-century history of failing to engage with human rights principles, the events of the late 1970s stand out in sharp relief. Just as striking, the definitions of human rights and policies associated with them narrowed considerably among Republicans in the late 1970s. At the 1976 convention, Republicans were in some sense a "big tent party" when it came to human rights. An ideologically splintered GOP offered multiple conceptions of human rights attached to a variety of policy agendas. Conservatives at the convention made much headway, though, in imposing their vision of human rights, in both foreign policy and in domestic affairs. The conservatives' chosen candidate, Ronald Reagan, sharpened this vision in the following years as he began his long march toward the presidency. Of course, Reagan's ascent in the GOP was accompanied by the marginalization of liberals and moderates within the party, and the marginalization of their version of human rights politics and policies.

By the end of the decade, then, a more conservative Republican Party—symbolized by Reagan—had embraced a particular set of human rights beliefs.

In foreign policy, the GOP argued that human rights were largely traditional political, civil, and legal rights. More important, Republicans linked these human rights to anticommunism and argued that the value of human rights lay largely in the American prosecution of the Cold War and the protection of American strategic interests relating to that conflict. In domestic affairs, Republicans increasingly saw human rights as part of their powerful advocacy of antistatism. Republicans held that honoring and supporting human rights in the United States could only be accomplished through the proper relationship between the state and the individual, one in which the former made limited demands upon the latter.

The development of a conservative Republican position on human rights had important consequences as the GOP assumed power in the 1980s. For one, the relationship between conservative Republicans and the neoconservatives matured as the neoconservative march into the Republican Party accelerated after 1980. Several prominent neoconservatives—including Richard Perle, Jeane Kirkpatrick, Elliott Abrams (who became assistant secretary of state for human rights and humanitarian affairs)—joined the Reagan administration and left the Democratic Party. The groundwork for that neoconservative-conservative partnership, though, was laid in the late 1970s, when conservatives and Reagan began articulating a human rights agenda very much in tune with neoconservative thinking.

The Reagan Administration put into action the human rights principles that conservatives trumpeted in the late 1970s. In the domestic realm, Reagan famously announced in his inauguration the foundational tenet of many of his policies: "Government is not the solution to our problem, government is the problem."[60] Although his inaugural pronouncement was not framed as a human rights message, it was a direct descendent of his late 1970s assertions that linked human rights to powerful antistatism. In foreign policy, the links between the 1970s and 1980s were even more direct. The Reagan administration during the first term turned a blind eye to human rights abuses committed by American allies. Nowhere was this more evident than in South and Central America, where anticommunist governments embarked on brutal campaigns that repressed leftist opponents, sometimes with genocidal results as in Guatemala. During its second term, the administration moved to a more aggressive human rights stance, mainly a policy of democracy promotion in the Americas that emphasized the protection of political and civil rights. In the Cold War, President Reagan called the Soviet Union to account for its human rights shortcomings: the suppression of political and civil rights; the lack of religious freedom behind the Iron Curtain; and the Soviet government's refusal to let dissidents emigrate. Indeed, even as Cold War tensions between the Americans and Soviets lessened in the mid to late 1980s, Reagan continued to press Soviet leaders on these human rights issues.[61] In these ways, the Reagan administration fulfilled the conservative human rights agenda of the late 1970s and completed the turn away from the breadth of human rights thinking that the GOP had displayed in 1976.

Chapter 10

The Polish Opposition, the Crisis of the
Gierek Era, and the Helsinki Process

Gunter Dehnert

When Edward Gierek succeeded Władysław Gomułka as first secretary of the Central Committee of the Polish United Workers' Party (PUWP) following the bloody suppression of the workers' uprisings on the Polish Baltic coast in late 1970, living conditions in Poland temporarily improved to a considerable degree. The 45 dead and about 1,100 injured at Gdańsk and Szczecin were a horrific way of conceding failure by Gomułka, who had returned as a beacon of hope to head the party in October 1956.[1] The revolts on December 13, 1970, came as a response to the drastic raising of food prices, which the Politburo saw as unavoidable. The price increases were due not least to the priority given to certain industries on ideological grounds. The preferred industries either represented opportunities for modernization or, as in the case of the heavy industry, were expected to continue the country's industrialization. In particular the already neglected food and consumer goods industries suffered from this bias. The price of meat occupied a symbolic status in the eyes of the public and would continue to do so during future crises in the People's Republic of Poland.[2] Besides poor provisions, the chronic housing shortage also proved to be a pressing issue.

Yet the appearance of an internationally famous Polish opposition after 1975 continues to surprise. Most accounts focus on 1976, when the Workers' Defense Committee (Komitet Obrony Robotników, KOR) was founded in response to the workers' uprisings in Ursus and Radom; this group helped make human rights and civil society world famous. Daniel C. Thomas described this phenomenon as the "Helsinki effect."[3] According to his interpretation, the signing of the Helsinki Final Act in August 1975 initiated a process that almost inevitably undermined the foundations of the socialist self-conception. Thomas sees this as the only perspective from which to adequately explain why Communist control was conspicuously dwindling from the mid-1980s on in the eastern part of Europe. After all, the Gorbachev factor[4] cannot on its own plausibly account for the emergence of democratic states during the process of transformation after 1989. The contemporaneous economic decline and falling living standards did not make themselves felt so quickly in the mid-1980s that they would have made the economic reforms inevitable, much less caused the revolutions of 1989: "Unsatisfied social demands and external geopolitical pressures also cannot explain why one-party Communist rule died in the way and when it did."[5] All the same, the agency of an international human rights regime—which is after all what the Conferenceon Security and Cooperation in Europe (CSCE) was, though not exclusively—cannot be reduced to that of a deus ex machina.[6]

Instead, its role should be analyzed in conjunction with the other factors and within a larger framework. Above all, it would be a gross overestimation of the reach of Moscow's centralized Communist power to interpret the global phenomenon of the Helsinki effect without differentiating between the situations in the individual member states of the Warsaw Pact.[7] As this essay will show, the economic crisis in the People's Republic of Poland developed already in the mid-1970s rather than only in the mid-1980s, making major concessions necessary. The emergence of the largest protest movement in the Soviet bloc can also hardly be regarded independent of that crisis. Long-standing traditional ties also played a vital role in the shaping of each key opposition movement, in Poland not least.

The Polish Opposition in National and Transnational Interpretations

In interpreting the transformation of the Polish opposition, two historiographical approaches have predominated. One is a nationalist perspective that places it in the continuity of Polish history. Another, most prominently represented by Thomas, assigns almost magical significance to the Helsinki

Accords. Both of these approaches are valuable, but neither is without its flaws.

One approach attempts to interpret the first real antiregime movement in a socialist country as a phenomenon determined by the inner logic of Polish national history. This historical narrative ascribes critical importance to what the opposition learned from the tactical and strategic mistakes of previous uprisings during the "Polish months": the de-Stalinization process within the PUWP in October 1956 in the aftermath of the bloody strikes in Poznań in June of that year; the student unrest in March 1968, which was accompanied by an anti-Semitic campaign by the government; and the riots on the Polish Baltic coast in December 1970, likewise overshadowed by fatalities.[8] This approach identifies 1976 as the pivotal year, not least owing to the KOR's founding.[9]

While this first interpretation places the emphasis on the pursuit of independence, a second interpretation focuses on universal human rights as the binding factor among oppositional tendencies. Without questioning the fundamentals of the internal Polish interpretation, which by now enjoys almost canonical status within Polish historiography and in the self-conception of most oppositional players, the following will attempt to produce a kind of synthesis between this explanatory model and the approach based strictly on foreign policy.

In my view, the Polish opposition's evolution up to August 1980 cannot be understood without taking into account its metamorphosis in the years following 1968. The opposition's success was nevertheless fundamentally determined by events that would not have been possible without the international reach of the new phase of détente, which manifested itself in the CSCE process. However, the decisive year is 1975, by which time the foundations of the new opposition movement were already in place. The new possibilities of oppositional behavior were tentatively being tested during the constitutional dispute that immediately followed the signing of the Helsinki Final Act. Moreover, the consumption-oriented socialist approach that Gierek had been advocating as the panacea to societal problems since December 1970, and which may be understood as the Polish equivalent of Czechoslovakian normalization and Hungarian "goulash communism," only further weakened Poland's already tenuous bond with socialist ideology.[10] In this sense the Polish attempt to achieve welfare socialism, with its astonishing degree of openness in the cultural sphere despite the presence of censorship, resembled Hungary more closely than either East Germany or Czechoslovakia, which were hardly willing to make ideological concessions.[11]

Moreover, it is crucial to integrate the insights of the existing literature into a larger framework that restores Eastern Europe to the history of the 1970s. In the last few years, historians have identified various social, economic, political as well as religious events and trends in an effort to emphasize the decade as a watershed that manifested itself in crisis phenomena.[12] Alleged symptoms of that crisis included the report published in 1972 by the Club of Rome, entitled *The Limits to Growth*,[13] and the oil price shock of 1973. In this account, the increasing secularization of society as well as the breakdown of traditional gender roles and the family unit sometimes also play a role. The awareness that an apparently ceaseless growth may come to an end—in addition to the unprecedented mass unemployment in the wake of increasing automation—is central to the search for historical classification.[14] But there is one large flaw with the current fashion: since this historiographical turn has focused solely on Western welfare states, it cannot contribute to explaining the collapse of the Soviet bloc or the reorganization of Europe after 1989–1991.[15]

An explanatory model according to which the Eastern economies lost contact with Western economic development and thus fell increasingly behind seems to be insufficient to account for the erosion of those economies for two reasons. First, it neglects the increasing integration between the various economies as a result of détente beginning in the early 1970s. At the time, it seemed plausible that the Eastern European states might catch up with the West on the basis of credit and technology transfers. However, there is the danger of losing sight of parallel though not equally strong tendencies in the development of individual societies when assessing the Eastern bloc's failures. Both of these objections are particularly relevant to the People's Republic of Poland in the 1970s. Although it can hardly be called a "post-boom" period since the Polish economy increasingly stagnated in the 1960s (the time of the "little stabilization"), Poland's palpable upswing in the early 1970s—sometimes referred to as the time of the "large stabilization"—culminated in a crisis by the middle of the decade, causing much deprivation and discontent.[16] This economic reversal proved decisive.

It was Gierek's leadership in navigating both the economic situation and the international diplomatic situation that created the conjectural situation in which the Helsinki effect became thinkable. His policies made clear that Poland suddenly cast its glance beyond the Eastern bloc in the second half of the decade, under the joint impact of economic and financial dependence and the incipient CSCE process.[17] That is the main reason for the Polish leadership's reluctance to deal with the opposition movement, which was steadily growing in plain sight. The new evolutionism that Adam Michnik promoted in his epoch-making speech in Paris in September 1976 was only applicable to the People's Republic of Poland in the mid-1970s and offered absolutely no solution for other societies of the Soviet bloc.[18] In fact, the balancing act that the Polish state and party leadership had to perform consisted, on the one hand, in sufficiently containing public dissatisfaction so that societal pressure would not erupt into riots and revolts against authority like those of the past. On the other hand, the government had to be careful not to put the system itself at risk by making even more ideological concessions in the People's Republic of Poland than those that had already been made and further extended through Gierek's new approach to politics.

In addition, the Helsinki agreements for the first time established a formal link between the degree of economic cooperation with the West and the observance of human rights at home. Whenever the supply situation worsened, as was the case from 1975 onward, the pressure on the Polish government grew accordingly. Responding to this pressure with unreasonably violent repression would have harmed the country's reputation on human rights issues and may have caused Western countries to revoke loans and economic aid. This would only have further exacerbated the supply situation and thus led to new potential conflicts. But when the government refrained from overt repression for this reason, the most active Polish opposition groups seized the opportunity to gradually expand their influence, as they would from 1976 to 1977 and after. They challenged the party's power monopoly as well as its hegemony over public opinion and as a consequence damaged the party's perception of its own role in a socialist state.

The Polish Opposition After 1968

Gierek, who had already acquired a reputation as a successful pragmatist in his home voivodeship in Upper Silesia, was the quintessential manager with a socialist slant. His willingness to set aside ideological concerns enabled him to address the fundamental grievances of the striking workers. Without apologizing for the harsh measures taken by the security forces, he announced in his first televised address on December 20, 1970, a new comprehensive social, wage, and economic policy. Wages would be increased, food prices frozen or even reduced, and the housing situation improved. In other words, Gierek put his predecessor's entire five-year plan into question.[19] Although isolated strike actions, such as the one in Łódź in February 1971, threatened from time to time to derail the reform process, Gierek managed to turn public opinion in his favor. Eventually the price increases from December were also revoked.[20] The Sixth Congress of the PUWP was moved up to December 1971, and the passage of the new five-year plan endorsed the revisions that had already been carried out during the course of that year. It was also now at least generally possible to honor the promises that had been made during the process.

As Gierek readjusted the economy, he was also propelled by the success of détente, especially after the signing of the Treaty of Warsaw with the Federal Republic of Germany in 1970. For instance, in the first five years of the Gierek government, that is, up to 1975, the gross domestic product grew by 39 percent, real wages rose by 41.5 percent, and industrial production doubled.[21] Turning away from a further expansion of heavy industry in favor of the consumer goods industry noticeably raised the quality of life. This rebound, however, came at a price of considerable new indebtedness and a huge trade deficit with Western states. It should consequently come as no surprise that crises in the Western industrialized nations had an impact—somewhat delayed—on Polish society.[22] Contemporary discourse on the internal state of the People's Republic of Poland was already dominated by the notion of crisis itself.[23] At the same time, it now became clear that economic and social reforms had been implemented without any political concessions—such as free trade unions, which had already been demanded during the strikes of 1970.

But the various strands of the Polish opposition remained unconvinced by Gierek's newly declared pragmatism. As in almost all societies of the Warsaw Pact, 1968 was a breaking point in Poland, first and foremost for groups critical of the system. There were two major events that left a lasting impact. First, there was the anti-Semitic campaign precipitated by the protests in March 1968 against the cancellation of national poet Adam Mickiewicz's play *Forefathers' Eve* in Warsaw; second, there was the crushing of the Prague Spring with the participation of Polish troops within the framework of the Warsaw Pact.[24] Especially affected were the progressive, more left-leaning members of the opposition surrounding Adam Michnik and Jacek Kuroń, who a few years earlier had still espoused a revisionist attitude. Many of these so-called nonconformist leftists had been devoted members of the PUWP themselves. They had derived hope from the Eighth Plenum of the PUWP's Central Committee in October 1956 that socialism in Poland was reformable.

When the day of reckoning had come for Stalinism and its aberrations, their optimism seemed justified as concessions were made toward a plurality of opinions.

But once the system had stabilized again, it soon became apparent that Gomułka was not willing to consent to genuine democratization. Kuroń's criticism reached its most potent expression with his 1964 open letter to the party, highly regarded in the West, which he coauthored with Karol Modzelewski.[25] Even this letter, however, reveals a desire to save socialism itself, as the authors decry the working class's lack of influence and the usurpation of power by a small caste of party officials. It was not the Western sense of democracy and human rights that dictated their actions at this stage.

All the same, they received lengthy prison sentences in 1965. During Kuroń's second term of imprisonment, which he served for taking a strong stance against Michnik's expulsion from Warsaw University, he reluctantly turned away from his earlier ideals: "I think that by November 1970 I developed my own model, and I saw with great regret that it was no longer compatible with Marxism. I came to the conclusion that I had to stop being a Marxist."[26] Adam Michnik made an attempt to put the Polish March in perspective during a public lecture in February 1981, at the height of the Solidarność (Solidarity) movement: "For most of those . . . who were involved with the March events, March 1968 marks the decisive end of the 'small stabilization' . . ., concluding an era in which their attitudes and expectations entirely coalesced around the circle of power and the establishment, and when only those of the highest principles concerned themselves with drawing the ethical line that was not to be crossed unless you were a swine. . . . In the consciousness of my generation, that March also signified the shattering of 1956's illusions."[27]

Michnik also connected the rapprochement between the Catholic milieu and the nonconformist left with the process of coming to terms with the March events. Both sides developed empathy for each other in the ensuing years, which prepared the ground for a dialogue.[28] Jan Józef Lipski, who as an interwar Polish social democrat belonged to the older generation within the opposition, also thought that the shift in consciousness that took place among the supporters of the unrest was critical: "March 1968 led to a dramatic change in consciousness, especially among the young student cohorts of the time. The movement of 'Airborne Troops' came into being within circles influenced by 'revisionist' ideology—the desire to renew, humanize and democratize Marxism—and by the conviction that the political order created by

Bolshevism was reformable. . . . A large portion of the youth was wrested away from Bolshevik ideology once and for all."[29]

East Central Europe's salutary shock over the true nature of communism was crucial for the formation of a genuine democratic opposition movement, a movement that would finally be prepared in the 1970s to reach out to the traditional forces in Polish society, especially to those within political Catholicism.[30] By 1976, Michnik considered the developing alliance solid enough for both sides within the opposition to adopt mutual objectives that were also to be jointly articulated. His book *The Church and the Left* documented the arrival at a common ground based on a set of shared values.[31] Moving beyond ideological differences, the cohesive force in this new venture was to be an ethos rooted in a commitment to basic human and civil rights.

A Helsinki Effect?

By the mid-1970s, at the latest, a profound process of intellectual disillusionment had reached its completion within the dominant oppositional milieu. Moreover, the organizational preconditions were largely already in place for the period after 1975. The tenor and modus operandi of the future opposition movement were anticipated most explicitly in Kuroń's essay "Polityczna opozycja w Polsce" (Political Opposition in Poland), which appeared in 1974 in *Kultura*, the most important émigré magazine that was also widely circulated in Poland.[32]

According to Kuroń, the "political opposition in Poland" was characterized by "an anti-totalitarian and independence-seeking attitude."[33] The article also mentions specific forms of action that could serve oppositional goals: expanding samizdat activity following the Soviet model as well as participating in a free and open literary, theater, and cabaret scene. In this context, the opposition itself was supposed to act in unison without thinking uniformly.[34] Its members were to subscribe to a common ethos that would allow them to "take a public stand against the despotism of the authorities—in various matters at official meetings as well as through writing letters and petitions in countrywide matters."[35]

Of course, some of the future trademarks of the new wave of opposition after 1975 were not present yet, such as its deliberately open way of taking action and its formal focus on civil and human rights. The latter, in any case, was never taken quite as rigorously in Poland as in the Helsinki Group in

Moscow; that is, their objectives and demands were seldom strictly and purely legalistic. Oppositional and dissident circles in most countries of the Eastern bloc, including the Soviet Union and Czechoslovakia, experienced a change of direction that was comparable to the one in the Polish opposition after 1968. There, too, the orientation of the movements became more pronounced and their oppositional activity much more intense starting with the mid-1970s. Many new groups were formed during this period, including the Helsinki Group in Moscow and Charter 77 in Czechoslovakia, which now clearly saw themselves as human and civil rights movements.

But the emergence of nonconformist groups in the Communist bloc—whether they now saw themselves as dissenters, dissidents, or oppositionists or were designated as such by the power structure—did not solely result from an internal intellectual process. Equally important was the presence of a favorable international environment. By signing the Final Act in Helsinki on August 1, 1975, all thirty-five participating states committed themselves to principles regulating the state's relationship to its citizens, which inevitably had to affect governmental and legal practice if applied consistently. Together with the seventh principle of the Decalogue, which was appended before the so-called first basket (dealing with matters of European security), the provisions of the third basket constituted the "human dimension" of the CSCE. The seventh principle, on "respect for human rights and fundamental freedoms, including the freedom of thought, conscience, religion or belief," could be read as a condensed catalogue of basic rights.[36]

To be sure, this principle did not offer much beyond the United Nations' Universal Declaration of Human Rights from 1948, which was explicitly invoked here. But the Final Act, although not a contract in terms of international law, was nonetheless more binding. Moreover, the Final Act was also affected by the principle of indivisibility, which applied to all baskets. In the following years, the United States in particular made ample use of a linkage strategy based on that principle in order to obtain concessions in the realm of human rights, artfully taking advantage of the Eastern bloc countries' competing interests in political as well as economic and security issues.[37]

There were also the provisions of the third basket for "cooperation in humanitarian and other areas" in matters of human contacts, information, culture, and education. They specified concrete steps that, if implemented, would have had an indirect effect on socialist societies, making them more open and accelerating processes that were already under way. If nothing else, the clause on the continuation of the CSCE as a process, which would be further discussed at follow-up conferences regarding the provisions' implementation and expansion, meant that the Helsinki Final Act was more than just a piece of paper.

The follow-up conferences in Belgrade (1977–1978) and Madrid (1980–1983) were intended to demonstrate that the implementation of human rights was central to the negotiations. Although the Warsaw Pact countries were well aware of the potentially explosive nature of the provisions that they signed, they nonetheless assumed that the benefits they would derive from the CSCE project were worth the risk.[38]

One should also bear in mind that the CSCE originally started out as a project of the Warsaw Pact. The successful conclusion of the conference therefore in itself represented a major propaganda victory.[39] Poland actually demanded to be recognized as one of the initiators of the conference, claiming that its origins went back to the Rapacki Plan of 1957. Human rights, however, did not initially play a role in the Polish and Soviet conception of a European security conference. In addition, the official propaganda tried to sell the accomplishments of the conference, specifically the recognition of the Oder–Neisse line, as a substitute for a long overdue peace conference.[40] It is likely that unofficially the economic advantages anticipated from the second basket's agreements (on economic cooperation) were of acute importance, especially since the Polish economy began to stagnate in the mid-1970s. Poland's use of the CSCE for propaganda purposes furthermore contributed to raising the Polish population's awareness of the Final Act.[41]

Thus two elements converged in 1975: the commencement of the CSCE process, which was actually conceived without any nongovernmental actors in mind, and a relatively well-consolidated oppositional milieu that was ready to take the offensive within this new framework. This observation is supported by an assessment that the Polish intelligence service put together in 1977:

Since autumn 1974, we have found symptoms of a revival domestically among persons and groups that have already risen up at different times in the past against individual decisions and courses of action connected to the party's policies in areas affecting the sociopolitical and economic life of the country. These symptoms have been reflected in the marked increase in the frequency of mutual meetings and discussions, which—except for the elaboration of a program of anti-Socialist activity—pertain to establishing a shared platform for the collaboration of people with different political histories and views. Participants range from revisionists, liberals, social democrats and the organizers of the 1968 student uprisings to former members of the illegal underground, clerics and other elements that continue to stand for extreme social Right positions.[42]

The report suggests that arriving at this integrated platform would have involved reflecting on the contents of the Helsinki Final Act.[43]

The Polish Opposition After 1975: Constitutional Dispute, the KOR, and the Founding Committees of Free Trade Unions

After the signing of the Helsinki Final Act on August 1, 1975, two events laid the groundwork for conciliation and consolidation with disparate milieus critical of the system, thus contributing to the emergence of the so far most powerful opposition in the Soviet bloc.

Already in 1975, the Central Committee of the PUWP announced constitutional amendments that could justifiably be seen to conflict with the commitments that the government had made voluntarily in Helsinki. Choosing this specific point in time to carry out these long-planned changes can only be attributed to outright misjudgment of the circumstances.[44] The first modification, publicized as an improvement, pertained to ensuring that the party's leading role was defined in the constitution. On the one hand, this measure was aimed toward catching up at last with the brethren states on the way toward higher levels of socialist development. On the other hand, the leadership wanted to resolve conflicts of responsibilities between the government and the party in a way that accorded with the PUWP. The proposed changes were made known at the Eighteenth Plenum of the PUWP's Central Committee on September 4, 1975.[45] A second amendment, which was to affirm the friendly ties of the People's Republic of Poland to the Soviet Union, was proposed in December 1975 at the Seventh Party Congress of the PUWP. A passage was also added that made civil rights contingent on civic obligations. All in all, the drafted amendments conflicted with at least the first, fourth, sixth and seventh principles of the Helsinki Final Act's Decalogue.[46]

In any case, the Central Committee's decisions presented the opposition with an opportunity, after an extended period of self-reflection, to engage once again in public action. In this phase, petitions and appeals to party and government offices were the preferred means to attract attention. The best-known act of protest was the "Letter of the 59" in December 1975.[47] Named after its number of signatories, the letter demanded basic human and civil rights. It also explicitly reminded the government of the Final Act's provisions, noting that "where there is no freedom, there is no peace and no security."[48] This was the first sign that the opposition had set aside its initial skepticism and was quickly recognizing and taking advantage of the opportunities that emerged from the CSCE process.

This trend was confirmed by the more moderate demands of the "Letter of the Seven," which called for the adoption of a new press law that would conform to the spirit of Helsinki.[49] Mieczysław F. Rakowski, a Central Committee member and editor of the progressive (within the official range) magazine *Polityka*, also had to concede in his diary: "It is hard to question these letter writers' reasoning."[50] And Andrzej Friszke, one of Poland's leading contemporary historians, holds that the protest activity surrounding the constitutional amendments had a key role in setting events in motion: "Without this collective experience, which characterized the constitutional campaign, the formation of KOR and other organized opposition groups would have been either impossible or much more difficult."[51]

Another phenomenon of equal importance also emerged in the course of these protests: for the first time, opposition figures with a socialist past marched side by side with the episcopate, which had also penned its own letter of protest in November. In order to appreciate the full significance of this, one has to perceive it in relation to the emergence of Solidarność in 1980. Already at this point, a movement transcending social boundaries was on the horizon, and its shared concern was the advancement of human rights in the People's Republic of Poland. By the first half of 1976, other oppositional tactics were also introduced; Radio Free Europe, the BBC, Voice of America, and the increased presence of samizdat literature galvanized the Western public and media as well as the Polish population.[52] The criticism of the constitutional amendments was equally motivated by unease over the country's lack of sovereignty and by concern for human and civil rights, creating a link between the two issues. The principles of the Final Act covered both concerns as well and established a logical connection on the international level between the observance of human rights and matters of security.

What this protest movement still needed was some form of organization akin to the Helsinki Group in Moscow, which had successfully been established on May 12, 1976, attracting much international attention. The necessary impetus was provided by the third major workers' uprising in Poland after 1945. As the end of the credit-financed economic boom was compounded by the bad harvest of 1975, price increases became unavoidable. On June 24, 1976, Prime Minister Piotr Jaroszewicz announced massive food price increases; the prices of sugar and meat especially soared. Riots broke out the next day at many companies nationwide, the fiercest taking place in the Warsaw suburb of Ursus, in Radom, and in Płock.[53] In Ursus, the workers occupied the important Łódź–Warsaw railway line, while in Radom they set fire to the headquarters of the PUWP's Voivodeship Committee.

The response of the power structure was decisive: the citizens' militia, Milicja Obywatelska, took violent action against the insurgents. In Radom, there were two deaths.[54] The workers involved in the unrest were subsequently browbeaten, harassed, dismissed, and convicted. The course of events thus initially followed the exact pattern of December 1970. What was new was that the official authorities failed to suppress the protest within the population, despite revoking the price increases and conducting a massive propaganda campaign.

The labor question—the central issue for a socialist state system—made its way onto the agenda of the oppositional Polish intelligentsia. The demand for free trade unions had already appeared in the Letter of the 59, and many of its signatories now rushed to the aid of the persecuted workers. They offered them financial and legal help, and, despite being harassed, attended the proceedings against the accused workers and published their reports worldwide. On September 23, 1976, the Workers Defense Committee, the KOR, was founded. The members of this committee—including Adam Michnik, Jacek Kuroń, Jerzy Andrzejewski, Edward Lipiński, Adam Szczypiorski, and Jan Józef Lipski, who were well known and highly respected in the West— covered nearly the entire political spectrum within the Polish opposition. Equally diverse were the members' professional backgrounds, from Catholic priests to lawyers to chemists. The workers themselves were nonetheless still absent.

In the KOR's founding appeal, which contained the names and addresses of all the signatories, the committee's objectives were explicitly tied to the cause of human rights:

> The repression against the workers is a violation of those basic human rights that are recognized in both Polish and international law as

mandatory and inalienable: the right to work, the right to protest, the freedom of expression, the right to assemble, and the right to demonstrate. Therefore, the committee demands amnesty for the condemned and detained workers and the reintegration of the victims of the repression into the workforce. These demands are in accordance with the resolutions of the Bishops Conference from September 9, 1976. The committee calls on the entire population to assert its rights. We firmly believe that by establishing this committee and taking action we are fulfilling a human and patriotic duty and serving a just cause on behalf of our country, its people, and humanity.[55]

This founding proclamation reveals another aspect of the KOR's strategy: the attempt to connect with other social groups as well as to make an impression on the wider population. In its appeal to patriotic sentiments, the text also signalled that the group's agenda could potentially be extended into the political realm, which was indeed carried out later. Like the Helsinki Group in Moscow, however, the KOR initially strove to draw attention to cases of government infringement upon national law or international commitments. In so doing, they were trying to avoid the appearance of a political association opposing the ruling regime. This so-called monitoring was central to all Helsinki Groups. Nonetheless, seeing that such a role was not recognized at all in the single-party state, even this minimalist approach can be regarded as political.

Initially, in the first half of 1977, the government largely met the specific demands concerning the persecuted workers. On February 3, 1977, the government issued a general amnesty for the jailed workers and, after numerous declarations of solidarity in the West, it announced another general amnesty for all political prisoners on July 22, 1977, the national day of the People's Republic of Poland.[56] Meanwhile, the security forces tightened the reins again starting in March 1977. They carried out a large number of house searches and arrests and murdered Stanisław Pyjas, a Krakow student associated with the KOR, even though for the time being this had little effect on the internal political situation. The original intent—to drive a wedge between the interests of the persecuted workers and those of the opposition through an asymmetric approach to the two groups—failed.

Paradoxically, it was precisely this success for the KOR that created a legitimacy crisis in the group. It now proved to be a temporary disadvantage that the KOR had abandoned the original idea of founding a committee for the defense of human rights and derived its own goals specifically from the events of June 1976 instead of following the Moscow example and basing them on the Helsinki process.[57] In retrospect, linking the human rights issue to the labor issue has to be regarded as one of the reasons for the Polish opposition movement's success, but in mid-1977 it presented a problem. By renaming KOR the Committee for Social Self-Defense (KSS "KOR"), the supporters of an active program to make human rights a reality and to build democracy finally gained the upper hand within the organization. They laid special emphasis, for instance, on the notion of the self-organization of society and on self-teaching programs for workers and students offered by the Society of Science Courses (Towarzystwo Kursów Naukowych).[58]

Since this path was mainly advocated by members with a revisionist past, groups were later formed that placed independence more at the center of their political program. An important factor in this process of diversification was a sense of mistrust toward KOR members, whose initial enculturation had been decidedly socialist. The new groups included the Movement for the Defense of Human and Civil Rights, ROPCiO (Ruch Obrony Praw Człowieka i Obywatela), and later the Confederation for an Independent Poland, KPN (Konfederacja Polski Niepodległej).[59] What all groups, including the increasingly important Catholic intellectuals, still had in common was their concern for the observance of human rights in Poland—ROPCiO even included the concept in its name. They incessantly emphasized human rights in their unofficial publications and their social activities and thus familiarized the general population with the concept.

Shortly before the first amnesty was declared in Poland on January 8, 1977, in the Moscow metro eight people were killed and more than forty others injured in a bomb explosion. The Soviet authorities tried to establish a connection between this terrorist act and, among others, the members of the Moscow Helsinki Group. This maneuver preceded a series of arrests and put an end to the general leniency toward the Helsinki movement within the Soviet Union. By imposing lengthy prison sentences and sending dissidents into exile, the government was able to silence the majority of opposition members and sympathizers. The operations of the Moscow Helsinki Group, the symbol of the international Helsinki movement, were reduced to a minimum by the early 1980s. In 1982, Elena Bonner, Andrei Sakharov's wife, together with the other two remaining members, finally put an end to the group's activities.[60]

That is to say, just when the KOR was able to claim its greatest success to date, the Moscow leadership delivered a powerful blow against the internal

Soviet dissidents. Charter 77, which was launched in Czechoslovakia in January 1976 and explicitly invoked the Helsinki Final Act in its founding statement, also encountered intense repressive measures from the start. The relatively subdued response of the Polish government to the opposition movements needs to be accounted for, all the more so since the Polish national security apparatus did apparently consider a similar solution at some point. The main reason was that the People's Republic of Poland was indirectly more dependent on its international reputation than the Soviet Union. The indivisibility of peace, a principle established in the Helsinki Final Act through the equal treatment of all three baskets, created a situation where Poland had to assume a pioneering role within the Soviet bloc in the observance of human rights so that a favorable economic climate would emerge.[61] Gierek and Rakowski, for instance, also clearly relished the demonstratively friendly relations with Western politicians, who were often invited to Warsaw as guests in the second half of the 1970s.

Forced by American president Jimmy Carter's aggressive human rights policy, Polish foreign policy now became constantly self-conscious about the country's international reputation. Certainly not everything could be directly attributed to the CSCE process, but none of this would have been conceivable without it, including the path that Carter took. As a report compiled by the Polish Interior Ministry put it: "The new administration sees the Helsinki Final Act as an important and welcome leverage point for placing political pressure on the Socialist countries."[62] This approach, as the report went on to explain, was only based on a selective reading of the Final Act's provisions, focusing only on the humanitarian concerns.[63] The common, decades-old objection among the socialist states that the West was interfering in their internal affairs no longer held water, for the Final Act was designed with the intention that the equal weight of all principles and provisions in the three baskets should be vital to the continuation of the CSCE process.

The interplay between the international framework and the difficult economic conditions in the People's Republic incidentally helped create a favorable environment for the Polish opposition. The relative restraint of the Polish security forces allowed the Polish opposition to plant their ideas in the public mind during the four and a half years following the middle of 1977. They drafted appeals to the signatory states of the CSCE, gave numerous interviews to Western television and radio stations as well as to the print media, and reached out to embassies in Warsaw.

In addition, exiled Poles in Western Europe and North America collected money to support the efforts within the country. They tried to report on their activities through Western radio stations offering Polish-language programs. Above all, they provided information on political persecutions and other human rights violations. All these efforts influenced public opinion in Western countries and thus also Western governments, which in turn applied pressure on the government in Warsaw. The exiled Poles also promptly utilized the information they received at the follow-up conferences in Belgrade and Madrid.

Taking over the monitoring function of the Moscow Helsinki Group, the KOR regarded itself as part of the international Helsinki network. They also made this clear by their expressions of solidarity with other dissident groups in the Eastern bloc. In 1978, there were even multiple meetings with representatives of Charter 77 at the Polish–Czechoslovak border in the Giant Mountains, and in 1981 Solidarność Polsko-Czechosłowacka was born.[64] Thus even though the Polish opposition groups took advantage of the opportunities provided by the CSCE process, they were not a Helsinki Group, not least because their aims went far beyond a mere monitoring function or the purpose of expediting the implementation of the Final Act's provisions.

Initially, the strict function of a Helsinki Group, that is, the documentation of human rights violations and the drafting of reports, was performed within the structures of the KOR by the Intervention Office. Then, prior to the Madrid CSCE follow-up conference, the Helsinki Commission took over with Zbigniew Romaszewski and Ludwik Cohn. The Helsinki Commission presented to the representatives of the signatory states at the beginning of the conference a comprehensive report on the human rights situation in the People's Republic of Poland.[65] Finally, from 1982 onward there was the underground Helsinki Committee with, among others, Lech Kaczyński. In 1986, Romaszewski was also assigned by Lech Wałęsa on behalf of the still illegal but increasingly resurfacing Solidarność to head the Commission for Intervention and the Rule of Law (Komisja d/s Interwencji i Praworządności NSZZ "Solidarność"). The Helsinki process thus went on beyond the period of martial law in terms of its framework, its import, and its personnel.

Conclusion

The fact that the Polish opposition of the 1970s did not constitute a Helsinki movement in the narrower sense cannot be grounds to infer that the CSCE process merely coincided temporally with the development of these groups. The point is to assess the parallels between the rise of the opposition and Helsinki using criteria that are neither too narrow nor too broad. Too narrow would mean that only the appeals that were made directly to the signatory states, along with the work of the intervention agencies and the Helsinki Commission, would provide the basis for an evaluation. Neither of these offers much insight into the opposition movement in the 1970s. Conversely, it would be wrong to trace back all developments that occurred against the backdrop of the 1975–1980 period to the initial spark of the Final Act. In this way Polish peculiarities such as the strong position of the Catholic Church or the residual impact of earlier revolts would be unduly ignored. Emerging from a long historical legacy, the problems and motivations of the opposition remained Polish, even after 1975. Viewed from this vantage point alone, 1975 does not represent a watershed in recent Polish history. The international environment after the signing of the Final Act, however, permitted strategies and approaches that previously would not have been possible. It set a process in motion that before long thoroughly eroded the legitimacy of the system.

For the opposition to be able to expand into a mass movement by way of the Founding Committees of Free Trade Unions and ultimately with Solidarność, society had to undergo further changes as a necessary precondition. Even if the welfare-socialist course was at no point and in no way attractive to oppositional circles, it did have a discernible stabilizing impact on the wider population. Implemented at an absolute low point, the improvements put the national Polish state model on a firmer footing.

At the same time, this was a process in which significant portions of Polish society moved away from socialist ideology. Together with the growing crises in 1975, this made the population more receptive to the Western model of human rights and democracy, which was propagated by the opposition. The disappointment over the economic situation was all the more extreme precisely because it followed a brief recovery period. Strikes broke out in August 1980, again because of the announced price increases (among other reasons). Unlike in December 1970 or in June 1976, demands for concrete improvements in the economic situation were now accompanied by calls for universal human and civil rights. The protesters had been sensitized to these issues by the opposition intelligentsia's publications and self-teaching programs. Above all, there was a growing understanding that one could not be achieved without the other. Among the strikers' thirty-six demands at the Szczecin shipyard was that the full text of the CSCE Final Act of 1975 should be published, which was subsequently carried out by the state publishing house for books and educational materials with a print run of fifty thousand copies.[66]

The crucial question remains why only the Polish opposition movement was already able to capitalize on the potential of the Helsinki process in 1980, instead of only in 1989. Exploring this question shows, if nothing else, how diverse the phenomena were that are every so often subsumed under the Helsinki effect. Basing his assessment on the correct assumption that at the time of the signing of the Helsinki Final Act neither the Warsaw Pact countries nor the United States anticipated the outcome of the human dimension, Thomas concludes: "They were trapped within their own commitments by the mobilization and arguments of non-state actors."[67] Thomas explains this development with the constructivist theory "that states seek legitimation by domestic and international audiences, and thus prefer to avoid glaring inconsistencies between their rhetoric and their formal normative commitments."[68] The endorsement of the human rights norms included in the Final Act, as well as related concessions later on in the CSCE process, can therefore not be attributed primarily to economic or security interests that the Polish government would have prioritized over fading ideological goals given the principle of indivisibility, which applied to all three baskets. Thomas suggests, in other words, that the country would have been unwilling to sacrifice these goals for the sake of a supposedly lesser evil. It was more a question of identity, meaning that "the value that states place on recognition and legitimation by international society reduces their willingness to defect from negotiations in the face of indications that they are unlikely to achieve other goals."[69]

This ultimately leads to a paradoxical situation where governments cooperate in the enforcement of standards that run contrary to their primary convictions, initially acting "as if" the Western human rights norms were compatible with their ideology.[70] As already mentioned, a progressive, cosmopolitan image coupled with personal conceits actually carried some weight for the new course of the Gierek team, both internally and externally. This could explain why the liberal policies of the state and the party were maintained for such a long period compared to other Eastern bloc countries in the 1970s, even at an apparent risk to the system itself. What Thomas's model cannot account for, however, is the abrupt turnaround in December 1981.

Only the Polish opposition movement was able to achieve a temporary victory against the Communist system already before the actual turning point of 1989–1991. There were two decisive reasons for this. First, the

Polish opposition movement was only able to seriously challenge the PUWP's monopoly on power and public opinion once it had managed to attract a "critical mass" in support of its notions of democracy and human rights. Furthermore, the PUWP·leadership was forced to pay more attention to the growing international sensitivity toward human rights than other Eastern bloc countries, because the People's Republic of Poland was dependent to a greater degree on Western financial and economic aid.

Even if one sets aside the specific political-cultural traditions in Poland that hindered the implementation of socialist structures from the beginning, the fragile social fabric can adequately be explained only by the social and economic turmoil that emerged during the second half of the Gierek government. It was this fabric that enabled the opposition groups to influence the working class and to establish first the Founding Committees of Free Trade Unions, and then Solidarność with its ten million members. While the Polish crisis of the 1970s differed in character from the crisis in the Western welfare states, the two were nevertheless connected. The crisis in Poland increasingly eroded the binding forces within Polish society, which also created fertile soil for the Western idea of human rights. None of these preconditions were present in the Soviet Union to the same degree. The Kremlin leaders also did not feel that they needed to take into consideration the same issues as the Gierek team in Warsaw.

The Polish opposition's concerns not only found sympathy among human rights activists, journalists, and trade unions in the West, but, with the Carter administration in the United States, it also found a determined advocate for the implementation of human rights in East Central Europe. Without this support, despite all exhibitions of sympathy, the issue of human rights would not have landed on the agenda of the CSCE follow-up conferences in Belgrade and Madrid and consequently would not have become the object of political struggles in multilateral arenas.

Chapter 11

"Human Rights Are Like Coca-Cola"
Contested Human Rights Discourses
in Suharto's Indonesia, 1968–1980

Brad Simpson

In April 1968, as students around the world were protesting their own governments and the Vietnam War, Iran hosted an international meeting to review progress made in promoting human rights, two decades after the signing of the Universal Declaration of Human Rights. The Tehran Conference has drawn justifiable criticism for being hosted and attended by authoritarian regimes whose commitment to human rights was dubious at best. In Indonesia, however, the Tehran meeting provoked wide discussion, with a variety of voices seeking to mobilize the gathering for their own ends. Officials with the National Family Planning Institute, seeking to assuage opponents of population control, noted that the Tehran Declaration endorsed family planning as a human right. Other Indonesians suggested that respect for fundamental human rights was the basis of freedom and independence for all postcolonial states, even Indonesia.[1]

A few months later, on International Human Rights Day, President Suharto chimed in, proclaiming that the development of human rights was Indonesia's "highest duty." Suharto darkly warned the country's student movement, however, that they should not take things to the point of sympathizing with the hundreds of thousands of suspected Communists arrested or killed in the aftermath of the alleged coup attempt of September 30, 1965, which had provided the pretext for Suharto's ascent to power. Lurking in the background was the growing criticism being directed at Indonesia by a nascent transnational network of human rights activists, who had begun to make the fate of political prisoners (*tahanan politik*, or *tapols*) one of the country's chief foreign policy challenges. Criticism of Indonesia's human rights record threatened to displace the narrative of rapid economic growth and modernization that Suharto's New Order regime carefully cultivated for both domestic and foreign observers.[2] At least in 1969, however, as a Lutheran World Mission official working in Indonesia observed, "the methods of operation of Amnesty International do not promise too much hope of success."[3] This would soon change.

Scholars of human rights and Indonesian politics have devoted substantial attention to the campaign against political imprisonment, in part because these events fit so well into recent narratives about the global surge of human rights activism in the 1970s.[4] But in order to insert Indonesia into the global history of human rights during this period we need to work both from the inside out and the outside in, crafting local narratives and seeking their points of contact with transnational social and political forces. We need to recover the diversity of Indonesian perspectives on human rights (which requires using Indonesian-language sources), explore why international activists selectively engaged with certain Indonesian rights discourses and not others, and trace how this selective engagement inflected domestic politics and Indonesia's human rights diplomacy.

Human rights politics did not emerge in Indonesia in the 1970s but rather reemerged, taking up concerns about economic justice and individual rights first raised early in the century and reasserted in the 1940s, but driven underground after the abrogation of parliamentary democracy in 1959.[5] Moreover, human rights talk inside Indonesia often ranged beyond civil and political rights to include economic and social equality, development, and Indonesia's place in the world economy, issues that some Western governments disparaged as a defense of cultural relativism or authoritarian rule. The Indonesian government's response to this pressure sometimes validated those critiques as it sought to prevent human rights concerns from seeping into its bilateral and multilateral relationships. But the incessant invocation by Indonesian officials of development and modernization as legitimizing tropes for Suharto's New Order created political space for local human rights activists to challenge the regime on the same grounds. These local dynamics can only be fully understood through their intersection with the international politics of human rights, in which they were deeply intertwined.

Indonesia's Post-Independence
Engagement with Human Rights

Like many postcolonial states, Indonesia's provisional 1945 constitution did not contain explicit references to human rights, though it did enumerate basic freedoms of speech, association, assembly, religion, equality under the law, and the right to work. Independence leaders such as Mohammed Hatta looked to Western constitutions with their protections for individual rights as potential models to follow, while others, such as Justice Minister Supomo and President Achmed Sukarno, advocated a more "integralist" constitution "based on the doctrine of family principle, not . . . on the doctrine of individualism."[6] In the early post-independence period, however, more liberal voices held sway, and the post-independence provisional constitutions of 1949 and 1950 referenced Western European constitutions and incorporated many articles of the Universal Declaration of Human Rights wholesale, providing far more explicit human rights protections.[7]

From 1956 to 1959 Indonesia's constituent assembly (Konstituante) engaged in lengthy debates about the form and content of a permanent constitution and the place that human rights would occupy in it. Women's groups, which had been active for decades, played an important role in these debates. They urged members to participate in elections for the assembly and launched petition drives all over the country on suffrage, marriage, and property rights. The 1955 Kongres Wanita Indonesia (Indonesian Women's Congress) "demanded that the constitution 'guarantee basic human rights included in the provisional constitution of 1950' and include article 16 of the UDHR [Universal Declaration of Human Rights]," which stipulated equal rights in marriage, as well as maintain provisions of the 1950 constitution guaranteeing equal citizenship.[8] Chinese-Indonesian organizations asserted that strong human rights provisions in the constitution would preserve minority rights and Pancasila (Sukarno's semi-official state ideology) values of religious tolerance, while Islamic scholars and organizations such as the Masyumi pushed to enshrine Islam as the basis of the state (Dasar Negara) and define human rights in terms compatible with Islamic doctrine on issues of marriage, property rights, and religious proselytizing.[9] While historians have tended to accept culturalist arguments that most Indonesians prioritized collective rights over individual rights and local or traditional values over universal values, the Konstituante ended up agreeing on a list of twenty-two civil and political rights found in the UDHR, showing that "even at a time when anti-Western sentiment was at its height, fundamental agreement could be reached about human rights."[10]

Indonesian diplomats officially joined these debates about the appropriate place of human rights at the United Nations and international forums such as the 1955 Afro-Asian Conference in Bandung, making the case for expansive conceptions of human rights that included self-determination, individual rights, and economic justice. Indonesian diplomat Artati Sudirjo, during discussion in the UN's Third Committee in 1950 about the draft human rights covenants, argued against inclusion of the so-called colonial clause limiting the reach of the UDHR in non-self-governing territories. Sudirjo, who later served as minister of education and culture under Sukarno, argued that doing so would be "betraying the ideal . . . unwearyingly pursued" in the Indonesian struggle for freedom." Others, such as delegate Nazir Pamontjak, insisted on national liberation and self-determination as "means essential . . . for ensuring those very [individual] human rights with which the Third Committee is concerned." Indonesian officials likewise endorsed the final communiqué of the 1955 Afro-Asian meeting, which cited the UDHR "as a common standard of achievement for all peoples and all nations" and endorsed self-determination as "a prerequisite of the full enjoyment of all fundamental human rights."[11]

Indonesians engaged in heated dialogue during the 1949 to 1965 period regarding the nature of human rights and their role in national and international politics. But the mass movements and organizations deploying rights claims usually did so in the context of popular mobilizations over issues such as land reform, rather than by creating institutions that would demand human rights on their own terms. When Sukarno abandoned parliamentary democracy in 1959 with support from the army and Western governments such as the United States, returning to Indonesia's 1945 Constitution and inaugurating the period known as Guided Democracy, the political space for debating human rights rapidly narrowed, with seemingly little protest. To punctuate the moment, the Indonesian president imprisoned human rights activist H. J. C. Princen (who had defected from the Dutch colonial army and fought on the side of Indonesia during its war for independence) in response to his criticism of the regime's authoritarianism and restrictions on freedom of speech and the press.

Human Rights and Indonesia's New Order

The year 1965, even more than 1959, marked a decisive rupture in Indonesia's engagement with the global politics of human rights. On September 30, 1965, elements of the Indonesian Communist Party (PKI) leadership and mid-ranking military officers moved against the army general staff, killing six. General Suharto, head of the army's Strategic Reserve Command KOSTRAD, quickly crushed the movement but exploited the opportunity it presented to launch a campaign of extermination against the PKI, killing perhaps five hundred thousand alleged Communists and imprisoning an estimated one million more, nearly all without trial.[12] Over the next decade some of the prisoners were executed, while the rest were held in local prisons under a three-tiered classification system, released with onerous restrictions or, beginning in 1969, "forcibly resettled to penal colonies in remote areas of the archipelago" such as Buru Island in the Moluccas.[13]

Western governments greeted Sukarno's overthrow with undisguised glee, showing little concern for the human rights impact of the PKI's annihilation. A search of nearly nine thousand pages of declassified U.S. State Department documents concerning the 1965–1966 killings, for example, yields not a single reference to human rights. Inside Indonesia many students, Catholics, anti-Communist intellectuals, and Sukarno-era dissidents looked to Suharto's ascendance with cautious optimism. For them, the first months of the New Order were a period of relative openness and fluidity, even amid the mass killings and imprisonments, and a variety of social forces mobilized in the expectation of a democratic revival.[14] When the MPRS (Indonesian People's Consultative Assembly) reconvened in mid-1966, among its first actions was the establishment of an ad hoc committee charged with drafting a bill of human rights, which it submitted for consideration in the next year's session. But the emerging New Order regime quickly shuttered this brief window of opportunity. Following his appointment as acting president in 1967, Suharto declined to take up the human rights bill, with support from his allies in the army and GOLKAR (Joint Secretariat of Functional Groups), his de facto political party. It soon became clear that the Suharto regime intended to practice a harsher authoritarian politics than its predecessor, equating any criticism with communism, discriminating against Chinese Indonesians, and using self-granted emergency powers to concentrate more authority in its hands and ruthlessly repress dissent. The mounting evidence of corruption and authoritarianism soured student activists and others who earlier cheered the destruction of the PKI. By 1968 the Student Action Front, KAMI, which had led demonstrations against Sukarno, was condemning political detentions and blaming Indonesia's economic problems in part on a lack of human rights and legal protections.[15]

Just a few months after the crushing of the September 30th Movement, in April 1966, H. J. C. Princen and lawyer Yap Thiam Hien cofounded Indonesia's first human rights organization, Lembaga Pembela Hak Asasi Manusia (Institute for the Defense of Human Rights). The institute was small, poorly funded, and politically weak, but Princen had returned to the Netherlands upon his release from prison to become a journalist, while Yap Thiam Hien was later invited to join the board of the World Council of Churches and the International Commission of Jurists, giving each valuable transnational contacts and some measure of protection. Simultaneously, Yap and a small group of private lawyers including former state prosecutor Adnan Buyung Nasution started Lembaga Pengabdi Hukum (Institute for Legal Service), part of a tiny movement "urging greater restraint on the exercise of the military's and the judiciary's powers" and seeking support for a "rule of law state," or *negara hukum*.[16] Yap quickly developed a reputation for courageous advocacy, taking on politically risky cases such as the defense of former foreign minister Subandrio, who had been accused of complicity in the alleged coup attempt of 1965, while Nasution deepened the organization's international connections, traveling to the United States, Germany, and Japan.[17]

As Indonesia's handful of human rights activists tried to gain a foothold, a wider range of NGOs and individuals began to direct attention to the country's detention practices. Amnesty International initiated a letter-writing campaign and visited the country in 1969, and the following year made Indonesia's political prisoners and the Buru Island forced resettlement program its major campaign.[18] About one-third of the one hundred Amnesty groups in the United States adopted *tapols* as prisoners of conscience, as did the entire West Germany country section. German activists took a particular interest in Indonesia due to the number of German missionaries who served there, ministering to prisoners and their families and working through the Indonesian Council of Churches.[19] Foreign scholars such as Frank Wertheim and Benedict Anderson began to write critically about the human rights situation under the New Order (prompting the regime to ban them from the country), as did exiled Indonesians living in the Netherlands, China, and elsewhere.[20]

The response of Indonesian officials and pro-regime intellectuals to these initial efforts suggests a human rights diplomacy still in formation. Some were bewildered by any criticism of the treatment of PKI prisoners, convinced as they were that the army had done its Western supporters a service by annihilating the party and deserved to be compensated for it.[21] Others variously acknowledged the legitimacy of human rights concerns, denounced critics such as Amnesty International as "pro-PKI," or painted universal human rights as a Western conceit representing interference in Indonesian affairs.[22] But the regime quickly began to adapt. Indonesian diplomats met with heads of mission in Jakarta, at the United Nations, and even with local Amnesty International groups to plead for understanding of Jakarta's position.[23] The relative silence of Jakarta's Western allies, meanwhile, suggested that human rights concerns could be contained within safe bounds. When remnants of the PKI in Blitar, East Java, tried to mount a campaign of armed resistance in 1968, local military commanders responded by executing up to three thousand political detainees. Aside from Lembaga Pembela Hak Asasi Manusia (LPHAM), virtually no one protested.[24] The U.S. Embassy in Jakarta recommended that "the USG [i.e., U.S. government] should in no way become directly involved in this sticky question," a position shared by the United Kingdom and other Western embassies.[25] The following year Jakarta heavy-handedly rigged a UN-sponsored "Act of Free Choice" in West Papua to ensure its incorporation with Indonesia, employing brutal counterinsurgency and police tactics to crush the territory's pro-independence advocates. Aside from the Netherlands, no Western government raised human rights concerns.[26]

In 1970 Adnan Buyung Nasution and Yap Thiam Hien responded to the worsening situation by founding Lembaga Bantuan Hukum (LBH), the Indonesian Legal Aid Society.[27] Nasution and others did not initially conceive of LBH as a human rights organization focused solely on "extension of legal, civil and political rights" but rather as seeking "social justice and popular participation" in national development. As political scientist Edward Aspinall has observed, "LBH figures argued that weaknesses in the rule of law were partly the result of cultural factors, notably the persistence of 'feudal' ideas in the general population, which in turn flowed from economic backwardness." In their early years both LBH and LPHHM thus couched their work within the rhetorical confines of the regime's nationalist project, presenting it as a contribution to the legal reform and modernization of the state rather than as a challenge to its legitimacy.[28] But lawyers like Yap were also firmly committed to "making the law more concrete for the interests of the poor." His young associate Todong Mulya Lubis later described legal aid as a "juridical response to injustice . . . for the poor as a class," rejecting an individual-centered approach as inappropriate to Indonesia's historical circumstances.[29]

Indonesian officials tolerated LBH but confined its activities to Jakarta and occasionally harassed or jailed its members, as when they tried to organize public discussions of political prisoners.[30] As LBH gained in prominence, however, it also developed transnational connections that provided it with some protection and, later, foreign funding. Shortly after LBH's founding, officials from the International Committee of the Red Cross made contact, as did lawyers associated with Amnesty International. Adnan Buyung Nasution was soon invited to join the International Commission of Jurists' Committee on Legal Services to the Poor in Developing Countries, inserting him into a stream of transnational legal aid activists who were forming the spine of local human rights organizations in dozens of countries.[31]

The legal aid approach of LBH and LPHAM appealed to international donors who were beginning to move beyond development assistance and fund human rights work.[32] The move to fund human rights work was a paradigm shift, reflecting a new way of imagining relations with the postcolonial world and a new moral ordering of the relationship between political change and stability at a time when many scholars, NGOs, and Western governments still prioritized economic development over human rights and even considered the two incompatible. The political science literature on modernization, going back more than a decade, had long theorized that authoritarianism was an acceptable, even necessary adjunct to rapid economic growth and the political instability it produced.[33]

The emerging literature on human rights often reflected the dominant assumptions of a declining but still potent body of modernization theory which argued that "short-run sacrifices" of human rights by developing countries "will foster growth and will ultimately be reversed as increased levels of economic welfare make possible the rebirth of freedom."[34] The U.S. Embassy in Jakarta put things more bluntly, arguing that "we should judge the political performance of the government on its contribution to long-range growth and modernization, and not on its support for the paraphernalia or formal procedures of parliamentary democracy."[35] In an influential 1973 treatise, Suharto confidante General Ali Murtopo extended this logic, dismissing democratic values and individualism as foreign to Indonesian culture and making the case for permanent military rule in the service of "accelerated modernization."[36]

In 1970 such assertions were commonplace; a few years later they would

be greeted with derision. What changed? Historians have cited the end of
colonialism, disillusionment in the West with utopian political schemes, or
technological transformations in explaining the emergence of human rights
politics in the 1970s. But the splintering of modernization theory and development as a global project played a crucial role in facilitating a reconsidera-
tion of the relationship between development and human rights.[37] The
unraveling of a broad postwar consensus on the basic goals and contours of
development among governments and scholars and at institutions such as the
World Bank spawned a variety of political and intellectual assaults, from assertions of a right to development or calls for a new international economic
order to the advancement of the "basic needs" paradigm by dissident economists such as Amartya Sen.[38] Critiques of Indonesia's development "miracle"
in the 1970s as either overblown or built on a foundation of political repression and economic exploitation nested within this broader set of challenges,
which were premised on the interconnection between development and
human rights, not their incompatibility. Whereas in the early 1970s human
rights activists would target the World Bank as a source of leverage for releasing Indonesian political prisoners, by the end of the decade they would be
targeting the institution itself for the impact of bank-funded programs such
as transmigration, offering human rights as an alternative framework for ap-
prehending development itself.

Unsurprisingly, the foundations that funded much of the social scientific
research on development in the 1950s and 1960s wrestled with this transition.
For the Ford Foundation these issues came into relief in 1974, after Board of
Trustees member Soedjatmoko was prevented from leaving the country following the Malari riots.[39] At an international gathering two years later of donors considering human rights grant making, Ford Foundation officials asked
of Indonesia: "Is the present level of repression necessary to maintain an or-
derly society and carry on the variety of development efforts?" To the extent
that the answer was no, they moved forward with human rights–related
grants, with others trailing in their wake. Initially, the Ford Foundation supported the International Commission of Jurists and International Committee
of the Red Cross, both of which worked with LBH and LPHAM to gather and
disseminate information about political prisoners, though only *outside* of Indonesia. The Ford Foundation later began funding the Jakarta Public Defenders office, the Institute for Legal Aid, and other programs to give higher
prominence to "legal aid and the rule of law" as a framework for human
rights advocacy and development.[40] Foreign donors soon came to dominate

human rights funding in Indonesia, helping to make NGO work an "alternative middle class career path for those with critical ideas" and serving as "transmitters into Indonesia of new paradigms for thinking about social, economic, and political change."[41]

By 1973 the elements of an international campaign against political imprisonment were falling into place. Campaigners began to generate sustained and critical global press coverage and political pressure in Western states, for the first time raising the prospect that Indonesia's foreign donors might use the economic aid to which they were committed as a lever for pressuring the regime on human rights. In February Amnesty International released a major report on political imprisonment in Indonesia, calling for an end to the Buru Island resettlement scheme and urging the UN Human Rights Commission to demand the trial or unconditional release of remaining political detainees. The International Labor Committee threatened to expel Indonesia over its forced labor practices in detention camps, and the International Commission of Jurists, World Council of Churches, and other organizations issued critical statements.[42] That December, Dutch development minister Jan Pronk became head of the Intergovernmental Group on Indonesia (IGGI), an aid consortium that disbursed more than $400 million annually in economic assistance to Jakarta. At an IGGI meeting in Amsterdam in December 1973 Pronk criticized Indonesia's detention policies, leading to student protests against him in Jakarta and numerous arrests (the jailed students were defended by LBH).[43]

Also important was the release from detention of British citizen Carmel Budiardjo, imprisoned in 1969 along with her husband, an economist and member of the PKI. After her release Budiardjo returned to Great Britain and founded the British Campaign for the Release of Indonesia's Political Prisoners, or TAPOL.[44] An indefatigable and skilled organizer, Budiardjo became one of the most important activists working on Indonesia. She corresponded with scores of left-leaning parliamentarians throughout Europe, Australia, and North America (where TAPOL support groups formed), gathered and published critical news on Indonesia's political prisoners and the Suharto regime more generally, and spoke before religious and secular audiences in dozens of countries about Indonesia and, after 1975, East Timor. For Western audiences Budiardjo cut a sympathetic and familiar figure: eloquent, attractive, determined, and able to bridge the psychological distance between ordinary human rights supporters and the people on whose behalf they advocated. For Indonesian officials and their Western supporters she was a formidable adversary, and they expended significant effort trying to discredit her or prevent her from speaking in prominent venues such as the U.S. Congress.[45]

The growing international drumbeat on human rights exacerbated existing bureaucratic and political disputes among New Order officials and policy elites, an understudied dynamic that Indonesia surely shared with other authoritarian regimes. Political scientist Greg Fealy argues that by the 1970s, detention of alleged PKI members served tactical rather than strategic goals, keeping alive the perceived threat of communism in order to justify continued authoritarian rule.[46] But some officials, such as Kopkamtib (Operational Command for the Restoration of Security and Order) chief General Sumitro, OPSUS (Special Operations) head Ali Murtopo, Foreign Minister Adam Malik, and others affiliated with the Jakarta-based Center for Strategic and International Studies (CSIS), recognized that foreign criticism might eventually produce real consequences. They sought a way out of Indonesia's "prisoners' dilemma" that would ease foreign complaints yet prove politically palatable at home, where critics were alert for signs that the regime was bowing to the West. It was not an easy task. Sumitro made modest efforts to improve conditions on Buru Island, inviting journalists and diplomats on guided tours intended to convince them that Indonesia was making progress on human rights, however slow.[47] But his half-hearted measures did not assuage activist concerns. In January 1974 the visit of Japanese prime minister Kakuei Tanaka and resentment of the growing influence of Japanese capital and foreign investors more generally sparked widespread rioting that led to the arrest of hundreds, the closing of major newspapers, and widespread international criticism. Following what became known as the "Malari incident," Foreign Minister Adam Malik privately encouraged Australian officials to urge greater press freedom and the release of Malari detainees such as Adnan Buyung Nasution and Hariman Siregar. He complained that insular officials "clearly are not aware" of the damaging impact of Indonesian detention practices, an assessment echoed by Intelligence Director for Foreign Affairs Sutopo Yuwono, who told British officials that he "had not understood the importance that the West attaches to the problem of political prisoners" until he visited the Hague.[48]

These splits extended to the wider populace. After traveling to France, where he witnessed protests against Suharto and "more questions about *tapols* than Bali," student activist Arief Budiman (later a prominent regime critic) warned that Jakarta could not simply denounce Amnesty and other groups as pro-Communist but needed to settle the *tapol* problem "before it is too late." Inside Indonesia, however, the suffocating nature of anti-Communist discourse made such advocacy nearly impossible. Former army chief of staff T. B. Simatupang, an ordained minister and in 1975 head of the Indonesian Council of Churches, told a gathering of U.S. and Indonesian church organizations they had to understand human rights from the perspective of state security, arguing that "we cannot take the risk to allow the possibility for a recurrence of this bitter experience [of 1965]." His U.S. counterparts, on the other hand, worried that "the 'cup of cold water' to prisoners and their families is hardly discharging the whole mandate of the Christian Church when human rights are so completely ignored." Simatupang's stance is noteworthy; in sermons given before American church audiences he described himself as an advocate of liberation theology concerned with economic and social rights and a preferential option for the poor. But in Indonesia his nationalism and anti-Communism trumped his theological liberalism.[49]

If Indonesia was becoming more vulnerable to international pressure in 1974 it was not only due to Amnesty's growing effectiveness, but also because a shifting economic and political landscape raised questions both internationally and domestically about Suharto's economic stewardship. Although oil revenues were skyrocketing due to OPEC price hikes, the country faced a major debt scandal involving the national oil company Pertamina, investigations into bribes paid by Ford Motor Company and Hughes Aerospace, mounting student protests against corruption and authoritarianism, preparations for the invasion of East Timor, and continued criticism over the Malari detentions.[50] When regime officials lobbied the IGGI for increased aid in early 1975, they faced sharp questioning on human rights for the first time, following a two-year campaign by Amnesty International targeting IGGI member governments and the World Bank. When Suharto visited the United States three months later the White House warned him that congressional human right activists would likely cut aid to Jakarta unless it made progress on the political prisoner issue.[51] British and Australian officials made similar entreaties, suggesting that, if for no other reason than to "appease public opinion" in their respective countries, Indonesia should try to release *tapols*.[52]

In October a delegation led by General Ali Murtopo and Lim Bian Kie of CSIS traveled to Washington to meet with senior officials and argue for closer U.S.-Indonesian ties. Murtopo and Lim also initiated quiet negotiations with the White House over the mechanisms of a prisoner release program. It is certain that they discussed the looming attack on East Timor as well, since the two were among the chief planners of the invasion and presumably expected concessions on political prisoners to mute criticism of Indonesia's takeover of the territory. Supporters in the U.S. Congress and in Western governments were pleased, but not human rights groups, who kept up their criticism.[53]

In early December 1976, however, Jakarta announced that it finally would begin a three-year, phased release of most of its thirty thousand political prisoners. The proposed prisoner release culminated a year-long process of negotiations with U.S., Japanese, and other policy makers spearheaded by Ali Murtopo, Admiral Sudomo, and Major General Benny Murdani.[54] The Ford administration greeted the announcement as a vindication of its quiet diplomacy, while Indonesian elites credited Adam Malik's negotiating skills, willingness to meet with critics, and courting of European capitals. Scholars disagree on the exact reasons for the change in policy, and Indonesian records remain closed. But abundant evidence suggests that the Suharto regime was concerned about Carter's human rights talk and the U.S. embassy in Jakarta's pending submission of its first human rights report.[55] Its concessions on *tapols* almost certainly also stemmed from a desire to soften the international opposition to the invasion of East Timor, and the implicit or explicit expectation that more economic and military aid would result.[56]

Their gambit seemed to pay off. Indonesia's prisoner release program muted congressional criticism of increased economic and military assistance to Jakarta amid emerging reports of mass killings in East Timor and evidence that Indonesian police and military forces were systematically torturing detainees. "Indonesia may escape relatively unscathed," crowed the British ambassador to the UN Human Rights Commission in Geneva, relieved that he would not have to vote against Jakarta at a time when London was negotiating substantial weapons deals with Suharto.[57]

Within a short period of time, the Suharto regime also learned to play the game of human rights diplomacy—not particularly effectively, but well enough to provide cover for its allies. Indonesian officials could not always mask the reality of arbitrary detention, extrajudicial killings, torture and other abuses, though they succeeded in barring reporters and most observers from East Timor for nearly three years after the invasion. But they doggedly engaged in multilateral and bilateral forums to defend Indonesia's human rights practices and claimed a commitment to improve them, giving their defenders in Washington, London, and elsewhere room for maneuver against domestic critics. Within the Non-Aligned Movement Jakarta emerged as a prominent proponent of the New International Economic Order (NIEO) and claims to development as human rights, even as it refused to sign the 1966 covenant on economic, social, and cultural rights. In 1977 Indonesian officials, like authoritarian counterparts elsewhere, hired a New York public relations firm, Hill and Knowlton, to trumpet positive news about the New Order's purported economic gains and deflect some of its critics.[58]

To international audiences, policy elites such as Jusuf Wanandi of CSIS argued that human rights must be viewed in the context of the trauma of 1965 and "Indonesian cultural values," which "as in many developing countries tend to emphasize communalism over individualism" but which would evolve as economic development accelerated.[59] Ironically this was the same argument many human rights activists made in attempting to explain the anemic state of legal and rights consciousness among ordinary Indonesians and the need to combine human rights advocacy with commitment to social and economic justice.[60]

Domestically, New Order officials and their defenders appealed to nationalism and attempted to mobilize resentment of alleged foreign interference in Indonesian politics. Amnesty International was a frequent target, and Indonesian intelligence and other regime officials fed newspapers a steady diet of inflammatory charges that Amnesty was pro-Communist, morally arrogant, blind to improvements in Indonesia's human rights situation, and seeking to impose Western values on an Islamic society, likening human rights to Coca-Cola. "Amnesty international is always raising its voice about PKI prisoners," an editorial in the newspaper *Kompas* complained, "but has nothing to say about the blood shed by the Communists in the 1965 coup" or the "terror of the Allende years" in Chile before General Augusto Pinochet came to power.[61]

The resort to red-baiting was hardly surprising given the central role that anti-Communism played in underpinning the New Order's political legitimacy, but attacks on Western interference were trickier, considering Jakarta's dependence on Western donors. This ambivalence was clearest when dealing with the United States. The election of Jimmy Carter caused genuine consternation among military officials in Jakarta, and even the perception that the United States would pursue aggressive human rights diplomacy increased pressure on British, Australian, and other Western embassies. Meeting with Indonesian ambassador to the UK Admiral Sudomo, British minister for overseas affairs Frank Judd observed that the "sensitivity of the interested British public on this subject had been increased by recent statements of the new U.S. administration that it was going to take a great interest in matters of human rights." Like President Sukarno before him, who famously told the U.S. government to "go to hell with your aid!," Indonesian officials wrote in newspaper editorials and told the U.S. embassy that President Suharto would refuse aid "if it's tied to human rights pressures." That was a bluff, to be sure, but it was indicative of their concern.[62] An editorial in the newspaper *Kompas* icily noted that "the United States is not the world's human rights police," while *Tempo*, the nation's leading newsweekly, reminded readers that "being a superpower was not the same as being a moral power."[63]

American views on human rights, however, could be put to many uses, and regime officials also seized on positive statements from Washington as rhetorical cover when it suited their purposes. After Assistant Secretary of State Robert Oakley praised Indonesia's improved human rights record in testimony before Congress, Indonesian newspapers trumpeted the news for days. As much as the concrete expressions of U.S. support that the Carter White House offered to Indonesia, such as accelerated arms shipments in 1978, these political signals emboldened the Suharto regime in its ongoing political battles with students, domestic human rights critics such as LPHAM and LBH, and international groups seeking to mobilize against it.[64]

As the decade drew to a close Indonesia's human rights movement began to look more like its counterparts elsewhere, at least in form. In 1979 LBH began issuing annual human rights reports on Indonesia, in addition to its ongoing programs of legal aid. Foreign donors such as the Ford Foundation and the Netherlands Organization for International Assistance funded an increasing number of Indonesian human rights, legal aid, development, and environmental NGOs, helping to shape their agendas and deepen their transnational links. Though nearly all 1965 detainees had been released, the Suharto regime's continued resort to political imprisonment—in 1978 of hundreds of protesting students and Muslims—kept the issue of *tapols* on the agenda of domestic and international human rights advocates, while the invasion and occupation of East Timor emerged as a driving force of transnational activism.[65]

Indonesia's experience, it seems, maps nicely onto the emerging narrative of the global human rights boom of the 1970s: struggling NGOs focusing on civil and political rights, gradually deepening and broadening their domestic and transnational bases of support, and through their work facilitating the sort of "boomerang effect" that Kathryn Sikkink and Margaret Keck have so powerfully described.[66] Yet Indonesia's human rights activists, NGOs, and the wider circle of movements and organizations that occasionally mobilized rights talk in the 1970s were not simply translating universal human rights into vernacular form.[67] They were drawing on a decades-old repertoire of ideas concerning social justice, the rights of the poor and marginalized, and the duties of the powerful. Jailed activists from the University of Indonesia and the Bandung Institute of Technology, for example, who were tried on subversion charges stemming from their participation in the 1977–1978 student movement, gave eloquent voice to a far broader conception of human rights. Their famous "White Paper on Student Struggle, 1978" offered a sophisticated critique of New Order political economy—characterized by technocratic rule, militarism, corruption, excessive reliance on the United States and the West more generally, and a government that was "only interested in achieving a bigger GNP and in the process . . . has forgotten the principles of social justice, self-respect [and] national culture."[68] As part of their mobilization, in December 1977 students at the University of Indonesia proclaimed "human rights month" and demanded from the Suharto government "protection and fulfillment of the basic rights of every citizen . . . freedom of expression, freedom from fear [and] freedom from poverty." While the students drew attention to the problem of political detention and the principle of equal justice under the law, they emphasized the social and economic dimensions of the problem, citing the harassment of peasants by local authorities for failing to repay loans for inputs needed to grow the "miracle rice" being promoted by the regime under the banner of the Green Revolution.[69]

Indonesian students were hardly alone in their understanding. Writing at about the same time, the Muslim religious and political leader Abdurrahman Wahid made the case for the universalism of Islamic conceptions of human rights, noting the shared commitment of nonreligious Soviet colleagues such as Andrei Sakharov to "morality on the side of the poor and powerless."[70] The first human rights report of LBH in 1979, placed alongside the same document from Amnesty International, is a study in contrasts. The Amnesty report focused entirely on political detention and barely mentioned East Timor and West Papua, where the army was engaged in extraordinarily brutal counterinsurgency operations. The LBH report asked "to what extent has development . . . succeeded in upholding the fundamental human rights" and welfare "of the whole Indonesian people?" To answer this question it examined progress in fulfilling the rights to education, health services, income, food, clothing and housing, jobs, and business opportunities, before arriving at the more familiar categories of freedom of press and information, the right to democratic participation, and the right to impartial justice, where it discussed detention practices.[71] Writing a few years later, Todong Mulya Lubis criticized both the narrow human rights horizons of Western NGOs and the blinkered vision of the Indonesian government and its Western supporters, who "privilege development over all else" and view human rights as an obstacle to its achievement. "Liberal understandings of equality before the law," he continued, "only work if there is equality to enjoy social, economic, political, and cultural life as well."[72]

Early LBH reports did not take on the mass killings taking place in West Papua and East Timor or challenge the basic legitimacy of the Suharto regime. Groups like LBH likewise downplayed gender concerns, though women's organizations mobilized effectively around coercive family planning policies employing a rights framework. But Indonesian human rights advocates could call the Suharto regime to account for failing to meet its self-professed commitment to a program of development whose benefits would be widely shared. The breadth of vision that the country's still tiny human rights community displayed is striking, bearing little resemblance to the "human rights orthodoxy" that Jean Quataert describes as ascendant in the period. This social democratic vision of human rights, so familiar in the 1940s, strikes a discordant note now because of the particular trajectory of human rights activism in the West in the 1970s with its focus on civil and political rights, an evolution that has been naturalized by existing historiography. Scholars and Western governments, meanwhile, routinely buttressed the arguments of authoritarian states such as Indonesia that the imperatives of development and the threat of Communism justified the subordination of human rights and democracy. Only after decades of struggle, from the bottom up and from the outside in, did they begin to think more broadly.

Conclusion

The historiography of human rights needs far more studies than we now have that take local sources and conceptions of human rights as their starting point. We should not be surprised to find that those engaging with global human rights politics in other parts of the world did not accept the artificial division between universally and locally derived conceptions of rights, or between civil and political and economic, social, and cultural rights. We should also not be surprised that activists in Indonesia and elsewhere viewed human rights—and rights violations—as intertwined in a complex web of social, economic, religious, gender, and ethnic relations. Figures such as Yap Thiam

Hien, seen abroad merely as "a fighter for human rights," were seen at home "as part of a developing movement for political reform and democracy"— devoted to human rights to be sure, but also to much more.[73] Accounting for the sometimes fractious human rights claims of Indonesians in the 1970s not only challenges diffusionist narratives in which civil and political rights radiate from the West outward to the postcolonial world, but helps to restore the very real sense of contingency that animated Indonesian political struggles and the role of human rights discourses in shaping them.

Chapter 12

Why South Africa?
The Politics of Anti-Apartheid Activism
in Britain in the Long 1970s

Simon Stevens

The global anti-apartheid movement, one scholar argues, "was the first successful transnational social movement in the era of globalization. . . . What is unique about the anti-apartheid movement is the extent of support it received from individuals, governments, and organizations on all continents. Few social movements garner anywhere near the international support mobilized against the racist apartheid regime in South Africa."[1] Such claims reflect the considerable interest scholars have recently begun to take in anti-apartheid activism. Despite this interest, however, and scholars' emphasis on "the extent of support" that the anti-apartheid movement received, historians have so far shown only limited interest either in examining and explaining how the extent of that support varied and changed over time or in addressing the question of why particular individuals and organizations came to direct their energies against apartheid in South Africa.

This chapter seeks to address the question of why South Africa became a focus of activism in Britain, the location of some (though by no means all) of the most high-profile overseas anti-apartheid campaigns. In doing so, it also seeks to throw light on three further themes: the chronology of anti-apartheid activism in Britain, the relationship between transnational and national explanations for that activism, and the role of concern for human rights in anti-apartheid activism in the 1970s.

Scholarship on anti-apartheid activism in Britain has taken off since the 2002 opening of the papers of the British Anti-Apartheid Movement (the organization that was formed in 1959 as the Boycott Movement and renamed the Anti-Apartheid Movement [AAM] the following year).[2] In the rapidly expanding literature on anti-apartheid activism in Britain, however, there has been remarkably little attention to the issue of the motivations and purposes of anti-apartheid activists, or the circumstances that led them to focus their attentions on South Africa rather than on other international or domestic issues. Such lack of attention appears to reflect a widespread assumption that those motivations and circumstances are self-evident. Other historians have recently made this point regarding the historiography of other activist campaigns. Jan Eckel notes in his study of the international campaign against the Pinochet regime in Chile in the 1970s, for example, that "in much of the historiography, the fact that the Pinochet regime was targeted for international action has not provoked much explanation. Historians have tended to describe the worldwide public concern as a kind of natural reaction to the atrocities committed, which by their horrendous nature forced politicians and private individuals into immediate action." Rejecting this as inadequate, Eckel instead directs his research toward the key question: "why Chile?"[3]

This chapter seeks to contribute to answering the equally important question, "why South Africa?" through a study of two prominent anti-apartheid campaigns in Britain that bracketed the "long 1970s."[4] Most of the existing scholarship tends to focus on the national organization of the AAM, and, to some extent, to treat the AAM as a single entity with a "hegemonic ideology."[5] This chapter shifts the focus to two of the groups that made up the broader anti-apartheid coalition in Britain and played key roles in organizing two of the most high-profile anti-apartheid campaigns in this period: Stop the Seventy Tour's campaign against South African sports tours to Britain in 1969–1970, and the City of London Anti-Apartheid Group's protests outside the South African embassy in Trafalgar Square, including its nonstop picket for eighty-six days in 1982. In both cases, I focus on the motivations and purposes of the organizers of the campaigns, rather than the rank-and-file activists who participated in them. My objective is to explain why it was that the campaigns were started at all.[6]

Explaining why particular groups came to mobilize around the issue of apartheid in this period is particularly important because, in general, anti-apartheid activism attracted relatively limited support in Britain in the 1970s, a period that Christabel Gurney characterizes as the British AAM's "difficult decade."[7] There had been considerable British public interest in and condemnation of apartheid in the late 1950s and early 1960s. In this period apartheid was seen in Britain as a "temporary aberration" being promoted by anti-British and Nazi-associated Afrikaner nationalists, which ran counter to British ideals of race relations and threatened both the stability of British rule elsewhere in colonial Africa and the unity of the British Commonwealth.[8] This interest and condemnation peaked in 1959–1960, with the result that the founders of the Boycott Movement in 1959 were able to mobilize considerable publicity and support for their consumer boycott of South African goods, even before the spate of worldwide attention and condemnation that followed the Sharpeville massacre, in which at least sixty-nine protesters were killed by South African police on March 21, 1960. From the early 1960s, British interest and activism on apartheid waned, however, for a number of reasons. Internal resistance was crushed following the banning of the African National Congress (ANC) and the Pan Africanist Congress in 1960, and the life imprisonment of Nelson Mandela and other key ANC leaders following the Rivonia trial in 1963–1964. Decolonization and disillusionment with the Commonwealth reduced British interests in Africa (and the perceived threat that apartheid could pose to them). Apartheid came to be seen as broadly supported by the white population of South Africa, including the English-speaking "British" population. And South Africa's seeming stability and prosperity appeared to contrast with the poverty and political turmoil of many postcolonial African states. The Anti-Apartheid Movement, as the Boycott Movement renamed itself, was unable for more than two decades to mobilize the kind of support it had received in 1960. The movement's demonstrations in London of between 6,000 and 15,000 people to launch its "month of boycott action" on February 28, 1960, and to protest the Sharpeville killings on March 27, 1960, were the largest anti-apartheid events held in Britain until the AAM's "Southern Africa—Time to Choose" rally in London of approximately 15,000 people in March 1982.[9]

Figures for the membership of the national AAM are very patchy and by no means reflect the total number of people prepared to take part in some form of anti-apartheid activism. Even many members of local anti-apartheid groups affiliated to the AAM were not members of the national organization, and the AAM was able to mobilize many more people to participate in campaigns and demonstrations and to sign petitions than to become members. Nevertheless, a graph of the national AAM's total individual membership following its decision to become a membership organization in 1963 provides a rough index of levels of interest and activism on this issue, especially when the membership figures are supplemented with figures for the AAM's total annual income from subscriptions. The graph shows that membership of the national AAM, though it may have spiked in the early 1970s following Stop the Seventy Tour's campaign in 1969–1970, appears to have remained fairly constant at between 2,000 and 2,500 members throughout the late 1960s and 1970s. Strikingly, although the Soweto uprising that began in June 1976 is often characterized as a turning point in international as well as domestic mobilization against apartheid, AAM membership appears not to have increased significantly in 1976 and actually declined the following year. British public reaction to Soweto appears to have been considerably more muted than it had been to Sharpeville in 1960, or would be to the uprising in South Africa's townships in the mid-1980s.[10]

Figure 12.1 suggests that AAM membership began to increase in the early 1980s and then took off in 1985–1986 following the township uprising that began in 1984. British public and media interest in apartheid—and in particular the issue of whether to impose economic sanctions on South Africa—reached by far its most intense level in 1985–1986. The AAM's success in rallying 15,000 people to demonstrate in London against apartheid in March 1982 was subsequently dwarfed by rallies of 50,000 people in June 1984 (to protest South African president P. W. Botha's visit to Britain), 150,000 in November 1985, and 250,000 in June 1986.[11] Membership in the AAM peaked in 1988–1989, however, as a consequence of the AAM's phenomenally successful "Nelson Mandela: Freedom at 70" campaign in 1988, which included a massive televised pop concert at Wembley Stadium on June 11, 1988.

In the long 1970s then, when anti-apartheid activism generally garnered relatively limited support in Britain compared to the mid- to late 1980s, why did particular groups come to focus their energies on South Africa, while many other seemingly similar groups did not? One of the key contentions of this chapter is that the question "why South Africa?" can only be answered comprehensively by disaggregating the anti-apartheid movement into its key constituent parts: opposing apartheid meant very different things for different people and served very different purposes.

This chapter suggests two conclusions regarding the origins and nature of the two campaigns studied here. First, the organizers of these anti-apartheid campaigns hoped that their campaigns would ultimately transform the political and economic order not only in South Africa but also in Britain itself. This is an interpretation rejected by Håkan Thörn, who instead focuses on the

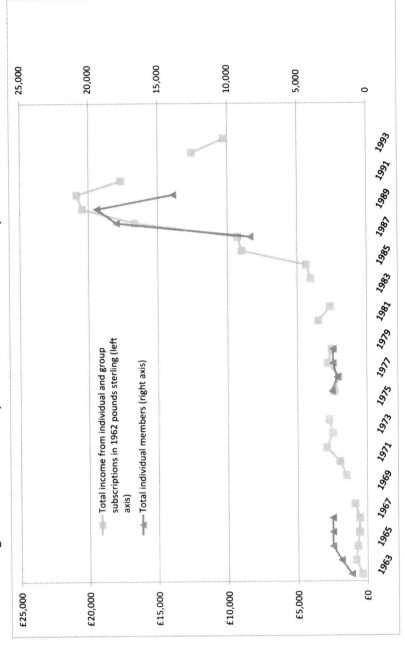

Figure 12.1 British Anti-Apartheid Movement Membership, 1963–1994

"transnational processes" responsible for enabling the "globalization of politics" of which the global anti-apartheid movement was a part: new means of transnational communication; new opportunities for international travel, making possible the creation of transnational networks of activists; and "the rise and consolidation of new 'global' organizations and institutions." These processes, Thörn argues, enabled the creation of an "imagined global community of solidarity activists."[12]

These transnational processes, however, are not sufficient to explain why particular groups within various countries came to focus on South Africa. While this chapter does not seek to diminish the significance of such transnational processes, it does suggest that they only became significant through their interaction with "the internal dynamics of the nation state" that Thörn explicitly dismisses, specifically the domestic political objectives of the individuals and groups that became heavily involved in anti-apartheid activism.

Second, the circumstance that led the particular British political groups studied here to make anti-apartheid activism one of their most prominent concerns was the initiative of South African exiles who were able to focus the attention of those groups on the issue of apartheid. There were many political groups in Britain whose ideologies could have predisposed them toward opposition to apartheid in South Africa. The fact that the Young Liberals came to focus a significant proportion of their energies on anti-apartheid activism in a way that the youth wing of the Labour Party or the Young Communist League did not, and that the Revolutionary Communist Group came to focus much more strongly on anti-apartheid activism than other far left and Trotskyist groups such as the Socialist Workers Party or Militant tendency, reflected the initiative of individual South African exiles who had established close relationships with members of Young Liberals and the Revolutionary Communist Group.

This second conclusion overlaps to some extent with Thörn's argument that "new possibilities of travel" facilitated the creation of transnational networks of activists. In particular, Thörn suggests that new possibilities of travel enabled South African exiles to play "an important role as organizers and mobilizers, travelling extensively around the world, making speeches at solidarity meetings and thus giving 'the other' a public face."[13] This chapter provides further evidence for the argument that exiled South Africans played crucial roles as organizers and mobilizers of anti-apartheid activism in Britain. At the same time, however, it also qualifies this argument: the South African exiles who were particularly significant in the cases studied here were not those who made use of new opportunities to travel but those who, having arrived in Britain (by sea, in one case), became most rooted in British politics.

Stop the Seventy Tour

On September 10, 1969, a new anti-apartheid organization calling itself the Stop the Seventy Tour Committee (STST) convened a press conference to announce its formation and objectives. Peter Hain, STST's spokesperson, called for the cancellation of the planned 1970 tour of Britain by South Africa's cricket team as a way of challenging racist selection policies in South African sport and, more broadly, of challenging apartheid itself. Hain threatened "mass demonstrations and disruptions throughout the tour" should it go ahead and warned British sporting authorities that "their complicity in apartheid sport will no longer be tolerated—all future tours, including the [South African] Rugby tour starting in November [1969], will be severely disrupted."[14] Subsequently, in what one scholar has characterized as "arguably the most successful mass action in post–World War II British history," STST was able to mobilize up to fifty thousand demonstrators during the twenty-five-fixture rugby tour, over four hundred of whom were arrested as they demonstrated at and attempted to disrupt games. One fixture was abandoned and two were forced to change their venues.[15] In May 1970, following a direct request from the British government, the English Cricket Council announced that it was cancelling the South African cricket tour.[16]

The 1969–1970 Stop the Seventy Tour campaign provides a clear example of the importance of South African exiles in mobilizing particular groups and organizations to focus their attention and energies on major campaigns against apartheid. In this case, the role of Peter Hain, STST's nineteen-year-old chairman, was crucial: one journalist commented in May 1970 that "Peter Hain may go down in history as the man who made apartheid a national issue in Britain."[17] Hain had grown up in South Africa, where his parents, both English-speaking white South Africans, had been prominent members of the anti-apartheid Liberal Party. The family had endured prolonged harassment from the South African police for their opposition to the National Party government. Both parents were briefly imprisoned in 1961 and were later served with banning orders.[18] The banning of his parents meant that as a teenager Peter was increasingly drawn into political activity, acting on their behalf. He passed messages to journalists and other banned people with whom they could not communicate, for example, and in April 1965 Peter, then aged fifteen, was drafted at the last moment to read the oration at the funeral of John Harris, a family friend and Liberal Party member who was hanged for having planted a bomb in a Johannesburg railway station. In early 1966 continued police harassment finally led the family to take a Union Castle liner into exile and move to London.[19]

Peter Hain's role in the Stop the Seventy Tour campaign was crucial not only because he founded STST, but because from the start he involved in it the Young Liberals, the youth wing of the Liberal Party, Britain's third largest political party after the dominant Labour and Conservative Parties. Hain was perhaps unusual among South African exiles in the extent to which he became involved in domestic British politics. He later recalled, "My father was quite clear: what we must do is become members of the community. There was among South African exiles—true of all exiles—a limbo existence. People were constantly waiting to go back and never settling. . . . We sunk ourselves into domestic politics. We were never going back."[20] The combination of his family's association with the South African Liberal Party, his disillusionment with the policies of Harold Wilson's Labour government on Rhodesia and Vietnam, and his perception that "the British Young Liberals were then a vibrant, irreverent force for radicalism," led Hain to join the Young Liberals.[21] By 1969 he had become chair of the Putney branch and vice-chair of the National League of Young Liberals.

In the mid- to late 1960s the Young Liberals became a prominent focus for student radicalism, especially on international issues. A small group of senior Young Liberal national officers decided in 1966 to convert their largely quiescent organization into a radical youth movement. This new approach first came to the attention of the national media at the Liberal Party's annual assembly in September 1966, at which the Young Liberals, soon dubbed the "Red Guards" in the press, played a major role in the defeat of the party's executive on the issue of Britain's role in NATO. Subsequently, the Young Liberals became particularly active in campaigning on two international issues: the Vietnam War and southern Africa. Southern Africa had become a particularly prominent issue in British politics following the Unilateral Declaration of Independence by white settlers in the British colony of Southern Rhodesia in November 1965, and what many on the British left perceived as the Labour government's weak and vacillating response to it. One of the Young Liberals' first actions on southern Africa was to organize a demonstration in London on the anniversary of the declaration in November 1966. Subsequently, the Young Liberals sought to organize a national campaign on South Africa in 1967 (though, as George Kiloh, their chair from 1966 to 1968, later recalled, this "essentially sunk") and established a Young Liberal Southern Africa Commission in early 1968 to coordinate activism on the issue.[22]

Though he had joined the Young Liberals only a few months earlier, Hain, the only South African involved, quickly came to play a leading role in the Southern Africa Commission, and was appointed vice-chair.[23] It was Hain who at a Southern Africa Commission meeting in January 1969 first proposed that the commission's members pledge themselves "to take direct action to prevent scheduled matches from taking place unless the 1970 [cricket] tour is cancelled."[24] The resolution passed, and to reinforce the threat Hain subsequently organized a series of "Young Liberal direct-action demonstrations" in July 1969 at the fixtures of the Wilf Isaacs XI, an all-white invitational South African cricket team then touring Britain, and at a Davis Cup tennis fixture in Eastbourne between Britain and South Africa. The protests were initially tiny: Hain and seven other Young Liberals occupied the pitch at the Wilf Isaacs XI's first game, and Hain and just three others invaded the court at the Davis Cup game.[25]

Part of Hain's purpose in founding STST in autumn 1969 was to "reach beyond the ranks of the Young Liberals and draw in all who were prepared to take action against apartheid sport." Organizations affiliated to STST included the National Union of Students, the United Nations Student Association, United Nations Youth, the radical Christian group CHURCH, the International Socialists, and the Young Communist League. Those who took part in STST protests in 1969–1970 reached far beyond the ranks of the Young Liberals.[26] Nevertheless, the Young Liberals continued to play a central organizing role. Hain himself cooperated closely with Louis Eaks, national chair of the of the Young Liberals in 1969–1970, and several of STST's regional organizers such as Simon Hebditch in London and Gordon Lishman in Manchester were also current or former officers of the Young Liberals and/or the Southern Africa Commission.

Why did the Young Liberals so enthusiastically target South Africa in the late 1960s? It seems highly likely that without Hain the Young Liberals would not have played nearly such a prominent role in anti-apartheid activism in 1969–1970. But for Hain to be successful in mobilizing the Young Liberals, both his objectives and his proposed tactics for achieving them had to appeal to them. Leaders of the Young Liberals framed their opposition to apartheid in strongly exceptionalist terms. South Africa was, George Kiloh argued, "the most outstanding affront to liberal values in the non-communist world," and even compared to communist countries it was "a special case. Its policies were utterly repugnant, in a way that was very different from those of Russia or China." The Young Liberals frequently compared South Africa to Nazi Germany: the theme of their 1967 campaign on apartheid was that the South African regime was "essentially Nazi."[27] Moreover, though Britain did not have the same kind of ongoing direct responsibility for South Africa that it did for the rebellious colony of Rhodesia, the Young Liberals contended that Britain nonetheless bore some responsibility for South African apartheid: Hain argued that Britain had "a great historical responsibility for the continuance of racialism throughout South African society."[28]

In general, the language of human rights appears to have played little role in how the Young Liberals framed their opposition to apartheid. In a "Background Briefing" on Southern Africa produced by the Southern Africa Commission in 1968, the commission's chair, Douglas Marchant, noted that the United Nations had designated 1968 as Human Rights Year and claimed that South Africa was "the only country in the world not only to have passed legislation in direct opposition to the Universal Declaration of Human Rights, but the only country to have violated every single one of the Universal Declaration's thirty articles."[29] Such language appears to have been uncommon, however. Much more frequently, Young Liberals and STST framed their campaign as one against "racialism." "Racialism" was, Hain wrote in 1971, "the issue on which we were campaigning." STST's objection to the proposed 1970 cricket tour was that the South African team was "selected on a racial basis and representing a racialist system."[30] For the Young Liberals and STST it was South Africa's "racialism" that made it exceptional in world politics: "We pick on apartheid because it is the one system in the world which is founded on the basis of racialism—and the cruellest, most institutionalized form of racialism the world has ever seen. We pick on the 'absolute tyranny' of racialism in South Africa because it condemns 14 million non-white South Africans to inferiority, exploitation and humiliation solely because of their colour, a factor beyond their control initially and which they can never change." When conservative critics demanded to know why STST was not also demonstrating against Russian sports teams, STST's standard response was that simply there was "no evidence that any Russian has been excluded from a Russian team for racial reasons. Russia has no racial laws similar to South Africa's, so that in this respect there is no comparison with apartheid."[31]

The particular form of anti-apartheid activism that STST adopted was also critical. Two key features of STST's campaign against the rugby and cricket tours were its emphasis on direct action—that is, the actual disruption of sports events—and its local orientation. Hain argued that "direct action tactics are much more sophisticated than stereotyped conventional demonstrations, because it involves people in such a positive and committed manner." He concluded afterward that "the whole momentum and strength of the campaign were helped by the fact that the target of protest was locally oriented. . . . we were not all coming to London to let off steam outside South Africa House, but were able to protest on our own doorsteps, as it were. No campaign has ever had quite this degree of local orientation and, so, of mass support."[32]

Both of these features of STST's campaign fitted closely with the focus of leading Young Liberals in this period on the interlinked ideas of direct action and community politics. From about 1967 on, Young Liberal leaders' rising frustration with their inability to influence the parliamentary Liberal Party prompted an increasing disillusionment with conventional parliamentary politics as a means of achieving the transformation of society they believed necessary. Instead, they came to argue—as did a memorandum on direct action probably written in late 1968 by Young Liberal chair Malcolm MacCallum—that Young Liberals must focus on organizing people "to solve their immediate problems in their schools, factories and local communities" through direct action. "Local direct action," the memorandum argued, was "the only way to persuade the public . . . that real change is needed." The memorandum concluded that Young Liberals "must look to non-violent direct action on a huge scale as the only way of mobilising people and achieving change."[33]

In November 1969, prominent Young Liberal members Gordon Lishman (STST's Manchester organizer) and Lawrence Freedman coined the term "community politics" to refer to this approach, which was then enshrined in the "community politics resolution" that the Young Liberals succeeded in having passed at the September 1970 Liberal Party conference. This committed Liberals "to help organise people in their communities to take and use power."[34] The ideologues of community politics saw the encouragement of participation in the solving of multiple different local issues as the first step toward the ultimate, if vague and usually undefined, objective of "community self-government." Lishman explained that "the most basic article of faith to the [community politics] movement is the belief that the aggregation and development of community activity will lead to the habit of participation. . . . The confrontation between the habit and the systems it confronts will lead to the development of new structures which are more open and more effective and clearly controlled." The starting point, then, was to mobilize people around single, usually local, issues. The habit of participating in local direct action—in what Hain called "the experience of taking and using power on their own behalf and on their community's behalf"—would give people the experience of achieving change for themselves and lead them to connect the local problem around which they had initially mobilized to broader questions of the organization of society.[35]

Much of the focus of Young Liberal community politics ideologues was on local community issues, such as solving problems in schools and workplaces. Nonetheless, local direct action against South African sports teams could clearly be accommodated by this approach, based as it was on the idea that, in MacCallum's words, "the key to real change is the praxis of dissent at local level."[36] Indeed, several of the most enthusiastic promoters of the concept of community politics, including Lishman, Hebditch, and Hain, were among the key STST organizers. Hain argued in 1971 that "the success of the [STST] campaign and its impact in Britain went far beyond the issue of apartheid sport, and indeed, beyond apartheid. The movement threw up a seemingly endless number of associated issues, and, in this light, the campaign was of immense importance almost because of itself." Hain and his fellow Young Liberals at the center of the anti-apartheid mobilization in 1969–1970 saw their campaign, as Hain told one journalist, as "a beginning, not an end, for protest movements in Britain for what you can do with direct action and militant non-violence."[37] They targeted South African sports tours with the hope of transforming society not only in South Africa but also in Britain itself.

The City of London Anti-Apartheid Group and the South Africa House Pickets

In the 1980s one of most visible forms of anti-apartheid activism in Britain were the pickets demonstrating outside the South African embassy in Trafalgar Square. The embassy picket line became a popular tourist attraction: former African National Congress (ANC) activist Paul Trewhela recalled in 2002 that "for thousands of visitors to London . . . the noisy picket . . . provided the most visible evidence of public opposition to apartheid." Journalist

Denis Herbstein recalled the "state of siege" the pickets created inside South Africa House when he visited it during the 1980s. Recent Freedom of Information Act releases show that the South African embassy repeatedly contacted the Foreign Office to complain about the "disruptive and abusive" demonstrations.[38]

The pickets outside South Africa House—which began with a nonstop day and night picket for eighty-six days from August 25 to November 18, 1982, followed by regular pickets every Friday thereafter, and later another nonstop picket from 1986 until 1990—were organized by the City of London Anti-Apartheid Group, which was founded in January 1982 as a local anti-apartheid group affiliated to the national AAM. Once again, a single South African exile played a crucial role. Norma Kitson (1933–2002) was born into a wealthy Jewish family in Durban and first began to turn against apartheid when she observed the crude racism and cruelty of her white colleagues toward black miners while she was working as a secretary in the mining town of Odendaalsrus in the Orange Free State in the late 1940s. She joined the Congress of Democrats, the white wing of the Congress Alliance, in 1953 and the underground South African Communist Party (SACP) in 1959.[39] Her husband, David Kitson, who was also an SACP member, joined Umkhonto we Sizwe (MK), the ANC's armed wing, when it was formed in 1961, and after the arrest of the MK leadership at Rivonia in 1963 he was drafted into the new four-person MK High Command, until he too was arrested a year later and sentenced to twenty years in prison.[40]

Suffering continued harassment from the security police following her husband's sentence, Norma Kitson and her two children left South Africa for London in 1967. Initially Kitson avoided political activity in Britain so as not to endanger the chances that she would be allowed to return to South Africa periodically to visit her husband in prison. After visiting him in 1976, however, she decided that she would never again return to South Africa, and on her return to Britain applied for admission to the ANC in exile. Though she was assigned to an ANC unit to work on propaganda, Kitson became increasingly frustrated with what she perceived to be the failure of the ANC, the SACP, and the AAM (with which the ANC and SACP cooperated closely) to mobilize Britons against apartheid. "Even after more than twenty years of existence," she wrote, the AAM's "membership was small, it had almost no influence or active support from any group of British people, and there was virtually no regular activity they could take part in."[41]

These concerns came to a head when Kitson's son Steven was detained in

South Africa in January 1982 during a trip to visit his father in prison. Frustrated with the response of the AAM and the ANC and convinced that her only hope was "to create an uproar of protest in England that would embarrass the South African authorities enough to force them to release Steven," Kitson formed on her own initiative a Free Steven Kitson Campaign, whose first activities included an emergency picket outside South Africa House. Steven Kitson was released after six days in detention, but in that short time the campaign had succeeded in mobilizing hundreds of people. Kitson was concerned not to lose the support of those who had joined the campaign for the anti-apartheid cause, and following Steven's release, the Free Steven Kitson Campaign converted itself into the City of London Anti-Apartheid Group (City AA). Norma Kitson became the treasurer, and most of the other members of the committee were drawn from the staff of Red Lion Setters, the women's typesetting cooperative that Kitson ran.

Reflecting its origins and Norma Kitson's concerns, City AA retained a particular focus on the issue of political prisoners in South Africa, including David Kitson.[42] Norma Kitson was convinced that the Free Steven Kitson Campaign's protests had been responsible for her son's rapid release from detention, and that demonstrations in Britain could have a direct effect on the conditions in which prisoners were held in South Africa and even achieve their release.

> Our experience over the years had shown that when there were campaigns for the prisoners, there were direct positive results. When activity died down, conditions for them worsened. . . . Whenever we managed to join or mount a campaign, there was always some result, sometimes tiny and seemingly insignificant, but always a result. The South African regime was forced to make little adjustments in the face of Western criticism. These small gains—better food, a film once a week, better clothing—seemed paltry to many hard-pressed campaigners in Britain who could not gauge whether their efforts were any use, but they made a difference to the lives of our prisoners. When the prisoners were upgraded, it meant a remarkable improvement in the quality of their lives.[43]

City AA's first nonstop picket, for eighty-six days in autumn 1982, was prompted by concerns for the health of David Kitson and other political prisoners, who had been moved into death row cells in 1979. The slogan used to advertise the picket was "Free All South African Political Prisoners: Save Dave Kitson's Life."[44] For Norma Kitson such campaigns were also an essential form of consciousness-raising: not only did they improve the conditions of prisoners in South Africa, but they also "made more British people aware of what was going on in South Africa and brought them into activity against apartheid."[45]

City AA's success in mobilizing considerable support for its campaigns reflected the organizational support it received from the Revolutionary Communist Group (RCG). Like the Young Liberals, RCG leaders believed that supporting and participating in anti-apartheid activism would enable them to contribute to the transformation of society not only in South Africa but also in Britain itself. The RCG was founded in 1974 after its members were expelled from the International Socialists (the British Trotskyist group that in 1977 renamed itself the Socialist Workers' Party) following an ideological dispute. The RCG saw its central role as creating and training a vanguard of the working class that would be able to break with bourgeois ideology, abandon the struggle for reforms within the capitalist system, and instead fight for state power.

The RCG's objective of creating a revolutionary vanguard led it to focus much of its energy on campaigns on international issues. As the RCG's October 1974 founding document put it, "a small cadre group such as ours must seek out those areas in which it can intervene to win cadres and develop the potential vanguard." Given that the RCG lacked the resources to mount such a campaign within the labor unions, the document concluded that "in Britain's present conditions a group such as ours can best employ its forces in work in international solidarity movements." By working alongside those who participated in such movements and highlighting the role of the British bourgeoisie "in aiding the oppression of other nations and their workers," RCG cadres would be able to demonstrate to British workers "how the Labour Party and the Trades Unions leadership attempt to throw the support of the [working] class behind defence of the national interest and behind the interest of the bourgeoisie, and at the same time we will show the necessity for an independent programme." In this way, the RCG hoped "to draw sections of the potential vanguard into work with us in these movements and convince them of the necessity of mounting a campaign in the class on these political questions. Through this we aim to begin to develop a base in the trades unions."[46]

Although the two international campaigns that the RCG's founding document mentioned were the Troops Out Movement, which campaigned for the withdrawal of British troops from Northern Ireland, and the Chile Solidarity Campaign, the RCG's arguments for working in international solidarity movements could also clearly be applied to the Anti-Apartheid Movement. The RCG first appears to have become interested in South Africa in 1976, when its theoretical journal republished a paper commissioned by the AAM entitled "South Africa: The Crisis in Britain and the Apartheid Economy" alongside a long piece by David Yaffe, the RCG's chief theoretician. Yaffe concluded his article by urging RCG members: "Above all, always link the struggle for liberation in South Africa with the struggle for socialism in Britain."[47]

Yaffe had emphasized that "support for the liberation struggle must go beyond resolutions." There appears to be no evidence, however, that the RCG went beyond rhetorical support of anti-apartheid activism until the arrest of Steven Kitson in 1982 and the decision by Norma Kitson to found City AA. Kitson had first come into contact with the RCG in the mid-1970s, when her cooperative typeset their publications. Though Kitson was a member of both the SACP and the Communist Party of Great Britain (which the RCG spent much energy attacking) she quickly developed a friendship with David Reed, one of the RCG's leaders, whom she considered "a brilliant Marxist-Leninist."[48] In 1976 Carol Brickley, another member of the RCG, joined Kitson's cooperative as an art worker and quickly became her closest friend. These connections played a crucial role following the arrest of Steven Kitson in 1982. As Brickley later recalled, the RCG was "centrally involved" in City AA. Brickley worked together with the Kitson family to found the group, and "together with other RCG members, we mobilized and worked to build events in London." Brickley herself was appointed the group's convenor.[49]

Once Norma Kitson had focused the RCG's attention on apartheid, the issue became one of the group's primary concerns, alongside its ongoing concern with Ireland. The RCG's focus on these two issues was vividly illustrated by the slogan on the front cover of the group's manifesto, published in 1984:

COMPLETE BRITISH WITHDRAWAL FROM IRELAND
SMASH APARTHEID
FIGHT RACISM!
FIGHT IMPERIALISM![50]

The manifesto itself contained long sections on "Ireland and British Imperialism" and "South Africa and British Imperialism." The manifesto justified its focus on these two issues in terms very similar to the RCG's founding document's emphasis on international solidarity movements a decade earlier:

> The working class in Britain, the Irish people and the black masses in Southern Africa have a common interest—the destruction of British imperialism. Only by making common cause with oppressed people fighting British imperialism can the British working class liberate itself. By uniting with the struggles of the oppressed in Ireland and South Africa the British working class not only hastens their victory but also weakens the grip of opportunist and pro-Imperialist Labour and Trades Union leadership over itself. By so doing it paves the way for the victory of communism in Britain.[51]

This orientation was generally much less explicit in the flyers and song sheets City AA produced to advertise its pickets of South Africa House. In these the language of human rights was sometimes used: one flyer explained that the South African government had "deprived the majority of the population in South Africa . . . of all democratic and human rights simply because they are black." One of City AA's picket songs asked in rhyme whether the listener was on the side of "racist whites" and "parasites" or "on the side of human rights." This was only one language among many that were used, however. City AA materials drew upon a number of different tropes in their virulent and wide-ranging condemnation of the South African regime. They routinely condemned the South African government as "racist" and "fascist" and placed great emphasis on its violent, brutal, and repressive character, particularly in its treatment of political prisoners, but also more broadly. The regime had "systematically murdered, tortured, imprisoned and detained its opponents"; the deprivation it imposed on the black population of South Africa amounted to "genocide"; apartheid was a system of "barbaric racism"; and the South African embassy represented "death and hate." City AA materials most commonly characterized the struggle of the ANC and the black population of South Africa as a "struggle for freedom and democracy," without examining further what they understood by either of those terms. They emphasized the importance of solidarity with the ANC and celebrated its armed struggle. One of the picket songs declared that the demonstrators would "not be moved" until Umkhonto we Sizwe had "won the war" and apartheid had been "completely smashed."[52]

At the same time, City AA sought to emphasize through its approach to anti-apartheid activism the need to campaign against what it saw as the op-pressive state in Britain, as well as that in South Africa. In response to what it perceived as the introduction of racist immigration and policing legislation by the Thatcher government, City AA campaigned under the slogan "Britain Out of Apartheid, Apartheid Out of Britain," and worked within the Anti-Apartheid Movement to have AAM campaign against racism in Britain as well as in southern Africa. At the movement's 1984 annual general meeting, for example, City AA succeeded in getting a resolution passed that declared that "the struggle against apartheid cannot be separated from the fight against racism in Britain."[53]

City AA also sought to expose what it perceived as harassment of anti-apartheid activists by the British police. In June 1983, when nine members of the group were arrested during a picket of South Africa House to protest South Africa's execution of three ANC cadres who had become known as the Moroka Three, City AA immediately formed a separate organization to de-fend them. The very name of the Trafalgar 9 Defence Campaign sought to establish equivalence between opponents of apartheid detained by the British state and its opponents detained by the South African state.[54] A year later, when the police imposed a temporary ban on demonstrations outside South Africa House, twenty-four members of City AA, including Norma and Steven Kitson, Carol Brickley, and other RCG members, deliberately violated the ban by crossing the street to the pavement in front of the embassy, and were arrested. Once again, City AA formed an organization, the South African Embassy Picket Campaign (SAEPC), to work for the lifting of the ban and to defend those arrested. An SAEPC flyer argued: "The ever more open alliance of the British government with the racist South African state is inevitably leading to greater attacks on democratic rights in Britain. To protest effec-tively against apartheid now means to fight to defend democratic rights in Britain."[55]

There is also considerable evidence that City AA sought to convert the many activists who participated in its pickets who were not members of the RCG to the RCG's political orientation. Though City AA strenuously denied to the national AAM that it promoted the literature of any British political organization, the AAM national office repeatedly expressed its concern about the promotion of the RCG's newspaper *Fight Racism! Fight Imperialism!* at City AA pickets. During the nonstop picket in 1982 a "Pavement University" was held every night, consisting of two or three ten-minute lectures and then discussion among the "Pickies." Though anyone could put down their name and the subject on which they wished to speak, and all those present voted each night on who should speak, the RCG apparently saw this as a means of educating the pickets about the connection it drew between the struggle against apartheid in South Africa and its own struggle for communism in Britain. City AA secretary Chris Fraser wrote in June 1983 that "often these 'university' sessions were addressed by 15-year-old youth about their own lives and many made the link between their oppression and the oppression of their peers in South Africa."[56]

Conclusion

In the long 1970s, British media and public interest in apartheid and in anti-apartheid campaigns was much lower than it would be in the mid- to late 1980s. Two factors in particular seem to have contributed to the explosion of interest in and campaigning against apartheid in the 1980s. First, the uprising in South Africa's townships between 1984 and 1986, and the South African government's attempts to suppress it generated sustained media coverage. Reports from South Africa were on Britain's television, radio, and newspapers daily for much of 1985. The South African government's high-profile efforts both to suppress the uprising and to counter the international condemnation the uprising generated—including its declarations of states of emergency in July 1985 and June 1986, and President P. W. Botha's notorious "Rubicon" speech in August 1985—only generated further media interest and public activism. Moreover, in contrast to the more amorphous character of the Soweto uprising in 1976, the formation of the United Democratic Front in South Africa in 1983 gave domestic resistance to apartheid a public face and media-savvy domestic spokesmen—most notably Bishop Desmond Tutu and Reverend Allan Boesak—who could articulate the demands of the South African opposition for an international audience.

Second, in the British context it was also important that Conservative prime minister Margaret Thatcher's outspoken opposition to imposing sanctions on South Africa and the perception that she was sympathetic to the South African regime helped to generate further British activism. The fact that Britain had a Labour government between 1974 and 1979 probably contributed to the relative lack of public support for anti-apartheid campaigns in the 1970s. Those on the left opposed to apartheid were more likely to believe that the Labour government's denunciations of the South African government were sincere, even if they believed its actions against it did not go far enough. Some may also have been more reluctant to campaign directly and openly against the policies of a Labour government. There were no such inhibitions to anti-apartheid activism under Thatcher, and, indeed, campaigning against apartheid probably garnered additional support precisely because it was a means of expressing opposition to the Conservative government.

The relatively limited support that anti-apartheid activism attracted in Britain in the long 1970s compared to the mid-1980s highlights the importance of paying attention to multiple chronologies in the histories of human rights and humanitarian activism. Not only did international campaigns on different issues follow significantly different courses, but international campaigns on the same issue, such as apartheid, may have followed significantly different courses in different countries. The mid-1980s witnessed an explosion of interest in and campaigning against apartheid not only in Britain but also in the United States and many other countries, a phenomenon that requires much further research. At other times, however, anti-apartheid activism appears to have followed distinctly national rhythms, depending on the interaction in each country of transnational factors with the kind of national factors examined here.

This chapter has highlighted the importance of disaggregating and paying attention to the motivations and purposes of the particular groups and individuals who initiated and led anti-apartheid campaigns in the 1970s, and to the circumstances that led them to focus their attention on South Africa rather than on other international or domestic issues. In the cases of the campaigns studied here, two key conclusions stand out. First, both the Young Liberals and the RCG believed that their activism against apartheid would transform the political and economic order in Britain itself, as well as in South Africa. For the Young Liberals, direct action against South African sports teams playing in Britain would not only deal a blow to apartheid by increasing South Africa's international isolation. It would also give those who took part the experience of participation in the exercise of power in their local community and would thus be a first step toward the establishment of "community self-government." For the RCG, participation in anti-apartheid activism would enable it to recruit and educate cadres who would form the vanguard of the working class and lead a communist revolution in Britain.

It was the combination of these domestic political concerns with outrage at apartheid that made the apartheid issue urgent enough for these groups to devote so much of their energy to campaigning against it. In neither case was that campaigning framed primarily in terms of human rights. Human rights appear rather to have been an incipient protest language. Both the Young Liberals and City AA did sporadically draw upon the language of human rights to express their opposition to apartheid, but this was only one of several languages used. In both cases, for example, the language of antiracism was much more prevalent.

What was perhaps to some extent unique about the issue of apartheid in South Africa, compared to some of the other repressive regimes of the period, was that it offered multiple entry points for activists of many different political persuasions and with a diverse range of international and domestic objectives. This was particularly the case in Britain, where the earlier imperial relationship with South Africa meant that there were a variety of long-standing ties between the two countries that activists could exploit. Those entry points ranged from the South African produce sold in British stores to the prominent British corporations with investments in South Africa, to the close sports relations targeted by STST, to the close diplomatic ties represented by the South African embassy right in Trafalgar Square (long a rallying point for protests and demonstrations), which provided a focal point for the campaigns of City AA.

In the cases of both the Young Liberals and the RCG there were many issues other than apartheid in South Africa that would have served equally well as means to promote community politics and communist revolution, respectively. Thus a second conclusion can be drawn from these cases. The turn of the Young Liberals and the RCG to apartheid as a major focus reflected to a large extent the initiative in each case of a single white South African exile. Peter Hain and Norma Kitson were each able to focus the attention of the Young Liberals and the RCG respectively on targeting South Africa as a means of promoting those groups' domestic, as well as international, objectives. Similarly, South African exiles and other individuals with personal connections to South Africa appear to have played a crucial role in other major anti-apartheid groups and campaigns in Britain. Britain's former imperial relationship with South Africa meant that many people had such connections, and many exiled opponents of the South African regime settled in Britain.

Anti-apartheid activism in Britain, then, must be understood as simultaneously both a transnational and a national phenomenon. At some moments, such as in the mid-1980s, developments inside South Africa itself played a crucial role in determining the chronology of anti-apartheid activism around the world. Anti-apartheid activists developed a range of techniques to exploit transnational connections between South Africa and the rest of the world—such as those developed by sports organizations and multinational corporations—in order to exert pressure on the South African regime. Ideas about such techniques circulated transnationally. But anti-apartheid activism in different countries also followed distinct national patterns and chronologies. The transnational processes highlighted by some scholars—such as the development of new forms of travel and communications—may have been necessary conditions for such activism, but they are not sufficient to explain why particular individuals and groups in Britain (and elsewhere) came to focus on apartheid, and why they did so at particular moments. The evidence from the British cases analyzed here suggests that such an explanation requires attention both to the specific objectives, including *domestic* political objectives, of the various groups and individuals who became heavily involved in anti-apartheid activism, and to the particular individuals—often South African exiles or others with personal connections to South Africa—who provided the initial impetus for those groups to focus on the issue.

Chapter 13

The Rebirth of Politics from
the Spirit of Morality:
Explaining the Human Rights
Revolution of the 1970s

Jan Eckel

In the past few years, the 1970s have rapidly moved to the center of scholarly interest. Interpretations have thrived at the same time as—and sometimes, it seems, even before—the contours of important events and developments are beginning to appear in research-based studies. Most historians have shaped the 1970s as a novel and distinctive phase in contemporary history and consequently accentuated the historical breaks that marked the transition from the 1960s to the following decade. Eric Hobsbawm many years ago diagnosed the "end of the golden age," which in his view inaugurated an era of long-term problems.[1] Those trends that have attracted most attention in recent historiographical discussion seem to largely confirm his early assessment. Most strikingly perhaps, the 1970s were a decade of pervasive economic insecurity. They saw the breakdown of the Bretton Woods system, two oil price shocks, a hitherto unknown "stagflation," and steep rises in unemployment. The optimistic belief in ongoing political progress secured by scientific planning quickly evaporated as consciousness of the "limits to growth" and acute perceptions of crisis spread.[2]

The tale is not entirely one of decline, though. In Europe, welfare states saw a vast expansion and mass consumerism continued unabated. On a global scale, democracy was strengthened while at the same time party systems in the Western world reconfigured, with the emergence of the new left and the rise of a populist right. Extra-parliamentary activism arguably left an even deeper imprint on the political scenes than in previous decades, as was most visibly manifested in the blossoming new social movements of various stripes. Not least, a cultural revolution, if there ever was one, occurred in the reshaping of relations between the sexes.

International relations, too, were subject to rapid change. The decade surprised observers with a rapid turnaround, as the era of détente reached its apex only to be followed by the outbreak of the "Second Cold War." But even though the superpowers reverted to their old bipolar antagonism, the clock was not fully turned back. In the 1970s, the field of international actors considerably diversified. China and the Arab countries emerged as potent players in the international arena. Moreover, both the impressive ascendancy of non-state actors in the international realm and the growing importance of transnational issues such as environmental protection or population control dramatically altered preconditions for foreign policy making. Looking back at many of these transformations, historians have discovered in the 1970s the roots of the world as we know it. They consider the decade to constitute the immediate prehistory, as it were, of our present.[3]

Human rights do not notably figure in these descriptions of the decade. Yet the 1970s saw a vigorous surge in the popularity of the idea and an impressive proliferation of political practices associated with it. The purpose of this essay is therefore twofold. On the one hand, I will suggest an explanatory framework for the new prominence that human rights gained in the international politics of the decade. On the other, I will place this conjuncture in the broader history of the period. Surveying some of the most important developments, I will argue that the 1970s did mark a new moment in human rights history. Nonetheless, this new moment should not be viewed as homogeneous and clear-cut but as an intricate and manifold shift. The decade presents a complex picture that cannot be traced back to a single cause and hardly lends itself to a grand narrative. To explain the diverse initiatives and various new departures shaping human rights politics in the 1970s, we need to understand both how they were related to more general transformations in international relations and political culture, and the inherent appeal they possessed for politicians and activists in different world regions. Human rights in the 1970s appear as a multifaceted promise of moral renewal that in view of the profound changes in the structure of national and international politics came to be seen as increasingly attractive, both ideologically and strategically. Their essential attractiveness lay in the fact that human rights seemed to provide a way of responding to the failure of older political projects, of transcending the logic of the Cold War, of basing political action on a moral foundation, and of reaching a vantage point that supposedly was above politics.

Human Rights in the 1970s

On the surface, the history of human rights in the 1970s neatly fits in the picture of profound upheaval that recent interpretations have drawn. The decade saw an astonishing confluence of developments, many of which clearly represented new political departures. This was true for the mushrooming of human rights groups in Western countries. In the 1970s, innumerable groups emerged, the vast majority of them rather ephemeral, loosely institutionalized, and organized on a grassroots basis. They differed considerably in their outlooks and fields of action, some rallying around countries or regions where human rights violations occurred, others dealing with issues such as torture or indigenous rights. Still others engaged on behalf of prominent human rights martyrs, such as Andrei Sakharov or Nelson Mandela. Their activism overlapped with the concerns of other movements. Human rights advocates at times adopted and reinforced the demands of feminist or Third World activists, for instance, and these in turn couched their demands in human rights language. Nevertheless, in the political jargon of the time "human rights" increasingly came to signify a type, or at least a current, of activism sui generis. Contemporary observers were amazed by the sudden upsurge and sardonically spoke of a "human rights industry" building up before their eyes.[4]

As far as the highly professional and politically potent human rights NGOs were concerned, the most important ones had been established in previous decades: the International League for the Rights of Man in 1941, the International Commission of Jurists in 1952, and Amnesty International in 1961. Yet these NGOs underwent profound institutional transformations that both testified to the growing attractiveness of their political project and significantly enhanced their impact on international politics. Amnesty International's development is a powerful case in point.[5] During the 1970s, the London-based organization saw a dramatic growth in membership and, leaving its sectarian beginnings behind, turned into a real mass movement. Perhaps even more tellingly, the organization expanded its geographical scope. Before the early 1970s, Amnesty was practically limited to four countries. Internal statistics reveal that almost 90 percent of local groups resided in Great Britain, Sweden, Denmark, and the Federal Republic of Germany.[6] It was only subsequently that the Amnesty movement took off and spread in many other Western countries.

In addition, the advent of Amnesty sparked a chain reaction that would deeply reshape the field of professional human rights NGOs. Beginning in the late 1960s, the New York–based International League for the Rights of Man initiated a reform process to modernize its institutional structures and to overcome some of the flaws that the board of directors thought hampered its activism.[7] To this end, the league copied many of the techniques that the London organization had forged. In particular, it was Amnesty's public relations work and its strategies of information gathering that the league chose to adopt. The only new major international human rights NGO that was formed in the 1970s, the later Human Rights Watch, vastly expanded after the turn of the decade. Even so, the Watch groups were also deeply indebted to Amnesty International in their use of the media, their ways of exerting pressure on governments, and their very reference to the idea of human rights.

The appeal of human rights was not limited to those who chose to defend the "rights of others," however. Among the most noticeable departures in the decade's human rights history, and even in its history of international politics at large, was the attempt of opposition groups to appropriate the idea in order to protect themselves from state repression and persecution. South America was one of the regions where this attempt resonated most strongly. Since the late 1960s, a wave of military coups had brought the subcontinent under the rule of a new type of military dictatorship. These regimes used an unprecedented level of violence to eradicate real or imagined Marxist tendencies and to kill or otherwise eliminate their political enemies.[8] The fact that in the international arena these regimes came to be closely associated with their "human rights violations," possibly more so than other states of the period, and certainly much more so than previous Latin American governments, is in itself revealing. An important reason lay in the struggle of opposition movements within the dictatorships. Comparably strong and well-organized groups emerged in Brazil, Chile, and Argentina, which strongly drew on human rights language and directed their appeals to international bodies. The Argentine Mothers of the Plaza de Mayo figure among the widely admired icons of the period's history of protest.[9] In Chile, the church-based Vicaría de la Solidaridad played a key role, particularly in the early years.[10]

Developments in Eastern Europe, the second region where human rights strongly came to the fore as a protest language, were similar insofar as dissidents used many of the same political strategies as South American opposition figures. They documented abuses, held their governments accountable to international norms and built up transnational networks with Western NGOs. Communist dictatorships arguably had a longer history of being confronted with human rights denunciations. The postwar decades had seen an international campaign against forced labor, partly supported by the United Nations, and the agitation of groups such as the Assembly of Captive European Nations, which had strongly relied on international human rights norms.[11] However, during these years of fierce internal repression, protests had mainly been waged from the outside. In the 1970s, by contrast, human rights groups emerged within Eastern European states, many of which rose to international prominence or even fame. The years 1976 and 1977, for instance, saw the formation of the Moscow Helsinki Group in the Soviet Union, the Workers' Defense Committee (KOR) and the Movement for the Defense of Human and Civil Rights (ROPCiO) in Poland, and the famous Charter 77 in Czechoslovakia.[12]

These new oppositional politics were in many ways linked to the Conference on Security and Cooperation in Europe (CSCE), a further and striking new development in international relations.[13] The conference, whose origins dated back to a Warsaw Pact proposal of 1969, constituted the first multilateral negotiations between the two Cold War camps since the immediate aftermath of World War II. Human rights formed an essential and strongly contested part of the negotiations. Both superpowers were initially skeptical as to their inclusion in the treaties, and the Soviet Union remained so throughout, being mostly interested in international guarantees of territorial integrity and of the postwar borders. Ultimately, it was the states of the European Community that in spite of strong resistance managed to keep human rights on the agenda. By signing the Helsinki Final Act in 1975, all participating states acknowledged that human rights were one of the "principles guiding relations between participating states." Further, they stipulated a set of so-called humanitarian provisions designed to facilitate "human contacts" across the West-East divide. Finally, states in Helsinki agreed to organize follow-up conferences, which were to take place in Belgrade (1977–1978), Madrid (1980–1983), and Vienna (1986–1989). Since Western governments regularly used these conferences as platforms to denounce violations behind the Iron Curtain, what came to be known as the CSCE process assured that the human rights situation in Eastern bloc countries remained under scrutiny until the very end of the Cold War.[14]

The extremely active role that Western states played in this process was partly related to the fact that in the 1970s human rights gained a new relevance in their foreign policy. Several governments set out to define or redefine their attitude toward the new catchword of the times. While some took the lead in incorporating human rights into the stated aims of their foreign policy, others felt compelled to react to the new wave of interest, occasionally taking human rights into consideration. They all contributed to a shift in international politics whose importance can hardly be overestimated. Human rights ceased to be a topic confined to states' policies toward international organizations, as it had been in the postwar decades. Now they entered the mainstream of bilateral relations to a much greater extent than before, moving human rights issues to the center of international relations.

The most influential of these new approaches was doubtless the policy adopted by the U.S. government under President Jimmy Carter, which probably did more than any other single actor to popularize the term in the international realm.[15] After embracing them late in his electoral campaign, Carter repeatedly declared human rights to be a central tenet of U.S. foreign policy and, for better or worse, identified his government's record with their protection worldwide. There is an ongoing discussion among scholars about the inconsistencies and shortcomings of Carter's approach—a discussion that essentially prolongs the contemporary debate, which had also centered around the supposedly selective application and counterproductive outcomes of the administration's policy. But irrespective of which side one takes in this debate, the Carter government unquestionably made human rights a systematic part and even an important pillar of its foreign relations. The archival record reveals that State Department planners reflected intensely on how to inject human rights in bilateral and multilateral relations and that they quite realistically discussed the means, prospects, and limits of this project.[16] Whatever the record after four years of government, the Carter administration had clearly attempted to fundamentally reorient U.S. policy in the world.

Furthermore, the United States was not the only state and, contrary to a widely held belief, not even the first one to develop a human rights foreign policy. Already in 1973, the leftist government of Joop den Uyl in the Netherlands had declared human rights to be an "integral part" of its international relations. Most notably, the foreign minister Max van der Stoel and the minister of developmental cooperation Jan Pronk incorporated human rights into their agendas during the four years of Den Uyl's premiership. Although both politicians at times pursued conflicting lines, human rights considerations came to strongly determine Dutch relations with several foreign states.[17] For Sweden, international human rights protection had an equally high priority in these years. Particularly the Social Democrat government of Olof Palme in the late 1960s and early 1970s lent much support to international campaigns. The Swiss government in the late 1960s and again toward the end of the following decade moved to emphasize the country's commitment to human rights norms. Interestingly however, it was Switzerland's still powerful self-image as a neutral country that in both cases prevented the government from leveling strong criticism against other states and thus from living up to its proclamations.[18] Even so, the new initiatives in the realm of foreign policy as well as in civil activism and multilateral relations clearly provided the idea of human rights with a new salience in international politics.

Complicating the Picture

Multiple Chronologies

Yet even though the new trends in international relations were marked, it would be wrong to assume that the 1970s constituted a coherent or homogeneous decade. To begin with, not all of the important impulses actually originated in the 1970s. Some emerged earlier, some later; several resulted from a longer evolution, while others sprang up abruptly and virtually unforeseen. A closer look at some of the human rights movements reveals multiple chronologies. Soviet human rights advocates in retrospect dated the first stirrings of their activism back to the mid-1960s.[19] In their accounts, the 1965 trial against the writers Andrei Sinyavsky and Yuli Daniel, which had sparked a series of public protests for freedom of opinion, constituted a moment of *prise de conscience*. Three years later, dissidents started to publish the *Chronicle of Current Events*, which meticulously documented government abuses and, translated by activists abroad, played a crucial role in publicizing the deplorable state of liberties in the Soviet Union. Although early demands for greater freedoms had mainly referred to the Soviet Constitution and thus to national legal norms, from the late 1960s on dissidents made use of their government's international commitments.[20] After 1968, dissidents increasingly invoked international human rights norms, and human rights groups emerged as early as in 1969. A Russian section of Amnesty International was established in 1971.

While the Soviet human rights movement took shape before the adoption of the Helsinki Final Act, the picture was different in Poland. Like in the Soviet Union, the Polish opposition of the 1970s had a longer history, dating back at least to the 1960s. And just like in the neighboring country, 1968 marked a turning point for opposition figures in Poland, provoking intense discussions about how to reevaluate their ideological beliefs and devise new political strategies. However, it was only the successful conclusion of the Helsinki negotiations that catalyzed their turn toward human rights.[21] In fact, the two years after 1975 saw the creation of Poland's most important human rights groups, KOR and ROPCiO.

Crucial as it was in the Polish case, the appeal of the CSCE process remained clearly limited elsewhere. The Helsinki Accords did not initiate sudden change in all the Eastern European states where human rights had not taken root before the mid-1970s. Already at the time, Western activists wondered why East Germany lagged so conspicuously behind.[22] The GDR in the wake of Helsinki saw a brief flurry of demands for freedom of movement, but these did not coalesce into a sustained and public protest movement.[23] It was not until 1985 that the first East German human rights NGO, the Initiative for Peace and Human Rights (IFM), was finally formed, giving rise to a widespread discussion among dissidents about the concept.

In South America, by contrast, human rights activism clearly responded to the advent of institutionalized military dictatorships and the shock waves that their brutal methods of repression sent through the continent. The time pattern therefore appears both more coherent and more discontinuous than the one in Eastern Europe. Scholars agree that human rights had played virtually no role as a protest language in the decades after the Second World War.[24] This began to change in the late 1960s, although the 1973 military coup in Chile would mark the decisive caesura. In Brazil, where the military established the first of the new South American dictatorships in 1964, opposition groups appear to have gradually adopted the idea of human rights in the last years of the decade.[25] This shift largely coincided with the most violent phase in the regime's history, between 1968 and 1973.[26] In Chile, developments unfolded much faster. Almost immediately after the overthrow of Salvador Allende, human rights became an important political device for the defense against state terror.[27] Toward the end of the 1970s, the human rights movement in Chile seems to have expanded further, a fact that testifies more to the relative slackening of the junta's repression than to a new appeal of the human rights idea. Events in Chile moreover resonated strongly beyond its borders, as can be inferred from developments in neighboring Argentina.[28] There, activists established human rights organizations even before the military takeover of 1976. Confronted with the near breakdown of public order, and amid increasing violence from both leftist guerrilla movements and right-wing terrorist groups, they created the Servicio para la Paz y Justicia (SERPAJ) in 1974 and the Asamblea Permanente por los Derechos Humanos in 1975. Both would remain active for the duration of the dictatorship. Even though the transition was more gradual than in Chile, human rights activism notably increased after the military established its devastating rule.

Finally, chronological comparison between the two regions not only reveals different geneses of human rights movements but also divergent trajectories. While their beginnings appear to have been less evolutionary in South America than in Eastern Europe, the movements proved more successful in staying on the scene. Communist rulers cracked down on practically all dissident human rights groups in the late 1970s and early 1980s. By contrast, many important organizations in the South American dictatorships managed to survive—at great cost, it should be added, since activists operated under permanent threat and many lost their lives. Human rights claims continued to be a rallying cry in the transitions to democracy that started in Argentina in 1983 and concluded with the elections in Chile in 1990. In the 1980s, human rights activism even spread beyond military dictatorships to formally democratic states such as Peru or Colombia, where advocates attempted to stem both state repression and the violence of guerrilla groups.

Other human rights causes followed even larger rhythms than the ones in South America and Eastern Europe. The most long-standing movement, if indeed it can be considered as a single continuous movement, was the one that fought against apartheid in South Africa. Some groups started to wage their campaigns as early as in the 1950s—such as the American Committee on Africa, in the United States, or the Movement for Colonial Freedom, in Great Britain. And to be sure, until the end of the white minority regime in 1994 transnational protest would never completely disappear. Anti-apartheid activism appears as a case par excellence to study the logic of protest cycles, since it points to the often contingent, strongly media related, and always multifarious causes behind the ebb and flow of international concern.[29] In many Western countries, organized protest against South Africa emerged in response to the African National Congress's demands in 1959 for an international boycott and would be fuelled by the Sharpeville massacre of the following year. The 1970s, particularly the second half, did have some significance in this story, as they marked a relative high point in anti-apartheid initiatives in several countries. After the Soweto massacre of 1976, various Western governments hardened their stance toward South Africa, the United Nations imposed a mandatory embargo, and NGOs redoubled their efforts at pushing their home governments to become active. However, the peak of mobilization against the racist regime was not reached before the mid-1980s. It was sparked by the vicious circle of increasing political unrest in South Africa and ever more violent state oppression. The regime declared a state of emergency and in 1985 committed the worst single killings since Sharpeville, leaving twenty-one dead. Against the backdrop of record media coverage, debate about possible sanctions against the racist state intensified in Great Britain, Sweden, and the United States. At the same time, nonstate groups mounted massive pressure through large-scale demonstrations, vigils, and boycott appeals. In 1988, several immensely popular rock bands participated in a birthday concert for Nelson Mandela, which an estimated audience of 600 million followed on television worldwide.

Different Forms of Appropriation

Temporal dynamics were not the only feature highlighting the diverse and anything-but-clear-cut patterns of the decade. Moreover, different forms of appropriation shaped the human rights history of the 1970s, even where actors were politically or culturally close or operated under similar circumstances. Although many Western governments displayed a new openness to international human rights claims, they remained far from developing a uniform morality in their foreign policies. Even Social Democrat governments, which came to be almost hegemonic in the 1970s, did not share anything like a common approach. The case of the West German government provides an illustrative example. Chancellor Helmut Schmidt's contempt for Jimmy Carter's supposedly idealistic approach to foreign relations was no secret even at the time. Schmidt was concerned, and not without reason, that human rights criticism leveled at repressive regimes might strain international politics.

More generally, the West German government in its foreign policy never went beyond a purely reactive approach.[30] On almost all occasions that Bonn included human rights considerations in its bilateral relations, it yielded to pressures from either domestic interests and human rights groups or from international partners, particularly the states of the European Community. At times human rights concerns became so important as to produce conflicts of interest. The government weighed moral convictions against their interest in the NATO alliance, in the case of the military junta that ruled Greece after 1967, or against trade relations, in the case of South Africa. Yet human rights never turned into a political end in itself or even received high priority.

If the relevance that actors attributed to human rights differed, so did the reasons why they adopted them and the meaning they invested in them. Global and transnational historians have in past years not tired of stressing that cross-national trends are usually shaped according to the circumstances prevailing in the national or even local realms. Their observations also apply to the way nonstate groups in Western states appropriated human rights and defined their engagement. Many derived at least part of their motivations from the historical traditions and political landscapes of their own countries. Activists often referred to their state's history of crime to justify and strengthen their fight against current injustices in faraway countries. German proponents of human rights, for instance, evoked National Socialist abuses, while Dutch activists pointed to Dutch colonial rule, which in fact was only terminated in 1975.[31] It deserves to be further explored, however, if and to what extent "Holocaust consciousness" and feelings of colonial guilt became themselves internationalized in the 1970s.

All Western human rights movements shared a highly critical attitude toward the foreign record of their own governments, pressuring them to support international norms and to take action against human rights violations abroad. Yet both the character and the urgency of these criticisms varied. While activists in countries such as West Germany or Switzerland mainly focused on their governments' trade relations, human rights groups in the United States far into the 1970s grappled with their government's covert and overt interventions in foreign countries. Many activists cited these experiences as a prime reason for getting involved in human rights work in the first place. To be sure, there was no lack of occasions. Beginning with the military intervention in the Dominican Republic in 1965, U.S. policy in the world drove many at home to engage in internationalist causes.[32] This was most notably true for the crucial support that the Nixon administration lent to the

Brazilian, Greek, and Chilean dictatorships—the latter was even widely believed to have been installed by a CIA-implemented coup.

Changing Constellations of Actors

The cold-blooded overthrow of Chilean president Salvador Allende and the ensuing repression met with a measure of international outrage and mobilization that was arguably more intense and more geographically widespread than in all previous cases of state terror. In fact, the international campaign against the Pinochet dictatorship, together with the one against the apartheid regime in South Africa, can be counted among the strongest and most prolonged ever waged against a single country.[33] It is from the history of these causes célèbres that political scientists have developed their concept of "transnational advocacy networks." They refer to coalitions consisting of governments, intergovernmental organizations such as the United Nations and the Organization of American States, and domestic and international NGOs all joining forces to end violence and aid victims.[34] In the abstract, this picture is certainly accurate. Similar networks were at work in all human rights campaigns against state repression since the 1960s and even earlier. However, this should not lead scholars to overlook the different composition of these networks in different cases. The fact that international human rights efforts were supported by changing constellations of actors constitutes another important facet of the decade's diversity. A brief look at the role of the church may suffice to highlight the varying degrees of support that a single actor lent to human rights struggles. In Chile, the Catholic Church formed the heart of the opposition to the Pinochet regime. It made use of its relative, if always precarious, immunity from state interference to provide shelter to the persecuted and build up crucial networks for legal advice and material aid. In Brazil, Catholic priests were likewise highly instrumental in organizing resistance and documenting human rights violations, particularly by disclosing evidence about endemic torture.[35] In Argentina, by contrast, the Catholic Church as an institution remained silent in the face of the military's fight against political opponents and at times even backed it.[36] Many activists embarked on the defense of human rights only after failing to receive church support. In Eastern Europe, Catholic priests played an important role in the context of the Polish opposition of the 1970s, as did the Protestant churches in the emerging human rights movement in East Germany in the 1980s. The same could not be claimed, however, for the Orthodox Church in the Soviet Union.

The fact that actor coalitions shifted is even more obvious when it comes to government actions. The decision whether or not to accuse another state of human rights violations unfailingly grew out of complex calculations about geostrategic priorities, economic needs, and humanitarian self-image. It may be argued that the state coalitions targeting South American dictatorships were exceptionally broad, precisely because these regimes came to represent a sort of lowest common denominator.[37] Even so, before 1977 the United States did not join these campaigns. Western European governments by and large supported international action against state crimes in South America. By contrast, they remained considerably more muted in their criticism of the military junta that ruled Greece between 1967 and 1974, careful not to endanger the NATO membership of this particularly important strategic ally. No human rights initiative managed to really surmount the political and ideological cleavages prevailing in the international arena. Human rights criticism of socialist state repression obviously did not receive encouragement from Eastern Europe. African states in the United Nations effectively blocked action on the mass murders in Uganda, Equatorial Guinea, or the Central African Republic, and the Organization of African Unity did not intervene. The appalling state crimes in Asia hardly even gave rise to any extended international effort at all, with China, Cambodia, and Indonesia figuring among the most glaring omissions.[38]

Limits of Human Rights Discourse

The role that African and Asian states played in this context suggests a final and particularly important modification in the picture of the 1970s, as they point to the limits of human rights discourse. The human rights history of the decade was marked by geographical divides that not only shaped the way in which actors adopted and defined the idea but also the degree to which it penetrated their ideological self-understanding and political practices. Africa and Asia are deplorably under-researched regions in this global story, but it seems safe to say that human rights did not acquire the same prominence there as in Western countries, either for governments or for nongovernmental organizations. A profound gap opened between the outlook of human rights NGOs in the global South and those in the global North. The former almost exclusively aimed at self-help and self-protection, whereas the latter embarked on a vigorous moral interventionism reaching into the world's remotest corners.

Similarly, no government in the global South drew as heavily on human rights rhetoric to justify its foreign policies as some Western states did. Nevertheless, attitudes of these governments are not easily categorized and on the whole reveal a certain ambiguity. On the one hand, the 1970s saw an attempt by African and Asian states to redefine the idea of human rights at the intergovernmental level. In the previous decade, nationalist movements and postcolonial states at the United Nations had mainly used the term to denounce colonial rule, and the Non-Aligned Movement continued to do so at its conferences throughout the 1970s.[39] Now an additional strategy emerged, however, since both the Afro-Asian bloc at the UN and the Non-Aligned Movement began to frame their concern for economic development in human rights language. Their initiative reacted to what they saw as the failure of the development model practiced by Western countries.[40] In their attempt to establish a "right to development," African and Asian countries employed human rights claims to expose the injustice of the postcolonial world order and to lessen Third World dependence on wealthy industrialized nations—largely unsuccessfully, as became evident by the mid-1980s.

On the other hand, an opposing discourse emerged on the African and Asian continents, rejecting human rights as a Western conception inappropriate to political and social realities in the global South. The vast majority of postcolonial governments, in their attempts to stabilize their newly gained power and to accelerate economic progress, had established harshly authoritarian systems relying on resolute suppression of opposition groups. Under these auspices, governments were hardly prepared to promote political freedoms and civil liberties internationally. But their new hostility toward human rights also responded to what they perceived as undue Western interference in their domestic affairs. Indeed, the surge of human rights politics in the West brought a flurry of criticism by both governments and NGOs that not only denounced political injustices but increasingly also cultural practices such as the treatment of women and children in supposedly "traditional" societies. At their 1979 conference, the Non-Aligned Movement strongly protested against Western states' attempt to use human rights accusations to patronize and ultimately prolong their domination over Third World countries.[41] Against this background, the view gained currency that human rights were a Western ideology designed to impose liberal and individualist norms on non-Western cultures. In the United Nations, so-called Third World countries as early as in the late 1960s began to contest the concept of civil and political rights as well as the universality of the human rights idea. During the

1970s, their contributions were largely limited to discrediting the human rights idea as an expression of Western imperialism and neocolonial designs.[42] Furthermore, toward the end of the decade a broad debate unfolded among African intellectuals about the meaning and relevance of human rights.[43] Some authors voiced a radical rejection of the idea. The dominant approach, however, was to counter the supposedly Western values with genuinely African legal concepts or even to construct an African tradition of human rights. These ideas encompassed "cultural relativism," the notion that legal and moral concepts were the product of distinct cultures; communitarian models emphasizing duties within the community over individual rights; and collective rights such as the right to development.

It was not only at the level of global divisions and conflicts, however, that human rights discourse remained restricted. Even the uses that Western movements made of the term during the high tide of the 1970s reveal limits. Human rights campaigns were seldom only human rights campaigns. In their efforts to shame foreign governments, activists harnessed a panoply of discourses separated by highly fluid and permeable boundaries. The campaigns against the Pinochet dictatorship and the South African apartheid regime, for instance, were strongly supported by people who thought of themselves as human rights advocates. The varieties of rhetoric that international opponents employed against both states were on the whole much more diverse, however. The hundreds of Chile solidarity groups emerging in the Western world after the military coup, coalescing into massive movements in countries such as Great Britain, Sweden or West Germany, clearly engaged in a leftist political critique of the emerging military regime. Antifascism was consequently a crucial point of reference in their campaigns. Anti-apartheid activists likewise couched their denunciations of the regime in anticolonial language or claimed the right to self-determination without necessarily referring to human rights. Many in addition relied on an ideology of antiracism.[44] Further, both movements strongly attacked transnational corporations and global capitalism for their supposed complicity in the crimes and both heavily drew on anti-imperialist discourse.

Finally, human rights advocates did not confront all forms of state injustice with equal vigor, nor did they always meet with the same measure of public support. The vastly heightened awareness of human suffering had a reverse side, as numerous issues that could have been considered human rights violations de facto fell out of its focus. Amnesty International, for instance, invested many resources in its "Campaign for the Abolition of the

Death Penalty," which was in fact one of the organization's major undertakings during the decade. Yet nowhere does this campaign seem to have resonated as strongly as its campaign against torture.[45] Certainly in the United States, where other human rights issues boomed in these years, Amnesty failed to mobilize the public—and even its own members—against the death penalty. Activities got off to a bumpy start and later attracted a fair amount of internal criticism precisely because the investments did not seem to pay off. State executions lacked the acuteness that torture, massacres, and other sudden eruptions of large-scale violence undoubtedly had. The death penalty was much more of a structural problem, deeply embedded in legal culture and administrative practice. Perhaps most important, American Amnesty members had numerous reasons to shy away from the topic. Some thought it would be hypocritical to become active as their own state resisted abolishing the death penalty, while others feared they would harm the organization's reputation in the American public. Still others believed that executing criminals was a just punishment.[46]

Explaining the 1970s Human Rights Moment: Extraneous Causes and Contexts

While the overarching trend in the decade's human rights history was a forceful global upsurge, a closer survey thus reveals a much more fractured picture. The "human rights revolution" of the 1970s can clearly not be viewed as a uniform shift. Rather, it evolved in a polycentric and fitful process, or perhaps more accurately in a set of processes mutually reinforcing each other but nevertheless distinct in themselves.

The complex nature and global reach of this breakthrough inevitably raises the question of what type of explanation may account for it. What seems obvious is that the new departures cannot all be traced back to a single historical cause. To reduce them to one or the other motive, be it at the level of ideologies, political strategies, or social movements, could not but brush over the very diversity that makes human rights politics during the 1970s so interesting. An explanatory framework has to be both more and less comprehensive than any monocausal interpretation could be: more comprehensive in that it needs to include a broad set of factors and various levels of analysis, less so in that each factor explains only part of the overall process and does not necessarily encompass the whole.

A good starting point might be to consider extraneous causes. Not all of the reasons for the rise of human rights resided in the meanings of the idea itself and its ideological or political substance. Human rights initiatives, like other social practices, were deeply embedded in the surrounding political culture, growing out of broader political and social trends and depending on opportunities. More specifically, it was a multidimensional political shift in world political and national constellations as well as in political styles that provided an important background to the decade's human rights conjuncture.

Decolonization

To begin with, two major trends in international relations deserve closer examination. Decolonization had by the late 1960s brought the virtual end of colonial rule, with some notable exceptions such as the Portuguese territories. For Western powers, loss of empire entailed a whole range of often arduous readjustments in their foreign policies. In the realm of human rights, however, it seemed to make things easier. As long as they had held on to their empires, Great Britain, France, or the Netherlands had often come under hard-hitting public attacks upon their human rights record.[47] This was most tangible in the United Nations, where postcolonial and socialist states almost ritually lambasted them for their oppressive and discriminatory behavior. The fear of opening the doors to anticolonial criticism worked as a heavy brake on the desire of these governments to formulate international human rights norms. Eager to shield their colonial policies from accusations, they were constantly on the defensive and acted warily. Consequently, a wide gulf opened between their rhetorical championship of human rights and the noncompromising stance that they assumed in practice. Colonial governments found themselves caught in a contradictory back and forth that severely damaged their international credibility, a fact of which foreign ministries were painfully aware.

From this perspective, the end of empire was a highly important tectonic change, ridding Great Britain, France, and the Netherlands of the main reason for their inconsistent policies and drastically improving their chances to present a positive self-image to the world. The precise effects of this turnaround are nevertheless far from clear. Historians have demonstrated that Great Britain and France, after withdrawing from their colonies in the 1960s, reformulated the premises for their policies at the United Nations.[48] They displayed a new openness toward international norms and started discussing new initiatives. However, no connections have so far been detected between the changed positions these states took in the UN discussions of the 1960s and the new approaches that they adopted in their foreign policies at large during the 1970s. It seems doubtful that France in its international relations developed anything like a strong and coherent human rights policy at all. The British Labour government that was elected in 1974 discussed giving human rights greater prominence in their foreign policy but without any apparent relation to the end of empire.[49] It was in the case of the Dutch government of Joop den Uyl that a direct influence most visibly came to the fore. The prime minister and several leading ministers appear to have acted under a sort of "guilt complex" that made them hastily engage in the decolonization of Surinam and also partly inspired their attempt to strengthen humanitarian considerations in foreign relations. Yet the country's colonial legacy was but one of several interlocking motives that spurred their embrace of human rights, and it ranked behind others.[50]

Détente

Whereas decolonization was largely completed by the beginning of the 1970s, the breakthrough of human rights overlapped with the peak years of détente between 1969 and the mid-1970s. The relationship between the two was by no means obvious. For the Western human rights movement, the waning threat of military confrontation was certainly an important backdrop. When the heads of the superpowers started to talk to each other and even entered into disarmament negotiations, the worst Cold War fears lost their immediate grip on political observers. The relaxation of international tensions set activists free to concern themselves with issues reaching beyond the clash between Western democracy and Eastern European socialism and helped to foreground problems that had long been overshadowed. In Amnesty International's work, these changing perceptions were reflected in the discussion about whether to abandon the principle of the "threes." A hallmark of the organization in its early years, this principle obliged local activist groups to adopt one prisoner each from the West, the Communist camp, and the Third World, thereby transcending the Cold War framework. Beginning in the mid-1970s, however, many activists saw this principle as no longer adequate to the changed world order and suggested dropping it.[51]

At the governmental level, a complex interplay developed between détente and human rights, as was manifested in the various and at times contradictory intentions that states pursued in the CSCE process. Human rights hardly played a significant role in the Nixon administration's conception of détente. The U.S. government clearly prioritized bilateral negotiations with the Soviet Union, and therefore the CSCE ranked low on its agenda. Only belatedly did Henry Kissinger start supporting the European initiative, as he became aware of its potential for destabilizing Soviet rule.[52] Western European governments, despite joining forces, had widely differing motives to include human rights in the conference program. The delegations of Canada and Denmark, and occasionally also those of Austria and the Netherlands, considered provisions for freedom of movement and free exchange of ideas as a way of making détente work on the ground.[53] The aim of at least some of their proposals was to alleviate the lot of Eastern European populations, not to win the Cold War by other means. This however was precisely the goal that some other delegations had in mind. The Netherlands by and large hewed to a subversive line in the CSCE process, realizing that humanitarian provisions provided a potentially useful means of undermining the Eastern bloc.[54] Growing out of staunch anti-Communism, Dutch advocacy of human rights and, even more importantly, self-determination was devised to erode socialist rule and promote the Eastern European satellites' independence vis-à-vis the superpower.

West Germany and France adopted an attitude in between these extremes. Initially, they shared parts of the subversive strategy. However, they were extremely skeptical about the chances of success—German chancellor Willy Brandt mused that it would be impossible "to force the Communists through negotiations to abolish themselves."[55] Moreover, both governments feared that putting the Helsinki provisions into practice would inevitably lead to conflict and thus endanger the achievements of several years of détente. Both therefore proceeded with extreme caution. The French deliberately stayed in the background throughout the negotiations, while the West German government after the Helsinki conference decided not to use the Final Act too offensively.

Only a few years later, the experience of the Carter administration proved that their fears were not groundless, demonstrating that human rights could indeed run counter to détente. When Carter set out to criticize the Soviet Union for its human rights violations and even bolstered the internal struggle against the regime by meeting with dissidents, the result was an immediate freeze in the temperature of bilateral relations.[56] Realizing that public criticism seriously threatened progress in the Strategic Arms Limitations Talks, the Carter government quickly changed course, toning down the human rights approach toward their Communist rival.[57]

Mass Media

Changes in the realm of politics—including ideological beliefs as well as political styles and practices—were preconditions for the breakthrough of human rights as important as the shifting cleavages in international relations. The rapid expansion of the mass media may be counted among the trends that most pervasively transformed the conditions of policy making from the 1960s on, most visibly if not exclusively in democracies. The diffusion of telephone and telex connections marked a quantum leap in both the speed and the reach of communication. Perhaps more to the point, the steep rise in the number of households equipped with television allowed for a much wider and almost instantaneous circulation of pictures.[58] Undoubtedly, image politics were an integral part of human rights campaigns in the 1970s. The military coup in Chile turned into a vivid reality when TV stations showed airplanes bombing the presidential palace in Santiago and fearful prisoners herded together in the city's sport stadiums. NGOs such as Amnesty International included photos in their reports to provide victims with a human face and to personalize the abstract process of political oppression. The Nigerian Civil War between 1967 and 1970 powerfully illustrates the ways in which images could stimulate international responses.[59] Leaders of secessionist Biafra deliberately employed pictures of starving babies to garner international support. A spokesperson later somewhat cynically recalled that the Biafran government had experimented with different strategies. It "had tried the political emancipation of oppressed people, it had tried the religious angle, it had tried pogrom and genocide . . . but the pictures of starving children . . . touched everybody, it cut across the range of people's belief."[60] In fact, news coverage of the war made extensive use of these pictures. Subsequently, the image of hungry African children would take on a life of its own, turning into an extremely popular icon of the perceived misery of the African continent. Similar pictures flooded newspapers and television reports time and again. Later they were popularized through music videos, most strikingly perhaps during the Ethiopian famine of the mid-1980s.

It is very plausible to assume that these and other images mobilized activists and literally shocked them into action. The photos of emaciated Biafran children reveal what art historian Horst Bredekamp calls the actor capacity of pictures: more than mere illustrations, they were appeals, activating deeply rooted cultural and religious frames of reference.[61] Children stood for innocent suffering, and their hunger evoked one of the archetypical situations of charity. Gazing at the viewer, often from below, they adopted a posture of begging for help. Images turned into powerful messages, condensing meanings and eliciting emotional responses. Very often, too, they stripped the events they depicted from their political contexts; photos could seemingly be grasped without the need of understanding the political and social intricacies that stood behind human rights violations.

Yet historians should be careful not to overestimate the significance of images. First, people did not automatically react in one way to pictures of violence or suffering. One and the same picture could stimulate a variety of responses that did not necessarily converge with the efforts of human rights groups.[62] Moreover, photos often merely activated political sensibilities rather than engendering them. Also, it remains to be discussed if and to what extent the interdependence of visual culture and social mobilization was a distinct phenomenon of the 1960s or 1970s. Antinuclear activists in the 1950s, for instance, used pictures of mushroom clouds, one of the most powerful cultural icons of the era, to symbolize the apocalyptic threat of atomic weapons. In the wake of the Second World War, humanitarian organizations employed photos depicting destitute European populations in order to request donations, albeit to a much lesser degree than later NGOs.[63]

Mass Mobilization and the Presence of Suffering

The comparison between social movements of the 1950s and those of the 1970s suggests another change in political practices that proved to be crucial for the strong resonance of human rights in the latter decade. NGOs springing up in the 1970s strongly benefited from techniques of mass mobilization and forms of public protest that only in the 1960s had become firmly entrenched in political movements' repertory of extra-parliamentary action. In the postwar decades, numerous international NGOs had dealt with human rights questions.[64] Some of them, such as religious or women's groups, had a broader focus, whereas others mainly or exclusively dedicated their work to human rights issues—this was true of anti-apartheid groups and of larger organizations such as the International League for the Rights of Man and the International Commission of Jurists. None of these groups, however, was able to leave nearly as strong an imprint on international relations as human rights groups would in the 1970s. Postwar NGOs working in the field of human rights remained small and elitist. Virtually all of them focused on developing legal norms at the United Nations and invested few resources in research or public relations work. In pursuing a largely nonpublic, high-level approach to politics they were typical of the social movements of the period. Few staged public events or organized rallies, such as the antinuclear movements in North America and Europe and, albeit only gradually, the civil rights movement in the United States. With the emergence of highly visible and mostly transnational protest movements—particularly of students, opponents to the Vietnam war, and American civil rights activists—the 1960s marked a decisive break whose long-term repercussions would continue to shape the practices of human rights groups in the following decade.[65] Many groups took their concerns to the streets, building up public pressure and engaging in symbolic manifestations, often using the same strategies of direct action and consciousness-raising that their 1960s predecessors had so successfully forged. In this respect, human rights activism bore a strong resemblance to other new social movements that perpetuated earlier political practices, adapting them to new circumstances and harnessing them for new political projects.

These new social movements were also exponents of another trend, which, however, was not confined to them. In Western countries, the 1970s saw the emergence of a conspicuous and pervasive culture of subjectivity shaping lifestyles as well as political attitudes and in fact often blurring the lines between the two.[66] The self-styled "alternative" milieu celebrated "post-materialist" values such as self-realization, autonomy, or self-organization. Members of this subculture crafted a virtually all-encompassing "politics of the self" that deeply penetrated their forms of political participation, cultural activities, work routines, and daily habits. This subjectivist turn came to be a powerful trend in intellectual life, too, with Michel Foucault developing his ideas about "technologies of the self" and sociologists such as Ronald Inglehart theorizing the nascent attitudes.[67] The topic has to be explored further, but it does not seem far-fetched to connect these trends to the increasing receptiveness to and public presence of depictions of suffering, which were decisive features of human rights advocacy. Empathy was key to the Western human rights movement and even at times spurred governmental actions. The capacity of activists and politicians to be shocked, to be moved, and to identify with "distant suffering" made helping others a moral imperative.[68] Very often it was the sheer fact of people being physically maltreated that propelled human rights activists to intervene—at least as much, it seems, as abstract notions of political injustice and oppression. This in part accounts for the impressive resonance of Amnesty International's antitorture campaign that targeted horrendously brutal forms of physical violence inflicted upon the completely defenseless.[69] Human rights NGOs, for their part, attempted to mobilize the public by deliberately appealing to sentiments of pity and moral outrage. In its reports on Chile and other countries, Amnesty International prominently inserted testimonies of victims who recounted their excruciating experiences of pain and humiliation.[70] Skillfully evoked in these accounts and often turning into a forceful impulse to help, empathy was part of a politics of the self.[71] It deeply involved individual activists, both morally and emotionally, and made their feelings the driving force for political action. Paradoxically, aiding those in need provided activists with an opportunity to engage in self-realization through altruistic behavior. This said, political uses of suffering were widespread in the period and not the exclusive domain of human rights groups. More and more groups started to refer to their own history of suffering to justify claims for political participation and nondiscrimination; victimhood formed an integral element of what came to be called "identity politics." This was notably true for Holocaust survivors but also for homosexuals and nativist groups, to name just a few.[72]

Transformation of the Political Left

The fact that most of the movements pushing these political and cultural shifts forward were associated with leftist politics raises the question of how the human rights revolution was related to the altered political landscape of the post-1968 period. While the position of human rights in the political spectrum remains somewhat elusive, it seems obvious that they were a project of the political left and much less a conservative project. What we can infer about the social composition of the Western human rights movement suggests that two constituencies were particularly important, apart from those activists who considered themselves to be leftists.[73] Many people joining human rights groups had strong religious ties, among them clerics but mostly laypersons active in their church communities or who simply practiced their religion. Furthermore, a fair number of members were nonpolitical in the sense that they had not engaged in political parties or organizations before entering the movement. These three groups can hardly be quantified, however, and obviously there was considerable overlap among them.

At the governmental level, human rights in the 1970s were decidedly not a conservative issue. With the possible exception of Dries van Agt's Christian Democrat–led coalition in the Netherlands, no conservative government strongly identified its foreign policies with human rights. In the United States, the Republican Party discussed its stance toward them intensively after mid-decade, laying the intellectual ground for the Reagan's administration later redefinition of the term.[74] While debate about the topic within the GOP had emerged independently of the Democrats' incipient embrace of human rights, the main purpose of Reagan's maneuvers was to appropriate the concept from the liberal left and to define it in the all-too-well-known terms of anti-Communist containment. Reagan would equate human rights with democracy and freedom and declare Communist totalitarianism vastly more dangerous to the worldwide survival of democratic rule than right-wing authoritarianism.[75] The fight against Communism in fact provided the main exception to the otherwise leftist coding of human rights politics. Conservative politicians in Western countries could agree with human rights criticism inasmuch as it was directed against Communist dictatorships. Therefore conservatives in Germany or the Netherlands came round to embracing the CSCE process as a new venue for discrediting the socialist system. Human Rights Watch would later attempt to use this negative consensus to support its human rights work on Eastern Europe, taking the Reagan administration by its anti-Communist word.

These observations suggest that the transformation of the political left since the late 1960s provided a particularly important framework for the reinvigoration of human rights politics.[76] After the energies of 1968 had dissipated, new leftist activism fractured and split up into differing and often competing factions. For activists who did not find their way back into the established socialist parties, two broad and heterogeneous directions came to predominate. Many engaged in the wildly proliferating range of sectarian groups; in Western Europe ultraleft Trotskyist and Maoist groups provided comparatively strong currents. Another offspring of 1968 was the fluid and ever-growing scene of alternative groups and new social movements rejected by radical leftists and revolutionary activists for their supposed bourgeois and reformist ideology. Many activists rallied around issues such as antinuclear protest, the ecological movement, second- or third-generation feminism, and later the new peace movement. Human rights groups can be counted among these movements. In most countries they were neither as large nor as publicly visible as others, which assembled tens of thousands of people for street marches and massive demonstrations. But they shared many features of the new social movements' conception of politics: they kept their distance from the parliamentary system, chose a confrontational style, experimented with distinct forms of participation, organized locally, and focused on concrete issues to bring about gradual social change. Interestingly, among new leftist groups a vigorous internationalism evolved that sometimes did and sometimes did not overlap with human rights initiatives. Mostly couched in anti-imperialist language, these campaigns often targeted the same regimes and events as human rights groups, such as the Chilean dictatorship, Portuguese colonial rule, the civil wars in Central America, apartheid, or the exploitation of the Third World.

The mythical year 1968 changed political perceptions in Communist countries, too. In the wake of the Soviet invasion of Czechoslovakia profound disillusionment spread among those who had hoped to alter the Communist system "from within." Not only in Czechoslovakia but also in the Soviet Union and Poland the ruthless smashing of the Prague Spring sounded the death knell for "reform Communism." Everywhere in the Eastern bloc regimes set out to strengthen their hold on power, buttressing central economic planning and restricting spaces of intellectual freedom. These events proved to be a crucial experience for many Eastern European intellectuals and dissidents and led them to reorient their ideological beliefs to include a new embrace of human rights. Repercussions also made themselves felt among Western European Communists. Most Western Communist parties distanced themselves from the Soviet Union, some clearly breaking with their Stalinist past, and redefined their position vis-à-vis democracy. Traditionally averse to what they considered as a bourgeois concept, some even seem to have made their peace with human rights. In their attempt to forge an independent "Eurocommunist" line, leaders of the Italian, Spanish, and French Communist parties at least occasionally demanded protection of basic rights and freedoms in Eastern Europe.[77] Yet the sobering effect of 1968 reached even further. In France, it prepared the ground on the left for a new attitude toward Socialist violence.[78] The Soviet crackdown on Dubček's "socialism with a human face" helped to erode the long-standing belief that repression was justified for the sake of building a Communist utopia. Informed by Solzhenitsyn's *Gulag Archipelago*, a book now suddenly attracting vast attention, intellectuals such as André Glucksmann and Bernard-Henri Lévy from the mid-1970s on started accusing the Soviets of state crimes. Dissidents emerged as celebrated figures on the French intellectual scene as elsewhere, personifying the unnecessary suffering that the Soviet system inflicted on its people. The "passing of an illusion," it seemed, awakened leftists to a new humanitarian awareness.[79]

The Transformation of the Churches

Considering the importance of church-related actors for human rights mobilizations, the transformation of the churches was no less fundamental than the changes on the political left. In the 1960s and early 1970s, both the Catholic and Protestant churches saw a dramatic redefinition of their role in world politics that entailed both their opening up to global issues and what has been called the politicization of their self-understanding and practical work. Historians are only beginning to grapple with the many consequences of this seminal process.[80] The starting point for much of what transformed the churches' activism was the Second Vatican Council between 1962 and 1965, convened to discuss the stance of Catholicism toward modernity and its role in "the world of today." Across confessional divides, the council sparked critical engagement with the traditions of ecclesiastical hierarchy and political aloofness, inaugurating the churches' transition "from a state-centered to a society-centered institution" and committing them to social change.[81] Developments in Latin America provided another strong impulse. Crystallizing at the second Latin American Episcopal Conference in Medellín in 1968, liberation theology gained strong intellectual influence among both Catholic and Protestant Christians worldwide. What united its various versions was its identification of the church with the struggle against poverty and oppression of the poor. The new prominence of the Latin American, African, and Asian churches moreover was an important reason why a forceful interest emerged among churches of the global North in the problems of the Third World. The ecumenical World Council of Churches at its conferences in the 1960s devoted increasing attention to issues such as economic inequalities and world hunger. Subsequently, the council initiated a comprehensive (and highly controversial) "Program to Combat Racism." But interest in these topics was also manifest at the grassroots level, where innumerable discussion and action groups emerged on both the Catholic and the Protestant sides. In ways that merit closer research, this spiritual upheaval provided a fertile breeding ground for the adoption of human rights claims, and a vigorous drive for international justice more generally. The Vatican had already in the 1960s revived and expanded its embrace of human rights. Pope John XXIII in his

1963 encyclical *Pacem in terris* expressed the church's commitment to a range of individual rights. He further acknowledged the Universal Declaration of Human Rights and the UN's efforts to protect human rights internationally. His successor Paul VI repeatedly articulated very similar positions. In a message to the UN General Assembly on the twenty-fifth anniversary of the Universal Declaration in 1973, for instance, he prominently declared the Vatican's "full moral support to the common ideal" contained therein. Eight years previously, the Second Vatican Council's declaration *Dignitatis humanae* had emphasized the protection of religious freedom as a human right.[82]

Explaining the 1970s Human Rights Moment: The Intrinsic Appeal of Human Rights

However important these structural changes were, the ascendancy of human rights in 1970s political culture cannot adequately be understood as the by-product of broader transformations in international relations, political practices, and ideological beliefs. These transformations created an environment propitious for the adoption of human rights. But without the intrinsic appeal of the idea, the resonance would hardly have been as widespread and as intense as it actually was. As mentioned before, the various actors had differing motives for embracing human rights that depended strongly on the political context in which they acted. Nevertheless, several transnational patterns shaped the human rights history of the period, each of which accounts for significant parts of why the concept came to be such a strong political impulse for activists and governments. The greatest common denominator of these patterns lay in the appearance of human rights as a profoundly moral yet multifunctional way of revitalizing politics, both as an ideal and as a practice.

Disillusionment and Rehabilitation

In several important instances, the turn to human rights followed the breakdown of previous political projects and grew out of the resulting political disillusionment. Samuel Moyn in his *Last Utopia* has made this observation the pivot of an interpretation of 1970s human rights. He frames the story as one of shifting idealisms, with human rights replacing lost hopes for social and political change that had dominated both the revolutionary and the democratic left in the United States, Latin America, and Western and Eastern Europe. It remains open to discussion whether this applies equally to all prominent new departures. Further, the question may be raised of how idealistic the collapsing concepts were in the first place. Nonetheless, the fact that politicians and activists resorted to human rights to reshape political approaches and redefine ideological projects provided an extremely important reason for the rise of human rights in the 1970s.[83]

This was reflected in the way the breakdown of the Prague Spring propelled Eastern European dissidents to seek new forms of political expression. Of course, no automatism was at work. Events of 1968 may have accelerated the disenchantment with Communism that had already been under way since the mid-1950s. There may have been less of a rupture in the Soviet Union than in Poland or Czechoslovakia. And the fact that dissidents seized upon human rights was certainly as much a matter of tactical choice as of ideological realignment, or even more so.[84] These observations notwithstanding, human rights formed an increasingly important part of a process of political reorientation. Many intellectuals and opposition figures in Eastern Europe perceived the post-1968 situation as dramatically new. Some literally had lost their faith: "I found that I had to stop being a Marxist," Polish dissident Jacek Kuroń said.[85] All realized that the possibility of reform would be forever precluded, and all faced much more severe repression as security apparatuses stepped up persecution. Human rights were part and parcel of the political conceptions and strategies that dissidents devised in reaction to these new circumstances. In essence, many dissidents jettisoned their ideas of changing the system and instead struggled to secure at least a minimum degree of freedom and a more humane treatment. They moved to smaller and more concrete aims, shifting "from theoretical counter-projects to the practical defense of civil and human rights."[86]

The Western human rights movement, too, searched for a new politics to deal with the sobering experience of earlier attempts at social change. The development of the U.S. section of Amnesty International provides an interesting example.[87] Beginning in the early 1970s, AIUSA saw a massive influx of new members securing the very survival of the hitherto struggling section and initiating an institutional success story that by the early 1980s would transform the section into the largest and richest of the worldwide organization. The vast majority of the new members had previously been engaged in the social and protest movements of the 1960s, particularly in the student, civil rights, and antiwar movements. They joined Amnesty precisely at the moment when these earlier undertakings had come to an end or even plainly failed. Their engagement on behalf of human rights essentially marked a departure from 1960s activism; they broke with the belief in social utopias, with the revolutionary fight against "the system," and with the inner polarization of the political scene.[88] Human rights activists consciously scaled down their political pretensions. At the grassroots level, their activism aimed at no more and no less than helping a few individuals. Groups did not set out to free the world from evil but wanted to assuage suffering in cases they had learned about and that promised a measure of success. Human rights activism, in this sense, grew out of a retrenched, postrevolutionary idealism. This attitude was summed up in the later statement of an AIUSA activist: "Sending a card . . . will not change the world very much. But it is surely worth investing a little time and postage to try to help two other individuals to secure justice, or at least to find courage."[89]

Finally, Jimmy Carter's new approach to foreign policy also fits in this pattern of political replacement. In the U.S. case, the political and psychological disasters of the Vietnam era formed the immediate backdrop. The Vietnam War, whose painful reverberations would be felt well up to the end of the Cold War, constituted the most profound break in the history of postwar America. It shattered the prevailing belief of the political elite and large parts of the population that the United States government had a mission to lead the democratic battle against Communist expansionism. Amid ever-growing protests, the "foreign policy consensus" dramatically collapsed that in the postwar decades had secured bipartisan support for the politics of containment.[90] At the beginning of the 1970s, the policy of President Nixon and Secretary of State Kissinger had come to appear as the very embodiment of a realpolitik devoid of ethical scruples. Nixon's moral bankruptcy assumed still greater dimensions when revelations of the Watergate scandal began after 1973 and the secret CIA operations to destabilize the Allende government in Chile came out into the open in 1975–1976.

Carter's championship of human rights was a deep-seated response to a foreign policy approach whose devastating outcomes were plain to see. In view of the severe loss of American credibility and a battered international reputation, Carter strove to depart from the excesses of ruthless Cold War power politics and tried to return to what he perceived as the best values of the American tradition. He sought to abandon violent interventions and secret operations, to distance himself from authoritarian allies, and to adhere to a democratic, transparent decision-making process. These had been the main themes of Carter's election campaign. He took up the term "human rights" relatively late in the day but then turned it into a pivotal element of his rhetoric of renewal, as expressed most strongly in his inauguration speech when he claimed that "our commitment to human rights must be absolute."[91] Human rights became a symbol for a fundamental reorientation of U.S. foreign policy encompassing its premises as well as its methods and aims.

Beyond the Cold War

What many proponents of human rights shared was a profound rejection of Cold War politics. They dismissed the ideological tenets and political methods that the superpowers and their allies had excessively upheld over decades to confront what they framed as an unrelenting threat to human existence. Exponents of human rights politics turned against the cherishing of power for its own sake, the cynicism of realpolitik, and a bleak Manichaean worldview that divided states into friends and foes. These impulses are manifest in the description already given of the Carter administration's new approach to international relations. With good reason have historians spoken of his attempt to develop a "post–Cold War foreign policy"—a spectacular attempt, it should be added, since it would remain singular until the very end of the Cold War.[92] Similar ideas shaped the human rights policy of the Den Uyl government in the Netherlands, albeit to a lesser degree. Dutch leaders converged with the U.S. approach in that they conceived human rights as a universal standard against which all governments would be measured, irrespective of their ideological leanings. This would help to relax the firmly entrenched bipolar order. In practice, the political conception of Dutch foreign minister Van der Stoel came much closer to this ideal than the forays of his colleague Jan Pronk. Pronk displayed some selectiveness in harshly criticizing military dictatorships while exerting much more restraint in relations with Cuba.[93]

Finally, the desire to leave Cold War cleavages behind also defined Western human rights activism. It was one of Peter Benenson's principal impulses in founding Amnesty International that Western governments too often overlooked the curtailing of democratic freedoms in right-wing regimes as long as these were allies in the struggle against Communism.[94] In later years, transcending bloc politics would remain one of the essential principles of Amnesty International's work. This did not only apply at the level of local groups, which based their advocacy on the above-mentioned system of threes. The International Secretariat consistently attached high importance to ideological equidistance. In its political interventions, Amnesty was extremely careful to retain the balance between the Western and Eastern camps and the nonaligned countries. In fact, it was Amnesty's credo, often repeated, that the guarantee of human rights was independent from ideological or political systems.

Morality as a Political Resource

In pursuing human rights, politicians and activists drew strongly on a set of arguments centered around ethical norms, altruistic beliefs, humanitarian needs, and religious notions of charity. These ideas saw a revival as human rights advocates complained that they had been subdued for too long by strategic or economic concerns and had fallen off the agenda of what politics were about. To be sure, much of this talk remained purely rhetorical. Very often actors did not live up to their promises and self-declared obligations; among the many objections raised against Carter's human rights policy, "inconsistency" was the most widespread and politically most costly. Moreover, when states and NGOs took initiatives in the name of human rights they always pursued various, and often competing, motives beyond humanitarian concerns. Yet the rise of human rights in the 1970s testifies to an increasing importance of morality as a political resource for both state and nonstate actors. This was most notably true for Western NGOs. To them, political action was about "doing the right thing" in situations of dire need, about pursuing "good" intentions and preventing unworthy concerns from overriding the fundamental obligation to help. In the last analysis, they strove to renew the very conception of what was political, reinventing it as a sort of moral politics.

Moreover, they were driven by a sense of global responsibility that crystallized in an ethics of interdependence. "The world is so small and so much more interdependent today than it used to be," a member of AIUSA stated in the early 1970s, "that it is morally right for citizens of all countries to feel responsible for possible political injustice anywhere on the globe."[95] A poem by Spanish philosopher and historian Salvador de Madariaga, which he apparently had written for Amnesty International in the early 1960s and which later circulated widely among activists, spoke of very similar notions. Characteristic of the Amnesty movement in its secularized Christian symbolism, the poem essentially expressed a single idea. The first stanza read: "For those who hopelessly latch on to the prison's bars / so that we can walk in freedom / a thought." Another very similarly read: "For those whose country lies in chains / so that our countries can be free / a thought."[96] The poem established a close mutual relationship between those who suffered—they were unambiguously represented as political prisoners—and those able to enjoy their freedom and basic rights, implying that the latter were morally obliged to help those who suffered from unjust punishment.

In the rhetoric of Western governments, the imperative of altruism was less acute, for obvious reasons, and would have been anything but easy to implement. For them, moral claims came to be important for projecting a positive self-image both in the international and domestic arenas. This was again tangible in U.S. foreign policy during the Carter presidency. At least in part responding to genuine shock at the excesses of power politics in the Cold War, his administration sought to regain confidence at home and abroad. Foreign observers found the moral standards that Carter introduced as conspicuous for what they said about American aims in the world as for what they said about the superpower's intention of taming its own power. Domestically, the administration hoped to have found in human rights the magic formula that could rally a large majority of Americans behind its policies and restore some degree of foreign policy consensus. That public opinion at home was particularly important for the moralistic reshaping of foreign policy was also highlighted by the behavior of the West German and Dutch governments before 1973, even though the context was fundamentally different. Yet both only started turning to human rights issues when they came under severe domestic pressure to intervene in state crimes abroad. The United States was the only country that needed human rights to work its way out of moral catastrophe. Others primarily used them to signal to the public that they considered the newly emerging humanitarian sensibilities as legitimate and that they were willing to take them into account as far as possible.

However, it should not be overlooked that these approaches also provided states with an opportunity to forge a new mission in international relations. Interference in the name of ethical principles in fact became an essential feature in the human rights politics of Western governments and NGOs alike. Citing a universal morality, activists and politicians worked for often profound changes in the political systems and even social practices of foreign countries.

Nonpolitical Politics

Yet another facet in the self-image of human rights advocates came to be decisive for their political project. Many proponents framed their struggle against injustice and for basic freedoms as nonpolitical or above politics. This view was ubiquitous in the rhetoric of NGOs, shared both by organizations that aimed at aiding others—that is, mostly Western NGOs—and those that used human rights claims to protect themselves from state terror. The tactical sense was obvious. Proclaiming their ideological impartiality, lack of hostility, and concern about "purely" humanitarian matters, these groups hoped to find repressive regimes more receptive to their actual demands or, respectively, tried to protect themselves from reprisals for unauthorized political activism. Of course, the contradictions inherent in this approach were not lost on repressive regimes. They were clearly aware that fulfilling activists' demands to guarantee basic rights would ultimately require installing democratic procedures and relinquishing absolute control of political life—both of which would undermine the very pillars of authoritarian rule.[97]

The tactical sense was not the only one involved in the idea that human rights were a nonpolitical concern. This idea furthermore helped to unite people from very different backgrounds in a common cause and to bridge, to some extent, the political, ideological, and religious gaps that had previously separated them. Amnesty members believed that their organization cut across party lines and transcended the many rifts besetting the political landscape of the period.[98] While available membership data clearly belies this view, it was the perception of working for an all-encompassing movement that accounted for much of Amnesty's appeal. For different reasons, the depoliticized language of self-protection also proved crucial in South America.[99] In Chile, Uruguay, and Brazil, opposition movements were extremely fractured, reproducing many of the conflicts that had so painfully polarized political life before the military coups. Leftists of various stripes, both moderates and revolutionaries, worked together with conservatives and relatives of victims who had no obvious connections to political parties. Both Christian activists and atheists joined the struggle against oppressive regimes. To agree that basic protections of life and freedom were the most urgent task at hand was a decisive step for these diverse groups to find some common ground.[100] Devoting themselves to what they considered a nonpolitical agenda, these groups finally managed to forge fairly unified coalitions.

All this was less true for states. Governments were hardly in a position to credibly portray themselves as nonpolitical actors. Their human rights criticism was always considered—and rejected—as highly politicized interference into domestic affairs. Nevertheless, government officials occasionally did revert to an apolitical rhetoric, promising oppressive regimes that they would refrain from condemning political and economic measures as long as the humanitarian situation showed signs of improvement.

Epilogue

Historians have so far mostly focused on the 1970s from the angle of what was lost—of economic certainties shattered, political aspirations abandoned, and social textures dissolved. The "age of fracture" emerged "after the boom."[101] The decade of the 1970s, in the tentative grapplings of both contemporaries and historians, constitutes the "post-" age—postindustrial, postmodern, poststructuralist—and human rights certainly formed an integral part of it. If they complicate the picture, it is by the shifting adjectives that follow the prefix. The decade was postrevolutionary for activists in the West but for no one else. Postcolonial framings emerged in the global South, not only contradicting Western uses but also contradictory among themselves. That human rights would inaugurate a post–Cold War era was what virtually all advocates hoped. The idea possessed a post-utopian flavor for the disillusioned activists of 1968 across the East-West divide and, in different senses, for politicians pulling back from the brink of catastrophe in the United States and in South America. Much of human rights' historical significance, then, consists in what they replaced and superseded.

Yet this view is only half the truth. "The general history of the 1970s is usually treated as a history of disaster or even 'nervous breakdown,'" Samuel Moyn writes in the introduction to this volume, "not of the moral breakthrough of human rights." Indeed what was striking about many—not all—of the decade's departures was the energies and hopes that proponents invested in creating a new mode of politics. They strove to redefine the boundaries of what was political, to enrich and dignify its very substance. Certainly this attempt had its limits and ambiguities; the rebirth of politics from the spirit of morality was perhaps a vision more than a reality. But as much as replacing what was no longer viable, human rights was about constructing new political causes, meanings, and futures.

Notes

Chapter 1. The Return of the Prodigal

1. See esp. Mary Ann Glendon, *A World Made New: Eleanor Roosevelt and the Universal Declaration of Human Rights* (New York: Random House, 2001), and Johannes Morsink, *The Universal Declaration of Human Rights: Origins, Drafting, and Intent* (Philadelphia: University of Pennsylvania Press, 1999).

2. See esp. Mark Mazower, "The Strange Triumph of Human Rights, 1930–1950," *Historical Journal* 47, no. 2 (2004): 379–398. The focus on the 1940s, only slightly decentered, remains obvious in the two standout historical collections in the field, Stefan-Ludwig Hoffmann, ed., *Human Rights in the Twentieth Century* (Cambridge: Cambridge University Press, 2011), and Akira Iriye, Petra Goedde, and William I. Hitchcock, eds., *The Human Rights Revolution: An International History* (New York: Oxford University Press, 2012).

3. See further my "Substance, Scale, and Salience: The Recent Historiography of Human Rights," *Annual Review of Law and Social Science* 8, no. 1 (2012): 123–140.

4. The three main sets of agreements, known as "baskets," dealt with security, economic cooperation, and humanitarian cooperation.

5. Compare Jan Eckel, "Utopie der Moral, Kalkül der Macht: Menschenrechte in der globalen Politik seit 1945," *Archiv für Sozialgeschichte* 49 (2009): 437–484; and Samuel Moyn, *The Last Utopia: Human Rights in History* (Cambridge, Mass.: Belknap Press of Harvard University Press, 2010), chap. 4; both authors propose somewhat different interpretations of why the decade was so pivotal.

6. Andreas Killen, *1973 Nervous Breakdown: Watergate, Warhol, and the Birth of Post-1960s America* (New York: Bloomsbury, 2006).

7. Daniel T. Rodgers, *Age of Fracture* (Cambridge, Mass.: Belknap Press of Harvard University Press, 2010).

8. See, e.g., Niall Ferguson et al., eds., *The Shock of the Global: The 1970s in Perspective* (Cambridge, Mass.: Harvard University Press, 2010), in which human rights has one cursory chapter.

9. Bruce J. Schulman, *The Seventies: The Great Shift in American Culture, Society, and Politics* (New York: Free Press, 2001).

10. Lynn Hunt, *Inventing Human Rights: A History* (New York: W. W. Norton, 2007).

11. Cf. Robin Blackburn, *The American Crucible: Slavery, Emancipation, and Human Rights* (New York: Verso, 2011); and Jenny Martinez, *The Slave Trade and the Origins of International Human Rights Law* (New York: Oxford University Press, 2011).

12. John Duffett, ed., *Against the Crime of Silence: Proceedings of the Russell International War Crimes Tribunal*, new ed. (New York: Simon and Schuster, 1970).

13. Daniel Patrick Moynihan, "The Politics of Human Rights," *Commentary* 64, no. 2 (August 1977); for my doubts about his reconstruction, on the grounds that no one noticed convergence around human rights at the time, see Moyn, *The Last Utopia*, chap. 4.

14. For the classic history of the United States and human rights in the 1940s, see Elizabeth Borgwardt, *A New Deal for the World: America's Vision for Human Rights* (Cambridge, Mass.: Belknap Press of Harvard University Press, 2006). For an extraordinary new investigation, see Barbara J. Keys, *Reclaiming American Virtue: The Human Rights Revolution of the 1970s* (Cambridge, Mass.: Harvard University Press, 2014).

15. Cf. Samuel Moyn, "Soft Sells: On Liberal Internationalism," *Nation*, October 3, 2011.

16. Oliver Bange and Gottfried Niedhart, eds., *Helsinki 1975 and the Transformation of Europe* (New York: Berghahn Books, 2008).

17. Sarah B. Snyder, *Human Rights Activism and the End of the Cold War: A Transnational History of the Helsinki Network* (Cambridge: Cambridge University Press, 2011).

18. Barbara J. Keys, "Anti-Torture Politics: Amnesty International, the Greek Junta, and the Origins of the Human Rights Movement in the United States, 1967–1970," in Iriye, Goedde, and Hitchcock, *The Human Rights Revolution, 201-22*; and Bradley R. Simpson, "Denying the 'First Right': The United States, Indonesia, and the Ranking of Human Rights by the Carter Administration, 1976–1980," *International History Review* 31, no. 4 (2009): 798–821.

19. Cf. Sally Engle Merry, *Human Rights and Gender Violence: Translating International Law into Local Justice* (Chicago: University of Chicago Press, 2005).

20. Compare "Declaration for the Establishment of a New International Economic Order," UN Gen. Ass. Res. 3201 (XXIV) (1974), and "Declaration on the Right to Development," UN Doc. A/RES/41/128 (1986). Bradley R. Simpson, *The First Right: A Global History of Self-Determination in the Twentieth Century* (New York: Oxford University Press, forthcoming).

21. Cf. David Cooper, *Qui sont les dissidents?* (Paris: Galilée, 1977).

22. It would be inaccurate to suggest that one story is ideological and the other "structural." Not all structural shifts are economic in nature. Ultimately, a full account would be phenomenological (capturing the self-understandings of diverse actors) as well as structural.

23. See also my "Substance, Scale, and Salience."

24. Cf. Michel Foucault, *"Society Must Be Defended": Lectures at the Collège de France, 1975–76*, trans. David Macey (New York: Picador, 2003).

25. See, e.g., Greg Grandin and Gilbert M. Joseph, eds., *A Century of Revolution: Insurgent and Counterinsurgent Violence During Latin America's Long Cold War* (Durham, N.C.: Duke University Press, 2011), which manages to give full coverage to dictatorship in the 1970s without posing human rights as a major alternative.

Chapter 2. The Dystopia of Postcolonial Catastrophe

1. "Nigeria's Civil War," *Time*, August 23, 1968.

2. I will use the spelling "Igbo," now widely common in English, unless spelled "Ibo" in original sources.

3. See Heerten, "A wie Auschwitz, B wie Biafra: Der Bürgerkrieg in Nigeria (1967– 1970) und die Universalisierung des Holocaust," *Zeithistorische Forschungen* 8, no. 3 (2011).

4. Thierry Hentsch, *Face au blocus: Histoire de l'intervention du Comité International de la Croix-Rouge dans le conflit du Nigéria, 1967–1970* (Geneva: Droz, 1973); Dan Jacobs, *The Brutality of Nations* (New York: Alfred A. Knopf, 1987).

5. The international history of the war remains poorly studied. The best work is still John J. Stremlau, *The International Politics of the Nigerian Civil War, 1967–1970* (Princeton, N.J.: Princeton University Press, 1977).

6. On Médecins sans Frontières, see Marie-Luce Desgrandchamps, "Revenir sur le mythe fondateur de Médecins sans Frontières: Les relations entre les médecins français et le CICR pendant la guerre du Biafra (1967–1970)," *Relations internationales* 146, no. 2 (April 2011): 95–108.

7. See Niall Ferguson et al., *The Shock of the Global: The 1970s in Perspective* (Cambridge, Mass.: Belknap Press of Harvard University Press, 2010); Michael Geyer and Charles Bright, "World History in a Global Age," *American Historical Review* 100, no. 4 (October 1995): 1034–1060; Charles S. Maier, "Consigning the Twentieth Century to History: Alternative Narratives for the Modern Era," *American Historical Review* 105, no. 3 (June 2000): 807–831.

8. Kenneth Cmiel, "The Emergence of Human Rights Politics in the United States," *Journal of American History* 86, no. 3 (December 1999): 1248; Jan Eckel, "Utopie der Moral, Kalkül der Macht: Menschenrechte in der globalen Politik seit 1945," *Archiv für Sozialgeschichte* 49 (2009): 437–484; Samuel Moyn, *The Last Utopia: Human Rights in History* (Cambridge, Mass.: Belknap Press of Harvard University Press, 2010).

9. Moyn, *Last Utopia*, 219.

10. This point was most recently emphasized by Stefan-Ludwig Hoffmann, "Introduction," in *Human Rights in the Twentieth Century*, ed. Hoffmann (Cambridge: Cambridge University Press, 2011), 1–26.

11. Christopher Leslie Brown, *Moral Capital: Foundations of British Abolitionism* (Chapel Hill: University of North Carolina Press, 2006), 2, 25.

12. Anthony H. M. Kirk-Greene, "Coups and Aftermath: January 1966–July 1967,"

in *Crisis and Conflict in Nigeria*, vol. 1, *January 1966–July 1967*, ed. Kirk-Greene (1971; Aldershot: Gregg Revivals, 1993), 25–111; Albert Wirz, *Krieg in Afrika: Die nachkolonialen Konflikte in Nigeria, Sudan, Tschad und Kongo* (Wiesbaden: Steiner, 1982), 134–147.

13. Morris Davis, *Interpreters for Nigeria: The Third World and International Public Relations* (Urbana: University of Illinois Press, 1977).

14. Roland Burke, *Decolonization and the Evolution of International Human Rights* (Philadelphia: University of Pennsylvania Press, 2010). See also Moyn, *Last Utopia*, chap. 3, and Jan Eckel, "Human Rights and Decolonization: New Perspectives and Open Questions," *Humanity* 1, no. 1 (Fall 2010): 111–135.

15. Ministry of Information of the Republic of Biafra, *The Concept of Territorial Integrity and the Right of Biafrans to Self-Determination* (Enugu 1967), 3, 1, 4. See also C. Odumegwu Ojukwu, *Biafra*, vol. 1, *Selected Speeches* (New York: Harper and Row, 1969), 225–244, and *Biafra*, vol. 2, *Random Thoughts* (New York: Harper and Row, 1969), 20–36.

16. Philipp Sarasin, "Die Wirklichkeit der Fiktion: Zum Konzept der 'imagined communities,'" Sarasin, *Geschichtswissenschaft und Diskursanalyse* (Frankfurt: Suhrkamp, 2003), 150–176.

17. Ross K. Baker, "The Emergence of Biafra: Balkanisation or Nation-Building?" *Orbis* 12, no. 2 (Summer 1968): 518–533; Benyamin Neuberger, "The African Concept of Balkanisation," *Journal of Modern African Studies* 14, no. 3 (September 1976): 523–529.

18. The most active was the Biafra Union of Great Britain and Ireland; see its "Statement on British Arms Supplies," in *Crisis and Conflict in Nigeria*, ed. Kirk-Greene, 2:151. See Andreas Olie Chegwe, ed., *Biafra* (Wiesbaden: F. Becker, ca. 1969) for the case of an Igbo activist in Germany.

19. For overviews of lobby group activities in Britain, where Nigerian and Biafran expatriates were the most numerous, see William A. Ajibola, *Foreign Policy and Public Opinion: A Case Study of British Foreign Policy over the Nigerian Civil War* (Ibadan: Ibadan University Press, 1978), 133–143; and Oladapo Fafowora, *Pressure Groups and Foreign Policy: A Comparative Study of British Attitudes and Policy towards Secessionist Moves in the Congo (1960–63) and in Nigeria (1966–69)* (Ibadan: Heinemann, 1990).

20. The number of victims is difficult to gauge; Axel Harneit-Sievers deems a number of one million victims to be realistic, whereas John W. Young considers around one hundred thousand to be more likely. Harneit-Sievers, "Nigeria: Der Sezessionskrieg um Biafra: Keine Sieger, keine Besiegten—Eine afrikanische Erfolgsgeschichte?" in *Vergessene Kriege in Afrika*, ed. Rolf Hofmeier and Volker Matthies (Göttingen: Lamuv, 1992), 284–285; Young, *The Labour Governments, 1964–1970*, vol. 2, *International Policy* (Manchester: Manchester University Press, 2003), 193.

21. See, for example, C. Odumegwu Ojukwu, letter to Members of Parliament, December 3, 1968, Churchill College Archives Cambridge (CCA) NBKR 4/41.

22. Ken Waters, "Influencing the Message: The Role of Catholic Missionaries in

Media Coverage of the Nigerian Civil War," *Catholic Historical Review* 90, no. 4 (October 2004): 697–718; Kevin O'Sullivan, *Ireland, Africa and the End of Empire* (Manchester: Manchester University Press, forthcoming), chaps. 4–5; Laurie S. Wiseberg, "Christian Churches and the Nigerian Civil War," *Journal of African Studies* 2, no. 3 (fall 1975): 297–331.

23. See Heerten, "The Biafran War in Britain: An Odd Alliance of Late 1960s Humanitarian Activists," *Journal of the Oxford University History Society* 7 (Special Issue Colloquium 2009), http://sites.google.com/site/jouhsinfo/issue7specialissueforinternet explorer.

24. See, for example, "The Land of No Hope" and "Children Wait to Die," *Sun*, June 12, 1968; and the front-page reports in *Life*, July 12, 1968; *Stern*, July 28, 1968; *Der Spiegel*, August 19, 1968; *Time*, August 23, 1968; *L'Express*, October 7, 1968.

25. Waters, "Influencing the Message," 697. The "age of televised disaster" began with the Biafran War, according to Michael Ignatieff in *The Warrior's Honor: Ethnic War and the Modern Conscience* (New York: Henry Holt, 1997), 124. For contemporary commentators, see "Nur beten," *Der Spiegel*, August 19, 1968, 71–76; and Hans Gresmann, "Mord ohne Gericht," *Die Zeit*, August 9, 1968.

26. See Heerten, "A wie Auschwitz."

27. *Hansard Lords*, August 27, 1969, column 700, http://hansard.millbanksystems .com/lords/1968/aug/27/nigeria.

28. Michael Kunczik, *Die manipulierte Meinung: Nationale Image-Politik und internationale Public Relations* (Cologne: Böhlau, 1990), 130–136; Suzanne Cronjé, *The World and Nigeria: The Diplomatic History of the Biafran War, 1967–1970* (London: Sidgwick and Jackson, 1972), 210–214.

29. See Margery Perham, "Reflections on the Nigerian Civil War," *International Affairs* 46, no. 2 (April 1970): 231–246.

30. B. O. Ogundipe, "Letter to the Director Leslie Kirkley," June 28, 1968, Oxfam Archives, Bicester, UK (OA) DIR/2/3/2/32, 1, 3.

31. H. Leslie Kirkley, "Letter to His Excellency the High Commissioner," July 5, 1968, OA, DIR/2/3/2/32, 1.

32. Young, *Labour Governments*, 193–217.

33. Joan Mellors, "What About Their Human Rights, Mr. Wilson?" *Tribune*, October 18, 1968, 6; "Biafra and Human Rights," in *Genocide Breaks Up Nations: Sow Genocide, Reap Disintegration: Genocide Broke Up Nigeria*, ed. Ministry of Information, Republic of Biafra (Enugu, 1968), 5–6 (published first in *Spectator*, London, November 15, 1968).

34. Auberon Waugh, *Britain and Biafra: The Case for Genocide* (London: Britain-Biafra Association, 1969), 8, 5, 7.

35. "Another More Murderous Harvest," *Spectator*, London, May 31, 1968, 729–730.

36. Aktionskomitee Biafra, "Resolution an die Bundesregierung," July 15, 1968, Political Archives of the German Foreign Office Berlin: B 34/747, 1.

37. Günter Grass, "Völkermord vor aller Augen: Ein Appell an die Bundesregierung," *Die Zeit*, October 11, 1968, 5.

38. Paul Connett, circular letter to Members of Congress, September 21, 1968, SCPC Clearing House for Nigeria/Biafra Information Records, 1968–1970, DG 168, Box 10.

39. Heinrich Tenhumberg, "Massenmord trotz Völkerrecht? Zur Problematik Nigeria/Biafra," in *Soll Biafra überleben? Dokumente, Berichte, Analysen, Kommentare*, 2nd ed., ed. Tilman Zülch and Klaus Guercke (Berlin: Lettner 1969), 229.

40. Hermann Kunst, "Brief an den Bundeskanzler," Political Archives of the German Foreign Office Berlin, B 34/747, 1.

41. "Menschenrechte (Vertraulicher Bericht): Anlage an den Brief an die Mitglieder des Arbeitskreises für Menschenrechte," 1968, Political Archives of the German Foreign Office, Berlin, B 34/747, 8. See also Zentralkomitee der deutschen Katholiken, "Entschließung zur Hilfe in Nigeria-Biafra," November 12, 1968, Political Archives of the German Foreign Office Berlin: B 34/747.

42. Mira Siegelberg, "Contending with Ghosts of the Past: Raphael Lemkin and the Origins of the Genocide Convention," *Columbia Undergraduate Journal of History* 1, no. 1 (January 2006): 30–48.

43. A good example is Tilman Zülch, "Plädoyer für die Republik Biafra," in *Soll Biafra überleben*, ed. Zülch and Guercke, 11–18.

44. Golo Mann, "Geleitwort," in *Soll Biafra überleben*, ed. Zülch and Guercke, 9.

45. "La France et le problème biafrais," in *La France et le Biafra*, ed. Ministère des Affaires Etrangères (Paris: Services d'Information et de Presse, 1969), 7–14. See also JM/HV, "Note: La France et la crise nigéro-biafraise," August 6, 1968, Centre des *Archives diplomatiques* La *Courneuve*: Afrique-Levant, Nigeria 1966–1970, 14.

46. Daniel Bach, "Le Général de Gaulle et la guerre civile au Nigeria," *Canadian Journal of African Studies / Revue Canadienne des Études Africaines* 14 (1980): 259–272.

47. Georges Henein, "Ojukwu est sûr de tenir," *L'Express*, August 12, 1968.

48. Raymond Offroy, "Editorial," *Biafra: Bulletin du Comité d'Action pour le Biafra* 1, no. 1 (April 1969): 1–2.

49. Nicolas Bancel, Pascal Blanchard, and Françoise Vergès, *La république coloniale* (Paris: Hachette, 2003); Todd Shepard, *The Invention of Decolonization: The Algerian War and the Remaking of France* (Ithaca, N.Y.: Cornell University Press, 2006).

50. G. S. Littlejohn Cook, "Memorandum," October 25, 1968, National Archives of the United Kingdom, Kew (NA), FCO 26/299, 1; W. R. Haydon, "Memorandum: Our Public Line on Nigeria," October 21, 1968, NA FCO 26/299.

51. John Peck, "Confidential Note," January 30, 1968 [1969], NA FCO 26/299, 1.

52. D. C. Tebbit, "Comment on Confidential Note by John Peck," January 28, 1969, NA FCO 26/299.

53. Egon Bahr, "Dokument 245: Ministerialdirektor Bahr an Bundesminister Brandt, z. Z. Hamar. 06.08.1968," in *Akten zur Auswärtigen Politik der Bundesrepublik*

Deutschland: 1968, vol. 1, *1. Juli bis 31. Dezember 1968*, ed. Rainer A. Blasius (Munich: Oldenbourg, 1999), 970.

54. John W. Young, *Twentieth-Century Diplomacy: A Case Study of British Practice, 1963–1976* (Cambridge: Cambridge University Press, 2008), 66–69.

55. R. E. Holloway, "Memorandum," October 24, 1968, NA FCO 26/299.

56. John Wilson, "Confidential Report by the Foreign and Commonwealth Office," November 24, 1969, NA FCO 65/446. See also L. C. Glass, "Confidential Minutes," October 7, 1969, NA FCO 65/446.

57. B. R. Curson, "Internal Report: Nigeria and Information Work in Europe," March 12, 1969, NA FCO 26/300; Arengo-Jones to Nigel Gaydon, January 17, 1969, NA FCO 26/299; Leslie Fielding to the West African Department, December 10, 1968, NA FCO 26/299. The government's practice did not go unnoticed among activists. In one of its leaflets, Peter Cadogan's Save Biafra Campaign claimed that "since 1961 the civil servants have briefed the Commonwealth correspondents of the national press almost daily and successfully shut them up." Save Biafra Campaign, "Whitehall's Guilty Men," 1969, NA FCO 65/250.

58. "Brockway and Griffiths Visit Ojukwu," in *Crisis and Conflict in Nigeria*, ed. Kirk-Greene, 2:341.

59. Fenner Brockway, "Letter to the Editor: War in Nigeria," *Times*, London, November 12, 1968; Bernard D. Nicholls, "Letter to Kirkley," December 21, 1968, OA, file OA/14: Nigeria / Biafra, vol. 2, 2.

60. Margery Perham, "*Why Biafran Leaders Should Surrender,*" *Times*, London, September 12, 1968, 9; Perham, "A Letter to General Gowon," *Spectator*, London, January 31, 1969, 132–133; for reactions to this move, see Haydon, "Memorandum," UK NA FCO 26/299; and Yakubu Gowon, "Letter to Dame Margery Perham," October 28, 1968, 2, OA, file COM 3/1/1: Confidential Papers on Nigeria/Biafra 1968-70.

61. Bernard D. Nicholls to Leslie H. Kirkley, December 5, 1968, OA, DIR/2/3/2/33.

62. Robert Smith, "Memorandum of Conversation: Relationship between Goldstein and Associates and the 'Republic of Biafra,'" February 14, 1968, The National Archives and Records Administration, College Park, MD, US (NARA), RG 59 General Records of the Department of State, Central Foreign Policy Files, Political Aff. and REL Biafra-NIG, Box 1872.

63. Cited in Davis, *Interpreters for Nigeria*, 114. See also Jules Chomé, *Le drame du Nigéria* (Waterloo: Tiers-Monde et Révolution, 1969).

64. Biafran Government, "Statement: Red Cross Relief Operations," June 27, 1968, OA, file OA/14: Nigeria / Biafra, vol. 1.

65. Bruce, "Telegram to Department of State," August 27, 1968, NARA RG 59 General Records of the Department of State, Central Foreign Policy Files, Pol 27 Biafra-Nigeria, Box 1876; *Hansard Commons*, August 27, 1969, column 693, http://hansard.millbanksystems.com/commons/1968/aug/27/nigeria.

66. Stremlau, *International Politics of the Nigerian Civil War*, 113.

67. International Observer Team to Nigeria, *No Genocide* (Apapa: Nigerian National Press, 1968).

68. See, for instance, "No Evidence of Genocide," *United Nigeria*, October 11, 1968; Odogwu Ozalla, *Ojukwu's "Self-Determination": A Reappraisal in the Light of International Politics* (Apapa: Nigerian National Press, ca. 1969).

69. For the Biafran efforts to counter these reports, see *Nigeria/Biafra Conflict: An International Commission of Jurists Find Prima Facie Evidence of Genocide*, 1969, Rhodes Library, University of Oxford, MSS.Afr.S. 2399; Ajibola, *Foreign Policy and Public Opinion*, 154–155. For a critical assessment of Whitehall's efforts to rebuke the genocide claims, see Karen E. Smith, *Genocide and the Europeans* (Cambridge: Cambridge University Press 2010), 66–81.

70. Tom Garrett, "Genocide—or Merely the Murder of Biafran Elite?" *Church Times*, October 18, 1968.

71. Ibid.

72. Stanley Diamond, "Who Killed Biafra?" *New York Review of Books*, February 26, 1970, repr. in *Dialectical Anthropology* 31, no. 1–3 (November 2007): 360, 359.

73. A. Dirk Moses, "Raphael Lemkin, Culture, and the Concept of Genocide," in *Oxford Handbook of Genocide Studies*, ed. Donald Bloxham and A. Dirk Moses (New York: Oxford University Press, 2010), 19–41.

74. Anthony Enahoro, "Chief Enahoro Writes to British MPs on Nigerian Civil War," June 12, 1968, CCA NBKR 4/41, 6.

75. Editorial, "The Bigger the Lie," *United Nigeria*, October 11, 1968.

76. Bernard D. Nicholls to Kirkley, December 5, 1968, OA, file OA/14: Nigeria / Biafra, vol. 2, 1. See also Akinwande Williams, "What a Policy of Calumny," *Economist*, September 14, 1968.

77. "Ein Kavalierskrieg," *Der Spiegel*, January 19, 1970.

78. "Ojukwu Flees as Biafra Faces Total Collapse," *Times*, London, January 12, 1970.

79. Young, *Labour Governments*, 210–211.

80. Karl-Heinz Janßen, "Das Ende mit Schrecken," *Die Zeit*, January 16, 1970.

81. Cronjé, *World and Nigeria*, 210.

82. Auberon Waugh and Suzanne Cronjé, *Biafra: Britain's Shame* (London: Michael Joseph, 1969), 115.

83. Paul Connett, "Conference Report," *International Conscience in Action* 1, no. 3 (June 1970), unpaged.

84. For a colorful example for such reproaches, see the letter of Kennedy Lindsay to the German Biafra activist Elfriede Reinke, August 8, 1970, Gesellschaft für bedrohte Völker Archives, Göttingen, Biafra allgemein 1968–1978.

85. See the organization's journal *Pogrom* or edited volumes, for example, *Von denen keiner spricht: Unterdrückte Minderheiten—von der Friedenspolitik vergessen: Kurden, Basken, Chicanos, Indios, Meschier, (Sowjetunion) u. a.*, ed. Tilman Zülch (Reinbek: Rowohlt, 1975).

86. Walter Schwarz, "Biafra's Embarrassing Ghost Lingers On," *Guardian*, January 28, 1970.

87. See, for example, Bernard Kouchner, "Préface: Le devoir d'ingérence," in *Le*

devoir d'ingérence: Peut-on les laisser mourir? ed. Mario Betatti and Bernard Kouchner (Paris: Denoël, 1987), 9-12.

88. See, for instance, Patrick Rotman and Hervé Hamon, *Génération*, vol. 2, *Les années de poudre* (Paris: Seuil, 1988), the narrative of which starts in Biafra.

89. See esp. O'Sullivan, *Ireland, Africa*.

90. Tim Allen and David Styan, "A Right to Interfere? Bernard Kouchner and the New Humanitarianism," *Journal of International Development* 12, no. 6 (August 2000): 825-842; Kristin Ross, *May '68 and Its Afterlives* (Chicago: University of Chicago Press, 2002), 155-169; Philippe Ryfman, "L'humanitaire, enfant de Mai?" in *68: Une histoire collective, 1962-1981*, ed. Philippe Artières and Michelle Zancarini-Fournel (Paris: La Découverte, 2008), 736-744; Bertrand Taithe, "Reinventing (French) Universalism: Religion, Humanitarianism and the 'French Doctors,'" *Modern and Contemporary France* 12, no. 2 (May 2004): 147-158.

91. Moyn, *Last Utopia*, 173.

92. On the New Left's Third-Worldism, see Christoph Kalter, *Die Entdeckung der Dritten Welt: Dekolonisierung und neue radikale Linke in Frankreich* (Frankfurt: Campus, 2011); and Quinn Slobodian, *Foreign Front: Third World Politics in Sixties West Germany* (Durham, N.C.: Duke University Press 2012).

93. This point is often emphasized by Frederick Cooper. See Cooper, "Possibility and Constraint: African Independence in Historical Perspective," *Journal of African History* 49, no. 2 (2008): 167-196, and "Reconstructing Empire in British and French Africa," *Past and Present*, no. 210 (2011): 196-210.

94. Jörg Fisch, *Das Selbstbestimmungsrecht der Völker: Die Domestizierung einer Illusion* (Munich: C. H. Beck 2010).

95. Jean-Loup Amselle and Elikia M'Bokolo, eds., *Au coeur de l'ethnie: Ethnies, tribalisme et état en Afrique* (1985; Paris: La Découverte, 1999).

Chapter 3. The Disenchantment of Socialism

I would like to express my gratitude to Jan Eckel and Samuel Moyn for discussing their work with me as well as for their helpful comments on this chapter.

1. Jan Eckel, "Utopie der Moral, Kalkül der Macht: Menschenrechte in der globalen Politik seit 1945," *Archiv für Sozialgeschichte* 49 (2009), 437-484; Samuel Moyn, *The Last Utopia: Human Rights in History* (Cambridge, Mass.: Belknap Press of Harvard University Press, 2010). The quotation comes from Peter Opitz (cited in Eckel, "Utopie der Moral," 437). Eckel uses the phrase "tectonic shift" in ibid., 459.

2. The first use of the term appears to have occurred in a prescient article by the literary critic Stanislav Rassadin in *Iunost'* [Youth], no. 12 (1960), as cited in Vladislav Zubok, *Zhivago's Children: The Last Russian Intelligentsia* (Cambridge, Mass.: Belknap Press of Harvard University Press, 2009), 162, 396.

3. K. Iu. Rogov, ed., *Semidesiatye kak predmet istorii russkoi kul'tury* (Moscow-Venice: O.G.I. Publishers, 1998), 9-12.

4. The strongest versions of this narrative can be found in Marshall S. Shatz, *Soviet*

Dissent in Historical Perspective (New York: Cambridge University Press, 1980), and Dietrich Beyrau, *Intelligenz und Dissens: Die russischen Bildungschichten in der Sowjetunion 1917 bis 1985* (Göttingen: Vandenhoeck and Ruprecht, 1993).

5. On the leading organizer of the glasnost meeting, see Benjamin Nathans, "The Dictatorship of Reason: Aleksandr Vol'pin and the Idea of Rights under 'Developed Socialism,'" *Slavic Review* 66, no. 4 (Winter 2007): 630–663.

6. A digitized collection of documents produced by the Initiative Group (*Dokumenty initsiativnoi gruppy*) was prepared in 2009 by the Memorial Society (Moscow) and is available online at http://www.memo.ru/history/diss/ig/docs/igdocs.html. A printed version is forthcoming. My thanks to Gennadii Kuzovkin for making this collection available to me.

7. Some of the committee's reports were published as *Dokumenty Komiteta prav cheloveka* (New York: International League for the Rights of Man, 1972).

8. Joshua Rubenstein and Alexander Gribanov, eds., *The KGB File of Andrei Sakharov* (New Haven, Conn.: Yale University Press, 2005), Document 23 (January 18, 1971), 114.

9. Many of these letters can be found in the Sakharov Archive in Moscow, f. 1, razdel 3.1.1, including several that mention having learned of the Committee on Human Rights from broadcasts by Radio Liberty.

10. Daniel C. Thomas, *The Helsinki Effect: International Norms, Human Rights, and the Demise of Communism* (Princeton, N.J.: Princeton University Press, 2001).

11. See Benjamin Nathans, "Soviet Rights Talk in the Post-Stalin Era," in *Human Rights in the Twentieth Century*, ed. Stefan-Ludwig Hoffmann (New York: Cambridge University Press, 2011), 166–190, especially 185–187.

12. *Dokumenty Initsiativnoi gruppy* (see footnote 7), Doc. 1.

13. See, for example, the November 28, 1971, and July 1, 1972, appeals by the Initiative Group in *Dokumenty Initsiativnoi gruppy*, Docs. 11 and 16. Many of the group's appeals were cast in the form of "Open Letters" or "Announcements" without specific addressees but implicitly destined for circulation via samizdat and *tamizdat* to readers inside and outside the USSR.

14. *Dokumenty Initsiativnoi gruppy*, Doc. 5 (January 17, 1970). The original phrase is "v zashchitu grazhdanskikh prav cheloveka." In Russian, the standard rendition of "human rights" is "prava cheloveka," literally "rights of the human being," hearkening back to the idea's eighteenth-century formulation as the "rights of man." For purposes of readability, I generally translate "prava cheloveka" as "human rights," except in cases such as this, where "civil human rights" would be too confusing.

15. This was a widespread misperception in the USSR, nourished by the fact that the Soviet Union never repudiated the UDHR and in fact repeatedly and publicly cited its principles in various international discussions of human rights. See *Dokumenty Initsiativnoi gruppy*, Note 124, and Jennifer Amos, "Embracing and Contesting: The Soviet Union and the Universal Declaration of Human Rights, 1948–1958," in *Human Rights in the Twentieth Century*, ed. Hoffmann, 147–165. Having entered the increasingly global conversation about human rights in the 1960s, it would have been extremely awkward

for Soviet leaders to distance themselves from the UDHR, which more often than not served as the point of departure for that conversation.

16. Leonard Ternovskii, "Taina IG [The Secret of the Initiative Group]," in *Vospominaniia i stat'i* (Moscow: Vozvrashchenie, 2006), 192. In the Soviet Union, one should note, foreign relations remained an exclusive "crown prerogative" to a greater extent than in contemporaneous democratic countries.

17. "Report on Political Prisoners in USSR" (1972), International Institute for Social History, Amsterdam (hereafter cited as IISH), Amnesty International Archive, Index Documents on the USSR (EUR 46), folder 438, p. 1.

18. Meeting of February 17/18, 1968, to discuss possible "Candidates for Prisoner of the Year from Communist Countries," IISH, Amnesty International Archive, International Executive Committee (EUR 46), microfilm reel 243, frame 330.

19. Columbia University, Butler Library, Rare Books and Manuscripts, Amnesty International USA Archive, Record Group II: Executive Director Files, 1967–1997, Series 5: National Section Memos, box 9, folder 23, document 3. I have retranslated the text into English in order to more closely conform to the Russian original, which circulated in samizdat. See *Arkhiv samizdata* vol. 25 (Munich: Samizdat Archive Association, 1977), document 1487.

20. "IEC/ 21–22 March 1970, Agenda Item 9D (iii)," IISH, Amnesty International Archive, International Executive Committee (EUR 46), microfilm reel 243, frame 780.

21. IEC internal memorandum, February 4–6, 1972, IISH, Amnesty International Archive, Index Documents on the USSR (EUR 46), folder 422, p. 1. On the controversy, see letter from Edward Kline urging Amnesty not to suspend publication of the *Chronicle*, June 15, 1976, ibid., folder 424.

22. Eckel, "Utopie der Moral," 462.

23. As is often the case in intellectual history, the unraveling of Marxist-Leninist thought (especially after 1956) has received far less attention than its origins. For the Soviet case, with special attention to the post-1985 era, see Archie Brown, ed., *The Demise of Marxism-Leninism in Russia* (New York: Palgrave Macmillan, 2004).

24. See for example Anatolii Marchenko, *Moi pokazaniia* (Frankfurt: Posev, 1969), 210–214; Petro Grigorenko, *V podpol'e mozhno vstretit' tol'ko krys . . .* (Long Island, N.Y.: Detinets, 1981), 490–492; Ludmilla Alexeyeva and Paul Goldberg, *The Thaw Generation: Coming of Age in the Post-Stalin Era* (Pittsburgh: University of Pittsburgh Press, 1993), 65–66, 74–76.

25. Richard Crossman, ed., *The God That Failed* (New York: Harper, 1949), 100–101.

26. Sidney Hook, "The Literature of Political Disillusionment," *Bulletin of the American Association of University Professors* 35, no. 3 (Autumn 1949): 450–467.

27. There were exceptions, especially among older dissidents who in their youth had taken part in the forced collectivization of the peasantry or other policies in the name of Marxism-Leninism. The best known example is Lev Kopelev, *Sotvoril sebe kumira* (Ann Arbor: Ardis, 1978).

28. Donna Bahry, "Society Transformed? Rethinking the Social Roots of Perestroika," *Slavic Review* 52, no. 3 (Autumn 1993): 512–554.

29. Iurii Orlov, "Vozmozhen li sotsializm ne-totalitarnogo tipa?" signed December 15, 1975, published in *Materialy samizdata* 11 (1976), AS #2425, repr. in P. Litvinov, M. Meerson-Aksenov, and B. Shragin, eds., *Samosoznanie: Sbornik statei* (Belmont, Mass.: Nordland, 1976), 279–303.

30. Max Weber, *Wissenschaft als Beruf: Studienausgabe* (1917; 1919; Tübingen: J. C. B. Mohr [Paul Siebeck], 1994), 22.

31. Jeffrey E. Green, "Two Meanings of Disenchantment: Sociological Condition vs. Philosophical Act—Reassessing Max Weber's Thesis of the Disenchantment of the World," *Philosophy and Theology* 17, nos. 1–2 (2006): 51–84.

32. On the "deterritorialization" of official ideology in late Soviet society, see Alexei Yurchak, *Everything Was Forever, Until It Was No More: The Last Soviet Generation* (Princeton, N.J.: Princeton University Press, 2006). For a critique of Yurchak's approach, see Kevin Platt and Benjamin Nathans, "Socialist in Form, Indeterminate in Content: The Ins and Outs of Late Soviet Culture," *Ab Imperio*, no. 2 (2011): 301–324.

33. Orlov, "Vozmozhen li sotsializm ne-totalitarnogo tipa?" 19.

34. This does not apply to social and economic rights, which attempt to specify the content of claims regarding such things as a living wage, access to education and housing, etc.

35. Yuri Orlov, *Dangerous Thoughts: Memoirs of a Russian Life* (New York: William Morrow, 1991), 189.

36. See, for example, Nathans, "The Dictatorship of Reason," 655, and more generally, Iurii Aikhenval'd, *Don Kikhot na russkoi pochve*, 2 vols. (New York: Chalidze Publications, 1982–1984).

Chapter 4. Dictatorship and Dissent

This research was made possible by support from the Berlin Program for Advanced German and European Studies. I am also deeply grateful to Kurt Sittmann for his help with several iterations of this chapter.

1. The Helsinki Accords were an international agreement meant to improve relations between the West and the Communist bloc. Thirty-three European states as well as the United States and Canada signed on to the accords in August 1975.

2. For the main work asserting the discontinuous effect of Helsinki Accords for the Eastern bloc, see Daniel Thomas, *The Helsinki Effect: International Norms, Human Rights, and the Demise of Communism* (Princeton, N.J.: Princeton University Press, 2001), as well as Michael Ignatieff, *Human Rights as Politics and Idolatry* (Princeton, N.J.: Princeton University Press, 2001), 19. Ignatieff argues that the Eastern bloc denied the validity of political and civil human rights prior to Helsinki. Works arguing that human rights were irrelevant to East German politics prior to 1975 include Christian Joppke, *East German Dissidents and the Revolution of 1989: Social Movement*

in a Leninist Regime (New York: New York University Press, 1995), 116; Jürgen Wüst, *Menschenrechtsarbeit im Zwielicht: Zwischen Staatssicherheit und Antifaschismus* (Bonn: Bouvier, 1999), 32; Steven Pfaff, "The Politics of Peace in the GDR: The Independent Peace Movement, the Church, and the Origins of the East German Opposition," *Peace and Change* 26, no. 3 (July 2001): 287.

3. Dirk Spilker, *The East German Leadership and the Division of Germany: Patriotism and Propaganda, 1945–1953* (Oxford: Oxford University Press, 2006), 28.

4. Allen E. Buchanan, *Marx and Justice: The Radical Critique of Liberalism* (Totowa, N.J: Rowman and Littlefield, 1982), 68.

5. Jürgen Kuczynski, *Menschenrechte und Klassenrechte* (Berlin: Akademie-Verlag, 1978), 20.

6. Alexander Schwitanski, *Die Freiheit des Volksstaats: Die Entwicklung der Grund- und Menschenrechte und die deutsche Sozialdemokratie bis zum Ende der Weimarer Republik* (Essen: Klartext, 2008).

7. Leszek Kolakowski, "Marxism and Human Rights," *Daedalus* 112, no. 4 (October 1983): 81.

8. "Kein Sozialismus ohne Menschenrechte," October 20, 1946, Archiv der Sozialen Demokratie, Bonn. 6/PLKA000150; and Arthur Schlegelmilch, *Hauptstadt in Zonendeutschland: Die Entstehung der Berliner Nachkriegsdemokratie, 1945–1949* (Berlin: Haude and Spener, 1993), 363.

9. Karl Polak, "Gewaltteilung, Menschenrechte, Rechtsstaat: Begriffsformalismus und Demokratie," *Einheit* 7 (December 1946), repr. in *Zur Entwicklung der Arbeiter- und Bauern-Macht* (Berlin: Staatsverlag der Deutschen Demokratischen Republik, 1968), 139–140.

10. Otto Grotewohl, *Deutsche Verfassungspläne* (Berlin: Dietz, 1947), 68. In the same year Grotewohl used the slogan in a speech at a SED party convention. Otto Grotewohl, *Im Kampf um Deutschland: Rede auf dem 2. Parteitag der SED* (Berlin: Dietz, 1947), 33.

11. On the development of the discourse of human rights in the Soviet Union, see Jennifer Amos, "Embracing and Contesting: The Soviet Union and the Universal Declaration of Human Rights, 1948–1958," in *Human Rights in the Twentieth Century*, ed. Stefan-Ludwig Hoffmann (Cambridge: Cambridge University Press, 2010).

12. The committee was originally named Das Komitee zum Schutz der Menschenrechte, gegen militaristische Willkür und Klassenjustiz in Westdeutschland, but this was soon simplified to Das Komitee zum Schutze der Menschenrechte, and then changed again in 1969 to DDR-Komitee für Menschenrechte. For the sake of clarity, it will be referred to throughout as the GDR Committee for Human Rights.

13. Siegfried Forberger, *Das DDR-Komitee für Menschenrechte: Teil 2, Kapitel I (1959–1967)* (Berlin: Self-published, 1997), 25.

14. "Rede des Regierenden Bürgermeisters von Berlin vor dem Deutschen Bundestag, 18. August 1961," *Das Parlament* 11, no. 35 (August 23, 1961): 3.

15. Bundesminister für Gesamtdeutsche Fragen, *Verletzungen der Menschenrechte,*

Unrechtshandlungen und Zwischenfälle an der Berliner Sektorengrenze seit Errichtung der Mauer (13. August 1961–15. August 1962) (Bonn: Bundesminister für Gesamtdeutsche Fragen, 1962); Kurt Rabl, *Die Menschenrechte und die SBZ* (Bonn: Mitteldeutscher Kulturrat, 1965).

16. Lora Wildenthal, "Human Rights Activism in Occupied and Early West Germany: The Case of the German League for Human Rights," *Journal of Modern History* 80, no. 3 (2008): 517.

17. Zusammengefasster Finanzplan 1961 des Komitees zum Schutze der Menschenrechte, Akademie der Künste, Pauls Wiens Archiv 2349.

18. Paul Fabian to Friedel Malter, February 10, 1964, Bundesarchiv Lichterfelde (hereafter cited as BArch-Lichterfelde) DY 46/ 394.

19. Presseveröffentlichung/Presseausschnitte 1965, BArch-Lichterfelde DZ 7/ 10.

20. Komitee zum Schutze der Menschenrechte in der Deutschen Demokratischen Republik, *Memorandum of the Committee for the Protection of Human Rights of the German Democratic Republic on the Violation of Human Rights in West Germany* (Berlin: Committee for the Protection of Human Rights, 1961), 6.

21. Ibid., 2.

22. On the centrality of antifascist biography to political legitimacy in the GDR, see Catherine Epstein, *The Last Revolutionaries: German Communists and Their Century* (Cambridge, Mass.: Harvard University Press, 2003).

23. Akademie der Künste, Pauls Wiens Archiv 2349; BArch-Lichterfelde, DY 46/ 394.

24. Informationen, Schriftwechsel, Vorlagen zu Fragen des Völkerrechts und Menschenrechte, Auswärtiges Amt-Politisches Archiv (PP-AA), MfAA A 9706.

25. Hermann Klenner, *Studien über die Grundrechte: Mit Dokumentenanhang* (Berlin: Staatsverlag der Deutschen Demokratischen Republik, 1964), 19–35.

26. Ibid., 78–88, 117–120.

27. Ibid., 108–116.

28. Ibid., 13.

29. William Glenn Gray, *Germany's Cold War: The Global Campaign to Isolate East Germany, 1949–1969* (Chapel Hill: University of North Carolina Press, 2003).

30. Hermann Klenner, "Frei von dreifacher Bürde: Eine Betrachtung über die Menschenrechte in unserer sozialistischen Verfassung," *Neues Deutschland*, March 30, 1968, 12.

31. "Beschluss des Staatsrates der DDR zur Erklärung der Bereitschaft der DDR zum Beitritt zu den UNO Menschenrechtskonventionen. 17. Juli 1968," BArch-Lichterfelde, DA 5/ 660. The GDR formally applied for UN membership in 1966 and was admitted with West Germany in 1973.

32. Roland Burke, "From Individual Rights to National Development: The First UN International Conference on Human Rights, Tehran, 1968," *Journal of World History* 19, no. 3 (2008): 296.

33. Erklärung der Regierung der DDR an die Internationale Konferenz über

Menschenrechte vom 22. April bis 13. Mai 1968 in Teheran, BArch-Lichterfelde, DY 30/ J IV 2/2/ 116.

34. See Bengsch, February 5, 1968, BArch-Lichterfelde, DY 30/ IV A2/13/ 46. Schönherr et al. letter, February 15, 1968, Evangelisches Zentral Archiv (hereafter cited as EZA) 104/687.

35. 218 Catholics in the town of Lenterode signed on to Letters no. 9669 and 9670, March 10, 1968, BArch-Lichterfelde DA 1/ 4157.

36. Mark Allinson, *Politics and Popular Opinion in East Germany, 1945–1968* (Manchester: Manchester University Press, 2000), 143.

37. Letter no. 1839, February 18, 1968, BArch-Lichterfelde DA 1/ 4079.

38. Dieter Blumenwitz, "Selbstbestimmung und Menschenrechte im Geteilten Deutschland aus der Sicht der Konferenz für Sicherheit und Zusammenarbeit in Europa," 11, BArch-Koblenz B 137/ 10780.

39. Bericht über die zweite Phase der Konferenz für Sicherheit und Zusammenarbeit in Europa und Direktive für das weitere Auftreten der Delegation der DDR, BArch-Lichterfelde DY 30/ J IV 2/2/ 1501.

40. Einschätzungen der Schlußdokumente der KSZE, 7, BArch-Lichterfelde DY 30/ IV B 2/20/ 614.

41. Bericht über den Hauptinhalt der an die Volkskammer und den Staatsrat gerichteten Eingaben im III. Quartal 1975, BArch-Lichterfelde DA 5/ 9026.

42. Bericht über die an den Staatsrat gerichteten Eingaben der Bürger im Jahre 1976, 10, BArch-Lichterfelde DA 5/11383.

43. Karl Wilhelm Fricke, *Opposition und Widerstand in der DDR* (Cologne: Verlag Wissenschaft und Politik, 1984), 169–170.

44. The third quarter of 1972 saw a 27 percent increase in written applications to travel to the FRG or West Berlin, while in-person applications jumped by 55 percent. In the fourth quarter of that year, applications climbed another 60 percent. Bericht über den Hauptinhalt der an die Volkskammer und den Staatsrat gerichteten Eingaben im III. Quartal 1972, and Bericht über den Hauptinhalt der an die Volkskammer und den Staatsrat gerichteten Eingaben im IV. Quartal 1972, BArch-Lichterfelde DA 5/ 9026.

45. Bericht über den Hauptinhalt der an die Volkskammer und den Staatsrat gerichteten Eingaben im IV. Quartal 1973, BArch-Lichterfelde DA 5/ 9026.

46. On the importance of 1977 as a breakthrough year for the international human rights movement, see Samuel Moyn, *The Last Utopia: Human Rights in History* (Cambridge, Mass: Belknap Press of Harvard University Press, 2010). Bericht über den Hauptinhalt der an den Staatsrat gerichteten Eingaben im Jahre 1978, Anlage 1, BArch-Lichterfelde DA 5/ 11385. Between 1977 and 1978 the number of letters from abroad jumped by 176 percent.

47. Thesen zum Menschenrechte. July 1978, EZA 687/ 48. Bund Evangelischer Pfarrer in der DDR: Eine Dokumentation über ihr Verständnis innerhalb des Ökumenischen Rates der Kirchen, BArch-Lichterfelde, BA DY 08/ 246.

48. Nationalkomitee des Lutherischen Weltbundes in der Deutschen Demokrati-

schen Republik, *Sorge um eine menschliche Welt: Normativität und Relativität der Menschenrechte*, 1973. Pg. 42–43.

49. Niederschrift über die Sitzung der ad hoc Gruppe Menschenrechte am 14.10.1976 in Berlin, EZA 687/ 47.

50. Manfred Stolpe, "Universale Menschenrechte," Potsdam, June 27 1976, 13, EZA 687/ 46.

51. Arbeitsgruppe Menschenrechte beim BEK 1975–1976. Auszug aus dem Protokoll der 55. Sitzung des Vorstandes der Konferenz der Ev. Kirchenleitungen in der DDR in Berlin am 30.Juli 1975, EZA 101/683.

52. See Lothar Tautz, ed., *Friede und Gerechtigkeit heute: Das "Querfurter Papier" - ein politisches Manifest für die Einhaltung der Menschenrechte in der DDR* (Magdeburg: Landesbeauftragte für die Unterlagen des Staatssicherheitsdienstes der Ehemaligen DDR in Sachsen-Anhalt, 2002).

53. Argumentation zur Auseinandersetzung mit politischen Provokationen pazifistischer Gruppen in den protestantischen Kirchen der DDR, July 1982, BArch-Lichterfelde DP 1/ 21439.

54. On the neutralization of the church's human rights debate, see Erhart Neubert, *Die Geschichte der Opposition in der DDR, 1949–1989* (Berlin: Christoph Links Verlag,1998), 356–359.

55. Repr. in Roger Woods, *Opposition in the GDR under Honecker, 1971–85: An Introduction and Documentation*, trans. Christopher Upward (New York: St. Martin's Press, 1986), 139.

56. Robert Havemann, *Ein deutscher Kommunist: Rückblicke und Perspektiven aus der Isolation* (Reinbek bei Hamburg: Rowohlt, 1978), 102.

57. Rudolf Bahro, *Ich werde meinen Weg fortsetzen* (Frankfurt: Europäische Verlagsanstalt, 1977), 13.

58. Fischer and Winkelmann to the Secretariat of the Central Committee of the SED, March 12, 1980, BArch-Lichterfelde DY 30/ 11642.

59. Cited in Thomas, *The Helsinki Effect*, 110.

60. Cited in Woods, *Opposition in the GDR under Honecker, 1971–85*, 196.

61. Wolfgang Rüddenklau, ed., *Störenfried: DDR-Opposition 1986–1989* (Berlin: BasisDruck, 1992), 37.

62. Ibid, 51.

63. Dirk Philipsen, *We Were the People: Voices from East Germany's Revolutionary Autumn of 1989* (Durham, N.C.: Duke University Press, 1993), 54.

64. Repr. in Rüddenklau, *Störenfried*, 56.

65. Ibid. 55.

66. Benjamin Nathans, "Soviet Rights-Talk in the Post-Stalin Era," in *Human Rights in the Twentieth Century*, ed. Hoffmann, 187.

67. Petition to the Eleventh Party Congress, April 2, 1986. Reprinted in Ferdinand Kroh, ed., *"Freiheit ist immer Freiheit": Die Andersdenkenden in der DDR* (Frankfurt: Ullstein, 1988), 222.

68. In comparison with other Eastern bloc countries, East German dissidents were not so disillusioned with the abstract ideal of socialism. See Celia Donert, "Charter 77 and the Roma: Human Rights and Dissent in Socialist Czechoslovakia," in *Human Rights in the Twentieth Century*, ed. Hoffmann, 193.

69. Moyn, *Last Utopia*.

70. For a representative expression of this optimism from loyal SED partisans, see the interview with Jürgen Kuczynski, "This Country Is Having a Revolution at Last," *Bulletin: GDR Committee for Human Rights* 15, no. 3 (1989): 6.

71. Die politische-ideologische Arbeit für Frieden und Abrüstung nach dem Genfer Gipfeltreffen, December 19, 1985, BArch-Lichterfelde, DY 30/ 11887.

72. Hörnig to Kurt Hager, March 3, 1987, BArch-Lichterfelde, DY 30/ 7495.

73. Heinz Mohnhaupt, ed., *Normdurchsetzung in osteuropäischen Nachkriegsgesellschaften. Bd. 5, Deutsche Demokratische Republik (1958–1989) Recht und Juristen im Spiegel der Beschlüsse des Politbüros und Sekretariats des Zentralkomitees der SED* (Frankfurt: Klostermann, 2003), 597.

74. Archiv demokratischer Sozialismus (AdS) Bestand Reißig-Berg Band 1. Multilateraler Wissenschaftlicher Problemrat von Bruderparteien sozialistischer Länder zu Fragen der Menschenrechte: Konzeptionelle Grundlagen der gegenwärtigen Politik der Bruderparteien sozialistischer Länder auf dem Gebiet der Menschenrechte. Studie, April 1989.

75. Cited in Frank Berg, *Menschenrechte: Der Autor im Gespräch mit Jürgen Weidlich* (Berlin: Dietz, 1990), 8.

Chapter 5. Whose Utopia?

1. Charlotte Bunch and Susana Fried, "Bejing '95: Moving Women's Human Rights from Margin to Center," *Signs* 22, no. 1 (Autumn 1996): 200–204.

2. Martha Chen, "Engendering World Conferences: The International Women's Movement and the United Nations," *Third World Quarterly* 16, no. 3 (September 1995): 477–493.

3. Jean H. Quataert, *Advocating Dignity: Human Rights Mobilizations in Global Politics* (Philadelphia: University of Pennsylvania Press, 2009).

4. Allida Black, "Are Women 'Human'? The UN and the Struggle to Recognize Women's Rights as Human Rights," in *The Human Rights Revolution: An International History*, ed. Akira Iriye, Petra Goedde, and William I. Hitchcock (New York: Oxford University Press, 2012), 133–155.

5. On the Mexico City conference, see Jocelyn Olcott, "Globalizing Sisterhood: International Women's Year and the Politics of Representation," in *The Shock of the Global: The 1970s in Perspective*, ed. Niall Ferguson et al. (Cambridge, Mass.: Belknap Press of Harvard University Press, 2010): 281–293.

6. Celia Donert, "Women's Rights in Cold War Europe: Disentangling Feminist Histories," *Past and Present*, no. 215 (Supplement 8, 2013, forthcoming); compare Catriona Kelly, "Defending Children's Rights, 'In Defense of Peace': Children and Soviet Cultural Diplomacy," *Kritika* 9, no. 4 (Fall 2008): 711–746.

7. More broadly on human rights in Soviet diplomacy, see Jennifer Amos, "Embracing and Contesting: The Soviet Union and the Universal Declaration of Human Rights, 1948–1958," in *Human Rights in the Twentieth Century*, ed. Stefan-Ludwig Hoffmann (Cambridge: Cambridge University Press, 2011), 147–165.

8. Laura Parisi, "Feminist Praxis and Women's Human Rights," *Journal of Human Rights* 1, no. 4 (December 2002): 571–585.

9. Nicholas Rutter, "Look Left, Drive Right: Internationalisms at the 1968 World Youth Festival," in *The Socialist Sixties*, ed. Anne E. Gorsuch and Diane P. Koenker (Bloomington: Indiana University Press, forthcoming 2013).

10. Francisca de Haan, "Continuing Cold War Paradigms in Western Historiography of Transnational Women's Organizations: The Case of the Women's International Democratic Federation," *Women's History Review* 19, no. 4 (September 2010): 547–573.

11. Herta Kuhrig, *A Contribution to International Women's Year: Equal Rights for Women in the German Democratic Republic* (Berlin: DDR-Komitee für Menschenrechte, 1973).

12. See chapters by Ned Richardson-Little and Benjamin Nathans in this volume; Paul Betts, "Socialism, Social Rights, and Human Rights: The Case of East Germany," *Humanity* 3, no. 3 (Winter 2012): 407–426.

13. Betts, "Socialism, Social Rights, and Human Rights," 408.

14. Daniel C. Thomas, *The Helsinki Effect: International Norms, Human Rights, and the Demise of Communism* (Princeton, N.J.: Princeton University Press, 2001).

15. Samuel Moyn, *The Last Utopia: Human Rights in History* (Cambridge, Mass.: Belknap Press of Harvard University Press, 2010).

16. Hilda Scott, *Does Socialism Liberate Women? Experiences from Eastern Europe* (Boston: Beacon Press, 1974).

17. Helen Laville, "A New Era in International Women's Rights? American Women's Associations and the Establishment of the UN Commission on the Status of Women," *Journal of Women's History* 20, no. 4 (Winter 2008): 34–56.

18. Leila J. Rupp, *Worlds of Women: The Making of an International Women's Movement* (Princeton, N.J.: Princeton University Press, 1997).

19. Ibid., 223.

20. Karen Offen, *European Feminisms, 1700–1950: A Political History* (Stanford, Calif.: Stanford University Press, 2000), 387.

21. Johannes Morsink, "Women's Rights in the Universal Declaration," *Human Rights Quarterly* 13, no. 2 (May 1991): 229–256.

22. Francisca de Haan, "Hoffnungen auf eine bessere Welt: Die frühen Jahre der Internationalen Demokratischen Frauenföderation (IDFF/WIDF) (1945–1950)," *Feministische Studien* 27, no. 2 (November 2009): 241–257.

23. Donert, "Women's Rights in Cold War Europe."

24. Melanie Ilic, "Soviet Women, Cultural Exchange, and the Women's International Democratic Federation," in *Reassessing Cold War Europe*, ed. Sari Autio-Sarasmo and Katalin Miklóssy (London: Routledge, 2011): 157–174.

25. Helen Laville, *Cold War Women: The International Activities of American Women's Organisations* (Manchester: Manchester University Press, 2002).

26. Jean H. Quataert, *The Gendering of Human Rights in the International Systems of Law in the Twentieth Century* (Washington, D.C.: American Historical Association, 2006).

27. De Haan, "Continuing Cold War Paradigms."

28. Arvonne S. Fraser, "Becoming Human: The Origins and Development Women's Human Rights," *Human Rights Quarterly* 21, no. 4 (November 1999): 899.

29. Ester Boserup, *Woman's Role in Economic Development* (London: Allen and Unwin, 1970).

30. Kristen Ghodsee, "Revisiting the United Nations Decade for Women: Brief Reflections on Feminism, Capitalism and Cold War Politics in the Early Years of the International Women's Movement," *Women's Studies International Forum* 33, no. 1 (January 2010): 3–12.

31. Kristina Schulz, *Der Lange Atem der Provokation: Die Frauenbewegung in der Bundesrepublik und in Frankreich 1968–1975* (Frankfurt: Campus, 2002), 74.

32. Sheila Rowbotham, *Women, Resistance, and Revolution* (Harmondsworth: Allen Lane, 1972); Rowbotham, "The Women's Movement and Organizing for Socialism," in *Beyond the Fragments: Feminism and the Making of Socialism*, ed. Sheila Rowbotham, Lynne Segal, and Hilary Wainwright (London: Merlin Press, 1979); Scott, *Does Socialism Liberate Women?*

33. Nancy Fraser, "Feminism, Capitalism, and the Cunning of History," *New Left Review*, n.s., no. 56 (March–April 2009): 103.

34. Information über eine Zusammenkunft leitender Funktionärinnen der Frauenbewegung aus der Sowjetunion, Bulgarien, Polen, der DDR, Ungarn, der CSSR und Rumänien, Berlin, den 11. Dezember 1968, SAPMO-BArch DY 30/IV A2/17.

35. Information über eine Beratung leitender Funktionärinnen der Frauenbewegung in Moskau vom 12.-15. 3. 1969, SAPMO-BArch DY 30/IV A2/17.

36. Raluca Popa, "Translating Equality Between Women and Men Across Cold War Divides: Women Activists from Hungary and Romania and the Creation of International Women's Year," in *Gender Politics and Everyday Life in State Socialist East and Central Europe*, ed. Shana Penn and Jill Massino (New York: Palgrave Macmillan, 2009), 59–74.

37. Ibid.

38. Cited in Popa, 65.

39. Karen Garner, *Shaping a Global Women's Agenda: Women's NGOs and Global Governance* (Manchester: Manchester University Press, 2010).

40. Ibid., 217.

41. SAPMO-BArch DY 31/646, 29.

42. Ausführungen des Genossen V. S. Schaposchnikov am 3.2.1975 auf der internen Beratung der 6 Bruderparteien zur Vorbereitung des Weltkongresses der Frauen,, SAPMO-BArch DY 31/646, 46.

43. Ständige Vertretung der DDR bei den Vereinten Nationen: Vermerk über einen Meinungsaustausch der sozialistischen UN-Mitgliedstaaten auf Expertebene über die Vorbereitung der Weltkonferenz zum Internationalen Jahr der Frau (IJF) am 23.4.1975 (New York, den 8.5.1975), SAPMO-BArch DY 31/636.

44. Ibid.

45. Ministerium für Auswärtige Angelegenheiten der DDR, Abteilung UNO, Bericht über die UNO-Konferenz in Mexiko im IJF, Berlin, den 8. Juli 1975, SAMPO-BArch DY 31/636.

46. Olcott, "Globalizing Sisterhood."

47. "Im Sozialismus sind Rechte der Frauen verwirklicht: Von der Konferenz der UNO im Internationalen Jahr der Frau," *Neues Deutschland*, June 25, 1975.

48. Abschlußbericht über die politisch-operative Sicherung des Weltkongresses im Internationalen Jahr der Frau und des VII. IDFF-Kongreßes (Aktion "Forum" gemäß Befehl Nr. 21/1975 des Ministers für Staatssicherheit), BStU, MfS, ZOS Nr. 2560, Zentraler Operativstab (hereafter cited as ZOS) Berlin, November 6, 1975.

49. Stand der Vorbereitung des Welt Kongresses im Internationalen Jahr der Frau in der Hauptstadt der DDR, Berlin, vom 20.10 bis 24.10.1975, BStU, MfS, ZOS Nr 2560. ZOS Berlin, October 8, 1975.

50. DFD Bezirksvorstand Berlin: Einzelmeinungen zum Weltkongreß, October 18, 1975, SAPMO-BArch DY 31/1557, bl. 3–4.

51. Robert G. Moeller, *Protecting Motherhood: Women and the Family in the Politics of Postwar West Germany* (Berkeley: University of California Press, 1993), 71.

52. Donna Harsch, "Society, the State and Abortion in East Germany, 1950–1972," *American Historical Review* 102, no. 1 (February 1997): 53–84; Benjamin Nathans, "Soviet Rights-Talk in the Post-Stalin Era," in *Human Rights in the Twentieth Century*, ed. Hoffmann, 166–190.

53. Kuhrig, *A Contribution to International Women's Year*.

54. Einschätzung der politische-operative Lage im Verantwortungsbereich der HA XX / Pressezentrum: Informationsdienst, BStU, MfS, ZOS Nr. 3344, Hauptabteilung XX, Berlin, October 21, 1975.

55. Donna Harsch, *Revenge of the Domestic: Women, the Family, and Communism in the German Democratic Republic* (Princeton, N.J.: Princeton University Press, 2007); Josie McLellan, *Love in the Time of Communism: Intimacy and Sexuality in the GDR* (Cambridge: Cambridge University Press, 2011); Dagmar Herzog, *Sex After Fascism: Memory and Morality in Twentieth-Century Germany* (Princeton, N.J.: Princeton University Press, 2007).

56. Kuhrig, *A Contribution to International Women's Year*, 9.

57. Kommission I, Arbeitspapier, SAPMO-BArch DY 30/vorl. SED 36900/1, SED Zentralkomitee (hereafter cited as ZK) Abteilung Frauen.

58. Ibid.

59. Betr: Bisher durchgeführte Treffen der AG für die K 9, 6, 2 und 1, 10.9.1975, SAPMO-BArch DY 30/vorl. SED 36900/1, SED ZK Abteilung Frauen.

60. Betts, "Socialism, Social Rights, and Human Rights."

61. Bulletin 1: Weltkongress im Internationalen Jahr der Frau: Grusssprache des Ersten Sekretärs des Zentralkomitees der SED Erich Honecker, SAPMO-BArch DY 30/vorl. SED 36902, SED ZK Abteilung Frauen.

62. Mark B. Smith, "Social Rights in the Soviet Dictatorship: The Constitutional Right to Welfare from Stalin to Brezhnev," *Humanity* 3, no. 3 (Winter 2012): 385–406.

63. Kommission I, Arbeitspapier, SAPMO-BArch DY 30/vorl. SED 36900/1, SED ZK Abteilung Frauen.

64. Kommission I, SAPMO-BArch DY 30/vorl. SED 36900/1, SED ZK Abteilung Frauen.

65. Olcott, "Globalizing Sisterhood."

66. Josie McLellan, "Glad to be Gay Behind the Wall: Gay and Lesbian Activism in 1970s East Germany," *History Workshop Journal* 74, no. 1 (Autumn 2012): 105–130.

67. Anja Mihr, *Amnesty International in der DDR: Der Einsatz für Menschenrechte im Visier der Stasi* (Berlin: Ch. Links Verlag, 2002).

68. Jocelyn Olcott, "Cold War Conflicts and Cheap Cabaret: Sexual Politics at the 1975 United Nations International Women's Year Conference," *Gender and History* 22, no. 3 (November 2010): 733–754.

69. Martin Klimke and Maria Höhn, *A Breath of Freedom: The Civil Rights Struggle, African American GIs, and Germany* (New York: Palgrave Macmillan, 2011).

70. Patrice G. Poutrus, "Asyl im Kalten Krieg: Eine Parallelgeschichte aus dem geteilten Nachkriegsdeutschland," *Totalitarismus und Demokratie* 2, no. 2 (Spring 2005): 273–288.

71. Kristen Ghodsee, "Rethinking State Socialist Mass Women's Organizations: The Committee of the Bulgarian Women's Movement and the United Nations Decade for Women, 1975–1985," *Journal of Women's History* 24, no. 4 (Winter 2012): 49–73.

72. Jean Quataert, "The Circuitous Origins of the Gender Perspective in Human Rights Advocacy: A Challenge for Transnational Feminisms," *Comparative Studies of South Asia, Africa and the Middle East* 31, no. 3 (2011): 639.

73. Janou Glencross, *How the International Women's Movement Discovered the "Troubles": Brokered and Broken Transnational Interactions During the Northern Ireland Conflict, 1968–1981* (Frankfurt: Peter Lang, 2011).

74. Bericht einer Minderheit an alle Kommissionen, angenommen auf einem inoffiziellen Treffen, October 24, 1975, SAPMO-BArch DY 30/vorl. SED 36900/1.

75. Abschlußbericht über die politisch-operative Sicherung des Weltkongresses im Internationalen Jahr der Frau und des VII. IDFF-Kongresses, November 6, 1975, BStU, MfS, ZOS Nr. 2560.

76. "Der Weltkongress ruft zur Aktionen," *Für Dich*, no. 45 (1975).

77. Bericht einer Minderheit an alle Kommissionen, angenommen auf einem inoffiziellen Treffen, October 24, 1975, SAPMO-BArch DY 30/vorl. SED 36900/1.

78. SAPMO-BArch DY 30/vorl. SED 36900/1.

79. Rebecca M. Kluchin, *Fit to be Tied: Sterilization and Reproductive Rights in America, 1950-1980* (New Brunswick, N.J.: Rutgers University Press, 2011).

80. "Der Weltkongress ruft zur Aktionen," *Für Dich*, no. 45 (1975).

81. Mihr, *Amnesty International in der DDR*, 172-173.

82. Torture of Women: Memorandum Presented to the World Congress for International Women's Year by Amnesty International, BStU, MfS, ZOS Nr. 3345.

83. MfS Dokumentation über Amnesty International, cited in Mihr, *Amnesty International in der DDR*, 173-174.

84. Mihr, *Amnesty International in der DDR*.

85. Ibid., 121.

86. Torture of Women: Memorandum Presented to the World Congress for International Women's Year by Amnesty International, BStU, MfS, ZOS Nr. 3345.

87. Judith P. Zinsser, "From Mexico to Copenhagen to Nairobi: The United Nations Decade for Women, 1975-1985," *Journal of World History* 13, no. 1 (Spring 2002): 147.

88. Quataert, *Advocating Dignity*.

89. Bernhard Graefrath, *Menschenrechte und internationale Kooperation: 10 Jahre Praxis des Internationalen Menschenrechtskomitees* (Berlin: Akademie-Verlag, 1988), 190.

90. Karen Garner, *Shaping a Global Women's Agenda: Women's NGOs and Global Governance, 1925-85* (Manchester: Manchester University Press, 2010).

91. Notiz zu den parallelen Konferenz nichtstaatlicher Organisationen (Tribune) während der UN-Konferenz aus Anlaß des Jahres der Frau in Mexiko-City 1977, June 28, 1980, SAPMO-BArch DY 30 / vorl. SED 36904/1.

92. *Report of the World Conference of the United Nations Decade for Women: Equality, Development and Peace (Copenhagen, 14 to 30 July, 1980)* (New York: United Nations, 1980), 9.

93. Quataert, *Gendering of Human Rights*; Nicola Lacey, "Feminist Legal Theory and the Rights of Women," in *Gender and Human Rights*, ed. Karen Knop (New York: Oxford University Press, 2004), 13-55.

94. Quataert, *Gendering of Human Rights*.

95. Margaret E. Keck and Kathryn Sikkink, *Activists Beyond Borders: Advocacy Networks in International Politics* (Ithaca, N.Y.: Cornell University Press, 1998).

96. Charlotte Bunch, cited in Elisabeth Friedman, "Women's Human Rights: The Emergence of a Movement," in *Women's Rights, Human Rights: International Feminist Perspectives*, ed. Julie Peters and Andrea Wolper (London: Routledge, 1995), 18-35.

97. Quataert, *Gendering of Human Rights*, 643.

98. Nancy Fraser, "Feminism, Capitalism, and the Cunning of History," *New Left Review*, n.s., no. 56 (March-April 2009): 97-117.

99. Keck and Sikkink, *Activists Beyond Borders*, 166.

Chapter 6. "Magic Words"

For guidance on this chapter, I am indebted to Mark Bradley, Michael Geyer, Mauricio Tenorio, Jim Green, Steve Stern, Diana Schwartz, Sam Moyn, and Jan Eckel.

1. Letter to President Emílio Médici from Rev. Frederick A. McGuire of the United States Catholic Conference, March 22, 1972. Online archive of the United States Conference of Catholic Bishops, http://old.usccb.org/sdwp/international/1972-03-22-ltr-brazil-medici-arrest-santos.pdf.

2. Statement of Ulf Sundvquist, Fundación Salvador Allende, Archivo Sergio Insunza, Santiago, Chile (hereafter cited as FSA, ASI), Ex. 9, C. 2.

3. "Protocolo Notarial," Archive of the Asamblea Permanente por los Derechos Humanos, Buenos Aires, Argentina (hereafter cited as APDH), file 198, B7.

4. The "long 1970s" is used by Bruce Schulman, *The Seventies: The Great Shift in American Culture, Society, and Politics* (New York: Free Press, 2001).

5. "Los derechos humanos en la Argentina," unpublished and undated article in the personal archive of Emilio Fermín Mignone located at the Centro de Estudios Legales y Sociales, Buenos Aires, Argentina, Subserie Ss 3.2 – DD.HH y Sociedad.

6. Jeri Laber, *The Courage of Strangers: Coming of Age with the Human Rights Movement* (New York: Public Affairs, 2002), 74; see more generally Samuel Moyn, *The Last Utopia: Human Rights in History* (Cambridge, Mass.: Belknap Press of Harvard University Press, 2010); on Uruguay, see Vania Markarian, *Left in Transformation: Uruguayan Exiles and the Latin American Human Rights Networks, 1967–1984* (New York: Routledge, 2005); on Chile, see Patrick William Kelly, "The 1973 Chilean Coup and the Origins of Transnational Human Rights Activism," *Journal of Global History* 8, no. 1 (March 2013): 165–86.

7. Many scholars tell stories that are, in my estimation, nothing but imagined genealogies. For an article that reaches shockingly far back, see Paulo G. Carroza, "From Conquest to Constitutions: Retrieving a Latin American Tradition of the Idea of Human Rights," *Human Rights Quarterly* 25, no. 2 (May 2003): 281–313.

8. For similar arguments about Argentine exiles, see Silvina Jensen, *Los exiliados: La lucha por los derechos humanos durante la dictadura militar* (Buenos Aires: Editorial Sudamericana, 2010), 15, 39, 179–180.

9. See Moyn, *Last Utopia*; Jan Eckel, "Utopie der Moral, Kalkül der Macht: Menschenrechte in der globalen Politik seit 1945," *Archiv für Sozialgeschichte* 49 (2009): 437–484.

10. Thomas E. Skidmore, *The Politics of Military Rule in Brazil, 1964–1985* (New York: Oxford University Press, 1990); Maria Helena Moreira Alves, *State and Opposition in Military Brazil* (Austin: University of Texas Press, 1985); James N. Green, *We Cannot Remain Silent: Opposition to the Brazilian Military Dictatorship in the United States, 1964–1985* (Durham, N.C.: Duke University Press, 2010); see also Elio Gaspari's works, *A ditadura envergonhada* (São Paulo: Companhia das Letras, 2002) *A ditadura derrotada* (2003), and *A ditadura escancarada* (2002), and *A ditadura encurralada* (2004).

11. Kenneth P. Serbin, *Secret Dialogues: Church-State Relations, Torture, and Social Justice in Authoritarian Brazil* (Pittsburgh, Pa.: University of Pittsburgh Press, 2000).

12. Peter Winn, "The Furies of the Andes: Violence and Terror in the Chilean Revolution and Counterrevolution," in *A Century of Revolution: Insurgent and*

Counterinsurgent Violence During Latin America's Long Cold War, ed. Greg Grandin and Gilbert M. Joseph (Durham, N.C.: Duke University Press, 2010), 239–275; Pamela Constable and Arturo Valenzuela, *A Nation of Enemies: Chile Under Pinochet* (New York: W. W. Norton, 1991).

13. See, for instance, Amnesty's "Report of the Mission to Santiago, Chile," November 1–8, 1973, Amnesty International of the USA Records, Center for Human Rights Documentation and Research, Columbia University (hereafter cited as AI-USA), RG I, Series I.1, Box 3, AMR 22 Executive Director Files, Americas-Chile.

14. Steve J. Stern, *Battling for Hearts and Minds: Memory Struggles in Pinochet's Chile, 1973–1988* (Durham, NC: Duke University Press, 2006); Pamela Lowden, *Moral Opposition to Authoritarian Rule in Chile, 1973–90* (London: Macmillan, 1996).

15. Iain Guest, *Behind the Disappearances: Argentina's Dirty War Against Human Rights and the United Nations* (Philadelphia: University of Pennsylvania Press, 1990), 85; for Amnesty's work related to Argentina, see AI-USA, RG I, Series I.1, Box 2 - Argentina; more generally, see Emilio F. Mignone, *Derechos humanos y sociedad: El caso argentino* (Buenos Aires: Ediciones del Pensamiento Nacional, 1991); Alison Brysk, *The Politics of Human Rights in Argentina: Protest, Change, and Democratization* (Stanford, Calif.: Stanford University Press, 1994); Marguerite Feitlowitz, *A Lexicon of Terror: Argentina and the Legacies of Torture* (Oxford: Oxford University Press, 1998); Marcos Novaro and Vicente Palermo, *La dictadura militar (1976–1983): Del golpe de estado a la restauración democrática* (Buenos Aires: Paidós, 2003).

16. See Kenneth Cmiel, "The Emergence of Human Rights Politics in the United States," *Journal of American History* 86, no. 3 (December 1999): 1231–1250. See also Stern, *Battling for Hearts and Minds*; Green, *We Cannot Remain Silent*; and Markarian, *Left in Transformation*.

17. Mario Sznajder and Luis Roniger, *The Politics of Exile in Latin America* (Cambridge: Cambridge University Press, 2009). See also Luis Roniger, James N. Green, and Pablo Yankelevich, *Exile and the Politics of Exclusion* (Sussex: Sussex Academic Press, 2012).

18. For an insightful transnational history of Allende's time in office, see Tanya Harmer, *Allende's Chile and the Inter-American Cold War* (Chapel Hill: University of North Carolina Press, 2011); Stern, *Battling for Hearts and Minds*, 92–93.

19. See Denise Rollemberg, *Exílio: entre raízes e radares* (Rio de Janeiro: Editora Record, 1999), for the best account.

20. Sznajder and Roniger cite the competing statistics in *Politics of Exile*, 200–201.

21. The conservative figure of two hundred thousand Chilean exiles comes from the Chilean Commission on Human Rights and the International Organization for Migration; Sznajder and Roniger suggest a vast range of two hundred thousand to two million in *Politics of Exile*, 230. See also Thomas C. Wright and Rody Oñate, eds., *Flight from Chile: Voices of Exile* (Albuquerque: University of New Mexico Press, 1998), *ix*, 8; Fernando Montupil, ed., *Exilio, derechos humanos y democracia: El exilio chileno en Europa* (Santiago: Casa de América Latina, 1993); José del Pozo Artigas, ed.,

Exiliados, emigrados y retornados: Chilenos en América y Europa, 1973-2004 (Santiago: RIL Editores, 2006); Marita Eastmond, *The Dilemmas of Exile: Chilean Refugees in the U.S.A.* (Goteborg: Acta Universitatis Gothoburgensis, 1997); Julie Shayne, *They Used to Call Us Witches: Chilean Exiles, Culture, and Feminism* (Lanham, MD: Lexington Books, 2009); Diane Kay, *Chileans in Exile: Private Struggles, Public Lives* (Wolfeboro, NH: Longwood Academic, 1987).

22. Sznajder and Roniger, *Politics of Exile.*

23. Sznajder and Roniger write of a fourth tier of exile politics that functioned as a "global arena preoccupied with humanitarian and international law and human rights." See *Politics of Exile,* 7.

24. See, for instance, Pablo Yankelevich and Silvina Jensen, eds., *Exilios: Destinos y experiencias bajo la dictadura militar* (Buenos Aires: Ediciones del Zorzal, 2007); Pablo Yankelevich, ed., *México, país refugio: La experiencia de los exilios en el siglo XX* (Mexico City: Plaza y Valdés, 2002); Silvina Inés Jensen, *La provincia flotante: El exilio argentino en Cataluña (1976-2006)* (Barcelona: Fundación Casa Amèrica Catalunya, 2007); and Jensen, *Los exiliados.*

25. Sznajder and Roniger, *Politics of Exile,* 212.

26. See Jensen, *Los exiliados,* 24-25.

27. Bobina E4: Solidarity in Latin America in Arquivo de Memória Operário de Rio de Janeiro, Coleção ASMOB, Rio de Janeiro, Brazil.

28. Denise Rollemberg, "Debate no Exílio: Em busca da renovação," in *História do marxismo no Brasil: Partidos e movimentos após os anos 1960,* ed. Marcelo Ridenti and Daniel Aarão Reis (Campinas: Editoria de UNICAMP, 2007).

29. Quoted in Katherine Hite, *When the Romance Ended: Leaders of the Chilean Left, 1968-1998* (New York: Columbia University Press, 2000), 139-140.

30. Sznajder and Roniger, *Politics of Exile,* 224; Pablo Yankelevich, "Memoria y exilio. Sudamericanos en México," in *La imposibilidad del olvido: Recorridos de la memoria en Argentina, Chile y Uruguay,* ed. Bruno Groppo and Patricia Flier (La Palta, Argentina: Ediciones al Margen, 2001).

31. Arquivo Público de Estado do Rio de Janeiro (hereafter cited as APERJ), Coleção Jean Marc van der Weid, Série Documentos Impressos De Circulação Interna, Dossiê DICI VI, Rio de Janeiro, Brazil; and Green, *We Cannot Remain Silent.*

32. See the Wisconsin Historical Society, Madison, Community Action on Latin America Records archive (hereafter cited as CALA).

33. Tom Quigley, correspondence with author, May 26, 2010.

34. Terence Turner, "Human Rights, Human Difference: Anthropology's Contribution to an Emancipatory Cultural Politics," *Journal of Anthropological Research* 53, no. 3 (Autumn 1997): 279-282.

35. Odd Arne Westad, *The Global Cold War: Third World Interventions and the Making of Our Times* (Cambridge: Cambridge University Press, 2007); see also U.S. Congress, Senate, Select Committee to Study Governmental Operations with Respect to Intelligence Activities, *Covert Action in Chile, 1969-1973,* Staff Report of the Select

Committee to Study Governmental Operations with Respect to Intelligence Activities, 94th Cong., 1st sess., December 18, 1975, Washington, D.C., 27–28.

36. See Harmer, *Allende's Chile*; on the Cold War stalemate and the global protests of 1968, see Jeremi Suri, *Power and Protest: Global Revolution and the Rise of Détente* (Cambridge, Mass.: Harvard University Press, 2003), 88–130.

37. Jan Eckel, "'Under a Magnifying Glass': The International Human Rights Campaign Against Chile in the Seventies," in *Human Rights in the Twentieth Century*, ed. Stefan-Ludwig Hoffman (Cambridge: Cambridge University Press, 2011); see also Consejos de Guerra, 1973–74, FSA, ASI, Ex. 22; Organización de las Naciones Unidas, Comisión de Derechos Humanos, 1975, FSA, ASI, Ex: 23.

38. Organizational Papers, 1971, CALA, Box 1, Folder 1. See also Green, *We Cannot Remain Silent*; and James Green, "Clerics, Exiles, and Academics: Opposition to the Brazilian Military Dictatorship in the United States, 1969–1974," *Latin American Politics and Society* 45, no. 1 (April 2003): 88–90.

39. Meeting notes from the National Coordinating Committee Meeting, November 1–2, 1975, CALA, Box 1, Folder 5, National Coordinating Center in Solidarity with Chile, 1974–75.

40. See Cmiel, "The Emergence of Human Rights Politics," 1249.

41. See untitled document #15, APERJ, Série Direitos Humanos, Dossiê Direitos Humanos I.

42. "Direitos Humanos, Posição dos Estudantes Socialistas," APERJ, Coleção Jair Ferreira de Sá, Série Ação Popular e a Sociedade Civil, Dossiê Ação Popular e o Movimento Estudantil.

43. "Uma nova fase para o ME do Grande Rio," APERJ, Coleção Jair Ferreira de Sá, Série Ação Popular e a Sociedade Civil, Dossiê Ação Popular e o Movimento Estudantil.

44. "Acerca del frente democrático," *Temas y Debates*, December 1973, no. 10, Bobina E3: Political Publications of Exiles in Chile, Arquivo de Memória Operário do Rio de Janeiro, Coleção ASMOB, Rio de Janeiro, Brazil.

45. "Plataforma de Luta," APERJ, Coleção Daniel Aarão Reis Filho, Ala Vermela, Documentos de Discussão Interna IV.

46. Jensen, *Los exiliados*, 39–40, 177.

47. Tom Quigley, correspondence with author, May 26, 2010.

48. See Moyn, *Last Utopia*, 144; Lowden, *Moral Opposition to Authoritarian Rule in Chile*; Lawrence Weschler, *A Miracle, A Universe: Settling Accounts with Torturers* (Chicago: University of Chicago Press, 1990).

49. See Van Gosse, "Unpacking the Vietnam Syndrome: The 1973 Coup in Chile and the Rise of Anti-Interventionist Politics," in *The World the Sixties Made: Politics and Culture in Recent America*, ed. Van Gosse and Richard Moser (Philadelphia: Temple University Press, 2003), 108–109.

50. For a fuller account of these Brazilian campaigns with an explicit emphasis on

Christian and academic activists in the United States, see Green, *We Cannot Remain Silent.*

51. Skidmore, *Politics of Military Rule in Brazil,* 79.

52. Cited in Green, *We Cannot Remain Silent,* 146.

53. Ibid., 146–147.

54. For references to the speech, see Sikkink, *Mixed Signals,* 58; and Green, *We Cannot Remain Silent,* 162.

55. "Terror in Brazil," copy obtained from Mr. Quigley's personal archive; Quigley, interview with author, November 19, 2010; correspondence with author, May 26, 2010.

56. Cited in Green, *We Cannot Remain Silent,* 157.

57. Jo Renee Formicola, *The Catholic Church and Human Rights: Its Role in the Formulation of U.S. Policy, 1945–1980* (New York: Garland Publishing, 1988).

58. Tom Quigley, interview with author, November 18, 2010; correspondence with author, May 26, 2010; See also Green, *We Cannot Remain Silent,* 206 and chap. 7.

59. Tom Quigley, correspondence with author, May 26, 2010.

60. Joe Eldridge, telephone interview with author, February 25, 2009; John Salzberg, telephone interview with author, March 6, 2009; Kathryn Sikkink, *Mixed Signals: U.S. Human Rights Policy and Latin America* (Ithaca, N.Y.: Cornell University Press, 2004), 65–68.

61. The International Commission reflected an enormous outpouring of support from northern European countries, most notably Sweden, Finland, Belgium, and Denmark. See Montupil, *Exilio, derechos humanos y democracia,* 20; see also Fernando Camacho Padilla, "La diaspora chilena y su confrontración en Suecia," in *Exiliados, emigrados y retornados,* ed. Pozo, 38.

62. The commission continued to meet throughout the early 1980s, but it never held another full session. Smaller audiences were held in Denmark (1979), Rome (1980), Athens (1982), and Helsinki (1983). See FSA, ASI, Ex. 20, C.1.

63. Stern, *Battling for Hearts and Minds,* 90–97.

64. Consejos de Guerra, 1973–74, C.1, FSA, ASI, Ex. 22; Ex: 23: Organización de las Naciones Unidas, Comisión de Derechos Humanos, 1975, C.1, FSA, ASI, Ex. 22.

65. The full name of the organization was the Comité Ecuménico de Cooperación para la Paz en Chile, but it was more colloquially known as the Comité Pro-Paz; see Stern, *Battling for Hearts and Minds,* 92, 113.

66. Pamela Lowden even goes so far to say that domestic human rights organizing was more about "secur[ing] international solidarity against the Pinochet regime . . . than within Chile itself." Lowden, *Moral Opposition to Authoritarian Rule in Chile,* 32, 40, 50.

67. On funding, see "Minutes, Human Rights Resources Office for Latin America," February 24, 1976, 429.02.02 – Minutes of HRROLA, Staff Advisory Group (1974–1996), World Council of Churches Archive, Geneva.

68. Lowden, *Moral Opposition to Authoritarian Rule in Chile,* 36, 50, 52–54, 73–74, 76.

69. José Zalaquett, interview with author, December 5, 2011, Santiago, Chile.

70. Lowden, *Moral Opposition to Authoritarian Rule in Chile*, 41n61.

71. In an attempt to build on the success of the Chilean campaigns, Argentine activists would talk of "Videla's Pinochetist dictatorship," conflating Argentine junta leader Jorge Videla with Chilean dictator Augusto Pinochet. See Jensen, *Los exiliados*, 48.

72. "Sobre la Paz y la Vida," document 1.36, C1–Cartas, Archivo de la APDH.

73. "El movimiento de derechos humanos en la Argentina," Subserie Ss 3.2–DD.HH y Sociedad, Archivo Personal Emilio Mignone, CELS.

74. Sznajder and Roniger, *Politics of Exile*, 222–224; Brysk, *Politics of Human Rights in Argentina*, 46–47, 51–56.

75. See Steve J. Stern, *Reckoning with Pinochet: The Memory Question in Democratic Chile, 1989–2006* (Durham, N.C.: Duke University Press, 2010), 9; on other lost visions of human rights, see Brad Simpson, "Denying 'The First Right': The United States, Indonesia, and the Ranking of Human Rights by the Carter Administration, 1976–1980," *International History Review* 31, no. 4 (2009): 709–944.

76. Juan Luis Segundo, "Derechos humanos, evangelización, e ideología," in *Carter y la lógica del imperialismo*, ed. Hugh Assmann (San José: Editorial Universitaria Centroamericana, 1978), 347.

77. Kathryn Sikkink, *The Justice Cascade: How Human Rights Prosecutions Are Changing World Politics* (New York: W. W. Norton, 2010).

78. See the "Exordio" from the Informe de la Comisión Nacional de Verdad y Reconciliación, http://www.ddhh.gov.cl/ddhh_rettig.html (accessed November 30, 2012). On the politics of truth and reconciliation in Latin America, see Greg Grandin, "The Instruction of Great Catastrophe: Truth Commissions, National History, and State Formation in Chile, Argentina, and Guatemala," *American Historical Review* 110, no. 1 (February 2005): 46–67.

Chapter 7. Shifting Sites of Argentine Advocacy and the Shape of 1970s Human Rights Debates

I am grateful to Jan Eckel, Samuel Moyn, Margaret Chowning, Mark Healey, Daniel Sargent, Brian DeLay, Daniel Immerwahr, my fellow graduate research seminar students, and conference participants for their suggestions and guidance.

1. Lucio Garzón Maceda, "Testimonio: La primera derrota de la dictadura en el campo internacional," in *Argentina 1976–2006: Entre la sombra de la dictadura y el futuro de la democracia*, ed. Hugo Quiroga and César Tcach (Rosario, Argentina: Homo Sapiens Ediciones, 2006), 267. Gustavo Roca died in 1997.

2. Tom Farer, "The Rise of the Inter-American Human Rights Regime: No Longer a Unicorn, Not Yet an Ox," *Human Rights Quarterly* 19, no. 3 (August 1997): 510–511.

3. Eduardo Blaustein and Martín Zubieta, *Decíamos ayer: The prensa argentina bajo el Proceso* (Buenos Aires: Ediciones Colihue, 1998), 23. See also Diana López Gijsberts and Martín Malharro, *La tipografía de plomo: Los grandes medios gráficos en la Argentina*

y su política editorial durante 1976–1983 (La Plata, Argentina: Ediciones de Periodismo y Comunicación, 2003).

4. See Marcos Novaro and Vicente Palermo, *La dictadura militar (1976–1983): Del golpe de estado a la restauración democrática* (Buenos Aires: Paidós, 2003), 164–165n110.

5. Héctor Ricardo Leis, *El movimiento por los derechos humanos y la política argentina*, 2 vols. (Buenos Aires: Biblioteca Política Argentina, 1989), 1:19–20; see also Margaret E. Keck and Kathryn Sikkink, *Activists Beyond Borders: Advocacy Networks in International Politics* (Ithaca, NY: Cornell University Press, 1998), 106; Silvina Jensen, *Los exiliados: La lucha por los derechos humanos durante la dictadura* (Buenos Aires: Editorial Sudamericana, 2010), 12–15; Emilio F. Mignone, *Derechos humanos y sociedad: El caso argentino* (Buenos Aires: Centro de Estudios Legales y Sociales, 1991), 118–119.

6. Alison Brysk, *The Politics of Human Rights in Argentina: Protest, Change, and Democratization* (Stanford, Calif.: Stanford University Press, 1994), 57; Novaro and Palermo, *Dictadura militar*, 279–280.

7. See Novaro and Palermo, *Dictadura militar*, 17–25.

8. See Brysk, *Politics of Human Rights*, 35–36.

9. Estimates of the disappeared range from nine thousand to thirty thousand. See John Dinges, *The Condor Years: How Pinochet and His Allies Brought Terrorism to Three Continents* (New York: New Press, 2004), 139–140; Brysk, *Politics of Human Rights*, 36–40.

10. See Brysk, *Politics of Human Rights*, 29–31; Patricia M. Marchak, *God's Assassins: State Terrorism in Argentina in the 1970s* (Montreal: McGill-Queen's University Press, 2003), 94; David Rock, *Argentina, 1516–1987: From Spanish Colonization to the Falklands War* (Berkeley: University of California Press, 1987), 187.

11. See Mauricio Chama, "Activismo social y político, represión estatal y defensa de 'presos Conintes': La experiencia de Cofade (1960–1963)," paper presented at V Jornadas de Historia Política "Las provincias en perspectiva comparada," Universidad Nacional de Mar del Plata, September 29–October 1, 2010, 3, available at historiapolitica.com, http://historiapolitica.com/datos/biblioteca/vj_chama.pdf; Iain Guest, *Behind the Disappearances: Argentina's Dirty War Against Human Rights and the United Nations* (Philadelphia: University of Pennsylvania Press, 1990), 51; Leis, *Movimiento por los derechos humanos*, 14; Mignone, *Derechos humanos y sociedad*, 100–101.

12. Brysk, *Politics of Human Rights*, 46, 196n58; Mignone, *Derechos humanos y sociedad*, 100; Alfredo Villalba Welsh, *Tiempos de ira, tiempos de esperanza* (Buenos Aires: Rafael Cedeño, 1984).

13. Brysk, *Politics of Human Rights*, 196n58.

14. See Corona Martínez [et al.], Federación Obrera Regional Argentina, *Justicia! Libertad! Defensa de los Dres Corona Martínez, F. Jorge, S. Shmerkin, R. A. Alfaro y S. Sheimberg* (Buenos Aires: Ediciones Federación Obrera Regional Argentina, 1936); Liga Argentina por los Derechos del Hombre, *¿Por qué están detenidos 500 presos políticos*

desde hace seis meses? 3 años bajo la llamada ley de "estado de guerra interno" (Buenos Aires: Liga Argentina por los Derechos del Hombre, 1954), both found in Biblioteca y Hemeroteca del Centro de Documentación e Investigación de la Cultura de Izquierdas en Argentina.

15. File on detained attorney, Subfondo Arturo Frondizi, Fondo Centro de Estudios Nacionales, Archivos y Colecciones Particulares, Biblioteca Nacional de la República Argentina.

16. Ernest Hamburger to Silvio Frondizi, Division of Human Rights, United Nations, May 20, 1952, Subfondo Silvio Frondizi, Fondo Centro de Estudios Nacionales, Archivos y Colecciones Particulares, Biblioteca Nacional de la República Argentina.

17. See Mauricio Chama, "La defensa de presos políticos a comienzos de los '70: Ejercicio profesional, derecho y política," *Cuadernos de Antropología Social*, no. 32 (2010): 195–217; Mauricio Chama, "Movilización y politización: Abogados de Buenos Aires entre 1968 y 1973," in *Historizar el pasado vivo en América Latina*, ed. Anne Pérotin-Dumon (Santiago, Chile: Universidad Alberto Hurtado Centro de Ética, 2007).

18. See *Nunca más: The Report of the Argentine National Commission of the Disappeared* (New York: Farrar, Straus, Giroux, 1986), 412–420.

19. *Nunca más*, 412–413.

20. Virginia Vecchioli, "Redes transnacionales y profesionalización de los abogados de derechos humanos en la Argentina," in *Derechos humanos en América Latina: Mundialización y circulación internacional del conocimiento experto jurídico*, ed. Angela Santamaría and Virginia Vecchioli (Bogotá: Editorial Universidad del Rosario, 2008), 41, 44–47; see also Viriginia Vecchioli, "Human Rights and the Rule of Law in Argentina: Transnational Advocacy Networks and the Transformation of the National Legal Field," in *Lawyers and the Rule of Law in an Era of Globalization*, ed. Yves Dezalay and Bryant G. Garth (New York: Routledge, 2011).

21. *Nunca más*, 386–387.

22. Brysk, *Politics of Human Rights*, 42–45.

23. Ibid., 7, 48.

24. See Jensen, *Exiliados*, 20.

25. See Brysk, *Politics of Human Rights*, 46; Paul H. Lewis, *Guerrillas and Generals: The "Dirty War" in Argentina* (Westport, Conn.: Praeger, 2002), 186; Mignone, *Derechos humanos y sociedad*, 101.

26. Mignone, *Derechos humanos y sociedad*, 105.

27. Brysk, *Politics of Human Rights*, 47–48; Leis, *Movimiento por los derechos humanos*, 19.

28. Mignone, *Derechos humanos y sociedad*, 105–107; Novaro and Palermo, *Dictadura militar*, 288; Brysk, *Politics of Human Rights*, 43.

29. See, for example, *¿Por qué el Profesor Alfredo Pedro Bravo sigue detenido?* (Buenos Aires: Asamblea Permanente por los Derechos Humanos, n.d.), 3, Archivo Institucional del Centro de Estudios Legales y Sociales, Fondo Archivo Emilio Mignone, APDH 1978–1995 2.2.2 Inv: 048–1995.

30. Keck and Sikkink, *Activists Beyond Borders*, 105. See also Patrick Kelly's chapter in this volume.

31. See Ann Marie Clark, *Diplomacy of Conscience: Amnesty International and Changing Human Rights Norms* (Princeton, N.J.: Princeton University Press, 2001), 74; Guest, *Behind the Disappearances*, 194–199, 216, 231–232, 439–441.

32. Keck and Sikkink, *Activists Beyond Borders*, 102.

33. Keck and Sikkink, *Activists Beyond Borders*, 105–106; Guest, *Behind the Disappearances*; and Kathryn Sikkink, "From Pariah State to Global Protagonist: Argentina and the Struggle for International Human Rights," *Latin American Politics and Society* 50, no. 1 (Spring 2008): 1–29.

34. See Lars Schoultz, *Human Rights and United States Policy Towards Latin America* (Princeton, N.J.: Princeton University Press, 1981), 3–4; Cynthia J. Arnson, *Crossroads: Congress, the President, and Central America, 1976–1993*, 2nd ed. (University Park: Pennsylvania State University Press, 1993), 3–13; Cynthia J. Arnson, "The U.S. Congress and Argentina: Human Rights and Military Aid," in *Argentina–United States Bilateral Relations: An Historical Perspective and Future Challenges*, ed. Arnson (Woodrow Wilson International Center for Scholars: Washington, D.C., 2003), 83–85; Kathryn Sikkink, *Mixed Signals: U.S. Human Rights Policy and Latin America* (Ithaca, N.Y.: Cornell University Press, 2004), 51–52.

35. David P. Forsythe, *Human Rights in International Relations* (Cambridge: Cambridge University Press, 2000), 175. See also Schoultz, *Human Rights and United States Policy*, 194; Sikkink, *Mixed Signals*, 49.

36. John P. Salzberg, "A View from the Hill," in *The Diplomacy of Human Rights*, ed. David D. Newsom (Washington, D.C.: Institute for the Study of Diplomacy, Georgetown University, 1986), 15. See also Sikkink, *Mixed Signals*, 65.

37. See Schoultz, *Human Rights and United States Policy*, 195–210, 250–266, 281–292; see also Sikkink, *Mixed Signals*, 65, 72; "Human Rights and U.S. Foreign Assistance Experiences and Issues in Policy Implementation: A Report / Prepared for the Committee on Foreign Relations, United States Senate, by the Foreign Affairs and National Defense Division, Congressional Research Service, Library of Congress," July 1979, 16–29.

38. See Claire Apodaca, "U.S. Human Rights Policy and Foreign Assistance: A Short History," *Ritsumeikan International Affairs* 3 (2005): 68; Sandy Vogelgesang, *American Dream, Global Nightmare: The Dilemma of U.S. Human Rights Policy* (New York: W. W. Norton, 1980), 128–133.

39. For earlier congressional efforts to cut military aid over human rights concerns in Latin America, see Schoultz, *Human Rights and United States Policy*, 250–253.

40. Salzberg, "View from the Hill," 17; Schoultz, *Human Rights and United States Policy*, 253; Sikkink, *Mixed Signals*, 69.

41. See Schoultz, *Human Rights and United States Policy*, 254, 258–259.

42. Schoultz, *Human Rights and United States Policy*, 106–108.

43. See Dinges, *Condor Years*, 1, 7, 176.

44. See Sikkink, *Mixed Signals*, 110.

45. I am grateful to Mark Healey for this insight.

46. See Chama, "Movilización y politización."

47. See Robert A. Potash, *The Army and Politics in Argentina, 1962–1973* (Stanford, Calif.: Stanford University Press, 1996), 246n22; José Campellone and Marisabel Arriola, *SMATA 50 años de vida—50 años de lucha* (Córdoba, Argentina: Lerner, 2006), 237.

48. Lucio Garzón Maceda, "Paso a paso, el Cordobazo," *La Voz del Interior*, Suplemento Temas, May 31, 2009; Carlos Sacchetto, "'El Cordobazo fue una expresión reformista, no revolucionaria," *Clarín.com*, May 29, 2009, http://www.clarin.com/diario/2009/05/29/elpais/p-01928450.htm; Potash, *Army and Politics*, 246n22; see Liliana de Riz, *Historia Argentina: La política en suspenso; 1966/1976* (Buenos Aires: Paidós, 2000), 74.

49. Chama, "Defensa de presos políticos," 208; Tito Drago, interview conducted for publication in *Cambio 16*, Paris, France, October 22, 1977.

50. Tito Drago, interview.

51. Garzón Maceda, "Testimonio," 234–236; House Subcommittee on International Organizations of the Committee of International Relations (hereafter cited as House Subcommittee), *Human Rights in Argentina*, 94th Cong., 2nd sess., 1976, 11.

52. See Guest, *Behind the Disappearances*, 66–69.

53. Garzón Maceda, "Testimonio," 233, 239, 245; Guest, *Behind the Disappearances*, 465n10.

54. House Subcommittee, *Human Rights in Argentina*, 11, 32; Guest, *Behind the Disappearances*, 66.

55. See Guillermo Mira Delli-Zotti and Fernando Osvaldo Estebán, "La construcción de un espacio político transnacional," in *Historia Actual Online*, no. 14 (2007): 61; Maria Luisa Bartolomei and David Weissbrodt, "The Effectiveness of International Human Rights Pressures: The Case of Argentina, 1976–1983," *Minnesota Law Review* 75 (1990–1991): 1016.

56. Schoultz, *Human Rights and United States Policy*, 106; Delli-Zotti and Esteban, "Construcción de un espacio político transnacional," 60–61. See Arnson, "U.S. Congress and Argentina."

57. Bartolomei and Weissbrodt, "Effectiveness of International Human Rights Pressures," 1016; Schoultz, *Human Rights and United States Policy*, 106; Guest, *Behind the Disappearances*, 49–75; Delli-Zotti and Esteban, "Construcción de un espacio político transnacional," 61.

58. Guest, *Behind the Disappearances*, 66–69.

59. Vecchioli, "Redes transnacionales," 41.

60. Garzón Maceda, "Testimonio," 240, 248.

61. House Subcommittee, *Human Rights in Argentina*, 42–43.

62. Garzón Maceda, "Testimonio," 240, 248.

63. House Subcommittee, *Human Rights in Argentina*, 31.

64. Ibid., 19.

65. Ibid., 12.

66. Ibid., 22–23, 41.

67. Guest, *Behind the Disappearances*, 67–69.

68. See ibid., 67–68.

69. House Subcommittee, *Human Rights in Argentina*, 12.

70. Ibid., 16.

71. Memorandum, Argentine Foreign Ministry, October 4, 1976, U.S. Department of State Argentina Declassification Project (1975–1984), 1–2, attachments (hereafter cited as ADP). This document and all other Spanish-language sources quoted here were translated by the author.

72. Cable, State Department to U.S. Embassy in Buenos Aires, "Sanctions Against Fraser Committee Witnesses," December 8, 1976, ADP, document no. 1976STATE298737.

73. Cable, U.S. Embassy in Buenos Aires to State Department, "Federal Judge Indicts Fraser Subcommittee Human Rights Witnesses," December 9, 1976, ADP, document no. 1976Buenos07975.

74. After Timerman was kidnapped by the junta in 1977, his cause was taken up internationally, and by the Carter administration in particular, which helped to secure Timerman's release in 1979. Timerman's account of his imprisonment and torture, translated as *Prisoner Without a Name, Cell Without a Number*, became a bestseller in the United States and played a singular role in publicizing the junta's human rights abuses. See Sikkink, *Mixed Signals*, 134.

75. See Dinges, *Condor Years*, 138. See also Novaro and Palermo, *Dictadura militar*, 23–25, 285.

76. Jacobo Timerman, "Una carta al Subcomité," *La Opinión*, October 1, 1976, SM 2426, Subfondo documental Secretaría de Medios—Departamento Archivo—Microfilm, Presidencia de la Nación (1934–1990), Archivo Nacional de la Memoria (hereafter cited as Subfondo documental Secretaría de Medios, ANM); Cable, U.S. Embassy in Buenos Aires to State Department, "Human Rights Round-Up No. 5," November 10, 1976, ADP, document no. 1976BUENOS07386. But see Guest, *Behind the Disappearances*, 154.

77. See Guest, *Behind the Disappearances*, 76–86.

78. "Entrevista con el director de 'La Opinión," *La Opinión*, November 12, 1976, SM 2426, Subfondo documental Secretaría de Medios, ANM.

79. "Verificación de los derechos humanos," *La Nación*, November 11, 1976, SM 2426, Subfondo documental Secretaría de Medios, ANM.

80. Letter, "Comisión de Familiares" to "La Comisión del Senado de EEUU que Estudia los Derechos Humanos en Argentina," October 1, 1976, ADP. This letter appears to have been destined for the Fraser subcommittee rather than to the Senate, as the subcommittee was the congressional body investigating human rights abuses in Argentina at the time.

81. See Robert K. Goldman, "History and Action: The Inter-American Human Rights System and the Role of the Inter-American Commission on Human Rights,"

Human Rights Quarterly 31, no. 4 (November 2009): 861; Farer, "Rise of the Inter-American Human Rights Regime," 514–515; David P. Forsythe, *The Internationalization of Human Rights* (Lexington, Mass.: Lexington Books, 1991), 98–99.

82. Article 9 of the Statute of the Inter-American Commission on Human Rights, approved by the OAS Council in 1960. See Organization of American States, *Handbook of Existing Rules Pertaining to Human Rights* (Washington, D.C.: General Secretariat, Organization of American States, 1979), 11–12; see also Goldman, "History and Action," 862.

83. Forsythe, *Internationalization of Human Rights*, 101; see also Jack Donnelly, *Universal Human Rights in Theory and Practice* (Ithaca, N.Y.: Cornell University Press, 2003), 142; Goldman, "History and Action," 867–868; Farer, "Rise of the Inter-American Human Rights Regime," 511.

84. Goldman, "History and Action," 870.

85. Forsythe, *Internationalization of Human Rights*, 101; see also Klaas Dykmann, *Philanthropic Endeavors or the Exploitation of an Ideal? Human Rights Policy of the Organization of American States in Latin America* (Frankfurt: Vervuert, 2004), 59–60.

86. Thomas Buergenthal, "The Revised OAS Charter and the Protection of Human Rights," *American Journal of International Law* 69 (1975): 828–836, 831–832.

87. Farer, "Rise of the Inter-American Human Rights Regime," 514–515; Buergenthal, "OAS Charter."

88. Farer, "Rise of the Inter-American Human Rights Regime," 512; Jensen, *Exiliados*, 77–79.

89. Guest, *Behind the Disappearances*, 173; Forsythe, *Internationalization of Human Rights*, 103.

90. Organization of American States, *Inter-American Commission on Human Rights: 10 Years of Activities, 1971–1981* (Washington, D.C.: General Secretariat, Organization of American States, 1982), 82, 251; Farer, "Rise of the Inter-American Human Rights Regime," 530–540; Goldman, "History and Action," 873.

91. See Farer, "Rise of the Inter-American Human Rights Regime," 531–532; Organization of American States, *Handbook of Existing Rules*, 42–43.

92. Guest, *Behind the Disappearances*, 447.

93. See Jensen, *Exiliados*, 49–52, 88.

94. Carlos Osorio, "The Dirty War's Declassified Documents: A New Perspective on Bilateral Relations," in *Argentina–United States Bilateral Relations*, ed. Arnson, 14.

95. Jensen, *Exiliados*, 93; Novaro and Palermo, *Dictadura militar*, 279, 300.

96. See Novaro and Palermo, *Dictadura militar*, 288–290; Osorio, "Declassified Documents," 21.

97. Guest, *Behind the Disappearances*, 175; Novaro and Palermo, *Dictadura militar*, 290.

98. Osorio, "Declassified Documents," 19–21; Keck and Sikkink, *Activists Beyond Borders*, 107; Schoultz, *Human Rights and United States Policy*, 311.

99. Novaro and Palermo, *Dictadura militar*, 294–295.

100. Interview with Joseph Eldridge, December 21, 2011.

101. Lewis, *Guerrillas and Generals*, 186; Mignone, *Derechos humanos y sociedad*, 112.

102. Newsletter, Centro de Documentación e Información sobre Derechos Humanos en Argentina, November 1, 1978, December 8, 1976, ADP.

103. Novaro and Palermo, *Dictadura militar*, 294.

104. Organization of American States (OAS), *Report on the Situation of Human Rights in Argentina*, Inter-Am. C.H.R., O.A.S. Doc. OEA/Ser.L/V/II.49, doc. 19 corr. 1, Chapter XI, "Status of Human Rights Defense Agencies," April 11, 1980, http://www .cidh.oas.org/countryrep/Argentina80eng/toc.htm.

105. OAS, *Report on the Situation of Human Rights in Argentina*, "Introduction."

106. Mignone, *Derechos humanos y sociedad*, 112.

107. OAS, *Report on the Situation of Human Rights in Argentina*, "Introduction"; Brysk, *Politics of Human Rights*, 54.

108. Servicio de Inteligencia de la Policía Federal, "Asunto: Viaje de familiares de DD.TT. desde la Pcia del Chaco hacia la capital federal," September 6, 1979, Área Centro de Documentación y Archivo de la Comisión Provincial por la Memoria, Archivo de la Dirección de Inteligencia de la Policía de la Provincia de Buenos Aires, Colección 10: Visita a la Argentina de la Comisión Interamericana de Derechos Humanos (1979–80), Documento 14391 (hereafter cited as CPM, Colección 10).

109. OAS, *Report on the Situation of Human Rights in Argentina*, "Introduction," "Activities of the Commission during its on-site observation."

110. Ibid.

111. Ibid., "Conclusions and Recommendations."

112. Jensen, *Exiliados*, 15.

113. Mignone, *Derechos humanos y sociedad*, 111.

114. Argentina, *Observaciones y comentarios críticos del gobierno argentino al Informe de la CIDH sobre la situación de los Derechos Humanos en Argentina (Abril de 1980)* (Buenos Aires: Círculo Militar, 1980), 7.

115. Argentina, *Observaciones y comentarios*, 22, 59.

116. Osorio, "Declassified Documents," 22; Brysk, *Politics of Human Rights*, 208n56, citing *Nunca más*.

117. Jensen, *Exiliados*, 119, 129; Goldman, "History and Action," 873.

118. See Goldman, "History and Action," 873.

119. Jensen, *Exiliados*, 75.

120. Brysk, *Politics of Human Rights*, 58; Guest, *Behind the Disappearances*, 69.

121. Jensen, *Exiliados*, 57; Brysk, *Politics of Human Rights*, 58.

122. See Novaro and Palermo, *Dictadura militar*, 167.

123. Patrick Buckley, "Al rechazar en la OEA las imputaciones sobre derechos humanos Montes exhortó a combatir el terrorismo," *La Opinión*, June 24, 1978.

124. Argentina, *Evolución de la delincuencia terrorista en la Argentina* (Buenos Aires: Poder Ejecutivo Nacional, 1980), 12–14.

125. Newspaper clipping, "Juicios de Vargas Carreño acerca del terrorismo," September 9, 1979 (handwritten date), "Inf. Periodisticas y difusión informes Inicio Actividades CIDH 7.9.79 al 10.09.79 Tomo I," CPM, Colección 10, documento 14458.

126. See Novaro and Palermo, *Dictadura militar*, 160; Jensen, *Exiliados*, 106–109.

127. See Jensen, *Exiliados*, 55–71, 103.

128. Secretaria de Inteligencia del Estado, "Ambito Subversivo, Situación—Marxismo," September, September 6, 1979, CPM, Colección 10, Documento 14413.

129. "Pronunciamientos por la visita de la CIDH," *La Nación*, September 21, 1979, SM 2428, Subfondo documental Secretaría de Medios, ANM.

130. Movimiento Ecuménico por los Derechos Humanos, *Informedh Suplemento*, May 1980, CPM, Colección 10, Documento 13242.

131. See Jensen, *Exiliados*, 64.

132. Cable, U.S. Embassy in Buenos Aires, August 24, 1979, ADP, document no. 1979BUENOS06961.

133. "'Visita lesiva' Oposición de Conservadores," *Crónica*, August 17, 1979, SM 2428, Subfondo documental Secretaría de Medios, ANM.

134. Asamblea Permanente por los Derechos Humanos, "Declaración del Consejo de Presidencia sobre el informe de la CIDH," August 7, 1980, CPM, Colección 10, Documento 16664.

135. Jensen, *Exiliados*, 83.

136. Letter, Emilio Mignone to Boris Pasik, June 3, 1994, Archivo Institucional del Centro de Estudios Legales y Sociales, Fondo Archivo Emilio Mignone, Corresp. Inst. Enviada 2.2.5.2; Mignone, *Derechos humanos y sociedad*; Keck and Sikkink, *Activists Beyond Borders*, 107; Guest, *Behind the Disappearances*, 118–119, 182–183.

137. Política obrera, "Concretemos la unidad de acción por la vida y libertad de presos y secuestrados políticos y gremiales," August 6, 1979, CPM, Colección 10, Documento 14106.

138. See Novaro and Palermo, *Dictadura militar*, 461–466.

Chapter 8. Oasis in the Desert?

1. Paul Gordon Lauren, *The Evolution of International Human Rights: Visions Seen*, 2nd ed. (Philadelphia: University of Pennsylvania Press, 2003), 5.

2. See, among others, John M. Headley, *The Europeanization of the World: On the Origins of Human Rights and Democracy* (Princeton, N.J.: Princeton University Press, 2008); Lynn Hunt, *Inventing Human Rights: A History* (New York: W. W. Norton, 2007); and Anthony Pagden, "Human Rights, Natural Rights, and Europe's Imperial Legacy," *Political Theory* 31, no. 2 (2003): 171–199. For an extended critique of the historiography's Eurocentrism, see Reza Ashari, "On Historiography of Human Rights: Reflections on Paul Gordon Lauren's 'The Evolution of International Human Rights: Visions Seen,'" *Human Rights Quarterly* 29, no. 1 (2004): 1–67.

3. Stefan-Ludwig Hoffmann, ed., *Human Rights in the Twentieth Century* (New York: Cambridge University Press, 2010), 4.

4. Samuel Moyn, *The Last Utopia: Human Rights in History* (Cambridge Mass.: Belknap Press of Harvard University Press, 2010).

5. Moyn, *Last Utopia*, 43.

6. Micheline R. Ishay, *The History of Human Rights: From Ancient Times to the Globalization Era* (Berkeley: University of California Press, 2004), 3.

7. Thomas W. Laqueur, "Bodies, Details, and the Humanitarian Narrative," in *The New Cultural History*, ed. Lynn Hunt (Berkeley: University of California Press, 1989), 177–205.

8. Hunt, *Inventing Human Rights*.

9. Thomas Hobbes, *Leviathan* (New York: Cambridge University Press, 1996); and Hugo Grotius, *The Rights of War and Peace* (New York: M. W. Dunne, 1901).

10. John Locke, *Two Treatises of Government* (New York: Cambridge University Press, 1988).

11. *Dred Scott v. Sanford*, 60 U.S. 393 (1857).

12. Aimé Césaire, *Discours sur le colonialisme* (Paris: Présence Africaine, 1989), 13–14.

13. Adam Smith, *The Theory of Moral Sentiments* (New York: Oxford University Press, 1976).

14. Cited in Lauren, *Evolution of International Human Rights*, 230.

15. Carol Anderson, *Eyes Off the Prize: The United Nations and the African-American Struggle for Human Rights* (New York: Cambridge University Press, 2003).

16. "Remarks of John F. Kennedy, Lincoln Monument Rally, Spokane, WA, September 6, 1960," in *The American Presidency Project*, ed. Gerhard Peters and John T. Woolley, http://www.presidency.ucsb.edu/ws/?pid=25656.

17. Jimmy Carter, "Universal Declaration of Human Rights Remarks at a White House Meeting . . . , December 6, 1978," in *The American Presidency Project*, ed. Gerhard Peters and John T. Woolley, http://www.presidency.ucsb.edu/ws/?pid=30264.

18. "Human Rights Coursepack," Frank Newman Papers, Bancroft Library, University of California, Berkeley, MSS 2005 / 175, Carton 1; and "To Banish Genocide," *New York Times*, February 26, 1976.

19. Arthur Schlesinger Jr., "Human Rights and the American Tradition," *Foreign Affairs* 57, no. 3 (1978): 513.

20. Gary J. Bass, *Freedom's Battle: The Origins of Humanitarian Intervention* (New York: Random House, 2008).

21. Marshall McLuhan, *The Gutenberg Galaxy* (Toronto: University of Toronto Press, 1962).

22. *Historical Statistics of the United States* (New York: Cambridge University Press), Series Dg., 117–130.

23. Sig Mickelson, "Communications by Satellite," *Foreign Affairs* 48, no. 1 (1969–1970): 67–79.

24. Contrast the following two sources: Akira Iriye, *Global Community: The Role of International Organizations in the Making of the Contemporary World* (Berkeley,

University of California Press: 2002), 98–100; Daniel Hallin, *The Uncensored War: The Media and Vietnam* (Berkeley: University of California Press, 1986).

25. Materials created for both Nigeria and the Republic of Biafra by foreign public relations firms are available in the papers of the Clearing House for Nigeria/Biafra, Swarthmore Peace Collection, Swarthmore College, Pennsylvania.

26. David Forsythe, *The Humanitarians: The International Committee of the Red Cross* (New York: Cambridge University Press, 2005), 66–68.

27. Roger Morris, *Uncertain Greatness: Henry Kissinger and American Foreign Policy* (New York: Harper and Row, 1977), 42.

28. On the relationship between technology and state development, see, among many others, Philip Bobbitt, *The Shield of Achilles: War, Peace, and the Course of History* (New York: Knopf, 2002); and Charles S. Maier, "Leviathan 2.0: Inventing Modern Statehood," in Emily S. Rosenberg, ed., *A World Connecting, 1870–1945* (Cambridge, Mass.: Belknap Press of Harvard University Press, 2012).

29. On this point, see James N. Rosenau, *Distant Proximities: Dynamics Beyond Globalization* (Princeton, N.J.: Princeton University Press, 2003).

30. The historiography on NGOs is growing fast. See William Korey, *NGOs and the Universal Declaration of Human Rights: "A Curious Grapevine"* (New York: Palgrave Macmillan, 1998); Margaret E. Keck and Kathryn Sikkink, *Activists Beyond Borders: Advocacy Networks in International Politics* (Ithaca, N.Y.: Cornell University Press, 1998); and Aryeh Neier, *The International Human Rights Movement: A History* (Princeton, N.J.: Princeton University Press, 2012).

31. "Role of Washington Office," September 16, 1976, Center for Human Rights Research, Columbia University, New York, Amnesty International–USA Papers, Executive Director Files, David Hawk Files, box 5.

32. Lester Brown, *World Without Borders* (New York: Random House, 1972).

33. Richard Falk, *Legal Order in a Violent World* (Princeton, N.J.: Princeton University Press, 1968), 75; and U.S. House, Committee on Foreign Relations, *Human Rights in the World Community: A Call for U.S. Leadership*, 93rd Cong., 2nd Sess. (Washington, D.C.: Government Printing Office, 1974), 246.

34. "U.S. Policies on Human Rights" (undated), attached to December 21, 1974, letter from Winston Lord to Mary Olmsted, National Archives II, College Park, Md., RG-59 Department of State, Policy Planning Staff, Director's Files, box 348.

35. "Remarks to the Trilateral Commission," October 25, 1977, Jimmy Carter Presidential Library, Atlanta, Georgia (hereafter cited as JCPL), Hendrik Hertzberg Materials, Speech Files, box 3.

36. "U.S. Foreign Policy and Human Rights," July 16, 1977, JCPL, Donated Historical Materials, Zbigniew Brzezinski Collection, Subject File, box 23.

37. On the Soviet dissident movement, see Valery Chalidze, *The Soviet Human Rights Movement: A Memoir* (New York: American Jewish Committee, 1984); Peter Reddaway, ed., *Uncensored Russia: Protest and Dissent in the Soviet Union: The Unofficial Moscow Journal, "A Chronicle Of Current Events"* (New York: American Heritage Press,

1972); Joshua Rubenstein, *Soviet Dissidents: Their Struggle for Human Rights* (Boston: Beacon Press, 1985); and Andrei Sakharov, *Memoirs* (New York: Knopf, 1990).

38. Richard Nixon, "Radio and Television Address to the People of the Soviet Union, May 28, 1972," in *The American Presidency Project*, ed. Gerhard Peters and John T. Woolley, http://www.presidency.ucsb.edu/ws/?pid=3437.

39. Minutes of Cabinet Meeting, February 21, 1974, Gerald Ford Presidential Library, Ann Arbor, Mich., National Security Adviser Files, Memoranda of Conversations, box 3.

40. Henry Kissinger, "Moral Promise and Practical Needs," October 19, 1976, *Department of State Bulletin* 75 (1976): 597–605.

41. "Operation Human Rights," JCPL, Hertzberg Materials, Speech Files, box 2.

42. Transcripts of phone conversations between the Moscow Human Rights Committee and the International League for the Rights of Man are available in the New York Public Library, International League for the Rights of Man, accession D 95M22, part 1, box 63.

43. Timothy Snyder, *Bloodlands: Europe Between Hitler and Stalin* (New York: Basic Books, 2010), 56–57.

44. U.S. Department of State, *Foreign Relations of the United States, 1969–1976*, vol. 26 (Washington, D.C.: Government Printing Office, 2012), no. 18.

45. Henry Kissinger makes this point well in "The Moral Foundations of Foreign Policy," July 15, 1975, *Department of State Bulletin* 73 (1975): 161–168.

46. U.S. House, Committee on Foreign Affairs, *Human Rights in Chile*, 93rd Cong., 1st Sess., (Washington, D.C.: Government Printing Office, 1974).

47. Transcript of conversation, June 8, 1976, *Digital National Security Archive*, KT01964, available at http://nsarchive.chadwyck.com.

48. "U.S. Foreign Policy and Human Rights."

49. "Greece, NATO, and U.S. Policy," June 13, 1973, Frank Newman Papers, Bancroft Library, BANC MSS 2005/175, Carton 2, Greece.

50. Robinson to Amnesty International, June 21, 1976, Columbia University, Center for Human Rights Research and Documentation, Amnesty International USA, II: Executive Director Files, Series II.1, David Hawk Files.

51. On this point, see Roland Burke, *Decolonization and the Evolution of International Human Rights* (Philadelphia: University of Pennsylvania Press, 2010), esp. chap. 2.

52. Moyn, *Last Utopia*, for example, 106, 116.

53. Henry Kissinger, "The Nature of the National Dialogue on Foreign Policy," in *Pacem in Terris III*, edited by Fred Warner Neal and Mary Kersey Harvey (Santa Barbara, Calif.: Center for the Study of Democratic Institutions, 1974), 6–17.

54. "U.S. Foreign Policy and Human Rights."

55. Clifford Geertz, "The Judging of Nations: Some Comments on the Assessment of Regimes in the New States," *European Journal of Sociology* 18, no. 2 (1977): 245–261.

56. Moynihan to Rogers, February 9, 1976, Library of Congress, Washington D.C., Daniel P. Moynihan Papers, Part I: United Nations File, Subject File, box 342.

57. Transcript of Conversation Between Kissinger and Ford, November 11, 1975, GFPL, NSA Files, Memoranda of Conversations, box 16.

58. "Epilogue," in *The Shock of the Global*, edited by Niall Ferguson, Charles Maier, Erez Manela, and Daniel Sargent (Cambridge, Mass: Belknap Press of Harvard University Press, 2010), 354. The argument is elaborated in Thomas Borstelmann, *The 1970s: A New Global History from Civil Rights to Economic Inequality* (Princeton, N.J.: Princeton University Press, 2012).

59. Martin Luther King Jr., *Where Do We Go From Here: Chaos or Community?* (Boston, Mass.: Beacon Press, 2010), 138.

60. John D'Emilio, *Lost Prophet: The Life and Times of Bayard Rustin* (New York: Free Press, 2003), 478–483.

61. *Brown v. Board of Education of Topeka*, 347 U.S. 483 (1954).

62. *Miranda v. Arizona*, 384 U.S. 436 (1966); and *Griswold v. Connecticut*, 381 U.S. 479 (1965).

63. *McDonald v. Chicago*, 561 U.S. 3025 (2010).

64. Mary Ann Glendon, *Rights Talk: The Impoverishment of Political Discourse* (New York: Free Press, 1991). For a sharp rejoinder, see Samuel Walker, *The Rights Revolution: Rights and Community in Modern America* (New York: Oxford University Press, 1998).

65. Podhoretz to Moynihan, September 2, 1975, Library of Congress, Daniel P. Moynihan Papers, Part I, UN File, box 339.

66. "The Carter Human Rights Policy: A Provisional Appraisal," JCPL, Donated Historical Materials, Brzezinski, Subject File, box 34.

67. "Address at the University of California, Berkeley," April 11, 1975, JCPL, Pre-Presidential Papers, 1976 Campaign Files, Issues Office (Eizenstat), Foreign Policy, box 16.

68. Carter to Eizenstat and Fallows, March 28, 1977, JCPL, Hertzberg Materials, Speech Files, box 1.

69. PRM/NSC-28, "Human Rights," and PDD/NSC-30, "Human Rights," available at http://www.jimmycarterlibrary.gov/documents/.

70. Author interview with former president Jimmy Carter, Plains, Georgia, August 2, 2009. Carter makes a similar point in *White House Diary* (New York: Farrar, Straus, and Giroux: 2010), 30.

71. Irving Kristol, "The Human Rights Muddle," *Wall Street Journal*, March 20, 1978, 12; Heritage Foundation, "Human Rights and Foreign Policy," August 22, 1977; and, most famously, Jeane J. Kirkpatrick, "Dictatorships and Double Standards," *Commentary* 68 (1979): 34–45.

72. "The Carter Human Rights Policy."

73. For recent historical perspectives, see Betty Glad, *An Outsider in the White House: Jimmy Carter, His Advisors, and the Making of American Foreign Policy* (Ithaca, N.Y.: Cornell University Press, 2009); Scott Kaufman, *Plans Unraveled: The Foreign Policy of the Carter Administration* (DeKalb: Northern Illinois University Press, 2008); Robert A. Strong, *Working in the World: Jimmy Carter and the Making of American Foreign Policy* (Baton Rouge: Louisiana State University Press, 2000).

74. Cited in "The Carter Human Rights Policy."

75. White House, *National Security Strategy of the United States* (2002), available at http://2001-2009.state.gov/r/pa/ei/wh/c7889.htm.

76. The author's survey of Berkeley undergraduates in February 2011 revealed that slim majorities believed employment and social security to be basic human rights. More than 90 percent said the same of free worship and speech. Contra Hobbes, fewer of them considered self-defense to be a human right. Some 86 percent of them considered basic (K–12) education to be a human right; only 41 percent said the same of higher education. On internet access and human rights, see *Report of the Special Rapporteur on the Promotion and Protection of the Right to Freedom of Expression, Frank LaRue*, May 16, 2011, UN A/HRC/17/27.

77. Patrick Caddell to Carter, October 21, 1977, and Hamilton Jordan to Carter, December 3, 1977, both in JCPL, Chief of Staff Files, Subject File, box 33.

Chapter 9. Human Rights and the U.S. Republican Party in the Late 1970s

I would like to thank the editors of this volume as well as Kristin Celello, Thomas F. Jackson, Stephen Porter, Patrick W. Kelly, Andrew Morris, Aaron Sheehan-Dean, and members of the Cornell University History Department for their comments on earlier versions of this essay.

1. Edward D. Berkowitz, *Something Happened: A Political and Cultural Overview of the 1970s* (New York: Columbia University Press, 2007).

2. Samuel Moyn, *The Last Utopia: Human Rights in History* (Cambridge, Mass.: Belknap Press of Harvard University Press, 2010).

3. Daniel Thomas, *The Helsinki Effect: International Norms, Human Rights, and the Demise of Communism* (Princeton, N.J.: Princeton University Press, 2001).

4. Kenneth Cmiel, "The Emergence of Human Rights Politics in the United States," *Journal of American History* 86, no. 3 (December 1999): 1231–1250; Barbara J. Keys, "Anti-Torture Politics: Amnesty International, the Greek Junta, and the Origins of the Human Rights 'Boom' in the United States," in *The Human Rights Revolution: An International History*, ed. Akira Iriye, Petra Goedde, and William I. Hitchcock (New York: Oxford University Press, 2011), 201–221.

5. Scott Kaufman, *Plans Unraveled: The Foreign Policy of the Carter Administration* (DeKalb: Northern Illinois University Press, 2008).

6. Moyn's *Last Utopia* provides an interesting rejoinder to this emphasis by demonstrating how European conservatives in the 1940s and 1950s employed human rights language in their effort to reconstruct the continent politically, socially, and economically. See Moyn, *Last Utopia*, 54–55, 72–81.

7. On domestic politics, see Kevin M. Kruse, *White Flight: Atlanta and the Making of Modern Conservatism* (Princeton, N.J.: Princeton University Press, 2007); Darren Dochuk, *From Bible Belt to Sunbelt: Plain-Folk Religion, Grassroots Politics, and the Rise of Evangelical Conservatism* (New York: W. W. Norton, 2010); Kim Phillips-Fein, *Invisible*

302   Notes to Pages 148–151

Hands: The Making of the Conservative Movement from the New Deal to Reagan (New York: W. W. Norton, 2009). On international politics, see Donald T. Critchlow, *Phyllis Schlafly and Grassroots Conservatism: A Woman's Crusade* (Princeton, N.J.: Princeton University Press, 2007); Adam Clymer, *Drawing the Line at the Big Ditch: The Panama Canal Treaties and the Rise of the Right* (Lawrence: University Press of Kansas, 2008); Jeremi Suri, "Détente and Its Discontents," and Julian Zelizer, "Conservatives, Carter, and the Politics of National Security," in *Rightward Bound: Making America Conservative in the 1970s*, ed. Julian E. Zelizer and Bruce J. Schulman (Cambridge, Mass.: Harvard University Press, 2008), 227–245, 265–287.

8. Moyn, *Last Utopia*, 54, 73–74.

9. Elizabeth Borgwardt, *A New Deal for the World: America's Vision for Human Rights* (Cambridge, Mass.: Belknap Press of Harvard University Press, 2007), 158–162; Harvard Sitkoff, "Willkie as Liberal: Civil Liberties and Civil Rights," in *Wendell Willkie: Hoosier Internationalist*, ed. James H. Madison (Indiana University Press, 1992), 71–101. For a different interpretation of Willkie and human rights, see Moyn, *Last Utopia*, 53.

10. Bricker cited in William White, "Senators Bid U.S. Hit Back for Oatis," *New York Times*, July 18, 1951, 1; Chester J. Pach Jr. and Elmo Richardson, *The Presidency of Dwight D. Eisenhower* (Lawrence: University Press of Kansas, 1991), 59–63; Robert D. Johnson, *Congress and the Cold War* (Cambridge: Cambridge University Press, 2006), 58–61.

11. Carol A. Anderson, *Eyes off the Prize: The United Nations and the African American Struggle for Human Rights, 1944–1955* (Cambridge: Cambridge University Press, 2003), 217–232; Mary Ann Glendon, *A World Made New: Eleanor Roosevelt and the Universal Declaration of Human Rights* (New York: Random House, 2002), 205.

12. "Enter Scranton," *New York Times*, June 14, 1964.

13. Kathryn Sikkink, *Mixed Signals: U.S. Human Rights Policies and Latin America* (Ithaca, N.Y.: Cornell University Press, 2004), 48–76; Moyn, *Last Utopia*, 120–175. On neoconservatism, see John Ehrman, *The Rise of Neoconservatism: Intellectuals and Foreign Affairs, 1945–1994* (New Haven, Conn.: Yale University Press, 1995); Justin Vaïsse, *Neoconservatism: The Biography of a Movement* (Cambridge, Mass.: Belknap Press of Harvard University Press, 2010).

14. Barbara J. Keys, "Congress, Kissinger, and the Origins of Human Rights Diplomacy," *Diplomatic History* 34, no. 5 (November 2010): 823–851.

15. Sikkink, *Mixed Signals*, 106–120.

16. Jussi Hanihimäki, *The Flawed Architect: Henry Kissinger and American Foreign Policy* (Oxford: Oxford University Press, 2004), 433–438; Jussi Hanhiimäki, "'They Can Write It in Swahili': Kissinger, The Soviets, and the Helsinki Accords, 1973–1975," *Journal of Transatlantic Studies* 1, no. 1 (March 2003): 37–59.

17. Cited in Peter Kornbluh, ed., *The Pinochet File: A Declassified Dossier on Atrocity and Accountability* (New York: New Press, 2004), 236.

18. John Robert Greene, *The Presidency of Gerald R. Ford* (Lawrence: University Press of Kansas, 1995), 157–173; Lou Cannon, *Governor Reagan: His Rise to Power* (New York: Public Affairs, 2003), 393–436.

19. Critchlow, *Phyllis Schlafly and Grassroots Conservatism*; Catherine E. Rymph, *Republican Women: Feminism and Conservatism from Suffrage through the Rise of the New Right* (Chapel Hill: University of North Carolina Press, 2006).

20. "The GOP Platform Process," Papers of the Republican National Committee, 1976 Republican National Convention, Box 683, Folder: "Republican National Convention News Briefs," National Archives, Washington, D.C.

21. "Democratic Party Platform of 1976," in *The American Presidency Project*, ed. Gerhard Peters and John T. Woolley, http://www.presidency.ucsb.edu/ws/index.php?pid=29606; Jimmy Carter, "Our Nation's Past and Future," in *The American Presidency Project*, ed. Peters and Woolley, http://www.presidency.ucsb.edu/ws/?pid=25953. On the Democrats in 1976 and human rights, see Moyn, *Last Utopia*, 152–155.

22. "Subcommittee: Human Rights and Responsibilities in a Free Society . . . Subject Matter Areas: Status of Women, Ending Discrimination, Native Americans, Hispanic Americans," Papers of the Republican National Committee, 1976 Republican National Convention, Box 679, Blue Binder, "Subject Matter Jurisdiction of Subcommittees," National Archives.

23. Conte press release quote from "SOC Remarks upon Being Released as Chmn of the GOP Convention Subcommittee," August 11, 1976, Box 252, File "August 1976," Papers of Silvio Conte, UMass-Amherst Special Collections Library; Conte quotes to a reporter from "Embittered Conti Scores Tactics Reagan Forces Used," *Holyoke (Mass.) Transcript-Telegram*, August 10, 1976, Scrapbook 31, Papers of Silvio Conte, UMass-Amherst Special Collections Library; R. W. Apple, "Ford and Reagan Backers Skirmish in Kansas City," *New York Times*, August 10, 1976; Richard Madden, "Ford Camp Loses Panel Chairmanship; Uncommitted Delegate Named to Post," *New York Times*, August 10, 1976; Sean Wilentz,"The Racist Skeletons in Charles Pickering's Closet," *Salon.com*, http://www.salon.com/2003/05/12/pickering_3/ (accessed November 21, 2012).

24. On Conte, see Robert Surbrug Jr., *Beyond Vietnam: The Politics of Protest in Massachusetts, 1974–1990* (Amherst: University of Massachusetts Press, 2009), 15–16, 118, 145–146, 208–221.

25. On Peterson, see William Grimes, "Elly Peterson, 94, a Leader of Moderate Republicans, is Dead," *New York Times*, June 20, 2008; Critchlow, *Phyllis Schlafly and Grassroots Conservatism*, 142–144, 252–253.

26. "Statement of Elly M. Peterson before Republican Platform Committee," August 9, 1976, Papers of the Republican National Committee, 1976 Republican National Convention, Box 680, National Archives.

27. "Remarks by Benjamin Fernandez, Chairman, the Republican National Hispanic Assembly of the United States," August 10, 1976, Papers of the Republican National Committee, 1976 Republican National Convention, Box 681, National Archives.

28. Michael Buryk, "Testimony on the Issue of Human Rights and Responsibilities . . .", undated, Papers of the Republican National Committee, 1976 Republican National Convention, Box 681, National Archives.

29. "Statement of Latvian-American Republican National Federation," June 21,

1976, Papers of the Republican National Committee, 1976 Republican National Convention, Box 680, National Archives.

30. "Filing of Minority Resolutions, Charles Coy, August 16, 1976," Papers of the Republican National Committee, 1976 Republican National Convention, Box 682, Folder: Unnamed, National Archives. For the platform, see "The Republican Party Platform of 1976, August 18, 1976," in *The American Presidency Project*, ed. Peters and Woolley, http://www.presidency.ucsb.edu/ws/index.php?pid=25843&st=&st1=. On the role of Helms and East, see William A. Link, *Righteous Warrior: Jesse Helms and the Rise of Modern Conservatism* (New York: St. Martin's Press, 2008), 160–164.

31. Greene, *Presidency of Gerald R. Ford*, 151–152, 166.

32. "Ex-U.S. Rep. Albert Lee Smith Dies," *Tuscaloosa News*, August 11, 1997.

33. "Meeting of the Temporary Committee on Resolutions (Platform Committee) of the Republican National Committee," Friday, August 13, 1976, Transcript Pages 496–502, Box 715, Papers of the Republican National Committee, 1976 Republican National Convention, National Archives.

34. "Meeting of the Temporary Committee on Resolutions (Platform Committee) of the Republican National Committee," Friday, August 13, 1976, Transcript Pages 516–525, Box 715, Papers of the Republican National Committee, 1976 Republican National Convention, National Archives.

35. Mike Berry, "Streetman, GOP Rose Together," *Orlando Sentinel*, September 24, 1992; "Meeting of the Temporary Committee on Resolutions (Platform Committee) of the Republican National Committee," Friday, August 13, 1976, Transcript Pages 563–566, Box 715, Papers of the Republican National Committee, 1976 Republican National Convention, National Archives.

36. Ehrman, *Rise of Neoconservatism*; Vaïsse, *Neoconservatism*; Jacob Heilbrunn, "The Neoconservative Journey," in *Varieties of Conservatism in America*, ed. Peter Berkowitz (Stanford: Hoover Institution Press, 2004), 105–128.

37. "Republican Party Platform of 1976."

38. Critchlow, *Phyllis Schlafly and Grassroots Conservatism*, 242.

39. Cannon, *Governor Reagan*, 444.

40. Ibid., 215, 437–476.

41. Ibid., 420.

42. Ronald Reagan, "Excerpts of Remarks . . . at the Phillips Exeter Academy," February 10, 1976, Ronald Reagan Presidential Library, Simi Valley, California (hereafter cited as RRPL), Series I: Hannaford/ California Headquarters, Box 21.

43. Ronald Reagan, "To Restore America," March 31, 1976, http://www.reagan.utexas.edu/archives/reference/3.31.76.html (accessed February 12, 2011).

44. Ibid.

45. Ibid.

46. Ronald Reagan, "Human Rights," radio broadcast, January 3, 1979, RRPL, Series I: Hannaford/ California Headquarters, Box 15.

47. Ronald Reagan, "Foreign Policy Association, Waldorf Astoria New York, June 9, 1977," RRPL, Series I: Hannaford/ California Headquarters, Box 22.

48. Ronald Reagan, "Human Rights," radio broadcast, March 6, 1979, RRPL, Series I: Hannaford/ California Headquarters, Box 15.

49. Ibid.

50. Ronald Reagan, "Foreign Policy Association, Waldorf Astoria New York, June 9, 1977," RRPL, Series I: Hannaford/ California Headquarters, Box 22.

51. Ronald Reagan, "Human Rights," radio broadcast, March 6, 1979, RRPL, Series I: Hannaford/ California Headquarters, Box 15.

52. Ronald Reagan, "Foreign Policy Association, Waldorf Astoria New York, June 9, 1977," RRPL, Series I: Hannaford/ California Headquarters, Box 22.

53. President Jimmy Carter, "University of Notre Dame, Address at Commencement Exercises at the University," in *The American Presidency Project*, ed. Peters and Woolley, http://www.presidency.ucsb.edu/ws/?pid=7552.

54. Vaïsse, *Neoconservatism*, 125–136.

55. Jeane J. Kirkpatrick, "Dictatorships and Double Standards," *Commentary*, November 1979.

56. Ronald Reagan, "Human Rights," radio broadcast, January 3, 1979, RRPL, Series I: Hannaford/ California Headquarters, Box 15.

57. Ronald Reagan, "Human Rights," radio broadcast, March 6, 1979, RRPL, Series I: Hannaford/ California Headquarters, Box 15.

58. Ronald Reagan, "Helsinki Pact," radio broadcast, December 2, 1978, RRPL, Series I: Hannaford/ California Headquarters, Box 15.

59. Ronald Reagan, "Foreign Policy Association, Waldorf Astoria New York, June 9, 1977," RRPL, Series I: Hannaford/ California Headquarters, Box 22.

60. President Ronald Reagan, "Inaugural Address," in *The American Presidency Project*, ed. Peters and Woolley, http://www.presidency.ucsb.edu/ws/?pid=43130.

61. Lou Cannon, *President Reagan: The Role of a Lifetime* (New York: Public Affairs, 2000), 676, 703–704; Frances FitzGerald, *Way Out There in the Blue: Reagan, Star Wars, and the End of the Cold War* (New York: Simon and Schuster, 2000), 422, 429, 452, 456; Sikkink, *Mixed Signals*, 148–180.

Chapter 10. The Polish Opposition, the Crisis of the Gierek Era, and the Helsinki Process

1. Cf. Andrzej Friszke, *Polska: Losy państwa i narodu* (Warsaw: Iskry, 2003), 308.

2. Cf. Peter Hübner and Christina Hübner, *Sozialismus als soziale Frage: Sozialpolitik in der DDR und Polen 1968–1976* (Cologne: Böhlau, 2008), 133–134, 273.

3. Cf. Daniel C. Thomas, *The Helsinki Effect: International Norms, Human Rights, and the Demise of Communism* (Princeton, N.J.: Princeton University Press, 2001). See also William Korey, *The Promises We Keep: Human Rights, the Helsinki Process, and American Foreign Policy* (New York: St. Martin's Press, 1993); and Sarah B. Snyder,

Human Rights Activism and the End of the Cold War: A Transnational History of the Helsinki Network (New York: Cambridge University Press, 2011). On the Helsinki process in general, see Andreas Wenger, Vojtech Mastny, and Christian Nuenlist, eds., *Origins of the European Security System: The Helsinki process revisited, 1964–75* (New York: Routledge, 2008); Leopoldo Nuti, ed., *The Crisis of Détente in Europe: From Helsinki to Gorbachev, 1975–1985* (New York: Berghahn Books, 2009); Peter Schlotter, *Die KSZE im Ost-West-Konflikt: Wirkung einer internationalen Institution* (Frankfurt: Campus Verlag, 1999); Wilfried von Bredow, *Der KSZE-Prozeß: Von der Zähmung zur Auflösung des Ost-West-Konflikts* (Darmstadt: Wissenschaftliche Buchgesellschaft, 1992); and Helmut Altrichter and Hermann Wentker, eds., *Der KSZE-Prozess: Vom Kalten Krieg zu einem neuen Europa 1975 bis 1990* (Munich: Oldenbourg, 2011).

4. Cf. Archie Brown, *The Gorbachev Factor* (New York: Oxford University Press, 1996).

5. Thomas, *Helsinki Effect*, 6.

6. Cf. Adam Michnik, "Verteidigung der Freiheit, Reflexionen über 1989," *Osteuropa* 59, no. 2/3 (2009): 9–18, 9–10.

7. Thomas, *Helsinki Effect*, 20, 91.

8. Cf. Jerzy Eisler, *"Polskie miesiące" czyli kryzyz(y) w PRL* (Warsaw: Instytut Pamięci Narodowej, 2008).

9. On the history of the KOR, see Łukasz Kamiński and Grzegorz Waligóra, eds., *Kryptonim "Gracze": Służba Bezpieczeństwa wobec Komitetu Obrony Robotników i Komitetu Samoobronej Społecznej "KOR" 1976–1981* (Warsaw: Instytut Pamięci Narodowej, 2010); Jan Józef Lipski, *KOR: Komitet Obrony Robotników, Komitet Samoobrony Społecznej* (1983; Warsaw: Instytut Pamięci Narodowej, 2006); Jastrzębski Andrzej, ed., *Dokumenty Komitetu Obrony Robotników i Komitetu Samoobrony Społecznej "KOR"* (London: Aneks, 1994).

10. "Goulash communism" or "Kadarism" describes the attempt to introduce economic and cultural liberalism in Hungary in the 1960s to consolidate the socialist regime after the 1956 uprising. The term "consumer socialism" is found, for example, in Friszke, *Polska*, 309. The 1970s are therefore sometimes referred to as a period of Bigos communism. Cf. Marcin Zaremba, "'Bigosowy socjalizm': Dekada Gierka," in *Polacy wobec PRL: Strategie przystosowawcze*, ed. Grzegorz Miernik (Kielce: Kieleckie Towarzystwo Naukowe, Akademia Świętokrzyska, 2003); Andrzej Paczkowski described this period as the "Belle Époque of real socialism." Andrzej Paczkowski, *Pół wieku dziejów Polski* (Warsaw: Wydawnictwo Naukowe PWN, 2005), 401.

11. Cf. Zaremba, "'Bigosowy socjalizm,'" 191; Leonid Luks, *Katholizismus und politische Macht im kommunistischen Polen 1945–1989: Die Anatomie einer Befreiung* (Cologne: Böhlau, 1993), 83–84.

12. Cf. Anselm Doering-Manteuffel and Lutz Raphael, eds., *Nach dem Boom: Perspektiven auf die Zeitgeschichte seit 1970*, 2nd ed. (Göttingen: Vandenhoeck & Ruprecht, 2010). Anselm Doering-Manteuffel, "Nach dem Boom: Brüche und Kontinuitäten der Industriemoderne seit 1970," in *Vierteljahrshefte für Zeitgeschichte* 55 (2007): 559–581;

Thomas Raithel, Andreas Rödder, and Andreas Wirsching, eds., *Auf dem Weg in eine neue Moderne? Die Bundesrepublik Deutschland in den siebziger und achtziger Jahren* (Munich: Oldenbourg, 2009).

13. Donella H. Meadows et al., *The Limits to Growth: A Report for the Club of Rome's Project on the Predicament of Mankind* (New York: Universe Books, 1972).

14. Cf. Thomas Raithel and Thomas Schlemmer, eds., *Die Rückkehr der Arbeitslosigkeit: Die Bundesrepublik Deutschland im europäischen Kontext 1973–1989* (Munich: Oldenbourg, 2009).

15. Cf. Doering-Manteuffel and Raphael, *Nach dem Boom*, 11.

16. Cf. Paweł Sasanka, *Czerwiec 1976: Geneza, przebieg, konsekwencje* (Warsaw: Instytut Pamięci Narodowej, 2006), 10.

17. Cf. Wanda Jarząbek, *Polska wobec Konferencji Bezpieczeństwa i Współpracy w Europie: Plany i rzeczywistość 1964–1975* (Warsaw: ISP PAN, 2008); Jarząbek, "Hope and Reality. Poland and the Conference on Security and Cooperation in Europe, 1964–1989," *CWHIP Working Paper* 56 (May 2008); Jarząbek, "Preserving the Status Quo or Promoting Change? The Role of the CSCE in the Perception of Polish Authorities," in *Helsinki 1975 and the Transformation of Europe*, ed. Oliver Bange and Gottfried Niedhardt (New York: Berghahn Books, 2008), 144–159. Zdzisław Lachowski, "Diplomatic File: Polish Diplomacy and the CSCE Process during the Cold War Period," *Polish Quarterly of International Affairs* 5, no. 4 (2009): 73–104.

18. Adam Michnik, "Der neue Evolutionismus," in *Polnischer Frieden: Aufsätze zur Konzeption des Widerstands* (Berlin: Rotbuch, 1985), 40–54; Thomas, *Helsinki Effect*, 92.

19. Thomas, *Helsinki Effect*, 160–161.

20. Ibid., 184.

21. Cf. Friszke, *Polska*, 320; Zaremba, "'Bigosowy socjalizm,'" 183–200, 196.

22. Cf. Friszke, *Polska*, 324, and Klaus Ziemer, *Polens Weg in die Krise: Eine politische Soziologie der "Ära Gierek"* (Frankfurt: Athenäum, 1987), 258–266.

23. Cf., for example, Jacek Kuroń, "Myśli o programie działania" (1977), in *Opozycja: Pisma Polityczne, 1969–1989* (Warsaw: Krytyka Polityczna, 2010), 77.

24. Cf. Jerzy Eisler, *Polski rok 1968* (Warsaw: Instytut Pamięci Narodowej, 2006); Andrzej Friszke, *Anatomia buntu: Kuroń, Modzelewski i komandosi* (Krakow: Znak, 2010).

25. Jacek Kuroń and Karol Modzelewski, "List otwarty do partii," in Jacek Kuroń, *Dojrzewanie: Pisma polityczne, 1964–1968* (Warsaw: Krytyka Polityczna 2009), 5–89.

26. Jacek Kuroń, *Glaube und Schuld: Einmal Kommunismus und zurück* (Berlin: Aufbau, 1991), 510.

27. Adam Michnik, "Reflexionen über die Märzereignisse," in *Polnischer Frieden*, 37–38.

28. Ibid., 39.

29. Lipski, *KOR*, 100-101; "Airborne troops" (*komandosi*) was the colloquial name for the rebelling students.

30. Cf. Adam Michnik, "The Prague Spring Ten Years later," in *Letters from Prison*

and Other Essays (Berkeley: University of California Press, 1985), 159. On the role of the Catholic Church in this process, see Luks, *Katholizismus.*

31. Adam Michnik, *The Church and the Left* (Chicago: University of Chicago Press, 1993).

32. Jacek Kuroń, "Polityczna opozycja w Polsce," *Kultura* 11 (1974): 3–21; cf. Hella Dietz, "Opposition der Siebziger in Polen. Ein Beitrag zur Integration neuerer Theorien sozialer Bewegungen," *Archives Européennes de Sociologie* 49 (2008): 236–238.

33. Kuroń, "Polityczna opozycja w Polsce," 8.

34. Ibid., 13.

35. Ibid., 14.

36. "The Conference on Security and Co-operation in Europe Final Act" (1975), Organization for Security and Co-operation in Europe, http://www.osce.org/mc/39501, 10.

37. Cf. Schlotter, *Die KSZE im Ost-West-Konflikt,* 107–115.

38. Cf. Jarząbek, *Polska wobec Konferencji,* 153.

39. Cf. Georges-Henri Soutou, *La guerre de Cinquante Ans: Le conflit Est-Ouest, 1943–1990* (Paris: Fayard, 2001), 560–561.

40. Cf. Gunter Dehnert, "'Eine neue Beschaffenheit der Lage': Der KSZE-Prozess und die polnische Opposition, 1975–1989," in *Der KSZE-Prozess,* ed. Altrichter and Wentker, 87–89.

41. The text of the Final Act itself was printed in 1975 in excerpts, including the text of the seventh principle, *Trybuna Ludu,* August 2–3, 1975. The complete text was found in the supplement to the special issue of the diplomatic journal *Sprawy Międzynarodowe* 10 (1975) dedicated to the results of the CSCE. The text was also published in *Wielka Karta Pokoju, materiały Konferencji Bezpieczeństwa i Współpracy w Europie* (Warsaw: Książka i Wiedza, 1975). Cf. Jarząbek, *Polska wobec Konferencji,* 162–163.

42. "Wybrane zagadnienia dywersji ideologiczno-politycznej przeciwko Polsce oraz działalności antysocjalistycznej w PRL/ Referat na sympozjum Krajów Socjalistycznych— Budapeszt, maj 1977 r.," Archiwum Instytutu Pamięci Narodowej (AIPN) 0296/133 t. 7, 97–98.

43. Ibid., 85.

44. Cf. Andrzej Friszke, "Protesty przeciw poprawkom do konstytucji w 1976," in *Przystosowanie i opór. Studia z dziejów PRL* (Warsaw: Więź, 2007): 231–255, 234.

45. Ibid., 231n2.

46. The mentioned principles are 1, 4, 6, and 7, "Final Act," 4–6.

47. "List 59," *Kultura* 1–2 (1976): 235–236.

48. Ibid., 236.

49. Cf. Friszke, "Protesty," 239. The text has been reprinted in *Aneks* 11 (1976): 14–15.

50. Entry of January 18, 1976, in Mieczysław F. Rakowski, *Dzienniki polityczne, 1976–1978* (Warsaw: Iskry, 2002), 20.

51. Friszke, "Protesty," 235.

52. Cf. Paweł Machcewicz, *"Monachijska Menażera": Walka z Radiem Wolna Europa 1950-1989* (Warsaw: Instytut Pamięci Narodowej, 2007), 311-335.

53. For a comprehensive discussion, cf. Sasanka, *Czerwiec 1976.*

54. Cf. Friszke, *Polska*, 341.

55. "KOR's appeal to the population and the authorities of the People's Republic of Poland, 23 September 1976," in *Das KOR und der "polnische Sommer": Analysen, Dokumente, Artikel und Interviews 1976-1981*, ed. Werner Mackenbach (Hamburg: Junius, 1982), 64.

56. In many European cities there were demonstrations in front of the diplomatic missions of the People's Republic of Poland. Cf. AMSZ, ZD 24/79, w. 15, t. 107: "15 czerwca, szyfogram ambasada w Paryżu o demonstracjach przeciw represjom w Polsce," in *Polskie Dokumenty Dyplomatyczne 1977*, ed. Piotr M. Majewski (Warsaw: Polski Instytut Spraw Międzynarodowych, 2009), 440. Besides the impressive names among Western supporters (including Arthur Miller, Noam Chomsky, Günter Grass, Heinrich Böll, Jean-Paul Sartre, and Jean Marie Domenach), the organized Polish minority in the United States appealed directly to Jimmy Carter, who in turn referred the matter to the U.S. Helsinki Commission. Cf. Lipski, *KOR*, 253-256.

57. Before the founding of the KOR in September 1976, Lipski favored the name Komitet Obrony Praw Człowieka i Obywatela [Committee for the Defense of Human and Civil Rights], "which would have tied in with the United Nations Charter, the final provisions in Helsinki, the key slogans of U.S. President Jimmy Charter and an older tradition, when the League for the Defense of Human and Civil Rights was active in Poland in the 1930s." Lipski, *KOR*, 136.

58. Cf. Ryszard Terlecki, *Uniwersytet Latający i Towarzystwo Kursów Naukowych 1977-1981* (Krakow: Instytut Europejskich Studiów Społecznych, 2000).

59. Cf. Grzegorz Waligóra, *Ruch Obrony Praw Człowieka i Obywatela 1977-1981* (Warsaw: Instytut Pamięci Narodowej, 2006).

60. Cf. Ernst Wawra, "The Helsinki Final Act and the Civil Rights Movement in the Soviet Union," in *Human Rights and History: A Challenge for Education*, ed. Rainer Huhle (Berlin: Fata Morgana, 2010), 150-151; Leonid Luks, "Idee und Identität: Traditionslinien im sowjetischen Dissens," *Osteuropa* 60, no. 11 (2010): 150-151.

61. Cf. AMSZ, ZD 24/79, w. 2, t. 13: "24 czerwca, szyfogram dyrektora PISM (z Belgradu) z oceną początkowej fazy obrad KBWE," in Majewski, *Polskie Dokumenty Dyplomatyczne 1977*, 447-448.

62. AIPN BU 01521/2231: "Wybrane zasady doktryny prezydenta Stanów Zjednoczonych Jimmy Cartera ze szczególnym uwzględnieniem praw człowieka, Warszawa 1980," 38.

63. Ibid.

64. Cf., for example, document no. 143: "Tłumaczenie informacji Federalnego MSW CSRS dotyczącej spotkania przedstawicieli KSS 'KOR' i Karty 77 na Śnieżce w dniu 2 września 1978 r." as well as Dokument Nr. 146: "Meldunek operacyjny dotyczący spotkania działaczy KSS 'KOR' w dniu 30 września 1978 r. oraz udaremnienia spotkania

polskich i czechosłowackich dysydentów w Karkonoszach w dniu 1 października 1978r.," in Kamiński/Waligóra, *Kryptonim "Gracze,"* 455, 460.

65. The English version of *Raport Madrycki* is Ludwik Cohn et al., eds., *Prologue to Gdansk: Report on the Observation of the Human and Civil Rights in the Polish People's Republic* (New York: Human Rights Watch, 1980).

66. The eighth demand was the "dissemination of the contents of the Helsinki Conference's Human Rights Charter in printed form," "Postulaty Załogi Szczecińskiej," accessed November 11, 2012, http://www.arcimboldo.pl/index.php?dir = 001_Postulaty; Jarząbek, *Polska wobec Konferencji,* 163

67. Thomas, *Helsinki Effect,* 270.

68. Ibid., 269.

69. Ibid., 267.

70. Ibid.

Chapter 11. "Human Rights Are Like Coca-Cola"

1. "Birth Control hak2 asasi," *Kompas,* May 10, 1968; "Hak-hak asasi manusia belum merata dijalankan," *Kompas,* April 26, 1968.

2. "Pengembangan Hak-hak Azasi Tugas Maha Besar dan Mulia," *Kompas,* December 11, 1968; Adam Malik, "1968 Promise in Indonesia," *Foreign Affairs* 46, no. 2 (January 1968): 292–303.

3. "Memo, the Problem of Political Prisoners in Indonesia," October 1969, Evangelical Lutheran Church in America Archives, Chicago (hereafter cited as ELCA Archives), ELCA Division for World Missions, Indonesia Program Files, 1951–1985, box 1.

4. Barbara Keys, "Anti-Torture Politics: Amnesty International, the Greek Junta, and the Origins of the Human Rights 'Boom' in the United States, 1967–1970," in *The Human Rights Revolution: An International History,* ed. Akira Iriye Petra Goedde, and William I. Hitchcock (New York: Oxford University Press, 2011), 201–223; Jan Eckel, "'Under a Magnifying Glass': The International Human Rights Campaign Against Chile in the Seventies," in *Human Rights in the Twentieth Century,* ed. Stefan-Ludwig Hoffmann (Cambridge: Cambridge University Press, 2010), 321–343; Bradley R. Simpson, "Denying the 'First Right': The United States, Indonesia, and the Ranking of Human Rights by the Carter Administration, 1976–1980," *International History Review* 31, no. 4 (September 2009): 798–821.

5. Elsbeth Locher-Scholten, "The Colonial Heritage of Human Rights in Indonesia: The Case of the Vote for Women, 1916–41," *Journal of Southeast Asian Studies* 30, no. 1 (August 2009): 54–73.

6. Todung Mulya Lubis, *In Search of Human Rights: Legal-Political Dilemmas of Indonesia's New Order, 1966–1990* (Jakarta: Gramedia, 1993), 75–85.

7. R. Supomo, *The Provisional Constitution of the Republic of Indonesia* (Jakarta: Equinox, 2009), 22–42.

8. Elsbeth Locher-Scholten, "The Colonial Heritage of Human Rights," 54; Elizabeth

Martyn, *The Women's Movement in Post-Colonial Indonesia: Gender and Nation in a New Democracy* (Auckland: Routledge Curzon, 2005), 117–121.

9. Teungku Muhammad Hasbi Ash Shiddieqy, *Islam & HAM (hak-hak asasi manusia)* : *Dokumen politik pokok-pokok pikiran Partai Islam dalam Sidang Konstituante 5 February 1958 / Teungku Muhammad Hasbi Ash Shiddieqy* (Semarang: Pustaka Rizki Putra, 1999), 36–79; Azizuddin Mohd, *Hak asasi manusia menurut pandangan Islam dan Barat, 1960* (Bentong Pahang Darul Makmur: PTS Publications, 2002).

10. Kuntjoro Purbopranoto, *Hak-hak dasar manusia dan Pantja-Sila Negara republik Indonesia* (Jakarta: Pradnja Paramita, 1960); Douglas E. Ramage, *Politics in Indonesia: Democracy, Islam and the Ideology of Tolerance* (New York: Routledge, 1995), 143–156; Adnan Buyung Nasution, *The Aspiration for Constitutional Government in Indonesia: A Socio-Legal Study Of The Indonesian Konstituante, 1956–1959* (Jakarta: Pustaka Sinar Harapan, 1992).

11. Sudirjo and Pamontjak cited in Roland Burke, *Decolonization and the Evolution of International Human Rights* (Philadelphia, University of Pennsylvania Press, 2009), 42, 119; *Final Communiqué of the Asian-African Conference Held at Bandung from 18th to 24th April, 1955*.

12. John Roosa, *Pretext for Mass Murder: The September 30th Movement and Suharto's Coup d'État in Indonesia* (Madison: University of Wisconsin Press, 2006); Justus van der Kroef, "Indonesia's Political Prisoners," *Pacific Affairs* 49, no. 4 (Winter 1976): 625–647.

13. Greg Fealy, *The Release of Indonesia's Political Prisoners: Domestic Versus Foreign Policy, 1975–1979* (Melbourne: Centre for Southeast Asian Studies, Monash University, 1995), 7.

14. Lubis, *In Search of Human Rights*, 5–6.

15. KAMI, *Simposium Masalah Ekonomi Beserta Pemetjahannja diambang pintu pembangunan.* (Jakarta: Senat Mahasiswa Fakultas Ekonomi Universitas Indonesia, 1968); "Masalah Tahanan," *Kompas*, December 13, 1968.

16. Van der Kroef, "Indonesia's Political Prisoners," 642; *Bantuan Hukum di Indonesia: Lima Tahun Lembaga Bantuan Hukum* (Jakarta: Lembaga Bantuan Hukum, 1976), 20–22.

17. "Indonesia: The Man on Trial," *Time*, October 14, 1966; Daniel S. Lev, *No Concessions: The Life of Yap Thiam Hien, Indonesian Human Rights Lawyer* (Seattle: University of Washington Press, 2011), 234–252.

18. "Memo from Secretary General, Amnesty International to all National Sections, Prisoners in Indonesia," January 30, 1970, Amnesty International USA Papers, Columbia University, Amnesty International National Office, Group II, Series 5, box 7.

19. State Department Circular Telegram 041420, February 24, 1975, Department of State, Freedom of Information Act (FOIA) Electronic Reading Room, http://foia.state .gov/SearchColls/Search.asp; on the work of German missionaries see Memo, Gregory to Lowry, "Political Prisoners Indonesia," October 15, 1975, ELCA Archives, Division for

World Mission and Ecumenism, Secretary for Southern Asia and the Middle East, Indonesia Program Files, 1951–1985, box 1.

20. See David T. Hill, "Knowing Indonesia from Afar: Indonesian Exiles and Australian Academics," paper presented to the 17th Biennial Conference of the Asian Studies Association of Australia, July 1–3, 2008, Melbourne.

21. Jeffrey A. Winters, *Power in Motion, Capital Mobility and the Indonesian State* (Ithaca, N.Y.: Cornell University Press, 1996), 79–82.

22. "Letter from Col. Ibrahim Adjie to Leo Abse, House Commons," July 14, 1969, United Kingdom National Archive (hereafter cited as UKNA), FCO 24-1699-1702, Political Detainees in Indonesia 1973–1974; Rachman Gunawan, "Aspek Universal Hak2 Manusia," *Kompas*, March 12, 1969.

23. Letter from RM Hunt, British Embassy Jakarta to FCO, January 17, 1971, UKNA, FCO 15-1941, Political Detainees in Indonesia 1974; Meeting with Indonesian Ambassador, Amnesty Bulletin 33, Melbourne Chapter, June 1972, Carmel Budiardjo Papers, London.

24. "Indonesia: The Killing Starts Again," *Economist*, November 30, 1968; Justus van der Kroef, "Indonesian Communism since the 1965 Coup," *Pacific Affairs* 43, no. 1 (Spring 1970): 34–60.

25. Airgram A-249 from Jakarta to State, "Indonesia's Political Prisoners," June 20, 1969, National Archives, College Park, SNF 1967–1969, POL 29 Indon; See also Letter from D. P. Aiers to Foreign and Commonwealth Office, July 20, 1970, UKNA, FCO 24-751, Political Detainees in Indonesia 1970.

26. John Saltford, *The United Nations and the Indonesian Takeover of West Papua, 1962–1969: The Anatomy of Betrayal* (London: Routledge, 2006); Brad Simpson, "U.S. Policy Toward Indonesia, West Papua, and the 1969 'Act of Free Choice,'" A National Security Archive Briefing Book, July 2004, http://www.gwu.edu/~nsarchiv/Indonesia.

27. Daniel Lev, *Legal Aid in Indonesia* (Melbourne: Monash Asia Institute, 1987); Takeshi Kohno, *The Emergence of the Legal Aid Institute in Authoritarian Indonesia: How a Human Rights Organization Survived the Suharto Regime and Became a Cornerstone for Civil Society in Indonesia* (Leiden: VDM Verlag Müller, 2010).

28. Edward Aspinall, *Opposing Suharto: Compromise, Resistance, and Regime Change in Indonesia* (Stanford, Calif.: Stanford University Press, 2005), 103–105; "Adnan Buyung Nasution SH: Dukungan dan Partisipasi yang Luas dari masyarakat adalah kunci untuk suksesnya Repelita," *Kompas*, January 30, 1969; Yap Thiam Hien, "Masalah Hukum dan Penyalah Gunaan Kekuasaan," *Prisma* 6 (1973): 21–29.

29. "Konperensi I, Lembaga Bantuan Hukum: Seleruh Indonesia, Djakarta Desember 10–12, 1971," n.d., LBH archives, Jakarta; *Bantuan Hukum di Indonesia: Lima Tahun Lembaga Bantuan Hukum* (Jakarta: Lembaga Bantuan Hukum, 1976), 29; "Record of Conversation with Mulya Lubis, Australian Embassy Jakarta," December 18, 1975, National Archives Australia (hereafter cited as NAA), A 1838, 3034-2-9-6, Part 14, Indonesia, Internal Security, Political Prisoners 1975.

30. "Diskusi 'tahanan politik di Indonesia' dilarang Kopkamtib," *Kompas*, May 24, 1971.

31. "Buyung Nasution Menjadi Anggota Bantuan Hukum Internasional," *Kompas*, September 8, 1972; "Direktur LBH ke AS," *Kompas*, Oktober 30, 1973.

32. William Korey, *Taking on the World's Repressive Regimes: The Ford Foundation's International Human Rights Policies and Practices* (New York: Palgrave Macmillan, 2007), 28–37; Rosalyn Higgins, "Human Rights: Needs and Practices," September 1973, Ford Foundation Archives, New York (hereafter cited as FFA).

33. Among many examples see Morris Janowitz, *The Military in the Political Development of New Nations: An Essay in Comparative Analysis* (Chicago: University of Chicago Press, 1964), 44; Moshe Lissak, "The Role of the Military: Modernization and Role-Expansion of the Military in Developing Countries: A Comparative Analysis," *Comparative Studies in Society and History* 9, no. 3 (April 1967): 233–255; Amos Perlmutter, "The Praetorian State and the Praetorian Army: Toward a Taxonomy of Civil-Military Relations in Developing Polities," *Comparative Politics* 1, no. 3 (April 1969): 382–404; Henry Bienen, ed., *The Military and Modernization* (Chicago University of Chicago Press, 1971).

34. Clarence Clyde Ferguson and David M. Trubek, "When Is an Omelet? What Is an Egg? Some Thought on Economic Development and Human Rights in Latin America," *American Journal of International Law* 67, no. 5 (November 1973): 203–204.

35. Airgram A-33 from Jakarta to State, February 16, 1970, National Archives, College Park, Md., RG 59 SNF 1970–1973, POL 1 INDON-US, box 2379.

36. Ali Moertopo, *Some Basic Thoughts on the Acceleration and Modernization of 25 Years' Development* (Jakarta: Centre for Strategic and International Studies, 1973), 82–87.

37. Most recently, see Samuel Moyn, *The Last Utopia: Human Rights in History* (Cambridge, Mass.: Belknap Press of Harvard University Press, 2010), 120–176.

38. Roger Normand and Sarah Zaidi, *Human Rights at the UN: The Political History of Universal Justice* (Bloomington: Indiana University Press, 2008), 289–316.

39. David D. Newsom, *The Diplomacy of Human Rights* (Washington: Potomac Books, 1986), 103.

40. Ford Foundation, "Notes on Human Rights and Indonesian Development," paper for Southeast Asia Development Advisory Group Seminar, May 14–15, 1976, Tamiment Library, New York University, ETAN Papers, box 14; "Human Rights and Intellectual Freedom," FFA, Ford Foundation Information Paper 005527, March 1978.

41. Aspinall, *Opposing Suharto*, 93–95.

42. Fealy, *The Release of Indonesia's Political Prisoners*,13–14; David Hinkley, "The Work of Amnesty International for Indonesian Prisoners of Conscience," *TAPOL US Bulletin* 1, October 1975; "ILO Given Indonesia Pledge on Prisoners," *Guardian*, June 17, 1976; on the International Commission of Jurists and World Council of Churches see *TAPOL Bulletin* 6 (1974), 6.

43. "Mahasiswa yang Menyambut Pronk dengan Poster Minta Bantuan LBH," *Kompas*, November 16, 1973; "Memo from Martin Innes, Secretary General, Amnesty International to National Sections of IGGI Member Governments," November 20, 1973, AIUSA Papers, AI National Office Group II, series 5, box 7.

44. Carmel Budiardjo, *Surviving Indonesia's Gulag: A Western Woman Tells Her Story* (London: Continuum, 1996); *TAPOL Bulletin 1* (January 1973): 2.

45. "Letter from J. L. Beaven, British Embassy Jakarta to FCO London," August 14, 1973, UKNA, FCO 24-1699-1702, Political Detainees in Indonesia 1973–1974; "Letter, Australian Embassy Jakarta to Canberra," April 2, 1974, NAA, A 1838, 3034-2-9-6, Part 4, Indonesia, Internal Security, Political Prisoners 1974; "Letter from Ali Murtopo to Donald Fraser," November 14, 1976, Minnesota State Historical Society, Donald Fraser Papers, Subject Committee Files 1976, box 149, G9.

46. Fealy, *The Release of Indonesia's Political Prisoners*, 9; Ron E. Elson, *Suharto: A Political Biography* (Cambridge: Cambridge University Press, 2002), 200–210.

47. Telegram 12266 from Jakarta to State, 16 October 1973, U.S. Department of State FOIA Electronic Reading Room, http://foia.state.gov/SearchColls/Search.asp.

48. Memo 434 from Australian Embassy Jakarta to Canberra, "Indonesia's Political Prisoners," May 6, 1974, NAA, A 1838, 3034-2-9-6, Part 4, Indonesia, Internal Security, Political Prisoners 1974; "Letter from J. L. Beavin, British Embassy Jakarta to FCO," September 3, 1974, UKNA, FCO 15-1941, Political Detainees in Indonesia 1974.

49. Arief Budiman, "The Problem of Political Prisoners: How to Handle It," *Tempo*, June 9, 1973; "Report of New Life Consultation held November 10–13, 1975 by the National Council of the Churches of Christ USA, on the Subject of Political Prisoners, Ex-prisoners and Their Families in Indonesia," March 22, 1976, ELCA Archives, Division for World Missions, Indonesia Program Files, 1951–1985, box 1; Memo from Paul Gregory to Boyd Lowry, "Political Prisoners in Indonesia," October 15, 1975, ibid.

50. *Indonesia: Economic Prospects and the Status of Human Rights* (Washington, D.C.: Center for International Policy, 1976); "Letter from David Munro, Australian Bar Association to Australian Minister for Foreign Affairs," February 11, 1974, NAA, A 1838, 3034-2-9-6-1, Part 2, Indonesia, Political Prisoners, Correspondence on, 1974.

51. Memo, Secretary General, "The Forthcoming Meeting of the Intergovernmental Group on Indonesia," November 20, 1973, AIUSA Papers, AI, RG II, box 7; Memo, "International Conference on Indonesia," October 11, 1974, ibid; memo, Ingersoll for Ford, "Visit of Indonesian President Suharto," July 1, 1975, Gerald Ford Library, Ann Arbor, Indonesia, box 6; Telegram 170357 from State Department to Jakarta, July 18, 1975, ibid.

52. "Record of Conversation with Ali Murtopo, Maj. Gen. Sudjono Humardani, David Yusuf of CSIS and Australian Minister for Foreign Affairs Don Willessee," March 14, 1974, NAA, A 1838, 3034-2-9-6, Part 4, Indonesia, Internal Security, Political Prisoners 1974; "W. I. Combs, Report on Meeting With Admiral Sudomo," June 10, 1974, UKNA, FCO 15-1940, Political Detainees in Indonesia 1974.

53. Citations from Fealy, *The Release of Indonesia's Political Prisoners*, 28; "Akhir 1975 Tapol C Sudah kembali ke masyarakat," *Kompas*, July 26, 1974; Telegram 252899 from State Department to Jakarta, October 23, 1975, U.S. Department of State FOIA Electronic Reading Room; Letter from Brian Burdekin, Permanent Mission of Australia to UN Office in Geneva to Mike Curtin, Indonesia Section, Department of Foreign

Affairs, August 8, 1975, NAA, A 1838, 3034-2-9-6, Part 14, Indonesia, Internal Security, Political Prisoners 1975.

54. Newsom, *The Diplomacy of Human Rights*, 101–111.

55. Telegram 15467 from Jakarta to State, November 30, 1976, U.S. Department of State FOIA Electronic Reading Room; Editorial, "UN Human Rights Commission," *Sinar Harapan*, February 7, 1977.

56. See Benedict Anderson, "Prepared Testimony on Human Rights in Indonesia and East Timor," Human Rights in Asia: Non-Communist Countries, Hearing before the Subcommittee on International Relations, House of Representatives, February 4, 6, and 7, 1980 (Washington, D.C.: Government Printing Office, 1980), 237–239.

57. Memo from FCO to Jakarta, FAG 015/1, "UN Sub-Commission Condemnation of Indonesia," September 22, 1977, UKNA, FCO 58-1163, Indonesia and Human Rights at UN 1977; Letter from Jan Pluvier to Cong. Donald Fraser, October 25, 1976, Minnesota State Historical Society, Donald Fraser Papers, Subject Committee Files 1976, box 149, G9, 8F; Report of Meeting with Father Verlaan re: Torture in Indonesia, July 15, 1974, Committee Against Torture Department, Amnesty International Archives, Amsterdam.

58. "Lebih Percaya Pers Asing, Pak?" *Tempo*, November 12, 1977.

59. Jusuf *Wanandi, "Human Rights: An Indonesian View," Far Eastern Economic Review*, December 2, 1977; "Antara 'human rights' dengan Bantuan Luar Negeri begi Indonesia," *Kompas*, April 25, 1977.

60. Yap Thiam Hien, "Masalah Hukum dan Penyalah Gunaan Kekuasaan," *Prisma* 6 (June, 1973): 21–29; Todong Mulya Lubis, "Bantuan Hukum Struktural: Redistribusi Kekuasaan dan participasi dari bawah," *Prisma* 5 (May 1981): 51–61.

61. Cited from "Amnesty International Berat-Sebelah," *Kompas,* November 6, 1976; "Kas Kopkamtib Tuduh: Lembaga Amnesty International Disusupi Unsur Komunis," *Kompas* October 19, 1976; "Kas Kopkamtib tanggapi kampanye AI: Transmigrasi untuk bekas tahanan G30S/PKI bukan 'penal colony,'" *Kompas*, October 22, 1977; Anja Jetschke, "Linking the Unlinkable? International Norms and Nationalism in Indonesia and the Philippines," in Thomas Risse, Stephen C. Ropp, and Kathryn Sikkink, eds., *The Power of Human Rights: International Norms and Domestic Change* (Cambridge: Cambridge University Press, 1999), 140.

62. Jusuf Wanandi, *Kebijakan Luar Negri Presiden Carter Dan Peranan Kongress AS* (Jakarta: Centre for Strategic and International Studies, 1978), 9–13; note of meeting between UK minister for overseas development and Indonesian ambassador to London, February 17, 1977, UKNA, FCO 58-1163, Indonesia and Human Rights at UN 1977; Memo for Zbigniew Brzezinski, *East Asia Evening Report*, January 18, 1977, Jimmy Carter Presidential Library, NSA SMFE, box 4.

63. "AS Bukan polisi dunia pengawas hak-hak asasi manusia," *Kompas*, February 13, 1978; "Pengakuan dan pelanggaran hak asasi manusia," *Tempo*, December 10, 1977.

64. "Hak Asasi Manusia di Indonesia Membaik," *Kompas*, October 24, 1977; "Surjono Darusman mengenai Kasus James Dunn: State Department di Belekung Kita," *Kompas*, March 18, 1977.

65. Brad Simpson, "Solidarity in an Age of Globalization: The International Movement for East Timor and U.S. Foreign Policy," *Peace and Change* 29, nos. 3/4 (2004): 453–482; Clinton Fernandes, *The Independence of East Timor: Multi-Dimensional Perspectives; Occupation, Resistance, and International Political Activism* (Sussex: Sussex Academic Press, 2011).

66. Margaret E. Keck and Kathryn Sikkink, *Activists Beyond Borders: Advocacy Networks in International Politics* (Ithaca, N.Y.: Cornell University Press, 1998), 12–13.

67. I borrow my formulation here from Jean H. Quataert, *Advocating Dignity: Human Rights Mobilizations in Global Politics* (Philadelphia: University of Pennsylvania Press, 2010), 161–169.

68. *Buku Putih Perjuangan Mahasiswa 1978* (Bandung: Dewan Mahasiswa, Bandung Institut Technologie, 1978), 16. A translated version appears in *Indonesia* 25 (April 1978): 151–182.

69. "Defense of the Student Movement: Documents from the Recent Trials," *Indonesia* 27 (April 1979): 29–32.

70. Abdurrahman Wahid, "Gus Dur—Moralitas: Keutuhan & Keterlibatan," *Tempo*, June 17, 1978.

71. *Amnesty International Report 1979* (London: Amnesty International, 1980), 92–94; *Laporan Tahunan Keadaan Hak-Hak Azasi Manusia di Indonesia 1979* (Jakarta: LBH, 1979), 1–2, 34–40.

72. Todong Mulya Lubis, *Hak Asasi Manusia dan Kita* (Jakarta: Sinar Harapan, 1982), 15–16.

73. Lev, *No Concessions*, 338.

Chapter 12. Why South Africa?

1. Francis Nesbitt, "A 'Postmodern' Interpretation of the Anti-Apartheid Movement," review of *Movement Matters: American Antiapatheid Activism and the Rise of Multicultural Politics*, by David L. Hostetter, *H-SAfrica* (June 2007), http://www.h-net.org/reviews/showrev.php?id=13284. Nesbitt is the author of *Race for Sanctions: African Americans Against Apartheid, 1946–1994* (Bloomington: Indiana University Press, 2004).

2. Roger Fieldhouse, *Anti-Apartheid: A History of the Movement in Britain* (London: Merlin Press, 2005); Christabel Gurney, "In the Heart of the Beast: The British Anti-Apartheid Movement 1959–1994," in *The Road to Democracy in South Africa: International Solidarity and Support* (Cape Town: Zebra Press, 2004), 255–351; Christabel Gurney, "'A Great Cause': the Origins of the Anti-Apartheid Movement, June 1959–March 1960," *Journal of Southern African Studies* 26, no. 1 (March 2000): 123–144; Christabel Gurney, "The 1970s: The Anti-Apartheid Movement's Difficult Decade," *Journal of Southern African Studies* 35, no. 2 (June 2009): 471–487; Håkan Thörn, *Anti-Apartheid and the Emergence of a Global Civil Society* (Basingstoke: Palgrave Macmillan, 2006).

3. Jan Eckel, "'Under a Magnifying Glass': The International Human Rights

Campaign Against Chile in the Seventies," in *Human Rights in the Twentieth Century*, ed. Stefan-Ludwig Hofman (New York: Cambridge University Press, 2011), 326.

4. The phrase "long 1970s" is borrowed from Bruce Schulman, who uses it to characterize the period 1969 to 1984 in the United States. See Bruce J. Schulman, *The Seventies: The Great Shift in American Culture, Society and Politics* (New York: Free Press, 2001). This periodization makes sense in terms of the chronology of British anti-apartheid activism discussed below: 1969 was marked by the upswing in public interest and activism on apartheid brought about by Stop the Seventy Tour's campaign against South African sports tours, while 1984 was the year in which anti-apartheid activism in Britain began to take off and reached previously unprecedented levels.

5. Fieldhouse, *Anti-Apartheid*, 466.

6. Stop the Seventy Tour was an entirely separate organization from the Anti-Apartheid Movement; the AAM collaborated with STST (and Peter Hain, STST's chairman, also sat on the AAM's National Committee), but concerns about STST's embrace of "direct action" also led the AAM to maintain its distance and stress that STST was independent. The City of London Anti-Apartheid Group was an affiliated local group of the AAM from City Group's founding in January 1982 until February 1985, when the ongoing tensions between City Group and the AAM National Office culminated in the AAM National Committee withdrawing its recognition of the group.

7. Gurney, "The 1970s."

8. Ronald Hyam and Peter Henshaw, *The Lion and the Springbok: Britain and South Africa Since the Boer War* (Cambridge: Cambridge University Press, 2003), 307, 314–320.

9. Ibid., 307–342; Gurney, "In the Heart of the Beast," 266, 317.

10. See also Gurney, "In the Heart of the Beast," 295; Gurney, "The 1970s," 481; Hyam and Henshaw, *The Lion and the Springbok*, 330–332.

11. Gurney, "In the Heart of the Beast," 324–330.

12. Thörn, *Anti-Apartheid*, 12, 4–5, 196–202.

13. Ibid., 199–200.

14. Peter Hain, *Don't Play with Apartheid: The Background to the Stop the Seventy Tour Campaign* (London: George Allen and Unwin, 1971), 121–122, 148.

15. Rob Nixon, *Homelands, Harlem, and Hollywood: South African Culture and the World Beyond* (New York: Routledge, 1994), 132; Hain, *Don't Play With Apartheid*, 148.

16. See Bruce K. Murray, "The Sports Boycott and Cricket: The Cancellation of the 1970 South Africa Tour of England," *South African Historical Journal* 46, no. 1 (May 2002): 219–249.

17. Christopher Ford, "Hain Stopped Play," *Guardian*, May 23, 1970.

18. Under the apartheid regime, such orders limited an individual's freedom of movement and association and prevented the publication of anything they said or wrote.

19. Peter Hain, *Sing the Beloved Country: The Struggle for the New South Africa* (London: Pluto Press, 1996), 32–43; Kevin Toolis, "Hain's World," *Guardian*, February 10, 2001.

20. Toolis, "Hain's World." See also Hain, *Sing the Beloved Country*, 44, and Hain, *Don't Play With Apartheid*, 115.

21. Hain, *Sing the Beloved Country*, 48. See also Ruth Fox, "Young Liberal Influence and Its Effects, 1970–74," *Liberal Democrat History Group Newsletter* 14 (March 1997): 16.

22. George Kiloh, "Forty Years Off: A Personal Account of the Young Liberals and the Liberal Party 1965–69," 47–50, George Kiloh Papers, London School of Economics and Political Science Library, London, UK (hereafter cited as Kiloh Papers), Bundle 12.

23. "National League of Young Liberals' Southern Africa Commission," Bodleian Library of Commonwealth and African Studies at Rhodes House, Oxford, UK (hereafter cited as Rhodes House), AAM 861.

24. Hain, *Don't Play with Apartheid*, 115; Ford, "Hain Stopped Play," 11.

25. Hain, *Don't Play with Apartheid*, 115–119.

26. Ibid., 120–121.

27. Kiloh, "Forty Years Off," 49–51, Kiloh Papers, Bundle 12.

28. Hain, *Don't Play with Apartheid*, 103, 88.

29. Douglas Marchant, "South Africa: The Kingpin," in "Southern Africa: A Background Briefing by Members of the Southern Africa Commission," Easter 1968, Rhodes House, AAM 861.

30. Hain, *Don't Play with Apartheid*, 200, 171.

31. Ibid., 87–88.

32. Ibid., 148, 199.

33. [Malcolm MacCallum?], "Direct Action," ca. late 1968, Kiloh Papers, Bundle 9.

34. John Meadowcroft, "The Origins of Community Politics: New Liberalism, Grimond and the Counter-Culture," *Journal of Liberal Democrat History* 28 (Autumn 2000): 3; David Boyle, "Communities Actually: A Study of Liberal Democrat Localism in Action," 16–17, http://www.libdemgroup.lga.gov.uk/lga/aio/989180.

35. Gordon Lishman, "The Framework for Community Politics," in *Community Politics*, ed. Peter Hain (London: J. Calder, 1976), 80; Peter Hain, "The Future of Community Politics," in *Community Politics*, ed. Hain, 21.

36. Malcolm MacCallum, "Officers Weekend Cambridge 12th/13th October: Summary of NLYL Problems," [circa October 1968], Kiloh Papers, Bundle 9.

37. Ford, "Hain Stopped Play," 11.

38. Paul Trewhela, "Norma Kitson," *Independent*, June 14, 2002, http://www.independent.co.uk/news/obituaries/norma-kitson-645283.html; Denis Herbstein, "Norma Kitson," *Guardian*, July 12, 2002, http://www.guardian.co.uk/news/2002/jul/12/guardianobituaries; "City of London Anti-Apartheid Group," Freedom of Information release, November 22, 2005, http://collections.europarchive.org/tna/20080205132101/http://www.fco.gov.uk/servlet/Front?pagename=OpenMarket/Xcelerate/ShowPage&c=Page&cid=1109172327551.

39. The Congress Alliance consisted of the African National Congress, the South African Indian Congress, the Coloured People's Congress, the Congress of Democrats, and the South African Congress of Trade Unions.

40. For Norma Kitson's account of her life, see Norma Kitson, *Where Sixpence Lives* (London: Hogarth Press, 1987).

41. Ibid., 214, 238.

42. See, for example, "The Free Steven Kitson Campaign Now to Become Impetus to Free Dave Kitson and Release Political Prisoners," January 17 [1982], Rhodes House, AAM 502.

43. Kitson, *Where Sixpence Lives*, 253, 260–261.

44. "Free All South African Political Prisoners: Save Dave Kitson's Life" (flyer), Rhodes House, AAM 502.

45. Kitson, *Where Sixpence Lives*, 261, see also 238, 284.

46. Political Committee of the Revolutionary Communist Group, "Our Tasks and Methods: The Founding Document of the RCG," *Revolutionary Communist* 1 (January 1975): 11.

47. David Yaffe, "South Africa: International Solidarity and the British Working Class," *Revolutionary Communist* (1976): 56–63.

48. Kitson, *Where Sixpence Lives*, 249–250.

49. Carol Brickley, "Norma Kitson," *Fight Racism! Fight Imperialism!*, August/September 2002, http://www.revolutionarycommunist.org/index.php/rest-of-the-world/907-norma-kitson--frfi-168-aug--sep-2002.html. See also Kitson, *Where Sixpence Lives*, 250.

50. *The Revolutionary Road to Communism in Britain: Manifesto of the Revolutionary Communist Group* (London: Larkin Publications, 1984). The cover was designed by Carol Brickley.

51. Ibid., 67–68, see also vii, 43–46.

52. South African Embassy Picket Campaign, "Close Down the Terrorist South African Embassy" (flyer); City of London Anti-Apartheid Group, "Songs" (flyer), Rhodes House, AAM 503; "No Talks with Botha While Mandela Is in Jail" (flyer), circa May–June 1984; City Anti-Apartheid Movement, "24 Hour Picket: Join Us!" (flyer); "We Shall Not Be Moved" (flyer); "One Week Picket: 26 May–1 June 1984: Songs" (flyer), Rhodes House, AAM 502.

53. Carol Brickley, Terry O'Halloran, and David Reed, *South Africa: Britain Out of Apartheid, Apartheid Out of Britain* (London: Larkin Publications, 1985); City of London Anti-Apartheid Group, "Mid-September Bulletin" (September 1984); "The Following Resolutions have been Received . . . ," Rhodes House, AAM 502.

54. "Trafalgar 9 Defence Campaign" (flyer); Chris Fraser to Trevor Huddleston, June 21, 1983, Rhodes House, AAM 502.

55. City of London Anti-Apartheid Group, "Police Attempt to Ban City of London Anti-Apartheid Group Pickets Outside South Africa House, Trafalgar Square," press statement, June 10, 1984; "We Shall Not Be Moved! Defend the Right to Demonstrate Outside the South African Embassy!" (flyer), Rhodes House, AAM 502.

56. Kitson, *Where Sixpence Lives*, 277; Chris Fraser to Trevor Huddleston, June 21, 1983, Rhodes House, AAM 502.

Chapter 13. The Rebirth of Politics from the Spirit of Morality

1. Eric Hobsbawm, *The Age of Extremes: A History of the World, 1914–1991* (New York: Pantheon, 1994).

2. See Bruce J. Schulman, *The Seventies: The Great Shift in American Culture, Society, and Politics* (New York: Free Press, 2001); Konrad H. Jarausch, ed., *Das Ende der Zuversicht? Die siebziger Jahre als Geschichte* (Göttingen: Vandenhoeck and Ruprecht, 2008); Daniel T. Rodgers, *Age of Fracture* (Cambridge, Mass.: Belknap Press of Harvard University Press, 2011).

3. Anselm Doering-Manteuffel and Lutz Raphael, *Nach dem Boom: Perspektiven auf die Zeitgeschichte seit 1970*, 2nd ed. (Göttingen: Vandenhoeck and Ruprecht, 2010).

4. Marguerite Garling, *The Human Rights Handbook: A Guide to British and American International Human Rights Organisations* (London: Macmillan, 1979), 5.

5. On Amnesty's early years, see Tom Buchanan, "'The Truth Will Set You Free': The Making of Amnesty International," *Journal of Contemporary History* 37, no. 4 (October 2002): 575–597. See also Stephen Hopgood, *Keepers of the Flame: Understanding Amnesty International* (Ithaca, N.Y.: Cornell University Press, 2006).

6. See IEC Correspondence, Film 555, International Executive Meeting, May 9–10, 1970, Internationaal Instituut voor Sociale Geschiedenis, Amnesty International, International Secretariat Archives, 1317.

7. See, e.g., Memo on the organization of the International League, January 1964, Frances Grant Papers, Rutgers University, Roger Baldwin, box 24.

8. See Guillermo A. O'Donnell, *Modernization and Bureaucratic-Authoritarianism: Studies in South American Politics* (Berkeley, Calif.: Institute of International Studies, 1979); Thomas E. Skidmore, *The Politics of Military Rule in Brazil, 1964–85* (New York: Oxford University Press, 1988); Thomas C. Wright, *State Terrorism in Latin America: Chile, Argentina, and International Human Rights* (Lanham, Md.: Rowman and Littlefield, 2007).

9. See Jean H. Quataert, *Advocating Dignity: Human Rights Mobilizations in Global Politics* (Philadelphia: University of Pennsylvania Press, 2009), 109–140.

10. See Patricio Orellana and Elizabeth Q. Hutchison, *El movimiento de derechos humanos en Chile, 1973–1990* (Santiago de Chile: Centro de Estudios Políticos Latinoamericanos Simón Bolívar, 1991).

11. See Daniel Maul, *Menschenrechte, Sozialpolitik und Dekolonisation: Die Internationale Arbeitsorganisation (IAO) 1940–1970* (Essen: Klartext-Verlag, 2007), 281–293; Sandrine Kott, "Arbeit—ein transnationales Objekt? Die Frage der Zwangsarbeit im 'Jahrzehnt der Menschenrechte,'" in *Unterwegs in Europa: Beiträge zu einer vergleichenden Sozial- und Kulturgeschichte*, ed. Christina Benninghaus et al. (Frankfurt: Campus-Verlag, 2008), 301–321.

12. See Daniel C. Thomas, *The Helsinki Effect: International Norms, Human Rights, and the Demise of Communism* (Princeton, N.J.: Princeton University Press, 2001), 159–194.

13. See Andreas Wenger, Vojtech Mastny, and Christian Nuenlist, eds., *Origins of the European Security System: The Helsinki Process Revisited* (New York: Routledge, 2008); Oliver Bange and Gottfried Niedhart, eds., *Helsinki 1975 and the Transformation of Europe* (New York: Berghahn Books, 2008); Helmut Altrichter, ed., *Der KSZE-Prozeß: Vom Kalten Krieg zu einem neuen Europa 1975 bis 1990* (Munich: Oldenbourg, 2011).

14. See Sarah B. Snyder, *Human Rights Activism and the End of the Cold War: A Transnational History of the Helsinki Network* (Cambridge: Cambridge University Press, 2011).

15. See Kathryn Sikkink, *Mixed Signals: U.S. Human Rights Policy and Latin America* (Ithaca, N.Y.: Cornell University Press, 2004), 48–180; David F. Schmitz, *The United States and Right-Wing Dictatorships, 1965–1989* (Cambridge: Cambridge University Press, 2006), 112–240.

16. See Presidential Review Memorandum/NSC-28, Human Rights, July 7, 1977, Jimmy Carter Library, Atlanta, Ga., Lipshutz Files, box 19; The Human Rights Policy: An Interim Assessment, January 16, 1978, White House Central File, Subject Files, Human Rights, box HU-1, Lake to Vance. See also David F. Schmitz and Vanessa Walker, "Jimmy Carter and the Foreign Policy of Human Rights: The Development of a Post-Cold War Foreign Policy," *Diplomatic History* 28, no. 1 (January 2004): 113–143.

17. See Peter Malcontent, *Op kruistocht in de Derde Wereld: De reacties van de Nederlandsde regering op ernstige en stelselmatige schendingen van fundamentele mensenrechte in ontwikkelingslanden, 1973–1981* (Hilversum: Verloren, 1998); Floribert Baudet, "*Het heeft onze aandacht": Nederland en de rechten van de mens in Oost-Europa en Joegoslavie, 1972–1989* (Amsterdam: Boom, 2001).

18. See Jon A. Fanzun, *Die Grenzen der Solidarität: Schweizerische Menschenrechtspolitik im Kalten Krieg* (Zurich: Verlag Neue Zürcher Zeitung, 2005).

19. See Joshua Rubenstein, *Soviet Dissidents: Their Struggle for Human Rights* (Boston: Beacon Press, 1980); Ludmilla Alexeyeva, *Soviet Dissent: Contemporary Movements for National, Religious, and Human Rights* (Middletown, Conn.: Wesleyan University Press, 1985).

20. See Benjamin Nathans's chapter in this volume.

21. See Gunter Dehnert's chapter in this volume.

22. See the memorandums and correspondence in the Human Rights Watch archives, Columbia University, New York, NY, series I.1, box 20.

23. See Ned Richardson-Little's chapter in this volume.

24. See Edward L. Cleary, *The Struggle for Human Rights in Latin America* (Westport, Conn.: Praeger, 1997).

25. See James N. Green, *We Cannot Remain Silent: Opposition to the Brazilian Dictatorship in the United States* (Durham, N.C.: Duke University Press, 2010).

26. See Skidmore, *Politics of Military Rule in Brazil*.

27. See Orellana and Hutchison, *Movimiento de derechos humanos en Chile*.

28. See Alison Brysk, *The Politics of Human Rights in Argentina: Protest, Change, and Democratization* (Stanford, Calif.: Stanford University Press, 1994).

29. See, e.g., Donald R. Culverson, "The Politics of the Anti-Apartheid Movement in the United States, 1969–1986," *Political Science Quarterly* 111, no. 1 (Spring 1996): 127–149; Roger Fieldhouse, *Anti-Apartheid: A History of the Movement in Britain: A Study in Pressure Group Politics* (London: Merlin Press, 2005); Håkan Thörn, *Anti-Apartheid and the Emergence of a Global Civil Society* (Basingstoke: Palgrave Macmillan, 2006).

30. See Philipp Rock, *Macht, Märkte und Moral: Zur Rolle der Menschenrechte in der Außenpolitik der Bundesrepublik Deutschland in den sechziger und siebziger Jahren* (Frankfurt: Lang, 2010).

31. See Lora Wildenthal, "Human Rights Advocacy and National Identity in West Germany," *Human Rights Quarterly* 22, no. 4 (November 2000): 1051–1059.

32. See Van Gosse, "Unpacking the Vietnam Syndrome: The Coup in Chile and the Rise of Popular Anti-Interventionism," in *The World the Sixties Made: Politics and Culture in Recent America*, ed. Van Gosse and Richard Moser (Philadelphia: Temple University Press, 2003), 100–113.

33. See Jan Eckel, "'Under a Magnifying Glass': The International Human Rights Campaign against Chile in the Seventies," in *Human Rights in the Twentieth Century*, ed. Stefan-Ludwig Hoffmann (Cambridge: Cambridge University Press, 2011), 312–342.

34. Margaret E. Keck and Kathryn Sikkink, *Activists Beyond Borders: Advocacy Networks in International Politics* (Ithaca, N.Y.: Cornell University Press, 1998).

35. See Joan Dassin, ed., *Torture in Brazil: A Report by the Archdiocese of São Paulo* (New York: Vintage Books, 1986); Green, "We Cannot Remain Silent."

36. See Brysk, *Politics of Human Rights in Argentina*, 42–62.

37. See Eckel, "Under a Magnifying Glass."

38. On Indonesia, see Bradley J. Simpson, "Denying the 'First Right': The United States, Indonesia, and the Ranking of Human Rights by the Carter Administration, 1976–1980," *International History Review* 31, no. 4 (2009): 788–826.

39. See Fabian Klose, *Menschenrechte im Schatten kolonialer Gewalt: Die Dekolonisierungskriege in Kenia und Algerien, 1945–1962* (Munich: Oldenbourg, 2009); Jan Eckel, "Human Rights and Decolonization: New Perspectives and Open Questions," *Humanity* 1, no. 1 (Fall 2010): 111–136.

40. See Roger Normand and Sarah Zaidi, *Human Rights at the UN: The Political History of Universal Justice* (Bloomington: Indiana University Press, 2008), 289–315.

41. See Odette Jankowitsch and Karl P. Sauvant, eds., *The Third World Without Superpowers: The Collected Documents of the Non-Aligned Countries*, vols. 1–5 (Dobbs Ferry, N.Y.: Oceana Publications, 1978–1984), 5:66–68.

42. See Roland Burke, *Decolonization and the Evolution of International Human Rights* (Philadelphia: University of Pennsylvania Press, 2010).

43. See Bonny Ibhawoh, "Cultural Relativism and Human Rights: Reconsidering the Africanist Discourse," *Netherlands Quarterly of Human Rights* 19, no. 1 (March 2001): 43–62.

44. See Simon Stevens's chapter in this volume.

45. See Report of the ICM Discussion Group on Action and Program, February

1979, Records of Amnesty International USA, Columbia University, New York, NY (hereafter cited as AIUSA Records), record group II, series 2, box 1; Barbara Sproul, Proposals for Death Penalty program, June 1982, AIUSA Records, record group I, series 1, box 4.

46. Board of Directors Meeting, May 1–3, 1981, AIUSA Records, record group I, series 1, box 3; Sproul, General Ideas, June 24, 1982, AIUSA Records, series 4, box 11.

47. See A. W. Brian Simpson, *Human Rights and the End of Empire: Britain and the Genesis of the European Convention* (Oxford: Oxford University Press, 2001).

48. See Klose, *Menschenrechte im Schatten kolonialer Gewalt*, 275–289.

49. See National Archives, Kew, FCO 58/1009–1011, 1143–1147, 1152, 1156–1157, 1395, 1414.

50. See A. E. Pijpers, " Dekolonisatie, compensatiedrang en de normalisering van de Nederlandse buitenlandse politiek," in *De kracht van Nederland: Internationale positie en buitenlands beleid in historisch perspectief*, ed. N. C. F. van Sas (Haarlem: Becht, 1991), 204–218.

51. See Growth and Development, ICM, September 24–26, 1976, AIUSA Records, record group I, series 4, box 7; Three-Year Growth and Development Plan, February 1977, AIUSA Records, record group I, series 4, box 7.

52. See Wenger, Mastny, and Nuenlist, *Origins of the European Security System*; Daniel Möckli, *European Foreign Policy During the Cold War: Heath, Brandt, Pompidou and the Dream of Political Unity* (New York: I. B. Tauris, 2009).

53. See the article in *Cold War History* 8 (2008); Wenger, Mastny, and Nuenlist, *Origins of the European Security System*.

54. See Baudet, "*Heeft onze aandacht*," 67–98.

55. Quoted in Rock, *Macht, Märkte und Moral*, 227.

56. See the correspondence between Carter and Leonid Brezhnev, Jimmy Carter Library, Atlanta, GA, Brzezinski Donated Material, Geographic File, box 18.

57. See William Korey, *The Promises We Keep: Human Rights, the Helsinki Process, and American Foreign Policy* (New York: St. Martin's Press, 1993).

58. See also Daniel Sargent's chapter in this volume.

59. See also Lasse Heerten's chapter in this volume.

60. Quoted in Alex de Waal, *Famine Crimes: Politics and the Disaster Relief Industry in Africa* (Bloomington: Indiana University Press, 1997), 74.

61. See Horst Bredekamp, *Theorie des Bildakts: Frankfurter Adorno-Vorlesungen 2007* (Berlin: Suhrkamp, 2010).

62. See Daniel Sargent's chapter in this volume.

63. See Lawrence S. Wittner, *The Struggle Against the Bomb*, vol. 1, *One World or None: A History of the World Nuclear Disarmament through 1953* (Stanford, Calif.: Stanford University Press, 1993).

64. See Jan Eckel, "The International League for the Rights of Man, Amnesty International, and the Changing Fate of International Human Rights NGOs," *Humanity* 4, no. 2 (Summer 2013): 183–214.

65. From the vast literature on the United States, see William H. Chafe, *The Unfinished Journey: America Since World War II* (New York: Oxford University Press, 2007), 290–328. On West Germany, see Roland Roth and Dieter Rucht, eds., *Die sozialen Bewegungen in Deutschland seit 1945: Ein Handbuch* (New York: Campus-Verlag, 2008).

66. See Sven Reichardt and Detlef Siegfried, "Das Alternative Milieu: Konturen einer Lebensform," in *Das Alternative Milieu: Antibürgerlicher Lebensstil und linke Politik in der Bundesrepublik Deutschland und Europa, 1968–1983*, ed. Reichardt and Siegfried (Göttingen: Wallstein Verlag, 2010), 9–26.

67. See Michel Foucault, *Technologies of the Self: A Seminar with Michel Foucault* (Amherst: University of Massachusetts Press, 1988); Ronald Inglehart, *The Silent Revolution* (Princeton, N.J.: Princeton University Press, 1977).

68. Luc Boltanski, *Distant Suffering: Morality, Media, and Politics* (Cambridge: Cambridge University Press, 1999).

69. See Barbara Keys, "Anti-Torture Politics: Amnesty International, the Greek Junta, and the Origins of the Human Rights 'Boom' in the United States," in *The Human Rights Revolution: An International History*, ed. Akira Iriye, Petra Goedde, and William I. Hitchcock (New York: Oxford University Press, 2012), 201–220.

70. See Amnesty International, ed., *Report on Torture* (London: Duckworth, 1973); Amnesty International, ed., *Chile: An Amnesty International Report* (London: Amnesty International Publications, 1974).

71. See "Humanitarian Governance and Ethical Cultivation: Médecins sans Frontières and the Advent of the Expert-Witness," *Millennium* 40, no. 1 (September 2011): 43–63.

72. See Peter Novick, *The Holocaust and Collective Memory: The American Experience* (London: Bloomsbury, 2000), 207–266.

73. Information can be found in the annual reports of adoption groups and members' correspondence scattered throughout AIUSA Records. On the German Amnesty, see Thomas Claudius and Franz Stepan, *Amnesty International: Portrait einer Organisation* (Munich: Oldenbourg, 1978).

74. See Carl Bon Tempo's chapter in this volume.

75. See Jeane J. Kirkpatrick, *Dictatorships and Double Standards: Rationalism and Reason in Politics* (New York: Simon and Schuster, 1982).

76. On the following see Geoff Eley, *Forging Democracy: The History of the Left in Europe, 1850–2000* (Oxford: Oxford University Press, 2002), 341–469; Roth and Rucht, *Die sozialen Bewegungen in Deutschland*; Reichardt and Siegfried, *Das Alternative Milieu*.

77. See Eley, *Forging Democracy*, 405–428.

78. Robert Horvath, "'The Solzhenitsyn Effect': East European Dissidents and the Demise of the Revolutionary Privilege," *Human Rights Quarterly* 29, no. 4 (2007): 879–907.

79. François Furet, *The Passing of an Illusion: The Idea of Communism in the Twentieth Century*, trans. Deborah Furet (Chicago: University of Chicago Press, 1999).

80. See Klaus Fitschen et al., eds., *Die Politisierung des Protestantismus: Entwicklungen in der Bundesrepublik Deutschland während der 1960er und 70er Jahre* (Göttingen: Vandenhoeck and Ruprecht, 2011); Pascal Eitler, *"Gott ist tot—Gott ist rot": Max Horkheimer und die Politisierung der Religion um 1968* (New York: Campus-Verlag, 2009).

81. José Casanova, *Public Religions in the Modern World* (Chicago: University of Chicago Press, 1994), 71 ff.

82. Pacem in terris: Encyclical of Pope John XXIII, April 11, 1963; Declaration on Religious Freedom "Dignitatis humanae," December 7, 1965; Message du Pape Paul VI. á M. Leopold Benites, Président de la XXVII Assamblée Générale des Nations Unies, December 10, 1973. All texts can be found in the Vatican's digital archives, http://www.vatican.va/archive.

83. Samuel Moyn, *The Last Utopia: Human Rights in History* (Cambridge, Mass.: Belknap Press of Harvard University Press, 2010). For his slightly differing discussion of the following examples see Moyn, *Last Utopia*, 120–175.

84. All these are Benjamin Nathan's convincing arguments in this volume.

85. Quoted from Gunter Dehnert's chapter in this volume.

86. See Detlef Pollack and Jan Wielgohs, "Comparative Perspectives on Dissent and Opposition to Communist Rule," *Dissent and Opposition in Communist Eastern Europe: Origins of Civil Society and Democratic Transition*, ed. Pollack and Wielgohs (Aldershot: Ashgate, 2004), 240.

87. See the scattered data in AIUSA Records, record group I, series 1, and record group IV, series 2.2.

88. See Teri Bardash, "Fight for World Human Rights Seeks Local Support," *Three Village Herald*, February 11, 1981, AIUSA Records, record group IV, series 2.2, box 15; "Amnesty International Goal to Free Prisoners," *Bangor Daily News*, May 21–22, 1983, AIUSA Records, record group IV, series 2.2, box 13.

89. Fred D. Baldwin, "Fight Political Jailing," *Sentinel Weekender*, April 3, 1983.

90. From the vast literature, see Charles DeBenedetti, *An American Ordeal: The Antiwar Movement of the Vietnam Era* (Syracuse, N.Y.: Syracuse University Press, 1990).

91. *Public Papers of the Presidents of the United States*, Jimmy Carter, Vol. 1977, 1, (Washington, D.C.: Government Printing Office, 1977), 2.

92. See Douglas Brinkley, "The Rising Stock of Jimmy Carter: The 'Hands On' Legacy of Our Thirty-ninth President," *Diplomatic History* 20, no. 4 (October 1996): 505–529.

93. See Malcontent, *Kruistocht in de Derde Wereld*, 179–204.

94. See Buchanan, "The Truth Will Set You Free."

95. Ethel Kweskin, letter to the editor, June 24, 1972, AIUSA Records, record group IV, series 2.2, box 2.

96. "Letanía para el 'Día de los Derechos Humanos,'" http://conlaspalabras.files.wordpress.com/2008/02/letania-para-el-dia-de-dchos-humanos-y-actividades.pdf (accessed November 17, 2012).

97. See Eckel, "Under a Magnifying Glass."

98. See Bardash, "Fight for World Human Rights"; "Amnesty International Goal to Free Prisoners."

99. See also Patrick Kelly's and Lynsay Skiba's chapters in this volume.

100. See Vania Markarian, *Left in Transformation: Uruguayan Exiles and the Latin American Human Rights Networks, 1967–1984* (New York: Routledge, 2005).

101. Rodgers, *Age of Fracture*; Doering-Manteuffel and Raphael, *Nach dem Boom.*

Carl J. Bon Tempo is associate professor of history at the University at Albany, State University of New York. He is the author of *Americans at the Gate: The United States and Refugees During the Cold War* (Princeton, N.J.: Princeton University Press, 2008).

Gunter Dehnert is Wissenschaftlicher Mitarbeiter at the Catholic University of Eichstätt, Germany, where he studies and teaches East European history. He is currently writing his doctoral thesis on the impact of the Conference on Security and Cooperation in Europe process on the Polish opposition movement.

Celia Donert is lecturer in twentieth-century history at the University of Liverpool. Her most recent publication is "Women's Rights in Cold War Europe: Disentangling Feminist Histories," *Past and Present* 215 (Supplement 8, 2013, forthcoming).

Jan Eckel teaches modern and contemporary history at the University of Freiburg, Germany. Among his publications on human rights history are "Human Rights and Decolonization: New Perspectives and Open Questions," *Humanity* 1, no. 1 (Fall 2010): 111–137, and "The International League for the Rights of Man, Amnesty International, and the Changing Fate of International Human Rights NGOs," *Humanity* 4, no. 2 (Summer 2013, forthcoming). He is currently finishing a book on the history of international human rights politics from the 1940s through the 1990s.

Lasse Heerten is a doctoral candidate in contemporary history at Free University Berlin. He is currently finishing a dissertation entitled "Spectacles of

Suffering: The Biafran War of Secession and Human Rights in a Postcolonial World, 1967–1970."

Patrick William Kelly is a doctoral candidate in international history at the University of Chicago. He is currently completing his dissertation, which examines the rise of transnational human rights activism in the Americas in the "long 1970s."

Samuel Moyn is James Bryce Professor of European Legal History at Columbia University. His most recent book is *The Last Utopia: Human Rights in History* (Cambridge, Mass.: Belknap Press of Harvard University Press, 2010).

Benjamin Nathans is Ronald S. Lauder Endowed Term Associate Professor of History at the University of Pennsylvania. He is completing a book on the history of the Soviet dissident movement.

Ned Richardson-Little is completing his doctorate in history from the University of North Carolina at Chapel Hill, with a dissertation entitled "Between Dictatorship and Dissent: Human Rights in East Germany, 1945–1990."

Daniel Sargent is assistant professor of history at the University of California, Berkeley. He is coeditor of *The Shock of the Global: The 1970s in Perspective* (Cambridge, Mass.: Belknap Press of Harvard University Press, 2010) and is completing a book on United States foreign policy in the 1970s.

Brad Simpson is associate professor of history and Asian studies at the University of Connecticut. He is the author of *Economists with Guns: Authoritarian Development and U.S.-Indonesian Relations* (Stanford, Calif.: Stanford University Press, 2008) and is currently writing a history of United States-Indonesian relations during the reign of General Suharto (1966–1998).

Lynsay Skiba is a doctoral candidate in history at the University of California, Berkeley. Her dissertation explores the development of human rights practice through an analysis of individual rights activism, executive power, and the law in twentieth-century Argentina.

Simon Stevens is a doctoral candidate in history at Columbia University. He is completing a dissertation on the forms of international pressure developed in the struggle against apartheid in South Africa.

Acknowledgments

The editors are grateful to the Freiburg Institute for Advanced Studies, and especially its former directors, Ulrich Herbert and Jörn Leonhard, for their kind funding and support. Along the way a number of scholars—Christian Albers, Frank Biess, Mark Philip Bradley, Dominique Clément, Benjamin Gilde, Michal Givoni, Veronika Heyde, Stefan-Ludwig Hoffmann, Barbara J. Keys, Konrad J. Kuhn, Gregory Mann, Jean H. Quataert, Sarah B. Snyder, and Lora Wildenthal—have also participated in our common intellectual project. Some discussions connected to this volume appeared in a slightly different form as *Moral für die Welt? Menschenrechtspolitik in den 1970er Jahre* (Göttingen: Vandenhoeck and Ruprecht, 2012). In preparing the English-language publication, Peter Agree of the University of Pennsylvania Press acted as deus ex machina, and it is thanks to his exceptional generosity and high standards that this volume appears. Noreen-O'Connor-Abel expertly shepherded the manuscript through production, and Dave Prout made a wonderful index. Thanks to all.

CPSIA information can be obtained at www.ICGtesting.com
Printed in the USA
BVOW05s0423080415

395184BV00002B/3/P